Muslim Spain and Portugal

Muslim Spain and Portugal

A Political History of al-Andalus

HUGH KENNEDY

Longman
London and New York

Addison Wesley Longman Limited
Edinburgh Gate,
Harlow, Essex CM20 2JE,
United Kingdom
and Associated Companies throughout the world

*Published in the United States of America
by Addison Wesley Longman Inc., New York*

First published 1996

ISBN 0 582 49515 6 PPR
ISBN 0 582 299683 CSD

British Library Cataloguing in Publication Data
A catalogue record for this book is available from the British Library

Library of Congress Cataloging-in-Publication Data
Kennedy, Hugh (Hugh N.)
Muslim Spain and Portugal : a political history of Al-Andalus /
Hugh Kennedy.
p. cm.
Includes bibliographical references and index.
ISBN 0-582-49515-6 (PPR). — ISBN 0-582-29968-3 (CSD)
1. Spain—History—711-1516. 2. Muslims—Spain—History.
3. Portugal—History—To 1385. 4. Muslims—Portugal—History.
I. Title.
DP102.K46 1996
946′.02—dc20 96-22764
CIP

Set by 35 in Baskerville 10/12pt
Produced by Longman Singapore Publishers (Pte) Ltd.
Printed in Singapore

Contents

List of Maps viii
Acknowledgements x
Note on Names and Dates xi
Glossary xii
Introduction xiv

1. *The Conquest and the Age of the Amirs, 711–56* 1
The Iberian background 1
The Muslim conquest, 711–16 3
The settlement of the Muslims 16
The early governors, 714–41 18
The coming of the Syrians, 741–56 23

2. *The Umayyad Amirate, 756–852* 30
'Abd al-Raḥmān I and the establishment of the Umayyads, 755–88 30
The reigns of Hishām I and al-Ḥakam I, 788–822 38
The reign of 'Abd al-Raḥmān II, 822–52 44
The administration of the early Umayyad amirate 49
The lands of the northern frontier, 788–852 54
The Iberian peninsula in the ninth century 59

3. *Muḥammad, al-Mundhir and 'Abd Allāh: the Slide into Anarchy, 852–912* 63
The accession and early years of the Amir Muḥammad 63
The growing crisis of the Umayyad amirate, 852–86 67
The reign of 'Abd Allāh and the decay of the amirate, 888–912 73

4. *The Golden Age of the Umayyad Caliphate, 912–76* 82

The policies and strategies of ʻAbd al-Raḥmān III 82
The years of expansion, 912–29 87
Umayyad intervention in North Africa 95
The later years of ʻAbd al-Raḥmān III, 939–61 97
The reign of al-Ḥakam II al-Mustanṣir, 961–76 99
The caliphate in Mediterranean society 106

5. *The ʻAmirids and the Collapse of the Caliphate of Cordoba* 109
The rise of al-Manṣūr, 976–81 109
Al-Manṣūr in power, 981–1002 115
The rule of al-Muẓaffar, 1002–8 122
The collapse of the Cordovan state, 1008–31 124

6. *The Taifa Kingdoms* 130
The emergence of the Taifa kingdoms 130
Arab patrician Taifas: Seville, Zaragoza and Cordoba 134
The 'old' Berber Taifas: Badajoz, Toledo and Albarracin 138
The *ṣaqāliba* Taifas of the Levante 140
The Zirids of Granada and other 'new' Berber Taifas 141
Taifa politics 143
The Christian advance, 1057–86 149

7. *The Empire of the Almoravids* 154
The origins of the Almoravid movement, c. 1050–86 154
The Almoravid conquest of al-Andalus, 1086–1102 161
The establishment of the Almoravid regime in al-Andalus 166
The reign of ʻAlī b. Yūsuf b. Tāshfīn: the years of victory, 1106–17 172
The structure of Almoravid government in al-Andalus 174
The reign of ʻAlī b. Yūsuf b. Tāshfīn: the years of decline, 1118–42 179

8. *The Second Taifas* 189

9. *The Early Almohad Caliphate* 196
The origins of the Almohad movement, c. 1100–30 196

'Abd al-Mu'min and the construction of the Almohad caliphate, 1130–63 200
The caliphate of Abū Ya'qūb Yūsuf: the early years, 1163–72 216
The Huete campaign, 1172 223
Abū Ya'qūb Yūsuf: the later years, 1173–84 231

10. *The Later Almohad Caliphate* 237

The caliphate of Abū Yūsuf Ya'qūb al-Manṣūr, 1184–99 237
The caliphate of al-Nāṣir, 1199–1213 249
The collapse of Almohad rule in al-Andalus, 1213–28 256
The twilight of al-Andalus, 1228–48 266

11. *The Nasrids of Granada* 273

Ibn al-Aḥmar and the foundation of the Nasrid kingdom, 1232–73 273
Nasrids, Merinids and Castilians, 1273–1333 280
The golden years of the Nasrid kingdom: Yūsuf I and Muḥammad V, 1333–91 288
Internal divisions and external threats, 1391–1464 292
The decline and fall of the Kingdom of Granada, 1464–92 299

Farewell to al-Andalus 305
Appendix 1: Governors of al-Andalus and Taifa Kings 309
Appendix 2: Family Trees of the Ruling Dynasties of al-Andalus 312
Bibliography 316
Maps 325
Index 329

List of Maps

1. Al-Andalus (Spain and Portugal) 326–7

2. Al-ʻUdwa (Morocco) 328

This book is dedicated to my daughter Katharine, in memory of happy days in Ubeda and Granada.

Acknowledgements

It is with genuine and heartfelt pleasure that I wish to acknowledge the help and encouragement given to me in the writing of this book by colleagues in Spain. In this context I would particularly like to mention Eduardo Manzano Moreno, Maribel Fierro, Manuela Marin and Mercedes Garcia-Arenal who have welcomed me at the Concejo Superior de Investigaciones Cientificas in Madrid, encouraged me in this work and introduced me to the writings of other Spanish authorities which I might otherwise have neglected. It has been a privilege to work with such a lively and interesting group of scholars.

I owe a major debt of gratitude to Andrew MacLennan of Longman, without whose encouragement this book would never have been written and without whose patience it might well have been cut off before it could be finished. It is easy to forget how important enthusiastic and knowledgeable history editors, like Andrew, are in the development of the subject.

I would also like to thank generations of St Andrews students who have sat through my courses on Christian and Muslim Spain and provided both audience and critique for many of the ideas presented here. My colleagues in the Department of Mediaeval History here have made this possible by encouraging the development of courses on Islamic History. I am grateful to the School of History for providing funds for visiting Spain and to Rob Bartlett for his companionship on a trip through the more remote parts of Extremadura. As always I must thank Helen and Robert Irwin for providing such a welcoming base in London. And last but not least my wife Hilary, for unfailing love and encouragement.

Note on Names and Dates

I have tried to make this book user-friendly to non-Arabists while remaining faithful to the evidence. Personal names are transliterated according to the *Cambridge History of Islam* system, now generally used in English language publications. Place-names are given in the modern Spanish and Portuguese forms for the Iberian peninsula, and standard modern transliterations for North Africa. Al-Andalus refers to those areas of the Iberian peninsula which were under Muslim rule at the time being described, so that, for example, it is much smaller in 1200 than in 1000. Andalucia always refers to the modern region of that name. I have used the English term Morocco to describe that part of the Maghreb which lies within the boundaries of the modern kingdom but which was known to the Muslims of al-Andalus as the ʿUdwa, the land on the other side of the Straits. I have also sometimes used the anachronistic Tunisia in place of the contemporary but more obscure Ifrīqīya. I have used Common Era (AD) dates. This sometimes leads to imprecisions when one Muslim year includes parts of two CE ones, and where there is uncertainty I have used both, so an event dated in the Arabic sources to 500 will be described as occurring in 1106/7.

Glossary

akhbār: short historical narratives
alcazaba: fortress, usually in a city (from Arabic *al-qaṣaba*)
baladī: local, a term used to describe those Muslims who settled in al-Andalus before the coming of the Syrians in 741
cortes: assemblies in Christian kingdoms of the Iberian peninsula, including lords, churchmen and representatives of towns
dhimmī: a protected person, a term used for Christians or Jews living under Muslim rule
dīnār: Muslim gold coin
dirham: Muslim silver coin
faqīh, pl. *fuqahā'*: a man learned in Muslim law
fatā: lit. young man, hence slave soldier (cf. *ghulām*)
ghāzī: warrior for Islam, one who participates in the *jihād*
ghulām, pl. *ghilmān*: page, hence slave soldier (cf. *fatā*)
ḥaḍra: capital city and surrounding area
ḥāfiẓ: lit. one who knows the Qur'an by heart, used as an administrative title in the Almohad caliphate
ḥājib: door keeper or chamberlain, title of chief minister
ḥashm: army
huerta: fertile irrigated area surrounding cities like Valencia, Murcia
'iqṭā': land or revenues given in payment for military service
jihād: Muslim Holy War (cf. *ghāzī*)
jizya: poll-tax paid by non-Muslims in an Islamic state
jund: lit. army, hence one of the districts in the south of al-Andalus settled by Syrian troops after 741
jundī: soldier recruited from one of the *jund*s
kātib, pl. *kuttāb*: secretary
kharāj: land-tax, sometimes used for tax in general
kūra: administrative division of al-Andalus
maghārim: taxes not sanctioned by Muslim law
mawlā, pl. *mawālī*: client or freedman, sometimes used of all non-Arab converts to Islam in the first century AH
muwallad: Muslim from native Iberian stock

qāḍī: Muslim judge
ra'īs, pl. *ru'asā*: chief
Reconquista: Christian reconquest of Muslim Spain and Portugal
rizq: rations given to soldiers as part of their payment
sāḥib al-madīna: administrator of an Andalusi city
ṣā'ifa: summer expedition of Muslims against Christians
sayyid: lord, title given to all members of the ruling Almohad dynasty
shaykh: old man, hence tribal chief or venerable teacher
shurṭa: police force
sijil: document, usually confirmation of office or property
ṣiqlabī, pl. *ṣaqāliba*: Slav, originally used of slave soldiers of eastern European origin who served in the armies of Cordoba, later of all white slave soldiers and mercenaries
sūq: market
ṭālib: lit. student, used as an administrative title in the Almohad caliphate
thughūr: areas of al-Andalus bordering on Christian territory, frontier zones
'ulamā: men learned in Muslim sciences and law
'ushr, pl. *'ushūr*: tithes paid by Muslims
Vega: fertile plain to the west of Granada
wālī: governor of province
wazīr: honorific title given to senior administrators in Umayyad times, vizier
za'īm: leader

Introduction

This book is intended to provide an account of the political history of al-Andalus, the parts of the Iberian peninsula under Muslim rule, between 711, the date of the first Muslim invasion, and 1492 when the last independent Muslim power, the Kingdom of Granada, was destroyed.

By political history I do not simply mean the narratives of rulers and battles, though these are of course important, but also the understanding of the structures which lie behind political events and decisions. The most obvious of these structures were the ruling dynasties, where they came from, who their most powerful supporters were and how they attempted to secure a justification and legitimacy for the exercise of power. The most important function of a pre-modern Islamic state was the raising and paying of the military forces. This determined the composition of the elite, the system of taxation and revenue raising and ultimately the success or failure of the regime. The structure of the military is an essential part of political history. Another concern is the reach and range of government and the extent to which the rulers in Cordoba, Seville or Granada were able to make their authority felt throughout al-Andalus. This in turn leads to the examination of local elites and pressure groups and to the consideration of their origins, nature and power.

This is not a history of the Reconquista. Of course the Christian powers to the north always affected the history of al-Andalus, and from the eleventh century onwards they became a threatening and dominant presence, but the struggle against the Christians was only one, and not always the most important, concern of the rulers of al-Andalus: maintaining their own authority in the Muslim-held areas was usually the first priority, and the affairs of North Africa were often as pressing as those of the Christian frontier. This work attempts to see al-Andalus as a Muslim political society among others like it. Its rulers and administrators were always keenly aware that their land was part of a wider Muslim commonwealth and it was to this commonwealth, rather than to their northern neighbours, that they looked for contacts and political ideas. The ultimate failure and extinction of al-Andalus should not be allowed to overshadow the whole of its 800-year history.

This book is not an intellectual and cultural history of al-Andalus. This is not because these things are unimportant, or that the Muslims of al-Andalus did not make a major contribution in these fields, but simply because they lie beyond the scope of this study except in so far as they affected, or illustrate, political developments. Similarly, there has recently been much fascinating work on such topics as rural settlement, landscape, irrigation technology and cuisine, but none of these are treated here.

There is a certain unavoidable inconsistency of texture in this work. At some periods we are comparatively well informed about political events and the scope and operations of government. At other periods our sources are much more limited and we can only discern a bare outline. Nor is it true that more recent parts of the history of al-Andalus are better known than the earlier ones: we are well informed, for example, about the reign of al-Ḥakam II (961–76) because of the survival of al-Rāzī's court chronicle, but the period 1184–1210 is an almost complete blank.

Any broad-brush history of this sort is bound to be heavily dependent on the works of others. For the history of al-Andalus we have two major political histories which are classics and remain the basis for all future research: E. Lévi-Provençal's celebrated *Histoire de l'Espagne Musulmane*, which covers the centuries when Cordoba was the capital (711–1031), and Ambrosio Huici Miranda's much less well known *Historia Politica del Imperio Almohade.* To these two can be added J. Bosch Vila, *Los Almoravides,* and Rachel Arié's *L'Espagne Musulmane au temps des Nasrides (1232–1492).*

The last two decades have seen a massive increase in the scope and intensity of research, which has meant that in many ways the history of al-Andalus is better known and understood than the history of any other part of the pre-modern Muslim world, and methodologies for treating some important aspects, prosopography and archaeological evidence for example, are more developed. It is perhaps invidious to single out individuals, but mention should be made of some of the main advances. The period up to 1031 has been the subject of intensive study in Spain and the works of E. Manzano Moreno on political structures, and Pedro Chalmeta and M. Barcelo on administrative and fiscal history, are fundamental. Also of major importance are the five volumes of the *Estudios Onomastico-Biograficos de Al-Andalus* edited by Manuela Marin and others which have added a whole new dimension to our understanding of the Umayyad regime. The period of the Taifa kings in the eleventh century has recently been superbly covered in *Los Reinos de Taifas: Al-Andalus en el Siglo XI,* edited by M.J. Viguera Molins as vol. viii of the Menendez Pidal, *Historia de Espana.*

In contrast, the periods of the Almoravids and Almohads have been studied more by French historians. The work of V. Lagardère has greatly increased our understanding of the Almoravid movement itself, while P. Guichard's *Les Musulmans de Valence* is an outstanding work of regional history. The archaeological evidence in its broadest context has been studied in A. Bazzana, P. Cressier and P. Guichard, *Les Châteaux Ruraux d'al-Andalus.* There has been less recent work on the Almohads and Nasrids, but important contributions have been made in R. Arié, *Nasrides,* L.P. Harvey, *Islamic Spain, 1250–1500,* and R. Manzano Rodriguez, *Los Benimerines.*

Numerous other authors, whose works are cited in footnotes and in the bibliography, have increased our understanding of the history of al-Andalus and I am dependent on and grateful to them all. If this work succeeds in providing an overview of the subject and recent research and introducing it to others, be they Orientalists, western mediaevalists or interested general readers, then it will have succeeded in its purpose.

CHAPTER ONE

The Conquest and the Age of the Amirs, 711–56

The Iberian background

The Iberian peninsula, divided into the great provinces of Tarraconensis, Carthaginensis, Baetica, Lusitania and Gallaecia, had been one of the richest and most developed areas of the western Roman Empire, but for three centuries before the coming of the Muslims it had been dominated by warrior aristocracies of Germanic origin. The most successful of these were the Visigoths who had first entered the peninsula in the early fifth century. With the accession of King Leovigild in 569 the Visigothic monarchy entered on a century and a half of stability during which kings, based in Toledo, exercised effective power.

The kingdom shared many of the characteristics of the post-Roman kingdoms in France and Italy. In general the Visigothic monarchy was a reasonably strong and effective instrument of government: it did not suffer the internal divisions and progressive debility of the contemporary Merovingian monarchy in France and, right up until the Muslim invasions, the kings maintained their control over most of the Iberian peninsula. In theory the monarchy was elective and successive church councils of Toledo in the mid-seventh century had laid down the rules: the king was to be elected by the bishops and nobles. He was to be a catholic Christian, a Goth by descent and of free birth. He was to be elected either in Toledo or on the site of the previous king's death, and before his accession he had to swear to uphold the laws of the realm. In practice, the choice of monarchs was confined to the most important lineages and there was a natural tendency for fathers to wish to pass their crowns to their sons, as Leovigild did to Recared in 586 and Egica did to Witiza in 702. At the same time, there seems to have been a strong feeling among the nobility against the establishment of a purely hereditary succession and perhaps that a lineage which had held the crown too long should be replaced.

Under the king, the chief men of the state were the nobles, mostly of Gothic origin, and the bishops, mostly recruited from the Hispano-Roman landowning class, although the distinctions between these two groups must have largely disappeared by the beginning of the eighth century. Besides providing spiritual leadership, the bishops were also among the largest landowners and most powerful political figures in the land. The nobles, who sometimes bore the title of *dux* (duke) or *comes* (count), were also owners of large, often underexploited estates cultivated by semi-free peasants. It was the nobles too who provided the army: apart from a royal guard, there was no standing army and the nobles brought their followers in response to the royal summons and the king might reward them with gifts of gold or silver. In general this simple military system seems to have functioned fairly successfully, but it probably meant that the bulk of the troops owed their first loyalties to their lords, rather than to the monarchy.

It is impossible to make any precise assessment of the population or economy of the peninsula. It has been plausibly suggested[1] that the population had been about six million in the early Roman period but had been reduced by plague and war to four million by the later Visigothic period. Archaeological evidence shows that the large open cities of the earlier period had shrunk into small fortified settlements. Country estates and their buildings were certainly more primitive than the great latifundia and villas of the imperial Roman period.

Economic life was almost entirely localised: there is little evidence of long-distance trade and both the small towns and the large estates were effectively economically self-sufficient. The circulation of coinage was extremely limited and most transactions were conducted by barter.

Later Visigothic Spain and Portugal was a fairly stable society and, apart from a limited Byzantine incursion around Cartagena in the south-east, there had been no outside invasion for a couple of centuries. On the other hand, we can picture a very empty landscape, where settlements were few, far between, poor and primitive. Agricultural resources were in many cases neglected or underexploited. There were areas, too, notably in the northern mountains

1. B. Reilly, *The Medieval Spains* (Cambridge, 1993), p. 7.

where the Basques and the Asturians lived, where the people were totally independent of any form of royal control and where a primitive mountain society vigorously resisted outside control. Such was the land the Muslims invaded.

The Muslim conquest, 711–16

The Muslim invasion of Spain and Portugal was in many ways the logical and necessary extension of the conquest of North Africa.[2] Before the coming of the Muslims the area of the modern states of Libya, Tunisia, Algeria and Morocco was occupied by two groups, the Byzantines and the Berbers. The Byzantines held a number of strongholds on the coast, notably Tripoli and Carthage, which they kept supplied by sea. When they reconquered the land from the Vandals in the reign of Justinian, they had established an elaborate system of defences on the southern frontiers of the settled areas, but these seem to have been abandoned by the mid-seventh century when the Muslims began to attack. The remaining Byzantine garrisons defended their coastal strongholds stubbornly and they held out much longer than the garrisons in Syria and Palestine had done a generation before, but they could easily be bypassed by overland invaders and were only a real threat when allied to the Berber tribes of the area.

The Berbers were the real power in the land. They were, and still are, the indigenous inhabitants of North Africa, with their own, unwritten, language, quite distinct from either Latin or Arabic. Their social structure was tribal and they seem to have owed their first loyalties to their kin. Apart from this, there were wide variations of lifestyle. Some Berbers were acculturated to the Byzantine world and many were Christians. Others seem to have lived a much more separate existence and some at least were still pagans. There were Berbers who lived in the cities, many more who lived as farmers in

2. The literature on the Muslim conquest of al-Andalus is vast and fairly uneven in quality. The classic account in E. Lévi-Provençal, *HEM*, i, pp. 1–89, is still a useful starting point. A.D. Taha, *The Muslim Conquest and Settlement of North Africa and Spain* (London and New York, 1989), is a meticulous, detailed but somewhat uncritical account. R. Collins, *The Arab Conquest of Spain, 710–797* (Oxford, 1989), contains important insights into Christian life and literature of the eighth century but is flawed by a contemptuous and uncomprehending attitude to the Arabic sources. A more balanced overview of the period by the doyen of historians of al-Andalus is P. Chalmeta, *Invasion e Islamizacion: la sumision de Hispania y la formacion de al-Andalus* (Madrid, 1994), and I have relied on this at many points.

mountain villages, some who kept sheep and goats in the steppe lands and yet others who wandered as the Touareg do today in the remote and awesome wastes of the Sahara. Berber genealogies are much less fully recorded than Arabic ones and it is difficult to gauge whether the scattered references we have reflect a static relationship or whether some groups were expanding at the expense of others.

According to Arab sources, the Berber tribes were divided into two groups, called Butr and Barānis, just as Arab tribes were divided into Qays/Muḍar and Yemen. Most of the Berbers who joined the Muslim conquest and settled in al-Andalus came from the Butr group. They seem to have retained their tribal identities and probably their pagan religion. In the sixth century these tribes were moving west from Tripolitania and putting pressure on the Byzantine settlements.[3] The Barānis, by contrast, were older-established tribes who had entered into closer relations with the Byzantines and had in many cases converted to Christianity. This suggests that the Muslims assumed the leadership and gave extra momentum to an existing movement of populations among the Berbers, and this goes some way to explaining the success and completeness of their conquests. In practice, the difference between Butr and Barānis seems to have had little effect on the politics of al-Andalus, unlike the murderous disputes between Qays/Muḍar and Yemen among the Arabs, and divisions among the Berber tribes were based on smaller units of individual tribes and extended families and their relationship to Arab groups.

The conquest of North Africa[4] had begun as early as 22/642 when the conqueror of Egypt, ʿAmr b. al-ʿĀs, led an expedition to Barqa in Cyrenaica. From there he dispatched an army to Zawīla, an oasis settlement to the south, led by ʿUqba b. Nāfiʿal-Fihrī. ʿUqba came from a branch of Quraysh, the Prophet Muḥammad's tribe, and his father Nāfiʿ had been one of the first Muslims to settle in Egypt. He came from the elite of early Islamic society and he used his position to make contacts among the Berber people of the area, alliances that were to make his family the most powerful in North Africa and al-Andalus before the coming of the Umayyads in the mid-eighth century. When ʿAmr returned to Egypt, he left ʿUqba in charge at Barqa.

The conquest of North Africa was difficult, partly because of

3. On this see E. Manzano Moreno, *La Frontera de Al-Andalus en epoca de los Omeyas* (Madrid, 1991), pp. 234–5.

4. For the conquest of North Africa see Taha, *Conquest and Settlement*, pp. 55–83, and Chalmeta, *Invasion e Islamizacion*, pp. 72–94.

political disputes among the Muslims but more because of the vigorous resistance put up both by the Berber tribes of the interior and the garrisons of Byzantine cities like Tripoli and Carthage on the coast. More than the other Arab commanders, ʿUqba seems to have understood that the key to subduing North Africa was to enrol the support of Berber tribes. In 50/670 he founded the Muslim settlement of Qayrawān, away from the coast, in the central plain of Tunisia. Like earlier Arab garrison cities at Kūfa, Baṣra and Fusṭāṭ, this was designed to be a settlement where the Muslims could preserve their identity and from which they could dominate the surrounding country.

In 681 ʿUqba led a spectacular raid to the west in which he reached Tangier and the Atlantic coast, although there were no Muslim settlements beyond modern Tunisia at this stage. This was his last and greatest achievement, but his memory lingered on and his sons continued to play a very important role in the Muslim politics of North Africa. There followed a period when the Arabs were almost driven out and Qayrawān itself fell to the Berber leader Kusayla. The Muslims did not recover the initiative until 74/694 when the Caliph ʿAbd al-Malik sent an army of Syrians led by Ḥassān b. al-Nuʿmān al-Ghassānī. He captured the last Byzantine outpost at Carthage and defeated the Berber leader, the priestess Kāhina, and in 82/701 established himself firmly in Qayrawān. He was able to do this, not only because of his Syrian troops, but because of his policy of working with the Berbers. Some tribes, like the Luwāta, seem to have remained allies of the Arabs throughout; many others came over after the defeat of Kāhina, including her own sons. They converted to Islam and were enrolled in the Muslim *dīwān*, receiving a share of the spoils like the Arabs.

Ḥassān was dismissed by the governor of Egypt, who supervised the western provinces in 704, probably because he was too successful, and was replaced by Mūsā b. Nuṣayr, a man of obscure origins who had risen in the financial administration of the Umayyad empire. He continued Ḥassān's policy of recruiting converted Berbers into the Muslim armies and using this new force to extend his control further to the west until, in about 90/708, he took Tangier and appointed a Berber supporter of his, Ṭāriq b. Ziyād, as governor.

The conquest of North Africa had been achieved by an alliance of Arabs and Berbers in the name of Islam. As the conquest proceeded, so the importance of the Berber contribution increased. By the time the Muslims were conquering the area of modern

Morocco, it is probable that the great majority of the troops in their army were Berbers, newly converted to Islam. These Berber troops received a share of the booty but, apart from Ṭāriq b. Ziyād in Tangier, they do not seem to have occupied positions of political importance. Many Berbers entered into *wālā'* agreements with important Arab groups or individuals. They were then described as *mawlā* (pl. *mawālī*) of so and so (Ṭāriq b. Ziyād, the Berber governor of Tangier and probably a man of considerable importance in his own community, for example, is described as *mawlā* of Mūsā b. Nuṣayr, the Arab governor of Qayrawān). This relationship can be described as a sort of clientage, by which members of the conquered peoples were converted (you could not be a non-Muslim *mawlā*) and given a position in the Muslim community in exchange for their loyalty and support.[5] These networks were very important in the fluid politics of early Muslim North Africa and al-Andalus and were often more useful than tribal followings in building up a power base: both the family of 'Uqba b. Nāfi' and the Umayyads depended heavily on their *mawālī* to support their political ambitions.

The governors (*wālī* or *'āmil* are the two Arabic terms used to describe this office), by contrast, were dependent for their authority on the governor of Egypt, and a change of command in Fusṭāṭ (Old Cairo) almost certainly meant a change in Qayrawān. This pattern became even more pronounced in al-Andalus, where the position of the governor was constantly threatened by changes of policies or personnel in Qayrawān or Fusṭaṭ. In these circumstances, it was difficult for a commanding personality to establish himself for long and the governors were often transient figures who made little impact on the country.

The conquerors fed off further conquests. It is true that subject Christian and pagan Berbers are said to have been obliged to pay *jizya* or poll-tax, but there is little indication of any formal tax-gathering machinery. Most of the soldiers must have served in the hope of booty and new lands rather than for a salary and Muslim dominion in North Africa had to expand to survive. If the booty dried up and no new opportunities appeared, then the groups and tribes would turn in on each other and disintegration would inevitably follow. The conquest of Tangier effectively meant the end of westward expansion; now only Spain could offer the sort of opportunities the state needed to be able to survive.

Our understanding of the Muslim conquest of al-Andalus and

5. For the role of *mawālī* in the Umayyad caliphate, see P. Crone, *Slaves on Horses. The Evolution of Islamic Polity* (Cambridge, 1980), pp. 49–57.

the establishment of Arab rule is hampered by the nature of the sources. No contemporary Arabic accounts of the conquest survive and the earliest major sources which have been passed down to us are collections of historical anecdotes (*akhbār*) preserved in a number of works dating from the tenth century onwards, notably the anonymous *Akhbār al-Majmūʿa* (*Collection of Anecdotes*) from possibly c. 940[6] and the *Taʾrīkh Iftitāḥ al-Andalus* (*History of the Conquest of al-Andalus*) of Ibn al-Qūṭiya (d. 977).[7] Both these collections arrange their materials more or less in chronological order but they are not annals and are more concerned with vivid and interesting stories than the careful ordering of events. The *Akhbār* is particularly important for the pre-Umayyad period, while Ibn al-Qūṭiya gives vivid and gossipy accounts of the courts of the Umayyad amirs.

In the tenth century these accounts were edited and systematised using the criteria of annalistic historiography developed in the eastern Islamic world by such authorities as al-Madāʾinī (d. 839) and al-Ṭabarī (d. 923). In al-Andalus this editing seems to have been the work of the Rāzī family, originally from Rayy in central Iran, who had come to al-Andalus as merchants in the late ninth century. According to his son ʿĪsā (d. 989), it was Aḥmad b. Mūsā al-Rāzī (d. 955) who took the *akhbār* which people in al-Andalus had not previously been very interested in and ordered them (*dawwana*) according to the rules of historical science.[8] The writings of the Rāzīs, father and son, have largely been lost but they were used, and often incorporated entirely, with acknowledgements, by the great eleventh-century compiler Ibn Ḥayyān (d. 1076). Much of Ibn Ḥayyān's work has in turn been lost, including the sections which dealt with the conquests and the early amirs. Some of his material has, however, been preserved in shorter works, like the anonymous *Fatḥ al-Andalus* of c. 1100,[9] and later abbreviated recensions in annalistic compilations like Ibn Idhārī's *Bayān al-Maghrib*[10] of about 1300.

The fact that the sources as they have reached us were written down at least two centuries after the events has meant that fierce

6. Ed. with Spanish trans., E. Lafuente y Alcantara (Madrid, 1867). I have used the dating suggested by Chalmeta (*Invasion e Islamizacion*, p. 50) because of the archaic nature of the text, but other authorities prefer an eleventh-century date. The text is analysed in detail in C. Sanchez-Albornoz, *El 'Ajbar Maymu'a. Cuestiones historiograficas que suscita* (Buenos Aires, 1944).

7. Ed. with Spanish trans., J. Ribera (Madrid, 1926).

8. Quoted in Chalmeta, *Invasion e Islamizacion*, p. 45.

9. Ed. L. Molina (Madrid, 1994).

10. The history of the conquest and the Amirs is covered in vol. ii, ed. G.S. Colin and E. Lévi-Provençal (Leiden, 1948).

controversy has raged about the relative merits and reliability of these sources. Opinions have varied between historians like Taha, on the one hand, who accept the Arabic narratives almost completely,[11] and Collins, who holds that the Arabic tradition is virtually worthless.[12]

It is important to attempt to assess the reliability of this material. Clearly these Arab histories are biased in the sense that they are in favour of Muslim victories and claimed that these were the result of God's support, but this sort of open partisanship does not present real problems to the modern historian. There are, however, a variety of other ways in which the material needs to be treated with caution.

There is material which is clearly legendary or folkloric, like the story of the locked chamber in Toledo which King Roderick was rash enough to open, only to find that the interior was covered by paintings of Arab warriors, and, probably, the story of Count Julian and the rape of his daughter by King Roderick. These stories, with their obvious predictive and entertaining functions, are unlikely to mislead historians. The use of topoi and conventional phrases, expressions and characterisation borrowed from eastern Islamic sources may also give a false impression of detailed accuracy.[13]

There may also have been more hard-headed reasons for being economical with the truth. The nature of the conquest affected the status of the lands conquered: if they were conquered by force (*'anwatan*) they became the property of the conquerors, the indivisible *fay'* (immovable booty) of the Muslims, and the proceeds from these properties were to be used for the benefit of the Muslims as their ruler saw fit. If the lands were taken peacefully (*ṣulḥan*), on the other hand, they continued to be the absolute property of the inhabitants and would only pass into Muslim hands by inheritance, purchase or conversion of the owner, in which case they would be the absolute property of their Muslim owners. There is some evidence of two historiographical traditions within the accounts of the conquests.[14] The first, reported by the Rāzīs and

11. See *Conquest and Settlement*, pp. 4–14. 12. *Arab Conquest*, pp. 34–5.

13. For these problems in early Islamic historiography in general, see A. Noth, *The Early Arabic Historical Tradition* (new edn with L.I. Conrad, Princeton, 1994); for a detailed discussion of similar problems in the historiography of al-Andalus, see B. Munzel, *Feinde, Nachbarn, Bundnispartner* (Munster, 1994).

14. For these ideas see Manzano Moreno, 'Arabes, berberes e indigenas: al-Andalus en su primer periodo de formacion', paper presented at the Congress on *Incastellemento*, French School in Rome, 1994, pp. 3–12. In press.

other sources close to the Umayyad court, emphasises the forceful nature of the conquest, since conquest by force would give the Umayyads the right to dispose of the lands, whereas other accounts talk of take-over by agreement and so emphasise the rights of the owners. This may account for disagreements in the sources about the nature of the conquest, and such details as the fall of Seville, which is said to have surrendered peacefully and then rebelled and had to be subdued by force, may be explained as attempts to conflate two contradictory traditions. In the end, however, it must be admitted that these divisions of opinion could simply be the result of genuine confusion over events which happened long ago.

The fact that these sources, in the form in which they have been handed down to us, are much later need not undermine their credibility. The Arabic historical tradition laid great emphasis on preserving the wording and forms of old accounts and much of the work of compilers like Ibn Ḥayyān was basically editing and republishing older materials, rather than composing a new account. Later chronicles can contain important nuggets of information which survive from much earlier times: the most important account of the nature of the settlement of the Syrian *junds* in al-Andalus after 741, for example, is found in fragments of al-Rāzī embedded in the late fourteenth-century *Iḥāṭa* of Ibn al-Khaṭīb, composed in its present form 650 years after the events it describes.[15]

In addition to the Arabic texts there are also Latin sources. Of these by far the most important is the so-called *Chronicle* of 754, also known as the *Mozarabic Chronicle.* This was composed in al-Andalus, probably in the mid-eighth century. Not surprisingly, its viewpoint is very different from the one presented by the Muslim chronicles, and for the Christian author, the invasion is a major disaster rather than a God-given triumph. There are differences over details, but there is a considerable measure of agreement about the broad outlines of events. Given its very early date, the evidence of the *Chronicle* of 754 must carry great weight and it is helpful that it tends to corroborate rather than undermine the outlines of the Muslim tradition.[16]

The sources for the Muslim conquest and establishment are as patchy as they are for most other areas of western Europe in the early eighth century. Accidents of survival may play a large part in shaping our understanding. There is always a danger in over-interpreting fragments of information and giving them more

15. See below, p. 50. 16. See Collins, *Arab Conquest*, pp. 26–34.

importance than they deserve. Despite all these qualifications, however, we can attempt a plausible reconstruction of events.

Most of the early Arabic accounts of the beginning of the conquest of al-Andalus tell of a Count Julian of Ceuta, perhaps a Byzantine official with close contacts with the Visigothic rulers of Spain across the Straits.[17] He had sent his daughter, as was the custom among the Visigothic nobility, to the royal court to complete her education. Here she was assaulted by King Roderick and complained to her father, upon which the outraged governor turned to the local Muslim commander as an ally in revenge. Whatever the literal truth of this story, it probably reflects a situation in which the Visigothic King Roderick was resented by an important section of society who were prepared to call in help from outside.

During the seventh century, the Visigothic monarchy was both elective and hereditary. In 693 Egica had associated his son Witiza in his rule, and when he died in 702 Witiza succeeded him as king. In his turn, he attempted to do the same for his own son Akhila and gave him the governorate of Narbonne, but when he died in 710 there was a *coup d'état* in Toledo, probably engineered by nobles who had no wish to see one family retaining the crown for too long. Power was seized by Roderick, not apparently a member of the ruling family, who was able to defeat the army of Akhila and his brothers Alamundo and Ardabast. In terms of Visigothic practice, Roderick was probably a legitimate king by election, but the circumstances did mean that there were a number of influential people at the court who felt themselves wronged; they might well have caused scandalous stories about the new king to circulate and would not have been sad to see him humiliated by outside invaders.

Like some other Muslim conquests, ʿAmr b. al-ʿĀṣ's expedition to Egypt, for example, the invasion of Spain seems to have been undertaken on local initiative without the approval of the hierarchy, represented in this case by the governor of Ifrīqīya at Qayrawān, Mūsā b. Nuṣayr, and ultimately by the Caliph al-Walīd b. ʿAbd al-Malik in Damascus. Majority opinion holds that Ṭāriq b. Ziyād, governor of Tangier, with a force of perhaps 7,000 to 12,000 men, mostly Berbers, crossed the Straits of Gibraltar in April 711 and established themselves first on the rock which still bears Ṭāriq's name, Gibraltar, before moving on to occupy Algeciras and the

17. For recent assessments of the Julian story, see Taha, *Conquest and Settlement*, pp. 84–8, and the full discussion in Chalmeta, *Invasion e Islamizacion*, pp. 112–20. Munzel, *Feinde, Nachbarn, Bundnispartner*, pp. 37–54, has a detailed discussion of the early sources.

surrounding countryside. Opinions differ as to whether they encountered any immediate resistance but are agreed that Roderick and the bulk of the Visigothic army were campaigning in the north of the country and it was not until the summer that he was able to lead his army south to counter the invasion.

There followed a battle which was to determine the future of the Iberian peninsula for the next eight centuries. It seems to have lasted for a number of days around 20 July 711. The exact site of the battle has been the subject of prolonged debate, but it probably lay to the south-east of Medina Sidonia. The sources give very large numbers for Roderick's army, between 40,000 and 100,000, and while these are certainly exaggerated, it is likely that Roderick's army was significantly larger than Ṭāriq's and may have amounted to between 24,000 and 30,000 men.[18] Arab sources suggest that there were divisions in the Visigothic ranks and that the brothers of Witiza at least hoped that the Muslims would defeat Roderick and then depart, leaving them to assume the crown they felt was rightly theirs. Whatever the reasons, the Visigothic army suffered a shattering defeat, Roderick was missing, presumed dead, and members of the army scattered throughout Iberia, spreading defeatist sentiment.[19]

If the brothers of Witiza had imagined that the Muslims would abandon the fruits of their victory, they were soon undeceived. In the aftermath of his victory, Ṭāriq moved with speed and confidence, aided by Count Julian. He dispatched a force under Mughīth al-Rūmī to Cordoba. Here Mughīth encountered serious resistance from the governor and a small garrison who defended themselves in a church after the Muslims had entered the city through a hole in the walls: it was three months before they surrendered and were executed. Malaga and the district of Elvira (the area around the later city of Granada, which did not really become important until the eleventh century) seem to have been taken by small units without much trouble, but Ṭāriq himself moved on quickly to the Visigothic capital at Toledo. There was no resistance. Most of the people, apart from the Jews, had abandoned the city and Ṭāriq was able to spend the winter of 711–12 there.

Ṭāriq's spectacular success attracted the attention of his superior, Mūsā b. Nuṣayr, in Qayrawān and he was understandably eager to associate himself and his supporters with the triumph and the booty which went with it. The next year he set out with a large

18. Chalmeta, *Invasion e Islamizacion*, p. 134.
19. For differing opinions on the site and course of the battle, see Taha, *Conquest and Settlement*, pp. 88–90; Chalmeta, *Invasion e Islamizacion*, pp. 132–44.

force, 18,000 men we are told,[20] which included many Arabs.[21] He landed at Algeciras and adopted a strategy which would enable him and his men to make conquests of their own. He went first to the great fortress of Carmona, which had been bypassed by Ṭāriq, which was captured with the help of some of Count Julian's men who pretended to be fugitives and so gained access to the city. He then went on to take Seville, which is said to have resisted for some months before being taken by force. We are given no more details about this siege and it may be that the resistance was 'invented' so that the city could be said to have been taken by storm and its lands confiscated. Mūsā subdued the neighbouring towns and went on north to Merida, where the Arab chroniclers comment on the splendour of the Roman remains. Here there was serious resistance, the garrison made a sortie and siege engines were required to force it into submission in July 713. While this was going on, Mūsā sent his son 'Abd al-'Azīz to the east; when he came to Orihuela, then the most important city in the Murcia (the city of Murcia itself was another later foundation) district, he was met by the local commander or *dux*, Theodemir, with whom he made a treaty whose lenient terms meant effective local autonomy and freedom of Christian worship in exchange for goodwill and a modest tribute to be paid in cash, wheat, barley, thickened grape juice, vinegar, honey and oil.[22] As a result of this, the Murcia area was known to the Arabs as Tudmīr for centuries afterwards.

After the fall of Merida, Mūsā headed for Toledo whence Ṭāriq came to meet him. Inevitably, when the two forces did join at Talavera there were tensions and reproaches, but they patched up their relationship and wintered together in Toledo. In the spring of 714 campaigning began again with expeditions which led to the nominal subjection of Galicia and the Ebro valley.

Their triumphant career was brought to a halt by a summons to present themselves before the Caliph in Damascus. Reluctantly, the two leaders left Spain in September 714, never to return, Mūsā leaving his son 'Abd al-'Azīz as governor.

While most of the peninsula had now been visited by Muslim armies, the conquest was by no means complete. The establishment

20. *Akhbār al-Majmū'a*, p. 15; other sources say 10,000: see Taha, *Conquest and Settlement*, p. 94.

21. For Mūsā's invasion and the conquests that followed, see Taha, *Conquest and Settlement*, pp. 94–102, and Chalmeta, *Invasion e Islamizacion*, pp. 168–205.

22. The full text and translation can be found in C. Melville and A. Ubaydli, *Christians and Moors in Spain. vol iii Arabic Sources* (Warminster, 1992), pp. 10–13.

of Muslim power seems to have occurred in two stages. The first was the take-over of the main cities and the fertile lands of the south and the Levante, in some cases with the assistance or at least agreement of members of the Visigothic nobility like the sons of Witiza and Theodemir. The second phase involved the conquest of the north-east, where there is some evidence that Visigothic rule continued under Akhila until the governorate of al-Samḥ (718–21) and the making of peace agreements with the Visigothic lords of the Ebro valley area and other remote districts like the mountains north of Malaga. In this way the conquest of al-Andalus resembled, on a smaller scale, the Muslim conquest of Iran where the main cities and lines of communication were first secured and only later were agreements reached with the inhabitants of outlying areas.

The reasons for the success of the Muslim conquest have been much debated. From the Muslim side the explanation was simple: God had willed it. For Christian commentators from the author of the ninth-century *Chronicle* of Alfonso III onwards, things were much more problematic and they were faced with the question: how could God have allowed this disaster to afflict a Christian people? For mediaeval authors the most plausible explanation was that the Visigoths were immoral and had disobeyed God's commandments, while more secular modern historians have tended to look for signs of political decay and weakness in the Visigothic kingdom.

For the author of the *Chronicle* of 754 the blame lay with the ambitions of Roderick, the treachery of Oppa, son of King Egica, who conspired with the Arabs, and the cowardice of the Archbishop of Toledo, Sindered, who fled to Rome rather than remaining with his flock.[23] For the *Chronicle* of Alfonso III it was the immorality of King Witiza, who besides having many wives and concubines himself, ordered his bishops and deacons to marry, and the treachery of his sons that led to the Christian débâcle.[24]

In fact, the evidence for the decadence of the Visigothic kingdom is non-existent.[25] In many ways it seems to have been stronger in its final years than ever before: the damaging religious division between Arian Visigoths and their Orthodox subjects had been laid to rest for more than a century and there is by the end of the seventh century no real sign of a split between Roman and Visigothic elements. The Jews certainly suffered severe legal disabilities and intermittent persecution and it is clear that they preferred to remain

23. Caps. 52–4. 24. Caps. 5–7.
25. For a good discussion of the arguments, see Collins, *Arab Conquest*, pp. 6–22.

in their cities and accept Muslim rule than to join their Christian fellow countrymen in flight, but there is no reliable evidence that they actively supported or encouraged the invaders. It is also true that the Basques remained outside effective Visigothic control, and indeed Roderick was campaigning in that area at the time of the first Muslim invasion, but separatism in the northern mountains had been a feature of political life for centuries and it was no more dangerous or more threatening than before. In fact, in some ways the very strength of the kingdom made it easier to conquer: if it had been divided into numerous local lordships and principalities, they would no doubt have put up stiff resistance. As it was, Visigothic Spain, like Anglo-Saxon England in 1066, was centralised to the extent that the defeat of the royal army left the entire land open to the invaders.

The Visigothic monarchy suffered a short-term political crisis at the accession of Roderick, resulting in the defection of important elements of the ruling class which may in turn have contributed to a major military defeat which left the country defenceless. The army he led against the invaders was certainly large enough for the purpose; its military worth is less easy to assess. Clearly the battle was lost, but this might have been the result of bad luck or bad decision-making on the day rather than long-term military weakness.

It is striking that there seems to have been little attempt to defend the cities effectively or to raise a second army. Apart from resistance in the northern mountains, which was at the beginning not conducted by the Visigoths, only Cordoba and Merida put up any effective defence. The smallness of the numbers is noticeable: Ṭāriq is said to have sent Mughīth against Cordoba with only 300 men, which might not have been effective if the governor had been able to raise more than 400 to defend it. The city seems to have been decrepit: the Roman bridge was broken and there was a major hole in the ramparts. When the Muslims arrived at Orihuela the governor Theodemir had so few men that he had to dress up women as soldiers and put them on the ramparts. No-one seems to have defended Toledo, a superb natural fortress. Perhaps this failure was partly a result of lack of population, or at least of arms-bearing population. When Saladin invaded the Kingdom of Jerusalem in 1187, the Crusaders mustered a large army to oppose him but to do so they had to empty their cities and fortifications of men. When they lost the battle of Hattin, their splendid castles were left virtually undefended and most of them soon fell to the invaders. This may well have been the same in the case of Visigothic Spain. It was not perhaps that numbers of the population in general were lacking, but rather that numbers of military men were inadequate. There seems to have been a sharp division in Visigothic society between military and non-military classes and there is no mention of popular or civilian resistance. In Cordoba the Muslims were informed by a shepherd they met that most of the people had fled and that only the garrison of 400 and the *ḍuʿafā* remained. *Ḍuʿafā* is an Arabic word which refers to the non-arms-bearing part of the population; it was clearly considered out of the question that such people would participate in the defence of the city.

Another factor in the lack of resistance may have been that the Visigoths did not take the invasion sufficiently seriously. It has already been noted that Roderick's opponents among the aristocracy were hoping that the invaders would defeat him and depart, leaving them in charge, and it is interesting to see that this attitude was shared by at least some of the invaders. It seems that Ṭāriq had to persuade Mūsā to allow the Muslims to settle in Spain and as late as 717 the Caliph ʿUmar b. ʿAbd al-ʿAzīz appointed a governor whose mission it was to evacuate the Muslims from the Iberian peninsula. It must have seemed to many in Spain that the logical response to the Muslim raiders was to retreat to their mountain fastnesses with what they could carry and wait for them to take their booty and go.

On the whole the Muslims offered generous terms which certainly made surrender a more attractive option, whereas unsuccessful resistance could, as the unfortunate defenders of Cordoba found, lead to death. In Andalucia the sons of Witiza seem to have been allowed to retain possession of the royal lands;[26] in the Murcia area the terms amounted to local autonomy; in Merida the inhabitants were allowed to keep their possessions but the property of those who had been killed in the battle for the city, those who had fled north and of the churches, was confiscated. In the later phases of the conquest many Visigothic lords in the Ebro valley area were allowed to retain their lands and status and soon converted to Islam: amongst the best known of these were the Banū Qasi (Casius) of Tudela and the Banū ʿAmrūs of Huesca, who formed dynasties which dominated the area for two centuries after the Muslim conquest.[27] Except for the action against church lands, this fits in well with what we know of Muslim terms elsewhere; the local people

26. Manzano 'Arabes, berberes e indigenas', p. 13. 27. Ibid., pp. 18–19.

were allowed to remain in possession of their lands as long as they paid a land tax and a poll-tax to the conquerors.

The settlement of the Muslims

In the event Spain proved too attractive to its conquerors and they did not leave but chose to settle in the new lands. In the eastern Islamic world it had been the intention that the Muslims should settle only in certain garrison towns, like Kūfa and Baṣra in Iraq, Fusṭāṭ (Old Cairo) in Egypt and Qayrawān in Ifrīqīya, and that they should live off the taxes of the land. No effort seems to have been made to develop such a system in Spain, and Muslim settlement seems to have been haphazard and determined by the interests of the settlers rather than any overall scheme. The conquerors settled down as property owners and do not seem to have received the *'aṭā'*, or pensions, which were such an important feature of early Muslim society in the Middle East. This in turn meant that there was no need for the elaborate and precocious bureaucracy which had grown up to service the system, nor any need to compile *dīwāns* or lists of those entitled to pensions. The slow development of bureaucracy in al-Andalus may in turn have been a reason for the slow development of a literary culture: not until the time of 'Abd al-Raḥmān II (822–52) did administration and a native literary culture begin to appear.

Cordoba became the capital shortly after the initial conquest and remained crucial to the politics of the period. Control of the capital was vital for anyone who sought to govern the country and no serious attempt was made to shift the capital elsewhere. The reasons for this are not clear at first. It was not the Roman or Byzantine capital and had little obvious strategic importance. It was, however, at the hinge of a number of important routes. To the north the roads ran through the passes of the Sierra Morena to Calatrava, Toledo and eventually to the Ebro valley. To the east the upper Guadalquivir valley gave access to the Levante, while south and west Elvira (Granada) and Seville were easily accessible. The geography of al-Andalus always made communications a problem, but Cordoba was probably the least inconvenient site for the centre of government.

Perhaps more important was the rich agricultural hinterland of the city and the fact that this was densely settled by the Muslims. These resources of supplies and men were often able to sustain the rulers when, in the reign of the Amir 'Abd Allāh (888–912) for example, other areas slipped out of their control. Toledo, another possible capital and the centre of Visigothic power, was clearly lacking in such local resources.

The non-Muslim population probably paid some taxes to Cordoba, probably a *jizya* or poll-tax and perhaps a land tax as well; a late source based on much earlier narratives recounts how a Christian count, Ardabast, son of the old king Witiza, rather than a Muslim bureaucrat was in charge of collecting the tax from the Christians.[28]

Naturally, people from the same tribal and ethnic backgrounds tended to settle in the same areas and in areas they considered appropriate for their lifestyle. On the whole the Arabs settled in the main cities and the fertile irrigated areas of the Guadalquivir valley, the Levante around Murcia and Zaragoza and the middle Ebro valley. In some places there were concentrations of men from the same tribes in the same area, Lakhm around Malaga for example, and the Judhāmīs and Tujībīs who settled in Zaragoza were to dominate the political life of the city and the surrounding area for centuries to come. Other tribes were more dispersed.

It would be wrong to think of these Arabs as Bedouin. Apart from the Qurashis, almost all of them belonged to the Yemeni group of Arab tribes. Some of these, like Lakhm and Judhām, had lived in the steppe lands of Jordan and southern Palestine, while others, like Khawlān and Maʿāfir, came from Yemen proper, a land of cities, well-built villages and carefully tended farms. In either case they would have been familiar with urban and agricultural life. Many of them were second or third generation immigrants to North Africa, reared in such urban settlements as Fusṭāṭ and Qayrawān and well placed to take advantage of the opportunities offered by their newly conquered lands. Tribal loyalties do not seem to have been strong. The settlers acquired land in absolute ownership, sometimes it would seem by inheritance, marrying the daughters of the previous Visigothic owners, as ʿAbd al-ʿAzīz b. Mūsā married Roderick's daughter and Sara, granddaughter of Witiza, married two Arab husbands in succession and founded a dynasty which produced, among others, the tenth-century historian Ibn al-Qutiya.[29] The integration of important elements of the Visigothic aristocracy into the new Muslim ruling class certainly accounts for some of the lack of opposition.

28. See the important passage in Ibn al-Khaṭīb, *Al-Iḥāṭa fi akhbār Gharnāṭa*, ed. M. ʾInan (4 vols, Cairo, 1973–77), i, pp. 100–5.

29. Manzano ʻArabes, berberes e indigenas', p. 15.

The Berbers were widely distributed throughout al-Andalus. Many settled in the central Meseta, Extremadura and the whole of the north and west apart from Zaragoza and its environs. Certain important cities like Toledo and Merida lay in areas with a predominantly Berber population. There was also a significant Berber presence in the Valencia area, where they probably practised transhumance, wintering flocks on the coastal plains and moving west into the mountains for the summer, and the Guadalquivir valley. These lands were in some ways less rich and inviting than the areas settled by the Arabs and it has been suggested that the Berbers were obliged to accept inferior lands despite the major contribution they had made to the conquests. However, there are reasons for thinking that this may not have been the case. As we have seen, there was no overall direction or system in the allocation of lands and, given the small numbers of the conquerors and the vast extent of the conquered lands, they would certainly have been able to take over richer areas had they wished to. Some Berbers were certainly farmers, used to irrigated agriculture, but the majority seem to have been pastoral people and it was natural that they should gravitate to the familiar pastoral environments of the Iberian peninsula. It is quite possible that many Berbers brought flocks with them with the result that they had no alternative but to look for pasture. This did not mean that there were not conflicts between Arabs and Berbers which eventually erupted in civil war, but there is no evidence that grievances over land were among the causes of this.

The early governors, 714–41

The years between the departure of Mūsā b. Nuṣayr in 714 and the installation of Balj b. Bishr al-Qushayrī as governor in 741 were the period when these early settlers enjoyed unopposed power. At first glance it is a period of great confusion: governors succeeded each other with bewildering speed and only one (ʿAnbasa b. Suḥaym al-Kalbī, 721–26) lasted for more than a year or two. Beneath this confusion, however, there are several common themes. The settlers wanted to control the riches of al-Andalus for themselves, and to increase that wealth by raiding areas in France, which were still in the Dār al-Ḥarb (the House of War, that is, non-Muslim territory) and from which booty could be obtained. It did not especially matter to them whether the governors who ruled the country were chosen by them, as sometimes happened, particularly when the previous governor had died a violent death, or appointed from outside, as long as they were responsive to their needs. In contrast to the period which followed 741, this first quarter of a century was comparatively free of internal strife and rebellion.

When Mūsā b. Nuṣayr departed, he left his son ʿAbd al-ʿAzīz in charge. He established himself as governor in Seville and married Roderick's widow. The story in the Arabic sources explains that she persuaded him to wear a crown and adopt other royal pretensions, as the Visigothic kings had, and that the Arab notables saw this as unIslamic and assassinated him. This certainly reflects their fears that he was attempting to make the governorship his family's property. They may also have been concerned that he was encouraging new settlers from North Africa and the Middle East who would demand a share of the wealth of the country. The struggle of the early arrivals to maintain their privileged status in the face of challenges from later immigrants was to be a major source of unrest in the period of the governors.[30] After ʿAbd al-ʿAzīz no governor died a violent death before 741 except at the hands of the infidel, and there were no rebellions of importance.

Muslim Spain was only loosely attached to the main body of the caliphate, but, given the vast distances involved, it is impressive to see how much influence the Umayyad caliphs in Damascus could exert on this, the newest and most distant of their provinces. Governors were in general appointed by the governor of Ifrīqīya in Qayrawān or sometimes, as in the case of al-Samḥ b. Mālik al-Khawlānī, by the Caliph in person, and they were almost always outsiders to the province with no local power base or following. This did not always mean that the wishes of the local people were ignored and the *Akhbār al-Majmūʿa* states, perhaps with exaggerated local patriotism, that if they did not like a governor or if he attempted to undermine their autonomy and privileged fiscal status, they would write to the Caliph who would send one who pleased them.[31] Sometimes, if the governor was killed, the settlers would 'elect' a successor, but such elections were not usually accepted by Qayrawān; when al-Samḥ b. Mālik was killed in the attack on Toulouse, they chose ʿAbd al-Raḥmān b. ʿAbd Allāh al-Ghāfiqī, but the governor of Qayrawān sent ʿAnbasa b. Suḥaym. When ʿAnbasa was himself killed while raiding in France in 726 the local people again 'elected' and again their nomination was rejected, but in 730

30. The assassination of Abd al-ʿAzīz is discussed in Chalmeta, *Invasion e Islamizacion*, pp. 245–54. Ibn ʿAbd al-Ḥakam's account of the event is translated in Melville and Ubaydli, *Christians and Moors*, pp. 14–17.

31. *Akhbār al-Majmūʿa*, p. 25.

an unpopular outsider was replaced by 'Abd al-Raḥmān al-Ghāfiqī as a sop to local opinion.

The Caliph in Damascus was remembered in the Friday prayers and his name appeared on the coins. Whether he received any more tangible benefits is not clear. In Muslim law a fifth of the wealth seized at the time of conquest belonged to the Caliph as a fifth had originally been reserved for the Prophet Muḥammad, but it is unlikely that the Caliph ever received any revenue from this fifth. Any attempts to secure a share of the revenues of al-Andalus for the Umayyad government were vigorously resisted by the early settlers.

In 718 the reforming Caliph 'Umar II (717–20) appointed al-Samḥ b. Mālik al-Khawlānī as governor to implement the fiscal reforms he had been introducing throughout the caliphate.[32] The governor arrived with a body of followers said to have been equal in number to the original conquerors. His first task, apparently, was to send to the Caliph 'a detailed description of al-Andalus, its rivers and its seas' – a sort of Doomsday Book. Then, in order to provide for his newly arrived followers, he intended to separate the land that had been taken by force (*'anwatan*) from the land that had been taken as a result of a treaty (*ṣulḥan*) and to take a fifth of the *'anwatan* as the government's share and distribute the remaining four-fifths among the new arrivals. Predictably, this aroused the indignation of the 'People of the Conquest' and they sent a deputation to the Caliph who responded by confirming the villages in the hands of those who had taken them as booty.[33] They would be liable to pay the *'ushr* or tithe on this land. The newcomers were accommodated by dividing the caliphal fifth among them in territorial concessions (*iqṭā'at*). For the first time the land was assessed for taxation, with the intention that the surplus should be sent to Damascus, as happened in other provinces of the caliphate. In the case of al-Andalus, al-Samḥ was allowed to use such revenue as remained after the payment of salaries and the expenses of the Holy War for the rebuilding of the bridge and city wall in Cordoba. In short, there is no unequivocal evidence that the caliphs received anything beyond gifts at the time of conquest from al-Andalus or that any financial strings bound the province to the central government. After the death of the Caliph in 720 and al-Samḥ in 721, these centralising measures seem to have been allowed to lapse.

32. I have followed the discussion of al-Samḥ's governorate in Chalmeta, *Invasion e Islamizacion*, pp. 259–68; see also Manzano, 'Arabes, berberes e indigenas', p. 21.
33. *Akhbār al-Majmū'a*, pp. 23–4.

The governors also issued coins from the earliest times in order to facilitate the distribution of booty and then the payment of taxes. The first of these date from immediately after the first conquests, 711–12.[34] Though they bear Latin inscriptions, such as the Islamic monotheist formula 'in nomine domini non nisi deus solus non deus similis', they are based not on Visigothic coins but on those issued by the Muslims in North Africa and ultimately on Byzantine originals. Under the governorate of al-Ḥurr (716–18) coins with bilingual Latin/Arabic inscriptions were minted, and in 720 al-Samḥ, as part of his fiscal reforms, minted the first purely Arab coins, with the sort of clear and elegant inscriptions which characterised Umayyad coinage throughout the caliphate. This suggests a development of financial administration, although it is not until the reign of 'Abd al-Raḥmān II (822–52) that we hear of an organised mint in Cordoba. Gold coins were struck in small numbers in the early years, but the use of gold was abandoned after 744–45 and thereafter silver *dirhams* were the standard issues.

This political establishment was typical of many areas of the early Islamic state, the conquerors and their descendants firmly in control, using the revenues of the province as they saw fit, obliging governors to work with them or be forced out and bitterly hostile to any attempts to undermine their position, either by central government or by any other group attempting to grab a share for themselves.

Attacks on France and the few remaining areas of resistance in the north of the Iberian peninsula were the major events. Many members of the Visigothic aristocracy had made their peace with the Muslims, but a few had fled northwards, among them Pelayo.[35] In the north these exiles joined forces with the local people, always resistant to any central government. Together they opposed the Muslims in the difficult and inaccessible mountain areas of the northern flanks of the Picos de Europa. Here they seem to have elected Pelayo as king and been victorious in a small encounter known to history as the battle of Covadonga and traditionally dated to 717. The reports of the Arab historians do not mention this trifling setback, but for later Christian sources the battle of Covadonga marks

34. The standard work on the early coinage of al-Andalus is A. Balaguer, *Las Emisiones transicionales Arabe-musulmanes de Hispania* (Barcelona, 1976). Early coins are also discussed and illustrated in Chalmeta, *Invasion e Islamizacion*, pp. 242–5.

35. For a full discussion of the history and historiography of Pelayo, see Collins, *Arab Conquest*, pp. 141–51, in which he suggests that Pelayo may have been a local lord like Theodemir with his power base in the north-west.

the first stage in the long struggle to expel the Muslims from Spain and has acquired a legendary importance.

At the time the Muslims were much more concerned to invade France, which offered prospects of booty wholly lacking in the inhospitable valleys of the Cantabrian mountains. Details are sketchy, but there were at least four expeditions, the first launched at the very beginning of the conquests, the other three led by the governors in person. In 721 al-Samḥ b. Mālik al-Khawlānī led an expedition against Toulouse on which he himself was killed, and in the summer of 725 ʿAnbasa b. Suḥaym al-Kalbī led a lightning raid right up the Rhone valley to Burgundy where the army pillaged Autun. Finally, the popular and well-respected governor of al-Andalus, ʿAbd al-Raḥmān b. ʿAbd Allāh al-Ghāfiqī, led an expedition through western France which was finally and disastrously defeated by Charles Martel at the battle of Poitiers (actually fought at Moussais la Bataille, to the north of Poitiers) in October 732.[36]

Historians from Gibbon onwards saw the battle of Poitiers as a major turning point and an event which marked the end of the great Muslim conquests which had begun a century before. More recently, scholars have tended to play down its effect: it was clearly significant in establishing the power of Charles Martel and the Carolingians in France, but it also had profound consequences in Muslim Spain. It signalled the end of the *ghanīma* (booty) economy. Up to this point pressure on resources in al-Andalus could be relieved by raiding and dissatisfied people had the opportunity to acquire more wealth. It was a popular activity: Ibn Idhārī, writing around 1300, looked back with nostalgia to the simplicities of these early, vigorous days: 'In those days the people of al-Andalus were admirable and excellent, determined in Holy War and eager for God's rewards so they threw themselves on the Christians (*Rūm*) in warfare and siege.' These were not wars of expansion and no attempt seems to have been made by the Muslims to settle any area north of Narbonne. The purposes of the raids were to take booty and to establish the prestige of the governor, whose most important public functions were the leadership of the Muslims in prayer in the mosque and in battle against the infidel. After 732 these opportunities were no longer available to anything like the same extent. The Muslims of al-Andalus were obliged to live off the finite resources of their own adopted country and competition for revenues and status soon gave rise to savage feuds.

36. For the Poitiers campaign see Lévi-Provençal, *HEM*, i, pp. 61–5; Chalmeta, *Invasion e Islamizacion*, pp. 284–8.

The coming of the Syrians, 741–56

This first phase of Muslim rule was brought to an end by a major upheaval in North Africa and its side-effects in al-Andalus. In 740 there was a Berber uprising against Arab rule. The main reasons for this seem to have been fiscal. During the period of conquest and expansion, the Arabs had been happy to grant their Berber followers the tax privileges which went with being full members of the Muslim community. With the end of expansion, the governor and financial administrator of Egypt, ʿUbayd Allāh b. al-Ḥabḥāb, tried to impose the *kharāj* (land tax) on these Berbers and reduce them to a subordinate status in order to increase the revenue yield now required to pay the Syrian army, the backbone of the caliphate. Further fuel was added to their justifiable resentment by the practice of taking Berber children for the harems of the Umayyad elite. Among some Berbers, these resentments led to the adoption of Kharijite beliefs. The Kharijites, a puritanical sect which tried to preserve the virtue of the earliest days of Islam, as they saw it, rejected the authority of the Umayyad caliphs and refused to pay taxes to them.

In a very short period of time, the whole Maghreb had slipped from the control of the governors. In response to the complete defeat of the local forces, the Caliph Hishām (724–43) set about recruiting a new army in Syria. Syria at this time was divided into a number of fairly small administrative units called *jund*s which were used as the basis on which the army was raised. Soldiers were recruited from the *jund*s of Qinnasrīn, Ḥims, Damascus and Jordan and on their way to North Africa they were joined by soldiers from Egypt who were held to form a separate *jund.* These *jund*s were divided by more than bureaucratic lines: by the middle Umayyad period all of them were dominated by one or other of the major tribal groups, Qays/Muḍar or Yemen.

The origins of the division between northern or Qays/Muḍar Arab tribes and southern or Yemen has been the subject of considerable controversy. In theory these groups were super-tribes, united by a common ancestry against their foes, but this genealogical theory disguised parties based on regional and political interests. To add to the confusion, it would seem that these labels meant different things in different areas. In Syria the division was basically between those tribes (Yemen) which were established in the area before the coming of Islam and the others (Qays/Muḍar) which migrated northwards from Arabia in the aftermath of the Muslim conquests. These divisions had been sharpened and made much more acute at the bloody battle of Marj Rāhiṭ in 684 when the Yemen supporters of the Umayyads had defeated their Qaysī opponents, inflicting injuries which were never forgotten. Subsequently there had been some reconciliation between the two parties and Qaysīs too supported the Umayyads, but the rift remained and increasingly undermined the power of the Umayyad caliphate. Of the *junds* at this time, Damascus and especially Qinnasrīn were Qaysī-dominated, Ḥims, Jordan and Palestine were Yemeni, as were most of the Egyptians.

The military expedition against the Berbers was led by a Qaysī commander, Kulthūm b. 'Iyāḍ, with his nephew Balj b. Bishr al-Qushayrī as second-in-command. It was not a success: in September/October 741 the Muslim army was defeated on the River Sebou in northern Morocco and the survivors, about 10,000 strong, now led by Balj b. Bishr, fled north to Ceuta. Here, completely cut off from their homeland, ragged and starving, they were in desperate straits. In vain they appealed to the governor of al-Andalus, Ibn Qaṭan, for help, but he refused.

Meanwhile, the Berber uprising in North Africa had resulted in a similar upheaval in al-Andalus. There had been rumblings of discontent in the peninsula before. According to the *Chronicle* of 754, a Berber (the *Chronicle* distinguishes the Berbers (Mauri) from Arabs (Saraceni)) called Munuz, hearing that his fellow Berbers in North Africa were being oppressed by the Arabs, raised a rebellion in the northern frontiers of al-Andalus, possibly trying to establish an independent lordship in Cerdaña. This was probably in 729. The next year Munuz made an alliance with Eudo, Duke of Aquitaine, but in 731 the governor, 'Abd al-Raḥmān al-Ghāfiqī, launched an expedition against him and he was finally surrounded in Cerdaña and was obliged to commit suicide in order to evade capture.[37]

The rebellion of 741 was much more serious. 'Ubayd Allāh b. al-Ḥabḥāb had appointed 'Uqba b. al-Ḥajjāj al-Salūlī as governor of al-Andalus to implement his strict fiscal policies. The Andalusi Arabs were fiercely opposed to him because the policies threatened their fiscal status and, perhaps, because they feared it would provoke the Berbers of al-Andalus to a similar rebellion.

In 740 there was a *coup d'état* in which 'Uqba was forced to resign

37. The only source which mentions this is the *Chronicle* of 754, cap. 79: for the chronology see Chalmeta, *Invasion e Islamizacion*, pp. 282–3.

and was replaced by 'Abd al-Malik b. Qaṭan al-Fihrī, a venerable figure chosen by the people of al-Andalus. It seems, however, that this change was too late to avoid an uprising. In the autumn of 741 there was a major revolt in the north-west and the Arabs were driven out of all the lands north of the Cordillera Central, so putting an end to the ephemeral Muslim occupation of this area.

The Berbers marched south towards Cordoba and Ibn Qaṭan found himself unable to resist them effectively. In his panic he looked across the Straits for allies. Balj and 'Abd al-Malik began to do business. Balj's men were so desperate that he was prepared to agree to almost any conditions which would see them fed, and he accepted that his men should fight the Berbers and then return to North Africa when their work was done. His only real stipulation was that they should return as a group, rather than be dispersed to be at the mercy of their enemies. In the spring of 742 the Syrians were helped to cross into al-Andalus.

The battle-hardened Syrians under Balj joined the Andalusi Arabs led by Ibn Qaṭan to defeat the Berbers in a fierce battle near Toledo. In the aftermath of victory, the Syrians were reluctant to leave this fertile and promising land, where, we are told, the Arabs lived 'like kings', and return to the hardships of North Africa. Relations between Balj and 'Abd al-Malik soon broke down and Balj launched a *coup* which left the old governor dead and himself and his Syrian followers in control. This could not go unavenged and the old-established Arabs (now called *Baladiyūn* (people of the country) in distinction to the *Shāmiyūn* or Syrians) launched a counter-attack, led by two of 'Abd al-Malik's sons. In August 742 this attempt was decisively defeated near Cordoba, but Balj was mortally wounded in the battle. Nonetheless, the Syrians remained in possession of Cordoba and chose a new governor from their own ranks who defeated the opposition, composed of both Arabs and Berbers, which had regrouped in the Merida area. Many Arabs of distinguished lineage were sold cheaply as slaves.[38]

The next year (743), a new governor was sent from Qayrawān by Ḥanẓala b. Ṣafwān, apparently in response to a petition from Andalusis of all parties who wanted peace. Abū'l-Khaṭṭar al-Ḥusām b. Ḍirār al-Kalbī was a member of the Yemeni aristocracy of Damascus (Kalb were one of the leading Yemenite tribes of Syria) and he attempted to solve the outstanding problems of the province. He first secured the release of all the Arab and Berber captives and

38. For these events see Chalmeta, *Invasion e Islamizacion*, pp. 307–27.

then set about providing for the Syrians who now clearly had to be accommodated in al-Andalus.

Abū'l-Khaṭṭār, perhaps on the advice of Count Ardabast, settled the Syrians in a methodical way. They were already organised in *jund*s and each *jund* was settled in a different area, chosen, allegedly, because it resembled their Syrian homeland. Thus the *jund* of Damascus was settled at Elvira (Granada), the *jund* of Jordan in Rayyu (Malaga and Archidona), the *jund* of Palestine in Sidonia, the *jund* of Hims in Seville and Niebla, the *jund* of Qinnasrīn in Jaen. The *jund* of Egypt, possibly the largest, was divided between the Algarve in the west and Tudmīr, the lands originally governed by the treaty with the Visigoth Theodemir which now seem to have been opened up for Muslim settlement, in the east. It is said that they were given a third of the property of the local people to live off, though again it is not clear whether this should be considered as revenues or actual lands to cultivate: certainly the image of these violent Syrian warriors suddenly settling down to plough the fields, prune the vines and dig the irrigation ditches is faintly improbable. It is most likely that the Syrians were given a third of the revenues paid by the people of the areas their *jund* was settled in. They were not concentrated in Cordoba or other garrison cities but dispersed throughout the area of the *jund*. The limited evidence suggests that they were responsible for collecting the revenues themselves and that they were obliged to pay the government *muqāṭaʿāt*, basically a fixed sum, from the revenues they collected. In exchange for this livelihood, the Syrians were obliged to do military service.[39]

The events of 741–43 profoundly changed the political character of Muslim Spain. It substantially increased the Arab element in the population, especially in those rural areas in the south which were to be the heartland of al-Andalus for centuries to come. It also increased the Syrian element. Most of the early settlers were ultimately of south Arabian origin, but the new arrivals came from Syria and the area the Arabs called al-Jazīra (the island), that is, the steppe lands of northern Iraq and Syria between the Tigris and Euphrates rivers. Many of these had long-standing loyalty to the Umayyad family. Along with the Arab tribesmen, there also arrived a significant number of *mawālī* of the Umayyad family, probably non-Arab native Syrians or prisoners of war from other regions of

39. See Chalmeta, *Invasion e Islamizacion*, pp. 331–5; for a full discussion of the settlement and fiscal obligation of the *junds*, see E. Manzano Moreno, 'El asentamiento y la organizacion de los ŷund-s sirios en al-Andalus', *Al-Qantara* xiv (1993), 330–8.

the Muslim empire. They formed an important group without tribal affiliations, owing their loyalty only to the ruling dynasty, and their presence in al-Andalus was vital to the later success of the Umayyads in establishing themselves as rulers.

The most immediate consequence was also the most destructive, the introduction into al-Andalus of the fierce Qays/Muḍar versus Yemen disputes. Previously the overwhelming dominance of Yemen had meant that there was little conflict, but the arrival of Balj, aggressively Qaysī, and his followers changed that. The defeat and temporary enslavement of many of the Yemenis added bitterness from their side to an already inflammatory mixture. It was difficult for any governor to break free from the constraints of the feud, since not to be generous to members of their own group would leave them without any reliable support. It was probably this insecurity which led Abū'l-Khaṭṭār, an outsider to al-Andalus without any local power base of his own, to rely on and favour the Yemenis. The Qaysīs could not afford to tolerate a governor who would only dispense favours to their hated rivals, and they found a new leader in al-Ṣumayl b. Ḥātim al-Kilābī, hard-bitten, brutal and fanatically devoted to the Qaysī cause.

War could not long be averted. The Qaysīs were fewer in number but stronger in the Cordoba area and possibly more effective militarily. Al-Ṣumayl set out to divide his enemies and succeeded in winning over the leader of the Yemeni tribes of Lakhm and Judhām. Both these tribes had long been settled in Syria and may have felt more in common with other Syrians than with the Yemeni tribes of South Arabia. This coalition rose in revolt and in April 745 defeated Abū'l-Khaṭṭār, who was taken prisoner but was soon rescued. There followed a period of confusion when different members of the coalition tried to take control as governor, until in January 747 al-Ṣumayl, who had remained behind the scenes, not claiming power for himself, produced an outside candidate, Yūsuf b. ʿAbd al-Raḥmān al-Fihrī.

It was a shrewd choice. Yūsuf was already an old man and al-Ṣumayl could expect him to be a pliable instrument. At the same time, he had positive advantages. He was a direct descendant of ʿUqba b. Nāfiʿ, hero of the early Muslim conquests in North Africa. Fihr, being a branch of Quraysh, were usually considered to belong to the Qaysī group, but Quraysh, being the Prophet's tribe, had always occupied an intermediate position somewhat outside tribal divisions and could hope to attract loyalty from all parties. In addition, the family had built up many contacts and alliances among the Berbers and could hope for support from some Berber groups. These assets recommended this otherwise rather undistinguished old gentleman to al-Ṣumayl and were also to mean that the Fihrīs were to be the only serious rivals to the Umayyads for control of the whole of al-Andalus.

Yūsuf began to exercise his power as his patron would have expected, excluding Yemenis from the fruits of office.[40] In 747 Yūsuf and al-Ṣumayl, aided, we are told, by the tradesmen of Cordoba including the butchers with their knives, defeated the Yemeni counter-attack at Secunda, on the south bank of the river opposite the city of Cordoba. Yūsuf began to grow in confidence. The collapse of the Umayyad caliphate of Damascus in 747–50 in the face of ʿAbbasid attacks from the east meant that he became an independent ruler. He felt strong enough to remove al-Ṣumayl to Zaragoza where he occupied himself helping victims of the terrible famine of the early 750s. But the old enmities were merely dormant. In 755 al-Ṣumayl was besieged in Zaragoza by Yemeni elements, Yūsuf was powerless to help him and he was only saved by an expedition of Qaysī volunteers from the south. It was into this environment of deadly factional conflict that the emissaries of ʿAbd al-Raḥmān b. Muʿāwiya, the Umayyad, arrived.

During this period of instability, the northern frontier of al-Andalus stabilised.[41] In the immediate aftermath of the conquest the Muslims penetrated as far as the north coast, leaving only a few upland valleys in the Pyrenees and isolated pockets of resistance on the northern slopes of the Picos de Europa; the sources even speak of a Muslim 'governor' in Gijon. Most of the plains of the Duero and the mountains of Galicia and Cantabria were occupied, in so far as there was a Muslim presence at all, by groups of Berbers, but we know very little about this and there is no record of permanent or significant occupation in these areas; nor were there any major campaigns, the Arabs finding France much more rewarding territory. Almost by default, the areas north of the Duero slipped out of Muslim hands after the Berber rebellion of 741 caused many of them to come south where they were heavily defeated in battle. A long famine which began in 750 seems to have caused many of the survivors to leave for North Africa. The Christian King Alfonso I (739–57) was able to establish some fortified outposts in the Duero plains and to raid even further south. The Cordillera Central marked

40. Yūsuf's governorate is described in Chalmeta, *Invasion e Islamizacion*, pp. 335–48.

41. For the historical geography of the frontier regions see Manzano Moreno, *Frontera.*

the most northerly limits of Muslim occupation in the western half of the peninsula, Coimbra, Coria, Talavera, Madrid, Guadalajara and Medinaceli all being frontier settlements. This position was hardly to change for three centuries. To the north of these settlements, the land seems to have been almost completely uninhabited except by wandering shepherds until the southernmost outposts of Christian settlement were encountered at places like Leon and Astorga.[42]

The eastern sector of the frontier presented a very different picture. Here Muslim settlement pressed up to and into the Pyrenees; Pamplona, Tudela, Huesca, Girona and Narbonne were in Muslim hands. Only in Narbonne, captured by Charles Martel's son Pepin, probably in 759,[43] was their rule challenged. The northern outposts of Muslim settlement lay not on an east–west axis but on a north-east to south-west line, and this was to remain the position until well into the twelfth century.

By 757 the Muslim presence in Andalus was clearly there to stay. Local resistance had effectively disappeared, a new generation of Arabs and Berbers born in al-Andalus was growing up and converts were beginning to be made among the indigenous people. But the new conquerors had conspicuously failed to develop a viable political system. After the 'Abbasid revolution of 750, al-Andalus was no longer part of a wider Muslim empire: it remained to be seen what alternative polity would emerge to fill the gap.

42. See C. Sanchez-Albornoz, *Despoblacion y Repoblacion del valle del Duero* (Buenos Aires, 1966).

43. Manzano Moreno, *Frontera*, pp. 75–7.

CHAPTER TWO

The Umayyad Amirate, 756–852[1]

'Abd al-Raḥmān I and the establishment of the Umayyads, 755–88

The Umayyad family were members of the Prophet's tribe, Quraysh, and distant cousins of Muḥammad himself.[2] In the early days of Islam, the Umayyad chief Abū Sufyān had been one of the leading opponents of the new religion, but, following the triumph of Muḥammad after 628, Abū Sufyān's son Mu'āwiya rapidly became one of the most important figures in the early Muslim state. After the conquest of Syria he was appointed governor and, in 661, with the assassination of Muḥammad's cousin and son-in-law, 'Alī, he became Caliph of the entire Muslim world (661–80). Mu'āwiya's direct line died out with his son Yazīd in 684. After a vigorous civil war between the supporters of the Umayyads and their enemies, the caliphate was seized by Mu'āwiya's second cousin Marwān b. al-Ḥakam (684–85) and his son 'Abd al-Malik (685–705), so inaugurating a second Umayyad dynasty, sometimes known as the Marwanids.

For half a century, the Umayyads ruled the whole of the Islamic world from Sind and Samarqand in the east to newly conquered al-Andalus in the west, but there was always opposition from those

1. Secondary sources for the early Umayyad amirate are very limited. For the reign of 'Abd al-Raḥmān I we have the final chapter of P. Chalmeta, *Invasion e Islamizacion: la sumision de Hispania y la formacion de al-Andalus* (Madrid, 1994), pp. 349–87. Thereafter, the fundamental account remains E. Lévi-Provençal, *HEM*, i, pp. 139–278. E. Manzano Moreno, *La Frontera de Al-Andalus en epoca de los Omeyas* (Madrid, 1991) is invaluable, not just for the study of the frontier zones but for wider questions of the political structure of the amirate.

2. For the role of the Umayyads in the eastern Islamic world, H. Kennedy, *The Prophet and the Age of the Caliphates* (London, 1986), pp. 82–123, and G.R. Hawting, *The First Dynasty of Islam* (London, 1986).

who felt that the hereditary monarchy of a family who had been among Muḥammad's leading enemies was unIslamic and those who resented the domination of the Muslim world by the Syrian military supporters of the dynasty. From 747 to 750 there was a vast upheaval, the ʿAbbasid revolution, which swept the Umayyads and their Syrian supporters from power. Most of the members of the ruling house were rounded up and executed, but a few, mostly less prominent, individuals were able to lie low and make their escape.

One such was ʿAbd al-Raḥmān b. Muʿāwiya, a young grandson of the great Caliph Hishām (724–43). After some hair-breadth escapes, he fled to North Africa, accompanied only by a few *mawālī*, among them Badr, later to be his right-hand man in al-Andalus. His first intention seems to have been to secure Ifrīqīya (Tunisia), but the governor, ʿAbd al-Raḥmān al-Fihrī, was hostile and he was obliged to seek refuge among his mother's relations, the Nafza Berbers. Thwarted in Africa, he sent Badr to make contact with the Umayyad *mawālī* among the Syrian *jund*s in al-Andalus. There were said to have been 500 of them in the *dīwān*, led by ʿUbayd Allāh b. ʿUthmān and ʿAbd Allāh b. Khālid of Damascus and Yūsuf b. Bukht of Qinnasrīn. At first they tried to attract the support of the Qaysī leader, al-Ṣumayl, then under siege in Zaragoza, but he refused, fearing that ʿAbd al-Raḥmān would like to make himself effective ruler, so they turned to the opposition Yemenis for support. In the early autumn of 755, after more than five years on the run, ʿAbd al-Raḥmān crossed to Almuñecar on the south coast of al-Andalus.

At first he was given refuge in the nearby homes of his *mawālī*, Ibn Khālid and Abū ʿUthmān, protected by 300 horsemen. After the attempt to reach a compromise with Yūsuf al-Fihrī and al-Ṣumayl, ʿAbd al-Raḥmān began to make contact with Yemeni leaders throughout the south. By the next spring (756) he had recruited an army of about 2,000 Umayyad *mawālī* and Yemeni *jundi*s and marched on Cordoba. Here his supporters fought and defeated the Qaysī army of Yūsuf and al-Ṣumayl and, in May 756, he entered the capital.

The proclamation of ʿAbd al-Raḥmān b. Muʿāwiya as Amir in the mosque of Cordoba on Friday 14 May 756 was not the end of the Umayyad seizure of power in al-Andalus, but only the end of the beginning. The new Amir was determined to build up a secure power base in al-Andalus which would enable him to survive and pass on the title to his descendants in a way no previous governor had been able to do. He also intended to establish himself as an independent ruler. After the first year, he no longer had the names of the ʿAbbasid caliphs of the east acknowledged in the Friday prayers in

Cordoba, and while he retained the fairly modest title of Amir, he acknowledged no temporal superior.

ʿAbd al-Raḥmān had a number of advantages over his rivals for power. He was a member of the Prophet's tribe of Quraysh and of the family of the Umayyad caliphs: no-one could deny his high descent. On the other hand there were many other Qurashīs in al-Andalus, notably Yūsuf al-Fihrī himself, and the Umayyad caliphs had been violently and completely rejected by the eastern Islamic world, which might have encouraged sympathy among the Syrians of al-Andalus but not much respect. The Umayyads were very much outsiders as well: as far as we can tell, no member of the extensive clan had ever visited al-Andalus before. ʿAbd al-Raḥmān's father Muʿāwiya had died when he was a boy and had not played an important role in the later Umayyad caliphate, and he himself was still a young man of 26 with no real political experience.

In addition to the reputation, being an Umayyad did bring ʿAbd al-Raḥmān a decisive advantage in terms of a small but committed band of supporters and the opportunity to recruit more. The band of supporters consisted of the Umayyad *mawālī* in al-Andalus with whom Badr had originally made contact, notably Abū ʿUthmān, his son-in-law ʿAbd Allāh b. Khālid and Yūsuf b. Bukht. To these were added ʿAbd al-Karīm and ʿAbd al-Malik, grandsons of one of the leaders of the original conquest of Spain, Mughīth al-Rūmī, himself said to have been a *mawlā* of the Umayyad Caliph al-Walīd, and Tammām b. ʿAlqama, who was probably a member or *mawlā* of Thaqīf, a tribe with close ties to the Umayyads. These *mawālī* seem to have had extensive possessions in Cordoba and the lands of Elvira and Rayyu, but they had little prestige in the tribal politics and rivalries which dominated al-Andalus and the arrival of the Umayyad gave them their only hope of real political power. But this group was not restricted to al-Andalus: there were Umayyad *mawālī* in other parts of the Muslim world who would be keen to come and support the new regime.

In addition to the *mawālī*, many members of the Umayyad family continued to arrive from the east and they too were committed supporters of the new Amir. The most important of these was ʿAbd al-Malik b. ʿUmar b. Marwān: it was he who advised ʿAbd al-Raḥmān to drop the name of the ʿAbbasid Caliph al-Manṣūr from the Friday prayers and he became governor of Seville and one of the Amir's most reliable generals. In this way, ʿAbd al-Raḥmān built up a following, based on the *mawālī* and his own clan and geographically centred in Cordoba and the south-east, that transcended the tribal followings which his opponents could command and which was entirely dedicated to his success. None of his rivals could achieve that.

ʿAbd al-Raḥmān b. Muʿāwiya was to reign as Amir for 33 years after his proclamation at Cordoba, and the length of his rule was a major factor in the success of the Umayyads; if he had died or been killed as so many other governors had been after a few years, the Umayyad regime would no doubt have followed its ephemeral predecessors into obscurity.

ʿAbd al-Raḥmān embarked on a policy of ensuring that he was acknowledged as Amir throughout the whole peninsula, but he faced many rivals in al-Andalus. In the Arabic chronicles, with their marked Umayyad/Cordovan sympathies, those who resisted are portrayed as rebels against a legitimate Umayyad authority; in reality they were local chiefs or strong men attempting to preserve their influence against expanding and encroaching Umayyad power. The previous amirs of Cordoba had had little coercive power beyond the strength of their own following: real influence in the provinces remained in the hands of the leaders of the *jund*s or other local notables. One of ʿAbd al-Raḥmān's main objectives was to expand the authority of Cordoba throughout the Muslim-held areas of the Iberian peninsula.

In these circumstances, it is hardly surprising that many people resented the attempts of the early Umayyad amirs to rob them of their autonomy and impose a measure of civil and fiscal control over them. There were other reasons for resentment too. The arriving members of the Umayyad family needed estates and, as the Syrian *jundī*s were not property owners, lands had to be confiscated from the Baladis and the Christians. It was at this time that the bulk of the estates of Count Ardabast were confiscated and, probably, that the areas covered by the pact with Theodemir were opened up for Muslim settlement.[3]

ʿAbd al-Raḥmān's first problem was to destroy the power of his predecessors, Yūsuf al-Fihrī and al-Ṣumayl, who still remained in the field despite their recent defeat. At first a compromise was arranged and Yūsuf was able to keep his possessions and reside in Cordoba, but it appears that he soon found this intolerable and he escaped to Merida where he raised a large army of Berbers. However, he was defeated by troops loyal to ʿAbd al-Raḥmān and in 759/60 was murdered near Toledo. The Fihrīs enjoyed extensive

3. See Chalmeta, *Invasion e Islamizacion*, pp. 262–3.

support among the Berbers and were the only family who could rival the Umayyads; they were not to give up easily. It was seven years before ʿAbd al-Raḥmān felt strong enough to challenge their hold on Toledo. In 764 he sent two of his most trusted commanders, Badr and Tammām b. ʿAlqama, against the city where Hishām b. ʿUrwa al-Fihrī was holding out and he was captured and executed. There were at least two other attempts by Fihrīs to establish themselves in the peninsula. The first of these came in 778–79 when ʿAbd al-Raḥmān b. Ḥabīb al-Fihrī, known as the Slav from his blond complexion and blue eyes, landed in the east of the country and attracted some support before being killed by one of his Berber supporters. Then, in the autumn of 785,[4] almost at the end of ʿAbd al-Raḥmān's reign, Yūsuf al-Fihrī's son Muḥammad gathered an army in the Toledo area. Defeated by the Umayyad troops, he fled west towards Coria where he was isolated and killed. ʿAbd al-Raḥmān went on to chastise the Nafza Berbers in the area, presumably because they had supported the rebel. The Fihrīs felt they had as good a claim to al-Andalus as the Umayyads and they could mobilise widespread support among the Berbers, but they seem to have been no match for the Umayyad *mawālī* and their allies among the Syrian *jundī*s.

Another threat was posed by agents of the ʿAbbasid caliph Abū Jaʿfar al-Manṣūr. Al-Manṣūr made one serious attempt to regain control of al-Andalus in 763. He sent no troops but a standard and a diploma of investiture as Amir of al-Andalus. The local leader was al-ʿAlā b. al-Mughīth al-Yaḥṣubī from Beja in southern Portugal, who gathered a large number of supporters in the west of al-Andalus. ʿAbd al-Raḥmān left Cordoba and moved west to the powerful fortress at Carmona, high on the hill where the castle still dominates the surrounding plains. Here he fought what was probably the most desperate encounter of his reign. The chronicler Ibn Idhārī takes up the story:[5]

> He fortified himself there with his *mawālī*, his faithful supporters [*thiqāt*] and the rest of his men and al-ʿAlā b. al-Mughīth began a close investment. When he had besieged the town for many days and the siege dragged on, al-ʿAlā's army began to get restless. ʿAbd al-Raḥmān knew that they were impatient and thinking of bridles and saddles and he ordered a fire to be built and he ordered his

4. For the dating of al-Rāzī, quoted by Ibn Idhārī, see *Al-Bayān al-mughrib fi akhbār al-Andalus wa'l-Maghrib*, ed. E. Lévi-Provençal and G.S. Colin (Leiden, 1948), ii, pp. 57–8.

5. Ibid., pp. 51–2.

companions to burn the scabbards of their swords and said to them, 'Come out with me against this crowd, determined never to return!' They were seven hundred of them, courageous men and famous heroes. So they took their swords in their hands searching for their enemy. The battle lasted long until God did His marvellous work and the army and companions of al-ʿAlā quaked and fled and their fate became a warning for the people of the world. Al-ʿAlā was among the first to be killed.

Only by such desperate actions did the Umayyad amirate survive. The dead head of the defeated rebel was enbalmed and sent east with a merchant who left it one night with a note attached in the markets of Qayrawān, the nearest ʿAbbasid outpost (in Tunisia, other accounts say it was taken to Medina and left outside the caliphal tent). When al-Manṣūr was informed he is said to have remarked, 'We all belong to God. We sent this miserable man to his death. Praise be to God who has put the sea between me and this devil!' It hardly needs to be said that this imaginative story appears only in Andalusi histories[6] and finds no place in ʿAbbasid chronicles. This débâcle meant the end of direct ʿAbbasid interference. After this there were exchanges of abusive correspondence, but the Umayyads of Spain posed no real threat to the Baghdad regime and the ʿAbbasids were soon preoccupied with problems much nearer home.

The rebellion of al-ʿAlā b. al-Mughīth was fuelled by local grievances as well as ʿAbbasid encouragement. ʿAbd al-Raḥmān was determined to assert his power over the Syrian *junds*. Before the coming of the Umayyads, the leaders (*ra'īs*, pl. *ru'asā'*) of the *junds* were either self-appointed or chosen by their followers: they were effectively independent and could make war or alliances as they saw fit. ʿAbd al-Raḥmān set out to replace the old-style leaders with his own supporters. The clearest example of this comes from the *junds* of Egypt and Hims settled in Beja and Seville. It seems that ʿAbd al-Raḥmān had appointed the Umayyad ʿAbd al-Malik b. ʿUmar b. Marwān as governor of Seville and the west and that this was resented by local leaders who felt that this was an encroachment on their power. Al-ʿAlā had attracted widespread support in the area and ʿAbd al-Raḥmān is said to have been worried that the soldiers from Seville in his own army would desert to the rebel cause.[7] In 766 one Saʿīd al-Maṭarī rebelled in Niebla and took over Seville

6. See for example *Al-Bayān*; *Akhbār al-Majmūʿa*, ed. and Spanish translation E. Lafuente y Alcantara (Madrid, 1867), p. 103.

7. Al-Banyān ii, p. 52.

before being killed by the Amir. In the same year he had another leader from the area, Abū'l-Ṣabbāḥ Yaḥyā al-Yaḥṣubī, executed in Cordoba. The dead man's followers sought revenge and the people of Seville joined his cousins in an attempt to take Cordoba by surprise. It was not until 774 that the rebellion was finally defeated by 'Abd al-Malik b. 'Umar. This seems to have completed the defeat of the *jundi* leaders in this area and their subjection to effective control from Cordoba.[8]

Another ideological challenge came from an 'Alid pretender. In the eastern Islamic world, the members of the house of 'Alī, first cousin to the Prophet and husband of his daughter Fāṭima, were the most powerful focus of opposition to both Umayyad and 'Abbasid caliphates. Most of their following, however, came from Iraq and points east and they had little support among the Syrians who formed the majority of the Arab settlers in al-Andalus. Heterodox religious opinions were more widespread among the Berbers, however. In North Africa at this time, these opinions usually took the form of Kharijism, but in 768 and 770 a Berber of the tribe of Miknāsa called Shaqyā b. 'Abd al-Wāḥid led a revolt, claiming to be related to the 'Alids.[9] His rebellion began in Santaver, in the hills around Cuenca, but for the next nine years he dominated much of the sparsely inhabited upland country between Santaver and Coria and Medellin far to the west. It was a guerrilla war, the Berbers retreating to the mountains on approach of the Amir's army and returning to the villages and plains when they had gone. The rebellion was an irritant, but the soi-disant Fatimid seems to have attracted no support amongst the Arabs or the town dwellers and 'Abd al-Raḥmān was also able to make an alliance with Hilāl al-Madyūnī, described as head (*ra's*) of the Berbers in the east of al-Andalus. In the end, in 776–77, Shaqyā was taken by treachery and killed. Although he clearly commanded support among the Berbers, there is little evidence that this, or indeed any other of the Berber disturbances of the time, were motivated by Berber resentment against Arab control. 'Abd al-Raḥmān had Berber supporters and Berber opponents just as he had Arab supporters and Arab opponents; the real distinction was between those who threw in their lot with Cordoba and those who were determined to maintain their own local independence.

8. For the chronology of these rebellions see Lévi-Provençal, *HEM*, i, pp. 110–12; for the political analysis see E. Mauzano Moreno, 'El asentamiento y la organizacion de los ŷund-s sirios en al-Andalus', *Al-Qantara* xiv (1993), 338–46.

9. The revolt is discussed in Manzano Moreno, *Frontera*, pp. 238–49.

There were areas of localised resistance in the west and north of the peninsula. Not surprisingly, ʿAbd al-Raḥmān had difficulty imposing his authority on distant Zaragoza.[10] The Arab notables of Zaragoza and the Ebro valley resisted Umayyad attempts to take the city as they had resisted the attempts of previous Amirs, and the tradition of local autonomy was well established. In about 774 Sulaymān b. Yaqẓān al-Aʿrābī, lord of Barcelona and Girona, and al-Ḥusayn b. Yaḥyā b. Saʿd b. ʿUbāda, descendant of a famous Madinan companion of the Prophet in Zaragoza, were the main powers in the area. In order to maintain his independent status, Sulaymān sent a mission to Charlemagne's court at Paderborn to ask his support, probably in return for the overlordship of Zaragoza. Charlemagne arrived in the Ebro valley in 778 but al-Ḥusayn refused to cooperate with the Emperor who, having no siege engines, had to withdraw, humiliated, from the walls of the city. It was during his return journey that the Basques attacked his rear guard in the Pyrenean pass at Roncesvalles, giving rise to the legends which are recounted in the Song of Roland, though the first text of this great epic does not appear for three centuries after the event and the historical detail has become wildly confused.

In the aftermath of this débâcle, Sulaymān was executed by his erstwhile ally al-Ḥusayn, but his sons inherited his position in Barcelona and Girona. It seems that the Amir ʿAbd al-Raḥmān was alarmed by this turn of events. In 781 he led a military expedition to demand the submission of al-Ḥusayn b. Yaḥyā and to re-establish Muslim control in the Upper Ebro valley. At first al-Ḥusayn accepted the Amir's authority and was confirmed as governor of the city, but the next year he threw off this allegiance. ʿAbd al-Raḥmān returned and assaulted the city with siege engines (*manjanīq*), and al-Ḥusayn was captured and executed and severe measures taken against the townspeople. The whole complex episode shows how the Umayyad Amir tried to establish his authority over the local magnates by a mixture of diplomacy and occasional force but that, as long as they were content to accept his overlordship, he was prepared to leave them in peace. By the end of his reign, Merida and Toledo were being governed by his sons, Hishām and Sulaymān, but it is not clear that the Umayyads exercised any direct control

10. The complex events in Zaragoza are discussed in Chalmeta, *Invasion e Islamizacion*, pp. 367–81, whose account I have largely followed. Manzano Moreno, *Frontera*, discusses the history and status of these local magnate families (pp. 208–23) and ʿAbd al-Raḥmān's attempts to control the city (pp. 315–18). M.J. Viguera Molins gives a simplified account of events (*Aragon Musulman*, Zaragoza, 1981, pp. 57–65).

in the Ebro valley. In one area they certainly did not: it was in 785, according to the *Chronicle* of Moissac,[11] that the inhabitants of Girona threw off the authority of the sons of Sulaymān b. Yaqẓān and handed their city over to the Carolingians. The event produced no reaction in Cordoba and is not noted by the Arab chroniclers.

Not all of 'Abd al-Raḥmān's energies were devoted to assuring his military control over al-Andalus. His reign saw the confirmation of the position of Cordoba as the capital of al-Andalus. The status of the city was confirmed when 'Abd al-Raḥmān built a country palace at al-Ruṣāfa to the north-east of the town, in addition to the Qaṣr in the centre of town, and in 785 he began the construction of the mosque which still survives, with many later additions, to the present day.

The reigns of Hishām I and al-Ḥakām I, 788–822

'Abd al-Raḥmān b. Mu'āwiya died on 7 October 788. His achievements had been enormous, but he had put them all in jeopardy by his hesitation about the succession. While it was clear he intended that the amirate should remain hereditary within the Umayyad house, it was not certain which of his sons should succeed him. The principle of primogeniture, which became so important to the ruling houses of mediaeval Christendom, was never established in the Umayyad family: designation by the previous ruler and acceptance by other members of the family and their supporters were the determining factors in deciding who amongst its members should succeed. 'Abd al-Raḥmān had three sons who emerged as possible candidates: Sulaymān, who had been born in the east and was now in his early forties, Hishām, who had been born in Cordoba in 757, and 'Abd Allāh, who does not seem to have been a serious candidate at this stage but was to become an important figure in years to come. Neither Sulaymān nor Hishām were at their father's deathbed, Sulaymān being in Toledo, Hishām in Merida. Some say that Hishām was his father's final choice, others that the dying Amir told 'Abd Allāh to acknowledge whichever of the two reached Cordoba first: Hishām, he said, had the advantages of piety and a good education, Sulaymān of age, bravery and the devotion of the Syrians.[12]

11. Quoted in Lévi-Provençal, *HEM*, ii, p. 128.
12. Ibn Idhārī, *Al-Bayān*, ii, p. 61.

It only took six days for Hishām to come from Merida, and 'Abd Allāh greeted him as ruler and handed over the seal of office, but his other brother was not prepared to accept this verdict and gathered his supporters to march south. There was a short, sharp conflict near Jaen and Sulaymān's men were defeated. It took almost two months for Hishām to reduce Toledo and oblige his brother to surrender, but in 789 Sulaymān was paid 60,000 *dīnār*s in cash, possibly half the annual income of the amirate at this time, and was forced to leave for North Africa and promise not to return: Umayyads might be defeated and disgraced but, at this time, they would not be executed like any common rebel, for that would undermine the status of the whole ruling house.[13]

As far as we can tell, the new amir faced little internal opposition after the defeat of his brothers. He had indirect dealings with the magnates of the Ebro valley. In 788/9 Sa'id b. al-Ḥusayn al-Anṣārī, whose father had held Zaragoza against the Umayyads in the previous reign, took the city again, proclaiming himself Amir. He was soon defeated, not by Umayyad troops but by Mūsā b. Fortūn b. Qasī, whose grandfather had been Count of the area in Visigothic times and one of the earliest and most distinguished converts to Islam.[14] In 791/2 Zaragoza was taken over by Maṭrūḥ, the son of Sulaymān b. Yaqẓān, and an expedition was sent from Cordoba to drive him out. The problem was solved, however, when Matrūḥ was murdered by one 'Amrūs b. Yūsuf while he was out hunting and the city was handed over to the Umayyad forces.

'Amrūs came from a *muwallad* (native Muslim) background and is first recorded as a *ghulām* (military page) in the service of Sulaymān b. Yaqẓān and his family. He now seems to have decided to throw in his lot with the Umayyads against his old masters: he and his family were rewarded by the favour of the ruling dynasty and during the next century they became one of the most powerful families in the Upper March.[15] The rise of the Banū Qasī and Banū 'Amrūs at this time, allied with the Umayyads against the leading Arab families of the area, marks the beginning of the entry of the *muwallad*s into the political life of al-Andalus.

The Arab chroniclers give Hishām a pious and ascetic personality

13. Lévi-Provençal, *HEM*, ii, pp. 139–41.

14. Ibn Idhārī, *Al-Bayān*, ii, p. 62: see art. 'Banū Kasī' by P. Chalmeta in *Encyclopaedia of Islam* new edn (Leiden, 1960–), and A. Cañada Juste, 'Los Banū Qasī (714–924)', *Principe de Viana* clviii–clix (1980), 5–90.

15. The origins of the family are discussed in Manzano Moreno, *Frontera*, pp. 219–22.

and say that he sought to exert his authority rather by personal example and by leading the Muslims against the Christians of the north.[16] His commitment to good works expressed itself in the completion of the first phase of the mosque in Cordoba, including the ablution facilities and the minaret and the repair of the bridge. Another manifestation of his piety was the sending of military expeditions against the Christians, among them a number of campaigns in the Asturias and Upper Ebro and a major attack on Narbonne and Carcassonne in 793, when the Count of Toulouse, William Short-Nose, was killed. Hishām himself did not lead these campaigns but entrusted command to the two brothers, ʿAbd al-Malik and ʿAbd al-Karīm b. ʿAbd al-Wāhid b. Mughīth. These campaigns were important in asserting the role of the Umayyads as leaders of all the Muslims of al-Andalus and of bringing Umayyad armies to parts of the country where they would not normally penetrate. In this Hishām was establishing a precedent which would be followed by many of his successors.

ʿAbd al-Karīm was Hishām's chief minister until his death fairly early in the reign. The inner circle also included the secretary ʿĪsā b. Shuhayd, whose father had served ʿAbd al-Raḥmān and whose family was to provide Cordoba with bureaucrats for the next three centuries as well as one of al-Andalus's greatest poets. Hishām's modest piety, attendance at funerals and visitations of the sick earned him such a reputation that the great Medinan scholar, Mālik b. Anas, whose work so profoundly affected al-Andalus, is said to have wished that Hishām could make the pilgrimage in person (which of course he could not, Mecca and Medina being in the power of the ʿAbbasid caliphs of Baghdad).

The connection with Medina was to prove very important. As far as we can tell, Andalusis never visited Damascus or Baghdad at this time, although there was a good deal of immigration from the eastern Islamic world, but they could and did go on pilgrimage to Medina and Mecca in comparatively large numbers, especially those who aspired to be *faqīh*s or *qāḍī*s. It was not surprising, therefore, that the knowledge of Muslim law that they picked up was the teaching of the pre-eminent Medinan master, Mālik b. Anas. Mālik (d. 795) was the founder of the oldest of the four 'orthodox' schools of Islamic law (the other three being the Ḥanbalī, the Shāfiʿī and the Hanafi, all developed in the ninth century). Māliki law, as expounded in the *Kitāb al-Muwaṭṭā'* of Mālik himself and later works,

16. See for example the character sketch in Ibn Idhārī, *Al-Bayān*, ii, pp. 65–6.

notably *al-Mudawwana al-Kubrā* of Saḥnūn of Qayrawān (d. 854), was essentially the codified practice of Medina. As such it was practical and much concerned with ordering everyday life and especially with the facilitating of trade and commerce. At the same time, the system left little room for abstract speculation and virtually none at all for innovation. The fact that it could be adopted as a fully worked out system no doubt increased its attractions for an isolated Muslim colony like that in al-Andalus, whose members wanted practical solutions rather than opportunities for debate. It also gave great power and status to a small, self-perpetuating group of scholars who were familiar with the doctrines, notably, in the first generation, Yaḥyā b. Yaḥyā al-Laythī (d. 848), a pupil of Mālik himself, who by his advice effectively controlled the appointment and dismissal of the *qāḍī*s of Cordoba. The adoption of the Malikite school so completely meant that al-Andalus was spared the sort of sectarian dissensions which tore Baghdad society apart in the third/tenth and early fourth/eleventh centuries. Malikism was hostile alike to Kharijism, Shi'ism and even to the more innocent forms of Sufism, and none of them really secured widespread support in al-Andalus. On the debit side, however, Malikism offered a rather formal and rigorist version of Islam, more concerned with correct performance than inspiration, and it discouraged speculation and discussion: if Cordoba was spared the conflicts that convulsed Baghdad, it also saw none of the intellectual excitement that accompanied them.

Hishām died on 17 April 796. He was careful to leave no uncertainty about the identity of his chosen successor and his son al-Ḥakam, now 26 years old, was duly accepted as Amir in Cordoba. The sources portray him as a very different character from his father. Tall, thin, haughty and strikingly dark in complexion, the new prince was to prove a formidable ruler. He was fond of women and wine, too much so some said, and was no mean poet, but he was remembered more for his cunning, his implacable ruthlessness and the awesome speed with which he reacted to news of disaffection.

And disaffection did not take long to become apparent. His father had been opposed by his two brothers, Sulaymān and 'Abd Allāh. Both these were still alive, in exile in North Africa, and they were now determined to regain their lost inheritance. The turbulent Sulaymān spent the next four years wandering the country, attempting to build up enough support, largely among the Berbers of the south, to dislodge his nephew. He was defeated in a number of encounters and was finally surrendered to al-Ḥakam by the Berber governor of Merida, Aṣbagh b. Wansūs. He was executed in 800, the first member of the ruling family to suffer this indignity.

'Abd Allāh was much more successful in establishing a position for himself and his family in the Umayyad polity. He tried to establish himself in the Upper March, even visiting Charlemagne in Aachen to solicit his support, without much success. In 800 he returned and attempted to establish himself at Huesca, but he was forced on to Valencia. Valencia was not, at this stage, a very important Muslim centre, but 'Abd Allāh was able to use the area as a base for negotiation with his nephew. In 802 an agreement was finally reached by which he was established in the city and given a salary (*rizq*) of 1,000 *dīnār*s a month, presumably to pay his supporters, and an annual bonus (*ma'ārif*) of 1,000 *dīnārs*.[17] This arrangement led to the Valencia area being effectively an appanage of this branch of the Umayyad family, and 'Abd Allāh was known thereafter as al-Balansī (the Valencian). In fact the arrangement worked well: this area had never been under the effective control of Cordoba and 'Abd Allāh's rule brought it within the Umayyad orbit, while his military ambitions, and those of his son 'Ubayd Allāh, were directed against the Christians of the north.

The most famous and dramatic events of al-Ḥakam's reign were revolts in Cordoba itself.[18] The causes of the widespread discontent are by no means clear but are probably connected with al-Ḥakam's autocratic determination to stamp his authority on this and other cities and to oblige the people to pay taxes. He had also distanced himself from the local elite by recruiting a private bodyguard commanded by a local Christian, al-Rabī' b. Theodulfo. Al-Ḥakam was basically trying to establish a reliable military and fiscal foundation for the amirate, but it was not surprising that some pious Muslims were numbered among the dissidents. Others said it was the natural restlessness of the Cordovans.[19] The unrest occurred in two stages. In 805 there was a conspiracy among certain notables of Cordoba to mount a *coup d'état* and put al-Ḥakam's cousin Muḥammad b. al-Qāsim on the throne. Unfortunately for the conspirators, Muḥammad did not share their enthusiasm for the project, which he revealed to the Amir. He sent his trusted secretary to overhear a clandestine meeting and record the names that were mentioned. This the secretary did, though being careful, according

17. The terms are given in Ibn Idhārī, *Al-Bayān,* ii, pp. 70–1.
18. These disturbances are discussed in full in Lévi-Provençal, *HEM,* i, pp. 160–73.
19. Ibn Idhārī, *Al-Bayān,* ii, pp. 85–6.

to Ibn al-Qūṭiya,[20] to reveal his presence before his own name came up. The conspirators were treated without mercy and 72 of them were executed. It seems to have been a movement within the elite, for the names that we have are either Arab or, like Masrūr al-Khādim, members of the palace staff, and it was in no sense anti-Umayyad or an attempt at social revolution, but was rather an attempt by leaders of Muslim society to preserve status and privilege which they felt the Amir was trying to undermine.

Numerous executions followed and Cordoba was surprised and shocked by the Amir's severity. His action alienated many who had not been actively involved in the *coup* attempt. For thirteen years discontent rumbled on and the Amir fortified himself in the city and became more and more dependent on his guards. Then in 818 opposition erupted again in a spectacular manner. There was a widespread uprising in the populous suburb, usually referred to simply as al-Rabaḍ (the suburb), which lay to the south of the city itself, across the Guadalquivir river. The uprising attracted support from such respectable figures as the jurist Yaḥyā b. Yaḥyā al-Laythī as well as the populace in general (called the *'āmma* or the *sawdā'* in the Arabic sources). The causes of the discontent are disputed. According to some sources there were complaints about taxation and especially the raising of 'unQuranic' taxes (*maghārim* or *waẓā'if*) to supplement the 'legitimate' tax base of the Umayyad amirs which was very limited. Al-Ḥakam is said to have been the first ruler of al-Andalus to acquire *mamlūk* (slave) soldiers, and recruiting and maintaining the sort of full-time guard al-Ḥakam built up would certainly have required additional sources of income. The combination of resentments among the Cordovans at being excluded from power and paying more taxes brought together a broad cross-section of the population to oppose the Amir.

If the cause of the rebellion is unclear, the results are not: the insurgents attempted to cross the bridge and storm the city proper but they were beaten off by loyal troops, led by the *ḥājib* (chief minister), 'Abd al-Karīm b. Mughīth, while two members of the ruling family with military experience, 'Ubayd Allāh b. 'Abd Allāh al-Balansī and Isḥāq b. al-Mundhir, led troops out of a side gate to attack the rebels from the rear. Their defeat was total and the vengeance of the Amir was terrible. After an initial slaughter, he ordered that the suburb south of the river be destroyed and its

20. Ibn al-Qūṭiya, *Ta'rīkh iftitāḥ al-Andalus*, ed. and trans. J.M. Nichols (unpublished PhD thesis, Chapel Hill, 1975), pp. 111–15.

inhabitants driven into exile. Only a few, like the jurist Yaḥyā b. Yaḥyā al-Laythī, went into hiding and were later pardoned. The most important consequence of this diaspora was that many of the refugees went to Morocco where they settled in Fes on the opposite bank of the river from the existing colony of immigrants from Qayrawān. In this way the twin settlements which still form the core of the ancient city of Fes, the quarter of the Qarawiyīn and the quarter of the Andalusiyīn, came into existence.

The events in Cordoba overshadowed the last years of al-Ḥakam's reign. He seems to have become something of a recluse before his death in 822, but he did establish the succession firmly. During his last illness, leading members of the court took the oath of allegiance (*bay'a*) to his son 'Abd al-Raḥmān in his house and then to his other son al-Mughīra, who became second in line to the throne. The taking of the oath was continued in the mosque in Cordoba where al-Mughīra remained for some days, receiving pledges of allegiance on the *minbar* (pulpit) of the mosque from the rest of the population. This public ceremonial was based directly on 'Abbasid models and reveals the increasing self-confidence and aspirations of the Umayyad amirs.

The reign of 'Abd al-Raḥmān II, 822–52

About 30 years old, the new ruler was already experienced in political and military affairs, having led expeditions to Toledo and the northern frontiers. He was tall and slightly stooping; people noticed his wide, dark eyes and full, henna-died beard. He was to rule al-Andalus for 30 years from 822 to 852, and his reign saw the coming of age of al-Andalus in terms of developing the mechanisms of a mature Muslim state and a genuine indigenous Muslim culture. 'Abd al-Raḥmān seems from the beginning to have tried to move away from his father's policy of repression and to be more responsive to Islamic susceptibilities. Even as his father was dying, he secured the execution of the commander of the Christian bodyguard, al-Rabī', and the demolition of the wine market in Cordoba, and during his reign this concern was to be expressed in a renewed enthusiasm for the *jihād* and a programme of mosque building.

The administration became more formal and bureaucratic and took on the structures it retained until the end of Umayyad rule in the early eleventh century.[21] At its head was the *ḥājib*, a word which

21. See Lévi-Provençal, *HEM*, i, pp. 256–9.

originally meant door-keeper or chamberlain, a meaning it retained in the Islamic east. In Cordoba, however, the *ḥājib* was effectively the prime minister, holding his own court or *majlis* at the palace gate where messengers or petitioners would report. Below him were the *wazīrs*: in the east, the *wazīr* of the 'Abbasid caliphate was the chief administrator and head of the civil servants (*kuttāb*, sing. *kātib*) who ran the bureaucracy. In al-Andalus, the *wazīrs* were much more general purpose officials who might well lead an army or govern a city, and the term was sometimes used as an honorary title. There was also a degree of overlap and the *ḥājib* could also be a *wazīr*. Under 'Abd al-Raḥmān the *wazīrs* were given salaries of 300 *dīnārs*. The Amir also had a personal secretary (*kātib*) who was often one of his closest advisers. A *dīwān* (administrative office) was organised to arrange the collection of taxes, and the standard Muslim institutions of the *sikka*, to mint coins, and the *ṭirāz*, to provide the official textiles, were set up.

For the first part of his reign he continued to make use of his father's advisers. The veteran 'Abd al-Karīm b. 'Abd al-Wāḥid b. Mughīth seems to have maintained his position as chief army commander and *ḥājib* as he had been for the previous two reigns, but after his death on campaign against the Christians in 824 his family seems to have disappeared from the scene. His place in the administration was taken by 'Īsā b. Shuhayd, famous for his incorruptibility, who became *wazīr* and *ḥājib* from 833 onwards and also commanded the horse at the time of the Viking attack on Seville in 844. 'Abd al-Raḥmān had gathered a number of trusted intimates in the years when he was heir apparent, among them Sufyān b. 'Abd Rabbihi, a Berber of obscure origins who became his *kātib*, and 'Abd Allāh b. Sinān, who rebuilt the walls of Seville after the Viking attack. From a military point of view, the most important of these newcomers were the two brothers, 'Abd al-Raḥmān and Muḥammad b. Rustam. These were scions of the Rustamid dynasty of Tahert (in Algeria) and were the first of many North African princelings brought over with their followers to serve the rulers of al-Andalus, Muḥammad particularly distinguishing himself against the Vikings. In the second half of his reign, 'Abd al-Raḥmān came to rely increasingly on the eunuch Naṣr, the first, but no means the last, eunuch to achieve major political influence in al-Andalus.

The simple household of 'Abd al-Raḥmān I was gradually transformed into the formal court of 'Abd al-Raḥmān II, with its courtiers sheltering a secluded and remote monarch who rarely appeared to his subjects. The Amir surrounded himself with a growing number of eunuchs and slave girls. This development of the court on eastern models had a cultural aspect to it as well. In this the Umayyads were helped by the catastrophe which overwhelmed the ʿAbbasid court between the outbreak of civil war in 811 and the final entry of al-Ma'mūn to Baghdad in 819: palaces were looted and burned and talented poets turned out on the streets. Among these was one ʿAlī b. Nāfiʿ, called Ziryāb. He was an Iraqi who had studied under the greatest of the early ʿAbbasid singers, Isḥāq al-Mawṣilī. According to the Andalucian story, he was forced to leave the ʿAbbasid court because of his master's jealousy and, after a spell in North Africa, he arrived in al-Andalus in 822. Here he set himself up not only as a musician but as an arbiter of taste in dress and food, remaining the uncontested Beau Brummell (the analogy is Lévi-Provençal's) of Cordovan society until his death in 857. Whatever the political vicissitudes of the reign, this period marks the first age of Andalucian culture, silver if not golden. Apart from al-Ḥakam II, ʿAbd al-Raḥmān was the most intellectual of the Umayyad sovereigns and encouraged scholars and poets, including the eccentric scientist ʿAbbās b. Firnās who, among other things, made himself wings and attempted to fly. Nor must ʿAbd al-Raḥmān's building work be forgotten. Apart from military architecture, there was the surviving extension of the mosque at Cordoba and the mosque at Seville, fragments of which can still be found in the court of the church of San Salvador, and a mosque at Jaen. Of course these buildings had a political value: just like the *jihād*, his commitment to mosque building showed the Amir as a truly Muslim ruler.

Perhaps the most picturesque indication of Cordoba as the heir of Baghdad is given in the story of the necklace of al-Shifāʾ. This necklace had been made for Zubayda, wife of Hārūn al-Rashīd, and during the dispersal of ʿAbbasid treasures during the civil wars which followed that caliph's death in 809, it was bought for 10,000 *dīnār*s by ʿAbd al-Raḥmān's agents and given by him to his favourite, al-Shifāʾ. With the collapse of the caliphate of Cordoba it passed to the Dhū'l-Nūnids of Toledo. After El Cid took Valencia in 1095, the necklace was handed over to him and given to his wife Jimena. It later appears among the possessions of Don Alvaro de Luna, Constable of Castile, and may even have been worn by Isabella the Catholic before it finally disappeared from record. Whether history or romance, the story of the necklace is symbolic of the changing fortunes of Baghdad and Cordoba, ʿAbbasids and Umayyads, in this period.[22]

22. Ibid., pp. 264–5.

The Amir had to cope with troubles in the area of Tudmīr in the east of the country. The old treaty arrangements of the time of the conquest had broken down and that meant that Arab settlers were competing for lands. They divided as ever into Muḍar and Yemen and fought not the government but each other. There was anarchy for seven years before the Yemen chief Abū'l-Shammākh Muḥammad b. Ibrāhīm al-Judhāmī finally surrendered to ʿAbd al-Raḥmān. He pacified the area in two ways: he offered Abū'l-Shammākh a position in his army, where we find him guarding Calatrava during one of the campaigns against Toledo, and he caused his governor to build a new capital, the city of Murcia, founded in 831, in which an Umayyad garrison could be stationed.

Two other notable events distinguish the reign of ʿAbd al-Raḥmān. The first of these was the Viking attack on Seville. In the summer of 844 (229), 80 Viking ships, having been driven away from Lisbon by the local governor, sailed up the Guadalquivir river, as they had sailed up so many other western European estuaries and, basing themselves on the island now known as the Isla Menor, attacked the unwalled city of Seville. This they looted and pillaged and, finding that the Guadalquivir was not navigable any higher, took to the land. ʿAbd al-Raḥmān, forewarned by the governor of Lisbon, acted swiftly and effectively: troops were summoned from all areas and even the recalcitrant Mūsā b. Mūsā b. Qasī led his followers from the Upper March. The Umayyad armies under Muḥammad b. Rustam and the eunuch Naṣr decisively defeated the invaders in a land battle; many were killed and most of the rest returned to their ships and fled. Some, however, remained and settled in the lower Guadalquivir area, where they converted by and by to Islam and lived reformed and blameless lives, selling cheeses to the Sevillanos.

The episode shows the effectiveness of the Cordovan state when faced with an unexpected attack by an unknown enemy, and it is only fair to contrast this swift mobilisation with the feeble and chaotic response of Anglo-Saxon and Carolingian contemporaries. The long-term response was equally effective. Seville was walled and a naval arsenal (*dār al-ṣināʿa*) established there which certainly frustrated further raids in 859 and 966. There were, of course, other reasons why the Vikings were not the menace in al-Andalus that they were in Britain or France. It lay further from their lands of origin and the lack of navigable rivers meant that they were unable to penetrate deeply into the country. The Vikings were defeated because they were fighting inland; if they had been able to bring their longships right up to Cordoba when they first arrived, the result might have been very different. As it was, the invasions which did so much to loosen the bonds of political society in northern Europe actually tightened them in al-Andalus, as the swift response of Mūsā b. Mūsā b. Qasī shows.

The other event also demonstrates the maturity of the Umayyad state in a different way. This was the series of Christian martyrdoms which took place in the capital.[23] In the normal course of events, Christian practices were allowed a wide degree of tolerance. Public and ostentatious displays of faith like processions and ringing of bells were discouraged, at least in the capital, but neither churches nor monasteries were directly threatened. There were, however, two practices which Islam could not tolerate: one was apostasy, which is punishable by death in Islamic law, the other was public insult of the Prophet. From 850 onwards a small group in Cordoba, led by the priest Eulogius and centred on the monastery of Tabanos outside the city, openly defied these prohibitions, by insulting the Prophet in public, even in the mosque or in the *Qāḍī's* court, or, in the case of converts to Islam, by publicly returning to the religion of their fathers. They refused to avoid the execution which would inevitably follow by repenting. Both the Muslim authorities and the Christian hierarchy sought to avoid the excesses, but to little avail. The motivation of the martyrs has been much debated. To an extent they were protesting against the Arabisation of the Christian community in Cordoba and its drift towards Islam by clearly asserting uncompromising Christian values, but the main motivation seems to have been the cult of self-sacrifice and martyrdom which developed around Eulogius and the small and very intense group at Tabanos. From 850 (235) onwards some thirteen were executed, all after public and formal trials. After the death of ʿAbd al-Raḥmān in 852, Eulogius left for the north and the martyrdoms ceased for a while, but when he returned in 853 they resumed and between then and March 859 there were fourteen more executions. Finally Eulogius himself, by now bishop of Cordoba, was decapitated and this seems effectively to have brought the movement to an end. Its historical importance is difficult to determine and it probably tells us little about the condition and attitudes of the bulk of the Mozarab population, though it does show the tolerance and essential reasonableness of the Muslim authorities, but it raises interesting moral and theological points about self-inflicted martyrdom which make the whole episode the subject of continuing debate.

23. On the martyrs see K.B. Wolf, *Christian Martyrs in Muslim Spain* (Cambridge, 1988), and J.A. Coope, *The Martyrs of Cordoba* (Nebraska, 1995).

The administration of the early Umayyad amirate

The reign of 'Abd al-Raḥmān saw the further development of the court and administration at Cordoba under the influence of eastern Islamic models. Despite political differences, the administrative and cultural examples set by Baghdad were eagerly adopted. The most important administrative function was the raising and paying of the army. In the 'Abbasid caliphate there was a steady move away from large armies of part-time Arab soldiers which had characterised the early Islamic state to reliance on much smaller groups of mostly Turkish professional soldiers, a process largely completed in the reign of 'Abd al-Raḥmān's contemporary, al-Mu'taṣim, 833–42. It is not surprising to find evidence of a similar development in al-Andalus in the first century of Umayyad rule, and the move from reliance on the *junds*, essentially unpaid part-timers, to a professional army recruited from outsiders, is the main feature of state formation at this time. 'Abd al-Raḥmān I is said to have formed a *shurṭa* (security police) from his *mawālī*, the Umayyads and some leading Berber families.[24] Al-Ḥakam I certainly had a guard of professional soldiers, and in an interesting passage the *Akhbār al-Majmū'a* explains why they were so highly valued:

> News reached him [al-Ḥakam] one day while he was in the park with some horsemen from his entourage disporting themselves with their mounts that Jābir b. Labīd was laying siege to Jaen. Al-Ḥakam had two thousand cavalry quartered on the bank of the river opposite the palace, grouped in two barracks, each of which housed ten *'arīfs*. Every *'arīf* was in charge of 100 horsemen who they supervised, supplied and changed those who needed to be replaced so that the force would be ready to deal with any emergency which might arise and it was as if they had a single mind. The Amir summoned one of these *'arīfs* and when he appeared before him, he secretly ordered him to set out for Jaen against Ibn Labīd immediately with his men and not to tell anyone where he was going. Then he returned to his pleasures. An hour later he summoned another of his *'arīfs* and gave him the same orders and went on until he had summoned ten and they all followed each other, none of them knowing the intentions of his fellows until they fell upon Ibn Labīd on the second day continuously from morning until night. When the enemy saw this, they were aghast and thought that they were surrounded by them and that all the regions of the country had combined against them. They

24. *Akhbār al-Majmū'a*, ed. p. 91; Chalmeta, *Invasion e Islamizacion*, p. 382.

> turned and fled immediately. The cavalry overran them, attacked their camp and returned with their heads on the third day. Al-Ḥakam was still with his *mawālī* in the park and none of them knew anything of the matter until he told them.[25]

No doubt this is an idealised picture of a system which did not always work so well in practice and is intended to demonstrate the power of the ruler, but it shows clearly the advantages of such a full-time, professional force stationed in the capital. This small force of cavalry was vastly superior to the irregulars of the *junds* who took time to assemble and often had political agendas of their own.

There is little evidence about the working of the *jund* system in the Umayyad period. The only account we have is a report from Aḥmād al-Rāzī (d. 955) who explains that the Syrian *jundis*, whose names were recorded in a *dīwān*, were divided into two groups, one which went on campaign and the other which stayed at home. After three months the two groups would change places. Those on campaign were paid a *rizq* of 5 *dīnārs* at the end of the campaign while their chiefs received 200. The *baladīs* had no *dīwān* and only their leaders were paid 100 *dīnārs*. The Syrians were exempt from the *'ushr* (tithe) and only had to pay a share of the revenues they collected from the non-Muslims; the *baladīs*, by contrast, were obliged to pay this tithe.[26]

When, and how far, this system worked in practice is doubtful. Certainly, if we look at the names of the commanders of armies, we find very few Syrian or *baladī* Arab names among them. Abū'l-Shammākh al-Judhāmī, the Yemeni leader, seems to have been the only Arab military commander employed by 'Abd al-Raḥmān, and if the *junds* had been used, they would certainly have been commanded by their own leaders. Instead we find *mawālī* like 'Abd al-Karīm b. Mughīth and 'Isa b. Shuhayd, a eunuch, Naṣr, who is said to have come from a *muwallad* family in Carmona, and Muḥammad b. Rustam, a North African of Persian origin but long settled in Berber country, as the principal generals. The origins of the leaders probably reflect the origins of the troops they commanded. In the process of state building, part-time tribal levies were phased out and replaced by professionals, mostly recruited from outside al-Andalus (and known by the Arabs as *al-khurs*, the silent ones, from their inability to speak Arabic), a process which

25. *Akhbār*, ed. p. 129; trans., pp. 116–17.
26. Al-Rāzī's account is given in Ibn al-Khaṭīb, *Al-Iḥāṭa fi akhbār Gharnāṭa*, ed. M. 'Inan (4 vols, Cairo, 1973–77), i, pp. 104–5, and discussed in Manzano Moreno, 'Los Yund-s Sirios', 348–9. See also above, p. 26.

was to determine the character of the later Umayyad state and account for much of its strengths and weaknesses.

The question of the collection of taxes is equally obscure. Under 'Abd al-Raḥmān II we find a mention of treasurers (*khuzzān*), though they probably looked after rather than collected the money. 'Abd al-Raḥmān II sent one of his *fatā*s (pages) from Cordoba to supervise the collection of the fifth after the sack of the Balearic Islands, and the Amir's fifth may have continued to be a significant source of windfall income. We have some details about the actual sums collected. Under al-Ḥakam, the districts around Cordoba paid 142,000 *dīnār*s, made up of payments to be excused military service, general taxes, and payments for the rights of falconry (*al-hashd, naḍḍ al-ṭabl,* and *naḍḍ al-bayzara*) as well as 53,000 *muḍḍ* of wheat and 73,000 *muḍḍ* of barley.[27] Figures are given for other areas: 35,000 *dīnār*s from Seville, 50,600 from Sidonia, 21,000 from Moron and 15,600 from Niebla.

All these were taxes paid by Muslims. A document describing the taxes paid by villages in the Cordoba area in the early ninth century, incorporated in the eleventh-century geography of al-'Udhrī,[28] suggests that 49.68 per cent of the revenue came from payment in place of military service, 45.61 per cent from *ṭabl* and a mere 4.71 per cent from *ṣadaqa* (alms) and falconry licences. In addition to these were the taxes collected from the Christians. In the apologetic literature for the Christian martyrs of Cordoba, it is claimed that 100,000 *dīnār*s (solidi) were collected from the Christians of Cordoba city alone.[29] The poll-tax was collected by the bishop Hostegesis who went around all the churches to find details of the Christian population in the parish registers. If these figures are not wildly exaggerated, they make it clear that the fiscal obligations of the Christians were very heavy in comparison with those of their Muslim compatriots.

This information is clearly incomplete and presents a number of linguistic problems, but it also has some interesting features. The most obvious is the relative importance of Cordoba and its district

27. Al-Bakrī, in appendix V of al-Ḥimyarī, *Rawḍ al-mi'ṭār fi akhbār al-aqṭār,* partial ed. with French trans., E. Lévi-Provençal (Leiden, 1938), pp. 250–1.

28. Al-'Udhrī, *Nuṣūṣ 'an al-Andalus min kitab Tarṣī' al-akhbār wa tawzī' al-āthār,* ed. A. al-Ahwani (Madrid, 1956), pp. 124–7. On this text see the important discussion in M. Barcelo, 'Un estudio sobre la estructura fiscal y procedimientos contables del emirato omeya de Cordoba (130–300/755–912) y del califato (300–366/912–976)', in *Acta Medievalia* v–vi (1984–85), 45–72.

29. Samson, *Praefatio* of *Apologeticus II,* quoted in Barcelo, 'Un estudio sobre la estructura fiscal', 56, 57.

as a source of revenue, since it contributed more than the other mentioned areas combined. If *ḥashd* does mean the payment of exemption from military service (and there seems no other possible interpretation), then this form of tax resembles practice in the Christian kingdoms of northern Spain at a later period when the *fonsadero*, which meant the same thing, was an important source of royal revenues. Payments for exemption from service form the basis of many western European mediaeval taxation systems (English scutage, for example), but are unknown in the eastern Islamic world. All the areas mentioned were ones which had been settled by Syrian *jundī*s who arrived with Balj in 741 and it is probable that they were paying to avoid the military service which would otherwise have been required in exchange for their lands. Similarly, payments for rights to fly falcons are alien to classic Islamic taxation and must reflect local practice. On the other hand the *kharāj* (land tax), which was the main fiscal pillar of eastern Islamic regimes, does not seem to have been established in Spain, nor, at this stage, do royal estates (*sawāfī*, *ḍiyāʿ*) appear as important sources of revenue.

The third interesting feature of this list is that all the revenues are said to have come from the south; as we might expect, neither the Marches nor the Levante are said to have made any contribution. It is true that this may well be no more than a gap in the evidence, but it certainly reflects the impression of other sources. The total sums of money available seem to have increased substantially, from 600,000 *dīnār*s per year under al-Ḥakam to 1,000,000 under ʿAbd al-Raḥmān II.

These areas in the Guadalquivir valley and further south were the *ḥaḍra*, the main resource base of the Umayyad amirs, but further away from the capital the position was very different. The Umayyads spent more time trying to assert their authority over the northern areas of al-Andalus than they did over the Christian lands. The areas on the Muslim side of the frontier were divided into Marches (*thaghr*, pl. *thughūr*), the Lower March based on Merida and Badajoz, the Middle March based on Toledo, and the Upper March in the Ebro valley with its capital at Zaragoza. The theory was that the Muslims of these marches had the responsibility of defending their areas against Christian attack and supporting any expeditions the Muslims might make into Christian territory. Like many of the administrative devices of al-Andalus, this had eastern Islamic parallels in the *thughūr* which were established along the Arab–Byzantine frontier in Syria and al-Jazīra. An important feature of these eastern *thughūr* was their fiscal immunity: in recognition of their role in the perpetual *jihād*, it seems that the people of these areas were not obliged to make any financial contribution to the central government of the caliphate and that, on the contrary, they received subsidies from the neighbouring areas. It seems likely that this system was continued in al-Andalus; in the information we have about the revenues of the Cordoba government, there is no mention of regular financial contributions from these areas, which suggests that a large area of al-Andalus remained outside the fiscal control of the government and, whereas in the eastern caliphate the *thughūr* were a comparatively small proportion of the state, in al-Andalus they must have formed at least a quarter of the whole area.

With this fiscal independence there went a broad measure of political separatism. In a way this was dictated by military considerations, since local commanders had to be able to respond to Christian raids without waiting for help from Cordoba. At the same time this was also a manifestation of more general ethnic diversity and separatist feeling.

In the last six years of ʿAbd al-Raḥmān's reign, Ibn Ḥayyān records Umayyad-appointed governors (*ʿummāl*, sing. *ʿāmil*) in Toledo, Zaragoza, Tortosa, Valencia, Tudmīr (Murcia) and Beja as well as Rayyu and Elvira in Andalucia. Despite the similarity of title, the nature of these appointments was very different. Rayyu, Elvira and Tudmīr are only recorded as being held by the Amir's sons and so were presumably within his power. Toledo saw frequent changes of governors chosen from members of Cordovan bureaucratic families (Banū Bazīʿ, Banū Sālim, Banū Basīl) who had, as far as we can tell, no local connections. This again suggests a fair degree of real authority from Cordoba. Valencia was governed by one Ibn Maymūn who is mentioned in the context of the expedition which forced the submission of the Balearic Islands in 848. After the fleet returned, the Amir sent one of his *fatā*s to supervise Ibn Maymūn's division of the booty and make sure that he got his fifth share. In the Upper March, ʿAbd Allāh b. Kulayb, the man who erected the citadel and inscription at Merida, was in charge in Zaragoza in 848 but had to compete against the rival power of Mūsā b. Mūsā b. Qasī in Tudela.

The case of Beja is different again. Here the governor, Faraj b. Khayr al-Ṭūṭāliqī, is said to have rebelled in 847/8. ʿAbd al-Raḥmān hastened in person to confront him. In return for acknowledging him as Amir, ʿAbd al-Raḥmān was generous to him and increased his status, formally appointing him as governor (*wālī*) of Beja. He soon reasserted his independence and in fact his sons continued to be powerful in the Algarve until the next century. Clearly Faraj was in a very different position from the governors of Toledo, appointed and dismissed at will; he was rather a quasi-independent local magnate and the power of Cordoba in his lands was strictly limited.

The lands of the northern frontier, 788–852

The consolidation of Umayyad power in the south and centre of the Iberian peninsula had not so far extended to the north. Here the pattern was much more of negotiation with independent potentates than of imposing Umayyad authority. The picture was complicated by the presence of independent Christian powers to the north and the complex interactions between them and the northern Muslim powers, and it is worth examining the changing nature of relationships between Cordoba and the north in the reigns of Hishām I, al-Ḥakam I and ʿAbd al-Raḥmān II (788–852).

In the western part of the peninsula, the Christian–Muslim frontier remained relatively stable; there were repeated raids by both sides in the no-man's land that divided the two sides but Muslim settlement did not advance beyond the Cordillera Central. The Christian kingdom of the Asturias was confined to the northern mountains, though Christians did manage to hold on, precariously, to some outposts on the northern edge of the plains like the old Roman fortifications at Leon and Astorga. Further east local Christians, with some support from the Carolingians, were able to take over Girona in 785 and Barcelona in 801, while in 799 Pamplona was taken by the Basques and gradually became the nucleus of the new Kingdom of Navarre. Barcelona and Girona were incorporated into the Carolingian empire and became the centres of the Spanish March (Marca Hispanica).

The early ninth century saw further Carolingian attacks as the Franks attempted to follow up the conquest of Barcelona with other gains.[30] According to Frankish sources Louis the Pious, then King of Aquitaine, made three attempts to conquer Tortosa in 804–7, 808 and 809, and Arab sources mention expeditions in 808 and 809, but Tortosa was successfully relieved by ʿAbd al-Raḥmān and ʿAmrūs b. Yūsuf and Frankish power was halted. From this point

30. Lévi-Provençal, *HEM*, i, p. 182.

Muslim control was limited to the Ebro plains, with Tudela, Huesca, Lleida and Tortosa being the most northerly significant settlements, and the frontier of 801 remained essentially unchanged in this area for the next 300 years.

Unlike the Christians, the Muslims made no substantial territorial gains, but they launched numerous raids on Christian lands. These usually took the form of a *ṣā'ifa,* or summer expedition. These raids could be directed at Galicia, the Leon area or Barcelona, but perhaps the most common objective was the area of Alava and the district that the Muslim authors began to refer to as al-Qilā', the land of the castles, which was later to become the nucleus of Old Castile. These raids were not, as far as we can tell, annual events but varied between periods of intense activity and spells when there are no expeditions recorded at all. Hishām I, in keeping with his policy of Islamic leadership, sent numerous expeditions between 791 and 795, but his successor, al-Ḥakam I, perhaps because he was preoccupied by internal dissent, was much less energetic. 'Abd al-Raḥmān II sent expeditions in 823, 825 and 826, but there was then a long gap until 838, when intermittent raids were resumed until the end of his reign.

Directing raids against the Christians was, in both eastern and western Islamic lands, an important sign of leadership and authority over the Muslim community and their purpose was as much ideological as military. Under Hishām the raids were usually led by one of the Banū Mughīth brothers, 'Abd al-Malik, 'Abd al-Karīm and 'Abd al-Wāḥid. This was continued under al-Ḥakam and into the reign of 'Abd al-Raḥmān II, with the Umayyad 'Ubayd Allāh b. 'Abd Allāh al-Balansī also prominent. When raids were resumed after 838 there was a marked difference. They were now led by members of the Amir's immediate family, including his brothers Sa'īd and Umayya and later his sons al-Muṭarrif, Muḥammad and al-Mundhir. In 840 the Amir himself, 'Abd al-Raḥmān II, led the expedition, the only time the ruler participated in person; we have no details, but the fact that the experiment was not repeated suggests that it may not have been a success. The *ṣā'ifa* was clearly being used at this time to enhance the prestige of the ruling family and to give the princes both experience and useful contacts; once again, Andalusi practice reflects eastern models.

There was no intention of conquering the Christian north, though attempts were made to regain lost lands like Pamplona and Barcelona. When the Leonese abandoned their city when faced by the mangonels of the Muslims in 846, the conquerors simply made breaches in the walls and then left the site abandoned;[31] of course, it was soon reoccupied and fortified again by the Christians. Destruction and booty were the main objectives, although the pickings from these impoverished and underdeveloped areas must have been quite limited. The one major expedition beyond the Pyrenees in this period, when ʿAbd al-Malik b. Mughīth defeated the Count of Toulouse near Carcassonne in 793, may have been more rewarding, and we are told of vast amounts of booty and slaves being taken, although, typically, it failed in its primary objective of retaking Girona.

Each of the Marches along the northern frontier of al-Andalus had a different physical and human geography.[32] The Lower March was centred on the open plains and wide landscapes of Extremadura. Apart from the capital at the old Roman city of Merida, it was a largely rural area where scattered castles and fortified villages were the only settled habitations. Few Arabs lived here and the bulk of the politically active population were Berbers and powerful *muwallad* landowners. Most of the Berbers were probably semi-nomadic or transhumant pastoralists, and tribal structures survived here for longer than in more settled areas: tribal chiefs exercised power throughout the Umayyad period. In the late eighth century the most important figure was the chief Aṣbagh b. Wansūs al-Miknāsī, who supported Hishām against the claims of his brother Sulaymān. After his death in 807/8, the leading role in the area was taken by a *muwallad*, Ibn Marwān al-Jilliqī (the Galician), whose family seem to have come from the area of northern Portugal. We know little about his power base, but he seems to have been accepted by the Umayyads and, along with the Banū Qasī and ʿAmrūs in the Upper March, was one of the first *muwallad*s to play an important role in the politics of al-Andalus. After his death at the hands of Berber and *muwallad* rivals in 828, ʿAbd al-Raḥmān took the opportunity to assert his control, sending troops to occupy Merida in 830 and appointing one of the Umayyad *mawālī* as governor. He built a citadel which still survives; an inscription records that it was constructed by the governor, ʿAbd Allāh b. Kulayb b. Thaʿlaba, and his *mawlā*, Jayfar b. Mukassir the architect (*ṣāḥib al-bunyān*), in 835 as a stronghold for Umayyad supporters (*maʿqil ahl al-ṭāʿa*) in the area.[33]

31. Ibid., p. 207.
32. The geography and population of the Marches are discussed at length in Manzano Moreno, *Frontera*.
33. E. Lévi-Provençal, *Inscriptions Arabes d'Espagne* (Leiden/Paris, 1931), no. 39 pp. 50–1.

The archaeological and literary evidence come together here to demonstrate both the reality and the weakness of the Amir's attempt to assert his authority: the fortress was impressive, but how far did Umayyad control extend beyond its walls? Away from Merida itself, rebels were still active, and the area was to slip out of Umayyad grasp after his death.

The Middle March was centred on Toledo. Again, there had been little Arab settlement here and the dominant group in the population of the old capital city were *muwallad*s who wished to keep power in the city in their own hands. Outside the city walls, it seems that the upland plains and mountains were dominated by Berber shepherd tribes. It may have been them rather than the people of the city whom the Fihrīs appealed to in their struggle against the Umayyads in the late eighth century. According to a tradition widely reported in the Arabic sources, al-Ḥakam I sent his son 'Abd al-Raḥmān to reduce the city and he summoned their leaders to meet him and had them executed at the 'Day of the Trench' (797). Recent research suggests that the story is legendary, and in fact borrowed from an eastern source describing a totally different incident,[34] but it probably reflects a brutal attempt by 'Abd al-Raḥmān, aided by the *muwallad* 'Amrūs b. Yūsuf, to impose Umayyad rule on Toledo. If it was, it was unsuccessful. For hard evidence of Umayyad control in Toledo we have to wait until the reign of 'Abd al-Raḥmān II (822–52). In the 830s the people of Toledo seem to have been causing disturbances by trying to assert their authority over the surrounding country and the Amir was obliged to fortify Calatrava to protect Cordoba and the Guadalquivir valley from their raids in 831/2. Calatrava lay near the old high-road from Toledo to Cordoba and this strategic site was, in the twelfth century, to become the eponymous seat of the oldest of the Spanish military orders. In 836/7 Toledo was finally occupied by Umayyad troops. As at Merida, the citadel was fortified and governors, usually Umayyad *mawālī*, appointed, but it is unclear how far Umayyad authority extended beyond the city walls.

The Upper March, based on the Ebro valley with its capital at Zaragoza, presents a more complicated picture. There were more urban settlements: besides the capital, Tudela, Huesca, Calatayud and Tortosa were all towns of some substance. The Muslims controlled the plains to the north of the Ebro, but Muslim settlement ended at the 1,000 metre contour line: the valleys and mountains

34. Manzano Moreno, *Frontera*, pp. 274–84.

to the north remained in the hands of the indigenous Christian inhabitants. There was a more complicated ethnic mix: as well as some Berbers and very powerful *muwallad* families, there was also a sizeable Arab population (or at least people who claimed Arab descent) especially in Zaragoza itself. To add to this, relations with the Christians, notably the rulers of Navarre and, for a period, the Carolingians, were much more complex.

Like his father, al-Ḥakam I attempted to extend his influence in this area not by direct military action but by an alliance with the leading *muwallad* ʿAmrūs b. Yūsuf of Huesca. In 797 al-Ḥakam invited him to keep the people of Toledo in check (he was obviously a powerful figure). After this, he was transferred to Zaragoza and then to Tudela to restrain the power of another *muwallad* family, the Banū Qasī, in 802. He died in 812, still an ally of the Umayyads, and his family remained influential in their native Huesca. It is interesting to note the power of local converts like ʿAmrūs and the Amir's reliance on him, rather than on any of the local Arab families.

The Banū Qasī retained their power and their quasi-autonomous state. By the end of the eighth century they appear in the Arabic sources as the leading magnates of the upper Ebro, and it is clear that they had close relations with the Christian kings of Pamplona, with whose family they intermarried and who may have provided them with Basque soldiers for their armies. Despite ʿAmrūs's occupation of Tudela, they retained their power. At first their relations with ʿAbd al-Raḥmān II were friendly, but after a quarrel on the *ṣāʾifa* of 842, Mūsā b. Mūsā b. Fortūn b. Qasī, the then leader of the family, defied the Umayyads, allying himself to the King of Navarre instead. In 844 he was able to do ʿAbd al-Raḥmān a good turn when the Vikings attacked Seville and he sent troops to help. By the end of the reign he had re-established his power and the Christian *Chronicle* of Alfonso III[35] says that he had himself called 'the third King of Spain' (the other two being the king of Oviedo and the Amir of Cordoba). He was able to use his local power base and pivotal position on the frontier to ensure that the Amir could not replace him or rule the area without his co-operation.

The city of Zaragoza itself was conquered by ʿAbd al-Raḥmān in person in 844 and entrusted to his son Muḥammad; it remained under Umayyad rule until the Amir's death in 852. So for the last eight years of his reign all three capitals of the *Thughūr*, Merida,

35. Cap. 25.

Toledo and Zaragoza, were under the direct control of Cordoba and ruled by supporters of the Umayyads sent from the capital. This did not mean, however, that they were undisputed rulers of all of al-Andalus: their rule may not have extended far beyond the walls of the capitals and, as events immediately after ʿAbd al-Raḥmān's death were to show, separatist forces were still very much alive in these areas. Great influence still lay with Berber tribal leaders and the *muwallad* nobles. The only area of the Muslim world which shows a parallel development at this time is Khurasān in north-east Iran, where local Iranian princes converted to Islam and acknowledged the Caliph's overall authority but were, in fact, independent rulers of their own areas who could, and did, defy the government if they felt their interests were threatened.

A further illustration of the devolved nature of power in this area can be seen from an account preserved in the surviving section of Ibn Ḥayyān's history of ʿAbd al-Raḥmān II's reign.[36] According to this, a certain ʿUbayd Allāh b. Yaḥyā, governor of Tortosa, wrote to ʿAbd al-Raḥmān II in 850/1 to say that he did not need any troops from the central government but would make do with 130 military pages recruited from his own *mawālī*. The Amir replied that he was satisfied with this arrangement and agreed that they should be paid from the government revenues (*māl al-sulṭān*). The governor was allowed to keep the cash collected from the poll-tax (*jizya*), tithes (*ʿushūr*) and other dues (*waẓāʾif*) in the area to ransom prisoners and keep the defences in good order. He was also given 200 *dīnār*s a month of this revenue for his own salary (*rizq*), with an annual bonus of 1,000 *dīnār*s. This shows that the governor enjoyed a large measure of fiscal autonomy: he could pay his own troops from the taxes collected in his area, and there is no suggestion that any money was paid to Cordoba. It is unlikely that ʿAbd al-Raḥmān was surrendering any real power with this agreement and more probable that he was simply regularising an existing situation.

The Iberian peninsula in the ninth century

By the time of ʿAbd al-Raḥmān's death in 852 the Umayyad state in al-Andalus was firmly established and had become one of the leading

36. Ibn Ḥayyān, *Al-Muqtabis min anbā ahl al-Andalus (Al-Muqtabis II)*, ed. M.A. Makki (Cairo, 1971), p. 147. The text is discussed in detail in Manzano Moreno, *Frontera*, pp. 330–1.

powers in the Mediterranean, maintaining diplomatic relations with the Byzantine emperor and a protectorate of sorts over some of the minor emirates of North Africa. But in many ways the strength of the state was dependent on the personality of the monarch; for all the wealth and culture of Cordoba, deep regional and social divisions remained and might easily reappear in response to feebleness or disturbances at the capital.

At the same time, the Christian communities on the northern side of the religious frontier were consolidating into recognisable political units.[37] The most important of these was the Kingdom of Oviedo and the Asturias. The earliest chronicles of the kingdom, which date from the late ninth century, recount how the noble Pelayo fled from the débâcle of the Visigothic kingdom to the northern mountains. Here he made contact with Peter, called Duke of Cantabria, whose daughter he married. This was an area where neither Romans nor Visigoths had been able to exercise any power; it was without cities or major churches and many of the people may still have been pagan. Pelayo is said to have rallied these people to defeat the Muslims at Covadonga and established a primitive kingdom based on the small settlement at Cangas de Onis. Alfonso I (739–57) was able to take advantage of the political troubles in al-Andalus from 741 on to establish his power over Galicia in the west and to raid as far south as the Guadarrama mountains. After the assassination of his son Fruela in 768 there was a period of succession disputes and short-lived kings which, combined with the establishment of the early Umayyad amirate, meant that this period of expansion came to a halt. Stability was restored during the long reign of Alfonso II (791–842). He moved the capital to Oviedo, a centre which offered easier access to the plains to the south, but the power of the Umayyads meant that the kingdom was unable to expand in that direction. However, two important ideological developments do seem to have taken place during his reign. According to the later sources, it was Alfonso II who set about restoring the institutions of the Visigothic monarchy in his kingdom. This could only have been an aspiration and the kingdom remained very limited in extent, but the Visigoths had ruled the whole peninsula and the claims to be successors of the kings of Toledo carried with it the implication that they were justified in reconquering lands which had unjustly been taken from

37. For an introduction to this process see R. Collins, 'Spain: the northern kingdoms and the Basques, 711–910', in *The New Cambridge Medieval History*, ed. R. McKitterick (Cambridge, 1995), ii, pp. 272–89.

their predecessors. The other event was the 'discovery' in about 830 of the tomb of St James the Apostle at the site later known as Santiago de Compostella, which provided the small kingdom with a powerful patron saint and an important focus of Christian belief.

The troubles of the Umayyad amirs in the second half of the ninth century gave Alfonso's successors, notably Alfonso III (866–910), the opportunity to extend the limits of Christian settlement into the plains of the northern Meseta, including the fortification of Zamora on the Duero. This period also saw the emergence of two subsidiary centres of Christian power in the area: to the west the County of Portugal emerged with the resettlement of Braga and Oporto, while to the east the County of Castile became firmly established with the settlement of Burgos in 880. The process culminated with the shift of the capital south over the mountains to the old Roman walled site at Leon after 910, a clear sign of the self-confidence of the emergent Christian polity.

To the east of the Kingdom of the Asturias lay the mountains of the Basque country. Even more than their neighbours to the west, the Basques had resisted incorporation into the Visigothic state and Muslim penetration had been minimal. The sources for the early history of what was to become the Kingdom of Navarre are very thin, but it is clear that from the end of the eighth century there developed a three-sided contest for control of the city of Pamplona. The three parties were the native Basque chiefs, the Franks and the Muslims. The Franks controlled the city for much of the period between Charlemagne's first invasion in 778 and 824, when they were finally driven out by the Basques. In the aftermath of their expulsion a rudimentary kingdom was ruled by a chief called Iñigo Arista (d. 851). For most of the ninth century the kings of Pamplona acted as allies with the Banū Qasī, to whom they were related by marriage, against both Franks and Asturians on one hand and the Umayyads of Cordoba on the other. The collapse of the Banū Qasī at the beginning of the tenth century and a change in dynasty in Pamplona in 905 put an end to this. In the tenth century the Kingdom of Navarre emerged as a fully fledged Christian monarchy embracing the area of Pamplona and the western Pyrenees.

The Franks had been more successful at the eastern end of the Pyrenees. The taking of Girona in 785 and Barcelona in 801 had been followed by the establishment of the Spanish March, a frontier region of the Carolingian empire, ruled by counts based in Barcelona. As in the rest of the Carolingian empire, the counts became increasingly estranged from imperial control in the ninth century, and by the time of Count Wilfried (873–98) the county was effectively independent.

By the beginning of the tenth century, al-Andalus was bordered on the north by a string of well-established Christian states. Compared with al-Andalus they were in many ways poor and backward: both literacy and the use of coined money were comparatively rare, and there was certainly no equivalent of the state apparatus that had been developed in the Muslim south. However, these states now had political and military structures, which meant that the Muslims were unable to subdue them or ravage their territories. This meant that a century later, these Christians were immediately able to take advantage of the break-up of the Cordovan caliphate.

CHAPTER THREE

Muḥammad, al-Mundhir and 'Abd Allāh: the Slide into Anarchy, 852–912[1]

The accession and early years of the Amir Muḥammad

Muḥammad b. 'Abd al-Raḥmān succeeded his father as amir without opposition on 23 September 852. There are two accounts of how this happened. The 'official' version, as recounted by Ibn Idhārī (the original version of Ibn Ḥayyān being lacking at this point), gives a brief account implying that there was no opposition.[2] According to gossipy Ibn al-Qūṭīya, on the other hand, the issue was decided by the palace eunuchs (*fatās*).[3] They kept the death of the old amir secret and held a meeting; many were in favour of appointing the prince 'Abd Allāh, who was the son of 'Abd al-Raḥmān II's favourite concubine, Turāb, who had been careful to be generous to them. One of them, called Ibn al-Mufrij, who, we are told, had been on the *Ḥajj* and was full of virtue, pointed out that 'Abd Allāh was quite unworthy and that if they appointed him, they would be criticised by the people and would lose power. He persuaded them to approach Muḥammad, a more vigorous person but one who had a reputation for meanness.

'Abd al-Raḥmān had died in the amir's official residence, the Alcazar, beside the mosque in Cordoba. The two candidates,

1. Apart from the general histories, there is no detailed account of this period. The best narrative remains E. Lévi-Provençal, *HEM*, i, pp. 278–396. For the history of the northern regions of al-Andalus see, as always, E. Manzano Moreno, *La Frontera de Al-Andalus en epoca de los Omeyas* (Madrid, 1991).

2. Ibn Idhārī al-Marrākushī, *Al-Bayān al-mughrib fi akhbār al-Andalus wa'l-Maghrib*, ed. E. Lévi-Provençal and G.S. Colin (Paris, 1948), ii, p. 94.

3. Ibn al-Qūṭīya, *Ta'rikh iftitāḥ al-Andalus*, ed. and trans. J.M. Nichols (unpublished PhD thesis, Chapel Hill, 1975), pp. 173–83.

Muḥammad and 'Abd Allāh, were each in their own houses nearby in the city. The key to success, the eunuchs realised, was to get Muḥammad to the palace so that he could take charge without arousing the suspicions of 'Abd Allāh and his supporters. The first problem was to convince Muḥammad that his father really was dead and that this was not a plot, then he was disguised as a woman and led through the darkened streets, past 'Abd Allāh's palace door where a riotous party was in progress, to a back gate of the Alcazar, where a suspicious doorman was induced to let the group in. Once in possession of the palace, the new amir had the oath of allegiance taken to him and he summoned the *wazīrs*, the servants and the *mawālī*. By dawn the *coup* was over and Muḥammad set about choosing his new ministers.

The story may have been embellished by Ibn al-Qūṭīya, and it certainly shows all his love of vivid narrative. At the same time, it reflects some interesting aspects of political life, notably the importance of the palace servants and the need to secure the Alcazar in Cordoba. Contrast this with what had happened after the death of 'Abd al-Raḥmān I less than a century before, when Hishām and his brothers summoned their supporters among the Arabs and Berbers and decided the issue by battle. The government of al-Andalus was now a palace-based bureaucracy, not a successful war-band.

Muḥammad was 30 at the time of his accession and was to rule for 34 years. It is difficult to assess his character or achievements because the sources are limited. The section of the manuscript of the great history of Ibn Ḥayyān which deals with his reign and that of his successor al-Mundhir was discovered in the recesses of the library of the Qarawiyin mosque in Fes, but was so badly damaged by damp and insects as to be effectively illegible.[4] This means we have to rely on the anecdotes in Ibn al-Qūṭīya and the abbreviated accounts of later chroniclers who give a factual but rather colourless account of the reign.

The new amir is said to have been pious and erudite and especially able at arithmetic, capable of checking all the accounts. He inherited his father's *ḥājib*, 'Īsā b. Shuhayd, whom the Ibn al-Qūṭīya describes as completely incorruptible (unlike his predecesor, 'Abd al-Karīm b. Mughīth, who was not above taking sweeteners),[5] and retained him as head of the administration until he was replaced by 'Ubayd Allāh b. Abī 'Abda. 'Īsa b. Shuhayd came from a family of *mawālī* already well established in the bureaucracy, and after his death his son Umayya, highly esteemed by Ibn al-Qūṭīya for his

4. Lévi-Provençal, *HEM*, i, p. 281. 5. *Iftitāḥ*, pp. 164–5.

shrewdness, continued the family tradition. Like the Banū Shuhayd, the Banū Abī 'Abda were another family of *mawālī* who claimed that their ancestors had fought on the Umayyad side at the battle of Marj Rāhiṭ in Syria in 684. They had served 'Abd al-Raḥmān I but really came into prominence at this time and during the reigns of Muḥammad, al-Mundhir and 'Abd Allāh, when they played a vital role in military command.

In addition to these, Muḥammad appointed other widely respected *wazīrs* including Muḥammad b. Mūsā, recruited by 'Īsā b. Shuhayd in Seville from the *mawālī* of the family of the early governor 'Abd al-Raḥmān al-Ghāfiqī (killed at the battle of Poitiers in 732), and al-Walīd b. Ghānim, who alternated with Umayya b. 'Īsā as commander of the city of Cordoba (*ṣāḥib al-madīna*), an office which had been introduced by 'Abd al-Raḥmān II and was assuming an increasingly important role. Around 875 Muḥammad started to rely heavily on another member of the *mawālī*, Hāshim b. 'Abd al-'Azīz, whom the *muwallad* Ibn al-Qūṭiya sees as the evil genius of the reign, accusing him of corrupting the entire administration.[6] His intolerance towards the *muwallads* certainly alienated leaders like Ibn Marwān al-Jillīqī who became determined enemies of the Cordoba government.

Ibn Idhārī and the other chronicle sources for his reign devote considerable attention to Muḥammad's contribution to the *jihād*, or Holy War. In fact this was at best spasmodic and petered out almost completely towards the end when internal pressures came to predominate. The Amir seems to have been content to leave leadership of the campaigns in the hands of Mūsā b. Mūsā, head of the Banū Qasī until his death in 862. This may have been convenient but it hardly increased the Amir's prestige or wealth and the Amir's fifth share of the booty from the Barcelona raid of 856 was spent on enlarging the mosque in Zaragoza, not sent to Cordoba. After Mūsā's death, Muḥammad pursued a more active policy, using the leadership of the *ṣā'ifa*, as his father had before him, to give his own sons experience and prestige: in 863 'Abd al-Raḥmān invaded Alava, in 865 al-Mundhir ravaged Old Castile and in 867 al-Ḥakam again made Alava his objective. Thereafter internal problems prevented any more expeditions until 878, when a raid was launched against Galicia to punish the King of Leon for supporting the rebels in Badajoz; the army seems to have been defeated and a fleet dispatched the next year was destroyed by bad weather.

A surviving passage of Ibn Ḥayyān's account of the reign[7] gives

6. Ibid., pp. 154–7. 7. Quoted in Ibn Idhārī, *Al-Bayān*, ii, p. 109.

details of the recruitment of horsemen for the *ṣā'ifa* of 863. The name of each *kūra* (district) is given with the number of men provided:

Elvira, 2,700
Jaen, 2,200
Cabra, 1,800
Priego (Bāghu), 900
Tākurannā (the Ronda district), 299
Algeciras, 290
Ecija, 1,200
Carmona, 180
Sidonia, 6,790
Rayyu (the Malaga area), 2,600
Faḥṣ al-Ballūṭ (Pedroche, north of Cordoba), 400
Moron, 1,400
Tudmīr, 156
(?) Reina (north-west of Cordoba), 106
Calatrava and Oreto, 387

There was also an unknown number from Cordoba. Ibn Ḥayyān explains that this was after the obligation to go on the *ṣā'ifa* was removed from Cordoba and some other places. Ibn al-Qūṭīya[8] relates a story in which 'Īsā b. Shuhayd goes to Seville, not mentioned in the list, to levy troops for the *jihād*.

The list is interesting, but it presents a number of puzzles. It is clear that the amirs were heavily dependent on Andalucia for military recruitment: the small contingent from Tudmīr (Murcia) are the only outsiders listed. There are none from north of Calatrava or west of Seville. These are precisely the areas in which the Syrian *junds* had been settled after 741. The army was assembled specifically for the *jihād* and the amirs probably had to rely on the full-time *ḥashm* army of professionals for campaigns within al-Andalus: only when they faced the infidel could the amirs command such widespread support. The differences between the contributions are very surprising: there seems no obvious reason why Sidonia should have supplied so many more than Elvira or Rayyu, or why Ecija should have contributed seven times as many as neighbouring Carmona. It looks in fact much more like a list of volunteers than an organised levy and, as Ibn Ḥayyān says of the Cordobans, 'they were each able to decide for themselves whether to volunteer for the *jihād* without any compulsion'.[9] In the short term, the move to

8. *Iftitāḥ*, pp. 166–7. 9. Ibn Idhārī, *Al-Bayān*, ii, p. 109.

make military service among the *jund* voluntary greatly increased Muḥammad's popularity, but the long-term effects may have been less beneficial: if this hypothesis is correct, then it marks an important stage in the demilitarisation of the native Andalusi population which was to be such an important, and ultimately disastrous, feature of the tenth- and eleventh-century history of al-Andalus.

The growing crisis of the Umayyad amirate, 852–86

Despite the attention given to the Holy War in the chronicles, it was increasingly irrelevant to the more general social and political crisis which enveloped the amirate in the second half of the ninth century and almost led to its complete collapse. The root of the problem seems to have lain with the increasing rate of conversion to Islam. Circumstantial evidence suggests that this was a period when large numbers of Andalusi Christians were becoming Muslims. These new converts, now full members of the Muslim community, sought to play a full role in the politics of al-Andalus. In doing so they inevitably came up against the opposition of established elite groups like the Umayyad *mawālī* and other Arab and Berber leaders. The evidence for the pace of conversion is very slight. We can be sure that before 711 there were no Muslims in the area and that by the twelfth century the Christians of al-Andalus were a small minority, but there is little direct evidence for the change. Using data from biographical dictionaries and comparisons with naming practices in Iran, Bulliet has postulated that there was a period of rapid conversion from 800 to 950, by which time about 50 per cent of the population of al-Andalus were Muslim.[10] Using the evidence of tax returns from the villages of the Cordoba area, Barcelo suggests that conversion was faster than this and that already by the mid-ninth century more than 70 per cent of the villages in the Cordoba area were Muslim.[11]

10. R. Bulliet, *Conversion to Islam in the Medieval Period: An Essay in Quantitive History* (Cambridge, Mass., 1979), pp. 114–27.

11. M. Barcelo, 'Un estudio sobre la estructura fiscal y procedimientos contables del emirato omeya de Cordoba (130–300/755–912) y del califato (300–366/912–976)', *Acta Medievalia* v–vi (1984–85), 51. Barcelo assumes that all villages were either Muslim or Christian, so a village which has Muslim taxpayers, which is what the evidence deals with, was entirely Muslim. There may, of course, have been many Christians living in such villages who would not appear in the record. Hence his method probably exaggerates the percentage of Muslims in the rural population at this time.

Of course, conversion to Islam had begun very early and some families, like the Banū Qasī and the family of Ibn al-Qūṭīya, had been integrated into the Muslim elite long before this. The pressures to convert among the elite are illustrated in a story in Ibn al-Qūṭīya.[12] According to this, when Muḥammad's secretary ʿAbd Allāh b. Umayya fell ill, he employed a Christian, Comes son of Antonian, to take his place. This caused considerable resentment and Hāshim b. ʿAbd al-ʿAzīz incited an Arab of distinguished descent, Muḥammad b. Kawthar, to complain to the Amir. Ibn Kawthar accordingly wrote, pointing out that the ʿAbbasids in the east would be full of scorn if they found that the Umayyads had to use a Christian secretary (though, in fact, the ʿAbbasids themselves often used Christian secretaries in this period) and that there were many well-qualified Muslims. The Amir responded by choosing the Berber Ḥamīd al-Zajjālī in his place. In another version, the Amir is made to say, 'If Comes were a Muslim, we would keep him in office', upon which he converted. This indeed seems to have happened, for he had a son with the typically Muslim name of ʿUmar, who served as a secretary to the Amir ʿAbd Allāh. The story makes the point that by the mid-ninth century, anyone who wanted a career in the expanding government bureaucracy had to be a Muslim.

Mass conversion, however, brought different problems: in particular, it undermined the fiscal basis of the Umayyad state. People who converted no longer had to pay the *jizya,* which was an important source of revenue for the amirs,[13] so conversion actually weakened the Muslim state apparatus. It may have gone further than that. At least until the changes in Muḥammad's reign, descendants of the Syrian *jund*s who had been settled in Andalucia had to do military service or pay the *hashd* to be exempt.[14] The new converts, in contrast, were not under any such obligation. In this way the new converts actually enjoyed a more favourable tax regime than the older Muslims. This was a sure recipe for tension. It may have been partly to assuage these grievances that Muḥammad relieved the Cordobans of the obligation to do military service. Further fiscal problems arose in times of famine in 865–68 and 873–74 when the collection of the *ʿushūr* (tithes) had to be abandoned. In Cordoba, the opposition to *muwallad* influence seems to have been led by Hāshim b. ʿAbd al-ʿAzīz, who became the Amir's chief minister in about 875 and whose rebarbative attitudes drove both Ibn Ḥafṣūn and Ibn Marwān al-Jillīqī into rebellion.

12. *Iftitāḥ,* pp. 182–7; Lévi-Provençal, *HEM,* i, pp. 289–90.
13. See above, p. 51. 14. See above, p. 50.

There are clear parallels with the tensions which led to the break-up of the rule of the ʿAbbasid caliphs in Iran in the ninth century. In both cases native Muslim elites emerged who wanted to exercise power in their own areas. They were not anti-Muslim (except in the last phase of Ibn Ḥafṣūn's revolt), but they resented being second-class citizens in a Muslim state and they resented attempts by Baghdad or Cordoba to impose their control.

Disaffection began in Toledo almost immediately after the death of ʿAbd al-Raḥmān II.[15] The city had always been a stronghold of independent-minded *muwallads* and had only been reduced to obedience in 836–37. On the death of the old amir, they drove out the governor he had appointed, Ḥārith b. Bazīʿ, and began to launch attacks on Cordovan territory. Muḥammad responded by fortifying and garrisoning Calatrava, but a relief force he sent was ambushed and defeated at Andujar, only a few kilometres from Cordoba itself, in 853–54, leading the government to fortify Ubeda as a refuge for the Arabs in case of further attacks. The Toledans were joined by many of the local Berbers and the rebellion was made more dangerous because the rebels entered into an alliance with the Christians and King Ordoño I of Oviedo sent a force to help them. The next year (854/5) the allies were defeated by Muḥammad's army on the Guazalete about 30 kilometres south-east of Toledo, though not perhaps as decisively as the Arabic sources would have us believe: certainly the victory was not followed up. In 870/1 the Toledans were described by Ibn Ḥayyān as being 'between rebellion and obedience'. In 873 they asked for peace and were given terms which hardly intruded on their autonomy: hostages and part of the *ʿushr* were to be sent to Cordoba, but the governor was to be chosen by the people of Toledo themselves.

Muḥammad's policy was to control the Toledans by garrisoning fortresses like Calatrava and by seeking alliances with neighbouring Berber chiefs, like the Banū ʿAbdūs of Zorita, where Muḥammad built a fortress, the Banū Sālim of Guadalajara and Medinaceli and, most important, the Banū Dhī'l-Nūn of Santaver and Ucles, whose dominance among the Berbers of this area was a result of this alliance with Cordoba. The Toledans also looked for outside support, notably from the Banū Qasī of the upper Ebro valley, perhaps because they were fellow *muwallads*. Members of the family appear on several occasions as governors of the city: in 859 Lubb b. Mūsā b. Mūsā b. Qasī appears as governor and is described by the Latin

15. The complex and often obscure history of Toledo in this period is discussed in Manzano Moreno, *Frontera*, pp. 284–97.

chronicle of Alfonso III as his father's prefect in the city.[16] At the end of the century we find another member of the family, perhaps based in Toledo, launching attacks in the Linares area close to Cordoba itself in 898. The influence of the Banū Qasī in the city seems to have come to an end with the unexplained assassination in 906 of Muḥammad b. Ismāʿīl. After this the Toledans seem to have made overtures to Alfonso III of Leon, but time was running out for Toledan independence and it is not clear that the alliance came to anything.

In the Lower March, too, the reign of Muḥammad saw the re-emergence of old separatist tendencies.[17] In 868 the Amir launched a surprise attack on Merida, which had been defying the authority of Cordoba under the leadership of the *muwallad* ʿAbd al-Raḥmān b. Marwān al-Jillīqī, whose father had been governor of the city until his murder in 828.[18] After some brisk fighting the city was taken and the leading horsemen (*fursān* – the word has a social significance here, somewhat like the English 'knight') were obliged to come and settle in Cordoba with their families, where it was presumably intended that these formidable warriors should form part of the Umayyad army. Muḥammad installed an Umayyad governor, Saʿīd b. al-ʿAbbās al-Qurashī, in the citadel his father had built, but the rest of the city is said to have been destroyed, and certainly for a later historian this event marked the end of Merida as an important urban centre: 'no vestige', he wrote, 'remained of that once opulent city'.[19]

The story might have ended there but for rivalries in Cordoba. We are told that Hāshim b. ʿAbd al-ʿAzīz, leader of the anti-*muwallad* faction, told Ibn Marwān in public that he was worse than a dog and had him slapped around the head.[20] In 874/5 Ibn Marwān fled along with his companions from the city where he was so obviously not wanted. Muḥammad led an expedition against him, but he was allowed to settle in Badajoz, still a village at this time, which he made his headquarters and from where he was able to defy Cordoba. He built mosques, a bath and walls for his new stronghold.[21] In 876 he was able to capture Hāshim b. ʿAbd al-ʿAzīz,

16. Cap. 25. 17. Lévi-Provençal, *HEM*, i, pp. 295–9.
18. See above, p. 00.
19. Al-Maqqarī, *History of the Mohammaden Dynasties in Spain*, trans. P. de Gayangos (2 vols, London, 1840–41), ii, pp. 127–8.
20. *Al-Bayān*, p. 102.
21. Ibn ʿAbd al-Munʿim al-Ḥimyarī, *Rawḍ al-miʿṭār fi akhbār al-aqṭār*, partial ed. with French trans., E. Lévi-Provençal (Leiden, 1938), cap. 48 (ed. p. 46; trans. p. 58).

who had been sent against him, and send him as a goodwill offering to King Alfonso III, a massive humiliation for Cordoba. Ibn Marwān was able to preserve his independence by disappearing, when he was under threat, into the no man's land north of the Tagus where Umayyad forces were unable to pursue him and biding his time until the danger had passed. He was also able to receive intermittent support from the Christians.

At the death of Muḥammad in 886, Ibn Marwān was powerful enough to be raiding as far as Seville. When he in turn died four years later, his little state partially disintegrated as his followers set up statelets in Beja and Santa Maria (Faro), but Badajoz itself remained in the hands of his family until, with typical thoroughness, 'Abd al-Raḥmān III took it from his grandson in 929/30.

A final vignette on the history of this area is provided by the story of the movement led by Ibn al-Qiṭṭ. Ibn al-Qiṭṭ was a member of the Umayyad family who, at the instigation of an adventurer called Abū 'Alī al-Sarrāj, proclaimed himself to be the Mahdī in 901. Mahdī can be loosely translated as 'Messiah', and there was a widespread belief throughout the Muslim world that such a figure would appear to sweep away oppression and lead the Muslims back to true Islam. Ibn al-Qiṭṭ chose to exercise his mission in the Merida area, notably among the Nafza Berbers, and to establish his credentials he mobilised them for the *jihād* against the newly fortified Christian outpost of Zamora. Sadly for him, the walls of the city did not collapse on his approach, as he had prophesied, and he was obliged to begin a siege. Meanwhile the established chief of the Nafza, Zu'āl b. Ya'īsh, began to fear that he was being supplanted in the chiefship (*ri'āsa*) of his tribe (*qawm*) and persuaded them to desert, leaving Ibn al-Qiṭṭ to his fate. The incident is revealing, partly because it is the first example in al-Andalus of anyone claiming to be the Mahdī, and it shows the appeal that such heterodox religious leaders could have among the Berbers, but partly too because it shows the power of tribal leaders and how tribal structures were still important in these remoter areas.[22]

The politics of the Upper March seem more complex,[23] partly because we are better informed: the surviving sections of al-'Udhrī's *Nuṣūṣ* give us more detail about this area than we have about either

22. For accounts of Ibn al-Qiṭṭ, see Lévi-Provençal, *HEM*, i, pp. 383–5; P. Guichard, *Structures sociales 'orientales' et 'occidentales' dans L'Espagne musulmane* (Paris, 1977), pp. 263–7; Manzano Moreno, *Frontera*, pp. 474–7.

23. Manzano Moreno, *Frontera*, pp. 332–40; M.J. Viguera Molins, *Aragon Musulman* (Zaragoza, 1981), pp. 91–104.

of the other two Marches. It seems that on his accession Muḥammad, faced with the dangerous disturbances in Toledo, entrusted the affairs of the Upper March to the local strong man, Mūsā b. Mūsā b. Qasī, thus formalising his position in the area. Al-ʿUdhrī says that Muḥammad *sajjalahu* (gave him a written contract),[24] and this may be an example of a fairly widespread practice of investing local dignitaries with independent governorates. He seems to have remained effective ruler until 860/1 when he was deposed. He was killed in 862 in conflict with the Banū Sālim Berbers of Guadalajara, probably supported by Muḥammad. With the Banū Qasī temporarily leaderless, Muḥammad seems to have been able to appoint his own governors in the Ebro valley for a while and send his sons to lead the *ṣāʾifa*, but in 871 Mūsā's four sons were able to capture the Umayyad governors of Tudela, Huesca and Zaragoza, where the Banū Qasī occupation is said to have been followed by a massacre of the Arab population, and restore the family's power in the area.

The power of the Banū Qasī was then restricted not by the Amir Muḥammad, who was increasingly preoccupied by problems much nearer home, but by other magnate families in the area, the Berber Banū Sālim, the *muwallad* Banū ʿAmrūs of Huesca and the Arab Tujībī family, who were installed by Muḥammad in the newly fortified towns of Calatayud and Daroca and were eventually to supplant the Banū Qasī in all their territories.[25] As in the case of Toledo, Muḥammad's policy was to try to create a balance of power in the province by supporting smaller lords against the Toledans and the Banū Qasī, rather than trying to impose the sort of direct control his father had done. The main reason for this retiring attitude was the growing threat posed by Ibn Ḥafṣūn's rebellion.

Of all the various protest movements against the Cordoba government which developed in the reign of Muḥammad, the rebellion of Ibn Ḥafṣūn was by far the most threatening. This was not because it was the most widespread – the power of Ibn Marwān in Badajoz or the Banū Qasī was certainly more extensive – but because it occurred in the heartland of Cordovan power.

ʿUmar b. Ḥafṣūn came from a family of property owners in the Ronda area.[26] They were of native Iberian stock and his grandfather had converted to Islam in the reign of al-Ḥakam I. The young ʿUmar seems to have broken with his family's respectable

24. Al-ʿUdhrī, *Nuṣūṣ ʿan al-Andalus min kitab Tarṣīʿ al-akhbār wa tawzīʿ al-āthār*, ed. A. al-Ahwani (Madrid, 1956), pp. 29–31.
25. Basilio Pavon, *Ciudades Hispanomusulmanas* (Madrid, 1992), pp. 155–7, 222–3.
26. For his early life see Lévi-Provençal, *HEM*, i, pp. 300–6.

lifestyle and killed a neighbour in a fight. After that he took to the wild hills to the east of Ronda and became an outlaw. Soon after he fled to Tahert in North Africa to escape reprisals and found work in a tailor's shop. While he was there he was approached by one of his fellow countrymen who urged him to return and lead a revolt. He found a base at Bobastro in the remote Guadalhorce gorge in the Serrania de Ronda. Here, from about 881, he became the focus for a growing band and they took to raiding the surrounding small towns. In 883 he made a temporary peace, but was soon back to his old tricks and came to dominate the hinterland of Malaga.

This was the position when the Amir Muḥammad died in August 886. In his last years he had seldom left Cordoba and action against Ibn Ḥafṣūn had been led by his son and successor al-Mundhir. Now in his early forties, the new Amir had had extensive military experience leading expeditions against the Christians in the north and rebels inside al-Andalus. The brief chronicle accounts of his reign present him as extremely effective, both as a military leader and as an administrator, and make the point that if he had reigned even a short while longer, the various separatist movements in al-Andalus would have soon been crushed.[27] At the end of his reign he was engaged on a determined siege of Ibn Ḥafṣūn's stronghold at Bobastro. In the event, he died in June 888 after a reign of just under two years.

The reign of ʿAbd Allāh and the decay of the amirate, 888–912

Al-Mundhir was succeeded without apparent conflict by his brother ʿAbd Allāh: the 'official' historiographical tradition represented by Ibn Ḥayyān and Ibn Idhārī leads one to assume that al-Mundhir died of natural causes, but Ibn al-Qūṭīya accuses ʿAbd Allāh directly of his brother's murder. If he did come to power through fratricide, the new Amir showed few signs of enjoying his ill-gotten power. He appears to have been pious to the point of asceticism but also morose, depressive and deeply suspicious: one is reminded of Mohun Lal's description of a nineteenth-century ruler of Herat: 'He is a gloomy and decrepit prince; he excites the pity of mankind.'[28] In

27. Ibn Idhārī, *Al-Bayān*, ii, p. 120; Ibn al-Qūṭīya, *Iftitāḥ*, pp. 227–9; Lévi-Provençal, *HEM*, i, pp. 306–10.
28. Quoted in R. Byron, *The Road to Oxiana* (London, 1937), p. 107.

891 Ibn Ḥafṣūn threatened Cordoba itself and for the first and last time the Amir was prodded into leading a military campaign himself; the rebels were driven away, but no lasting gains were made.[29] Apart from this, 'Abd Allāh failed to offer any military leadership to the Cordovan forces. He only seems to have left his palace to go to the mosque (having a covered way constructed so that people could not see him) and for the chase. He became something of a recluse, and people who trespassed on his privacy did so at their peril: in 910 a number of members of the Umayyad family were taken into custody by the prefect of the city (*ṣāḥib al-madīna*), Mūsā b. Muḥammad b. Ḥudayr, for daring to use the bridge on a day when the Amir was wanting to cross it to go hunting.[30]

Dissatisfaction with his rule may lie behind the family bloodshed at the beginning of his reign. In 891 he was responsible for the murder of his eldest son Muḥammad, stabbed by his brother al-Muṭarrif with his father's encouragement.[31] In 895 it was al-Muṭarrif's turn: accused of conspiring with the rebels in Seville, he was murdered after defending himself in his house for three days. The vindictive Amir also had two of his brothers, Hishām and al-Qāsim, killed. It is likely that these purges, unprecedented in the history of the Umayyads of al-Andalus, were a response to understandable impatience within the ruling family at the Amir's lack of effective leadership.

For the Umayyad amirate faced a challenge that almost completely destroyed it. Ibn Ḥafṣūn's revolt had clearly demonstrated the ineffectiveness of Cordoba's military power and 'Abd Allāh's accession seems to have been the signal for almost universal rejection of Umayyad authority as one place after another was taken over by local lords. The nature of these challenges to Umayyad rule in the Guadalquivir valley and the southern mountains has been thoroughly investigated recently.[32] There is no real evidence that there was a general uprising of the *muwallad*s against the Arabs and Berbers (though, as we have seen, there were many *muwallad*s with grievances against Cordoba), still less was there a Spanish 'nationalist' movement involved. The alliances the usurpers made cut across ethnic boundaries to suit political expedience. It seems

29. Ibn Ḥayyān, *Al-Muqtabis fi ta'rīkh rijāl al-Andalus (Al-Muqtabis III)*, ed. M. Antuña (Paris, 1937), pp. 93–102, gives a full account; Lévi-Provençal, *HEM*, i, pp. 372–6.
30. Ibn Idhārī, *Al-Bayān*, ii, p. 146.
31. See Lévi-Provençal, *HEM*, i, pp. 333–4, for the evidence.
32. See M. Acien Almansa, *Entre el feudalismo y el Islam: 'Umar Ibn Ḥafṣun en los historiadores, en las fuentes y en la historia* (Granada, 1994).

that the usurpers were reacting against the more systematic taxation developed by 'Abd al-Raḥmān II; they all seem to have appropriated the dues which previously went to Cordoba for their own use. They also built strongholds (*ḥuṣūn*) from which to exercise control over the areas (often no more than a few villages) that they had taken over and they often passed this power on from father to son. In this process, we can see parallels with the contemporary disintegration of Carolingian authority under the impact of civil war and Viking invasion and the passing of power to local dynasts.

More substantial and permanent than these local lordships were the 'states' set up in Murcia and Seville. One would like to know more about Daysam b. Isḥāq, described by Ibn Ḥayyān as 'loved by all classes of people, a friend [*rafīq*] of his subjects, open-handed and showering favours on poets and literary men', who ruled in Lorca, Murcia and the district of Tudmīr.[33] He is said to have had an army of 500 and ruled his principality until his death in 906. A more unsavoury character was Ibrāhīm b. al-Ḥajjāj, ruler of Seville, about whose rise to power Ibn Ḥayyān tells us more than is good for his reputation.[34]

Seville was the largest city in al-Andalus after Cordoba and an important port for communications with Morocco. It was ruled by a well-established urban patriciate with houses in the city and extensive properties in the country, notably in the attractive olive-covered hills of the Aljarafe to the west where many of these urban aristocrats chose to spend part of the year. At the beginning of 'Abd Allāh's reign, the two leading Arab families were the Banū Khaldūn (distant ancestors of the great historian Ibn Khaldūn) and the Banū'l-Ḥajjāj,[35] who, as well as a distinguished Arab lineage, also claimed descent from the Visigothic kings through the female line. There were also two important *muwallad* families, the Banū Angelino and the Banū Savarico. These groups seem to have lived together in peace if not harmony until the breakdown of government under the Amir 'Abd Allāh. Only one year after his accession, in 889, Kurayb b. Khaldūn decided to take advantage of the unrest. He left the town and established himself on his estate in the Aljarafe, making alliances with other dissidents, including Ibn Marwān al-Jillīqī, defeating the Umayyad governor and attacking the suburbs

33. Ibn Ḥayyān, *Al-Muqtabis*, ed. Antuña, p. 9; Lévi-Provençal, *HEM*, i, p. 340.
34. Ibn Ḥayyān, *Al-Muqtabis*, ed. Antuña, pp. 68–85; Lévi-Provençal, *HEM*, i, pp. 356–68.
35. On the Banū'l-Ḥajjāj see J.M. Carabaza, 'La Familia de los Banu Haŷŷaŷ', in *Estudios Onomastico-Biograficos de Al-Andalus* v (1992), 39–55.

of the city. A leading *muwallad*, Muḥammad b. Ghālib, approached the Amir, who appointed him to maintain order on the road between Seville and Cordoba. This enabled Ibn Khaldūn to enlist the support of the leader of the other main Arab family, the Banū'l-Ḥajjāj, and the feud began in earnest, the Arab lords seizing Coria and Carmona while the Amir sent his son Muḥammad to try to make peace. The unfortunate *muwallad* leader Ibn Ghālib was sacrificed to expediency and executed, but this only gave rise to further civil strife in Seville.

By 891 the Arabs had seized control, the leading *muwallad*s had been slaughtered and the Umayyad governor, Umayya b. 'Abd al-Ghāfir of the Banū Abī 'Abda, had fallen in battle. Preoccupied with Ibn Ḥafṣūn, Cordoba could do nothing. Predictably, by 899 the Banū Khaldūn and the Banū'l-Ḥajjāj were at loggerheads, but Ibrāhīm b. al-Ḥajjāj arranged a dinner-time massacre of his rivals and became undisputed ruler of Seville. From this position of strength he negotiated with Cordoba. 'Abd Allāh acknowledged him as king (*malik*) of Seville and Carmona, in exchange for some revenues, military support on the *ṣā'ifa* and a promise not to help the Amir's enemies, and Ibrāhīm established a small but cultured court in the city. He had a standing army of 500, appointed the *qāḍī* and the *ṣāḥib al-madīna* and had the *ṭirāz* (official robes and textiles), though not coins, inscribed with his name. Among the literary men who benefited from his patronage was Ibn 'Abd Rabbihi, author of the great cultural encyclopaedia known as the *'Iqd al-Farīd*, which sought to lay all the riches of eastern Islamic literary life before the Andalusi public. Ibrāhīm survived in peace and prosperity, dying just before the Amir 'Abd Allāh in 910/11.[36]

An interesting exception to the general run of local war-lords is the story of the confederation of the sailors of Pechina, unearthed for the first time by Lévi-Provençal.[37] Pechina became wealthy in the ninth century as the maritime entrepôt in south-east Spain for North Africa, especially for Tenes, the main port of the Rustamid amirate of Tahert, with which relations were close. Pechina, with its nearby harbour under the watchtower (al-Māriya, now known as Almeria), was inhabited by a mixture of Ghassānī Arabs, who farmed the rich Andarax valley, and sailors of Spanish origin, some Muslim, some Christian. Before the death of the Amir Muḥammad in 884, they had formed a self-governing community and set about

36. Ibn Ḥayyān, *Al-Muqtabis*, ed. Antuña, pp. 11–13.
37. *HEM*, i, pp. 348–56, largely based on Ibn Ḥayyān, *Al-Muqtabis*, ed. Antuña, pp. 53, 87–9.

beautifying their city on the model of Cordoba. During the reign of 'Abd Allāh this community, led by the sailor 'Abd al-Razzāq b. 'Īsā, succeeded in avoiding attempts by the predatory Arab chiefs of Elvira to take it over, and it survived, an oasis of peace and growing prosperity, until in the mid-tenth century the settlement moved to Almeria, which became, in its turn, one of the leading ports of al-Andalus.

Ibn Ḥafṣūn remained the most dangerous among the many enemies Cordoba faced. He was the only one who attempted a direct assault on the capital and he was accepted as the leader of the *muwallad* faction (*da'wa al-muwalladīn*, as Ibn Ḥayyān calls it[38]) way beyond his own sphere of control. The high point of his power came in 891 when he established his base at Aguilar de la Frontera and raided the countryside around Cordoba, his forces reaching the walls of the city itself. At this stage he also tried to enlist support from outside the Iberian peninsula, writing to the Aghlabids of Qayrawan and suggesting that he offer his allegiance to the 'Abbasids. His defeat in that year at the hands of the Amir 'Abd Allāh only temporarily reduced his power and he soon recovered Archidona and other towns he had lost, but it seems to have damaged his prestige and his power ceased to expand.

In 899 he announced that he had converted to Christianity. The reasons for this are not clear and in many ways it made his position much more difficult: while some Mozarabs no doubt joined his cause, many *muwallads*, who were after all sincere Muslims, abandoned him. His conversion meant that compromise with Cordoba was no longer possible. In Muslim law the penalty for apostasy is death and it was inconceivable that he could be recognised as a legitimate governor. It also meant that campaigns against him took on the aspect of a *jihād* or holy war and made it more difficult for him to find Muslim allies. During the last decade of 'Abd Allāh's reign his power was under continuous attack from expeditions from Cordoba, but despite this, the Amir's death saw him still in control of Bobastro and his mountain fastness. There is no indication that Ibn Ḥafṣūn had any vision of overthrowing Arab rule or of establishing a government in Cordoba. He tried to make alliances with other opponents of the Amir ranging from Ibn al-Ḥajjāj of Seville to Alfonso III of Leon, but he was essentially an opportunist rather than a long-term planner. He sometimes accepted offers of peace and position under Cordovan rule, but in the end the temptations

38. *Al-Muqtabis,* ed. Antuña, p. 24.

of independence were too strong. Whatever his vacillations and weaknesses, however, Ibn Ḥafṣūn survived because he spoke for the interests of a powerful constituency of the disaffected.

Credit for the survival of Umayyad rule despite these assaults should go, not to the torpid Amir himself but to a small band of dedicated Umayyad *mawālī* and some members of the Umayyad family. The key figure among them was Aḥmad b. Abī 'Abda, whose family had long connections with the Umayyad family.[39] He, and his sons 'Īsā and 'Abbās, were indefatigable leaders of military expeditions to drive back rebels and to collect taxes. He collected a small group of soldiers, only 300 strong, but they were said to have been the equal of any army in al-Andalus. Virtually every year, usually under the formal leadership of one of the Amir's sons, Abān or al-'Āṣī, the Banū Abī 'Abda would set out to do battle.

A typical expedition is described by Ibn Ḥayyān in the year 896.[40] The small army, commanded by the Amir's uncle Hishām b. 'Abd al-Raḥmān and Aḥmād b. Muḥammad b. Abī 'Abda, left Cordoba at the end of Rabī I (17 May) when the harvest would be beginning. They pursued a very winding route through the mountains east of Jaen to Guadix. At first they headed south to Ḥiṣn Qamarat Jaysh (an unidentified site on the river Guadalbullon near to Jaen[41] controlled by Ibn Hudhayl) where they set about ravaging the agricultural lands and cutting down the trees until Ibn Hudhayl appeared to do battle. After some inconclusive fighting Ibn Hudhayl asked for peace and it was agreed on condition that his father was sent as a hostage to Cordoba. They then moved on to Bakhtwīra (unidentified) in the lands of another war-lord, Hurayz b. Hābil, where the horses were allowed to graze in the crops and inflicted considerable damage. After that they went to Baeza (at this time loyal to the government) where they collected the *'ushūr*. They stayed there for three days during which time the troops went off to Tashkar (Castillo de Tiscar) which they found deserted so they burned it and took the harvest.

By this time the weather had worsened dramatically and, despite the fact that it was high summer, the army was drenched and demoralised by continuous torrential rain. They returned to Bakhtwīra, stronghold of Hurayz b. Hābil. After some fierce fighting they drove him out of the suburb, which they burned, and into the castle.

39. See above, p. 65. 40. Ibn Ḥayyān, *Al-Muqtabis*, ed. Antuña, pp. 114–18.

41. Some, but not all, of the sites mentioned in this account have been identified in J. Vallvé Bermejo, 'La Cora de Jaen', in *Al-Andalus* 34 (1969), 55–82, and idem, 'La Cora de Tudmir', in *Al-Andalus* 37 (1972), 145–89.

From here he negotiated peace on the condition that he handed over his son as a hostage and agreed to pay 2,500 *dīnār*s in cash and compensation for eight military horses which had been hamstrung in the fighting. He was given a written agreement (*aman*). The bedraggled expedition (it was still raining hard, with thunder and lightning) pushed on, stopping at Munt Shāqir (Montejicar), Al-Banyūl (Albuniel) and Ḥiṣn al-Liqūn (Alicun de Ortega) which they quickly captured and where they took horses, equipment and a lot of food; they ejected the partisans of Ibn Hudhayl from the fortress and installed a garrison of Arabs and Berbers. At Guadix they paused for a few days to receive the caravan bringing the tithes (*'ushūr*) from Pechina and the taxes (*jibāya*) of Hiṣn Bashīra before crossing the border into the province of Tudmīr (Murcia) to Balsh (Velez Rubio). The weather was still as bad but they persevered, fighting the locals and destroying houses and fruit trees until, in August, they reached the River Segura where they first came into conflict with the supporters of Daysam b. Isḥāq. When they finally reached Murcia they stayed there for ten days collecting the taxes (*maghārim*) from the people.

At the beginning of Rajab (26 August) they set off on the return journey. It was not easy. Having been drenched on the way, they now suffered from terrible thirst and some 30 men and numerous animals perished. Daysam himself was at Lorca, but they passed the city and made no effort to take it. Daysam pursued them and there was some skirmishing in which the Cordoba forces took horses and seven coats of mail. Then they returned via Jaen to Cordoba, reaching the capital three months and 21 days after setting out.

The long account throws very interesting light on the government in 'Abd Allāh's reign. It is quite clear that the systematic taxation and administration had almost completely broken down. It is true that taxes were collected from Pechina and in Murcia but, at least in Murcia, this only happened because the army visited. In addition to the money, the expedition was concerned to secure supplies of food, horses and military equipment, presumably to see it through the winter in Cordoba as well as for the expedition. The Cordoba forces could extract hostages from lesser war-lords, but, faced with Daysam at Lorca, they could not even attempt to reduce him to obedience. Basically, this was government by pillage and the Umayyad army was no more than a marauding band living off the country: its main objective was not to uphold the authority of the state, but simply to feed itself. This was the reality of power when 'Abd al-Raḥmān III became amir.

Against this background, it is not surprising that ʿAbd Allāh's government made very little impact in the *Thughūr*. We know very little about Toledo and Badajoz during the reign, but it is clear that Toledo maintained its independence and that Badajoz continued to be ruled by the family of Ibn Marwān al-Jillīqī. The power of the Banū Dhī'l-Nūn was consolidated, both in their upland possessions around Ucles and Huete and in their domains in the Levante including Valencia and Jativa. These different areas were ruled by different branches of the family, but they were probably bound together by ties of transhumance. In the next two centuries, agricultural development was to make Valencia one of the richest and most fertile parts of al-Andalus, but it seems that at this time it was sparsely populated by Berbers dependent on transhumant pastoralism rather than settled agriculture, and it was these transhumants who looked to the Banū'l-Dhī'l-Nūn for leadership. The reign of ʿAbd Allāh saw a prolonged conflict between the people of Toledo and the Banū Dhī'l-Nūn, who seem to have wanted to take over the city. In 887 Mūsā b. Dhī'l-Nūn led an army of 20,000 (much larger than any of the Umayyad armies of the period) against Toledo and defeated the army of the city, taking a vast amount of booty but not, as far as we know, occupying it. After this defeat, the Toledans seem to have looked to the Banū Qasī of the Ebro valley for protection and members of the family appear as governors in the scattered notices we have. In 908 Mūsā b. Dhī'l-Nūn died and his domains were divided among his sons, one of whom, al-Fatḥ b. Mūsā of Ucles, continued the struggle for Toledo. The eventual Dhū'l-Nūnid take-over of the city in the eleventh century was the culmination of 150 years of struggle.[42]

In the Upper March, there was a major change in the balance of power. As before, al-ʿUdhrī gives us more detail than we have for the other two Marches, but it is not always easy to make a consistent picture of events. The Amir al-Mundhir had appointed as governor of Zaragoza to keep a check on the Banū Qasī a member of the Umayyad family called Aḥmād b. al-Barā', who seems to have been able to maintain himself in this difficult outpost. For reasons which are not clear, ʿAbd Allāh decided to replace him by the Tujībīs. This family of Arab extraction had been entrusted with Calatayud and Daroca by the Amir Muḥammad. According to Ibn al-Qūṭīya, Muḥammad b. ʿAbd al-Raḥmān al-Tujībī was a close friend of the Amir's, and in 890 ʿAbd Allāh secretly invested him with

42. For these confused events see Manzano Moreno, *Frontera*, pp. 299–304.

Zaragoza and may have helped in the governor's subsequent murder. Whatever the ins and outs of this murky episode, the end result was clear: Zaragoza now had new masters and neither the Banū Qasī nor the Umayyads were able to remove them. For almost 150 years, Zaragoza and the central Ebro valley remained in the hands of this dynasty. By contrast, the power of the Banū Qasī declined rapidly in the early tenth century, partly because of the growing importance of the Tujībīs but even more because of their own internal divisions, though Muḥammad b. Lubb remained an important figure in the Upper Ebro valley until his death in 907 and was invested with the family's hereditary stronghold at Tudela. The dynasty retained a toe-hold in Tudela until the reign of 'Abd al-Raḥmān III, but the real power in the Upper March was now the Tujībīs.

The feebleness of 'Abd Allāh's government allowed the fissiparous tendencies in Andalusi society to come to the fore. Most of the local 'barons' who took over were men with long-established roots in their own areas and the local separatism they brought into the open was as old as Muslim Spain itself. Vigorous amirs like 'Abd al-Raḥmān II with his castles and his garrisons had temporarily been able to overlay it: now, with or without the *sijil* of formal investiture, these local magnates, just like the counts and castellans of northern France in the same period, took formal power from the faltering government into their own hands.

CHAPTER FOUR

The Golden Age of the Umayyad Caliphate, 912–76

The policies and strategies of ʿAbd al-Raḥmān III

ʿAbd al-Raḥmān b. Muḥammad b. ʿAbd Allāh succeeded to the Umayyad amirate on 16 October 912 without open opposition.[1] He was not the obvious candidate: his father Muḥammad had been executed by his grandfather, the Amir ʿAbd Allāh, almost immediately after his birth. Furthermore he had paternal uncles, notably Abān and al-ʿĀṣī, sons of ʿAbd Allāh, who were already experienced in military and political affairs. But ʿAbd Allāh seems to have preferred his young grandson and educated him for the succession from his earliest days. The young prince had been born on 7 January 891. He was of comparatively short stature and, like many of his family, had fair hair and blue eyes, inherited from his Frankish or Basque mother Muzna and his grandmother Iñiga, daughter of King Fortun Garces of Navarre (deposed 905). Whatever his grandfather's other failings (and they were many), his choice of his young grandson to succeed him could not be faulted. He was not a brilliant general, nor a charismatic religious leader, but rather a methodical and determined politician who systematically restored the power of the amirs until the Umayyads of Cordoba had much more extensive power over al-Andalus than ever before.

The position he inherited was not an encouraging one. The authority of Cordoba scarcely extended beyond the city itself and the Campiña which surrounded it. The administration seems to have been much reduced, for there were very few assets to administer,

1. For the political history of his reign see E. Lévi-Provençal, *HEM*, ii, pp. 1–164; J. Vallvé Bermejo, *El Califato de Cordoba* (Madrid, 1992), pp. 131–200.

and the army was more like a war-band living off the proceeds of an annual pillaging expedition than an organized military force.

It is clear that the new Amir had his strategy worked out in advance, for he moved into action with remarkable speed. His policy was to expand the area under the control of Cordoba gradually and carefully. In order to do this, he had to destroy the power of many local lords, some controlling a large town (*madīna*) like Seville or Badajoz, others just a single castle (*ḥiṣn*) on some remote, rocky Andalucian pinnacle. His first moves were modest enough, but he was careful to make sure that they were permanent. He was skilful at organising systematic sieges. He used blockade, economic warfare (the cutting down of fruit trees at Badajoz and Toledo[2]) and siege engines: in 929 at Beja he prepared mangonels which demolished some of the towers of the walls of the city, forcing the local lord, ʻAbd al-Raḥmān b. Saʻīd, to surrender. At Bobastro in 927 and Toledo in 930 he built permanent siege camps with their own *sūq*s.[3] He did not always stay to prosecute the siege himself, but always left a trusted lieutenant, returning later himself (Bobastro, Badajoz and Toledo). His determination and ability to maintain a siege meant that no castle in al-Andalus could resist him forever. When his forces captured a fortress and forced the local lord to 'come down' (*istanzala*), he was careful to leave a garrison behind or to demolish the stronghold. He did the same with larger cities: Seville, Badajoz and Toledo were all supplied with troops and governors appointed by ʻAbd al-Raḥmān.

But while he was efficient at wielding the big stick, he also offered carrots to persuade his opponents to surrender. Those who submitted were treated well and often given posts in the Cordoba military. When Muḥammad b. Ibrāhīm b. al-Ḥajjāj gave up Seville, he was temporarily installed among the *wazīr*s in Cordoba as a mark of favour.[4] When the last of the Banū Marwān of Badajoz finally surrendered in 930,[5] he and his followers were moved to Cordoba and given senior positions in the military. This applied even to the most bitter of ʻAbd al-Raḥmān's opponents: when Ḥafṣ b. Ḥafṣūn finally surrendered Bobastro in January 928, he was allowed to enrol in the army.[6] In most cases the defeated rebels were kept well away

2. Ibn Ḥayyān, *Al-Muqtabis V*, ed. P. Chalmeta, F. Corriente and M. Sobh (Madrid, 1979), pp. 188–9; Spanish trans. M. Viguera and F. Corriente (Zaragoza, 1981), pp. 213–14; Ibn Idhārī al-Marrākushī, *Al-Bayān al-mughrib fi akhbār al-Andalus wa'l-Maghrib*, ed. E. Lévi-Provençal and G.S. Colin (Leiden, 1948), ii, pp. 200, 203.

3. Ibn Ḥayyān, *Al-Muqtabis V*, pp. 145–6, 188–9; trans., pp. 171–2, 213–14.

4. Ibid., pp. 53–4; trans., p. 73. 5. Ibid., p. 179; trans., p. 205.

6. Ibid., pp. 137–8; trans., p. 164; Lévi-Provençal, *HEM*, ii, p. 20.

from their bases, but an exception was made in the case of Khalaf b. Bakr, the lord of Ocsonoba (Faro). He had such a good reputation among his subjects that when he surrendered his little principality to 'Abd al-Raḥmān in August 929[7] he was allowed to keep it on payment of tribute. It was this combination of dogged determination on the one hand and flexibility on the other that enabled 'Abd al-Raḥmān to achieve the pacification of al-Andalus.

Another important feature of 'Abd al-Raḥmān's policy was his use of the *jihād* or holy war. He himself led five main expeditions, in 917, 920, 924, 934 and 939, the last of which resulted in a disastrous defeat at al-Khandaq (Alhandega) after which the monarch did not participate any more in person. As with previous expeditions, the purpose of these raids does not seem to have been to conquer Christian Spain, and no effort seems to have been made to garrison and settle new areas. Some of the campaigns were launched, at least ostensibly, to protect Muslim communities on the frontiers in the face of Christian advances – thus in 924, the campaign which resulted in the sack of Pamplona was a response to the defeat of the Banū Qasī and other frontier lords by Sancho Garces of Navarre[8] – but sometimes the expeditions were undertaken for reasons which had much more to do with internal policies than threats from the north.

The obligation to lead the *jihād* against unbelievers was an important part of 'Abd al-Raḥmān's claim to be the legitimate ruler of all the Muslims of al-Andalus. In 929 he took the title of Commander of the Faithful, or Caliph. We do not know how long he had been considering the move, but the fact that he had led and was continuing to lead the Muslims against the infidels, whether against Ibn Ḥafṣūn in the south or the ancient enemy to the north, certainly increased his claims to the title. The public relations side of his campaigns is clearly indicated by the way he took care to have the heads of his slaughtered enemies delivered to Cordoba for the people to admire and accounts of his triumphs read out in the mosque. (This is possibly another borrowing from 'Abbasid practice. When al-Muwaffaq was conducting his campaigns against the Zanj rebels of southern Iraq between 879 and 883, he always had progress reports read out in the mosques of Baghdad and Samarra.)

There were also more practical reasons why the *jihād* helped expand his authority. Somewhat like the progess of a mediaeval

7. Ibn Ḥayyān, *Al-Muqtabis V*, pp. 163–4; trans., pp. 188–9.
8. Lévi-Provençal, *HEM*, ii, pp. 44–7.

European monarch, it enabled the ruler to keep in touch with important people who never usually came to court. In his expedition of 924, for example, he made his way up the east coast through Tudmīr and the *kūra* of Valencia to Tortosa, which he brought under Umayyad control. It may well have been the first time a reigning member of the Umayyad dynasty had ever visited the Levante. While in the north he granted the Tujībī ruler of Zaragoza, Muḥammad b. ʻAbd al-Raḥmān, a *tasjīl*, a diploma of authority. After the sack of Pamplona he took a more direct route back, passing through the upland territories of the Dhū'l-Nūnids. The leaders of this clan had been conspicuous by their absence from the campaign, but when the monarch arrived at Ucles, Yaḥyā b. Mūsā and other members of his family felt obliged to come and make their excuses. As we shall see, this did not mean that the Tujībīs or the Dhū'l-Nūnids became submissive vassals, but the expedition had provided ʻAbd al-Raḥmān with an important way of demonstrating his leadership.[9]

As the area under ʻAbd al-Raḥmān's control expanded, so did his revenues. *Kūras* (districts) which accepted his rule were obliged to pay a tribute, generally referred to as a *jibāya*. In order to administer his expanding assets and lead his armies, ʻAbd al-Raḥmān made use of a corps of devoted administrators. These were divided into two distinct groups. The first were members of a number of what can be described as mandarin dynasties, the Banū Abī ʻAbda, whose veteran leader Aḥmad died a martyr's death fighting the Christians at San Esteban de Gormaz in September 917,[10] the Banū Ḥudayr, the Banū Shuhayd, the Banū ʻAbd al-Ra'uf and the Banū Futays. These families, mostly claiming to be descended from Umayyad *mawālī*, occupied most of the important posts in the administration, as secretaries, treasurers (*khuzzān*), administrators of the city (*aṣḥāb al-madīna*) and supervisors of military equipment (*khuzzān al-ṣilāt, aṣḥāb al-ʻarḍ*), and they also provided the *wazīrs*, the general purpose title given to the highest ranks. They were a rich and cultivated group who contributed much to the cultural milieu of Cordoba, and one gets the impression of an exclusive and very influential clique. Family ties were very important: uncles and brothers were frequently employed in the administration at the same time and sons succeeded fathers.[11]

The second group were *ṣaqāliba*, who were mostly recent arrivals

9. Ibn Ḥayyān, *Al-Muqtabis V*, pp. 121–8; trans., pp. 146–53.
10. Ibid., pp. 88–9; trans., pp. 110–11.
11. Lévi-Provençal, *HEM*, iii, pp. 192–6.

in al-Andalus. These had been employed by the Umayyads since the reign of ʿAbd al-Raḥmān II, but it was not until the time of ʿAbd al-Raḥmān III that they became a prominent force in the administration and the military, and their numbers are said to have increased from 3,750 to 13,750 in the course of the reign. These slaves were generically known as *ṣaqāliba*, a word which was usually applied to the Slav peoples of eastern Europe, although it was also more loosely applied to slaves of northern European origin. From the ninth century it seems that pagan Slavs captured in the eastern campaigns of the Franks were exported to Spain. The time of the Ottonian emperors of Germany in the tenth century saw the trade reach its height, slaves being bought in Prague or Verdun by Jewish merchants and taken south. Some of them were castrated and these eunuchs were used for both domestic and administrative functions by the Caliph. Some clearly remained intact, as dynasties of *ṣiqlabī* origin were to appear in the next century. According to Ibn Ḥawqal, some of these were re-exported to the east.[12]

Those who remained in al-Andalus were often referred to as *ghilmān* (sing. *ghulām*). This word originally meant young man or page, but it was used throughout the Muslim world from the ninth century onwards to describe such slave soldiers, usually of Turkish origin in the east and Slavic in the west. Senior individuals were still known as *fatā* (young man), however old and battle-hardened they might be, and they were given distinctive personal names like Badr (Full-moon), Najā (Deliverance) or Durrī (Brilliant) which were quite different from the conventional Arabic names. The most senior of these was Badr b. Aḥmad, old servant of the Amir ʿAbd Allāh who continued to be *ḥājib* and a leading military figure until his death in 921. Other *fatā*s were recruited to fill important military posts, like Durrī, Aflaḥ and the most important of them, Ghālib. Sometimes this provoked resentment among other members of the military, and resentment at Najā being given command of the army may have been a contributory factor in the disastrous Muslim defeat at Al-Khandaq in 939. In general, the *fatā*s did not occupy important positions in the civil administration and are mostly found in military commands or holding positions in the para-military *shurṭa* or police. Al-Andalus did not at this stage, however, show the sharp division between military and civil elites characteristic of later Islamic societies like Mamluke Egypt.

12. On the *ṣaqāliba* see G. Verlinden, *L'esclavage dans l'Europe Medievale* (Bruges, 1955), pp. 211–27; Lévi-Provençal, *HEM,* ii, pp. 117–30.

The rise in importance of the *ṣaqāliba* as the Caliph's most trusted military assistants led to the partial eclipse of members of the ruling family, so long a main prop of Umayyad power. There were exceptions, like Sa'īd b. al-Mundhir, a distant cousin, who was entrusted with a number of important commands and held the prestigious title of *wazīr* until his death in 938. Other Umayyads clearly felt dissatisfied, and this feeling of exclusion from power may be the background to the few political executions of the reign. In 921 al-'Āṣī b. 'Abd Allāh, 'Abd al-Raḥmān's uncle and a man who had led numerous campaigns in the previous reign, was put to death for aspiring to the amirate, and in 936 Aḥmad b. Isḥāq al-Qurashī (a descendant of the Umayyad Caliph Marwān I) was executed, apparently for stirring up the lords of the Upper March against the Caliph.[13]

The rise of the *ṣaqāliba* also led to a reduction in the importance of the Syrian *junds* as sources of military power. Although they were still present in the armies sent against the Christians and appeared at ceremonial occasions in court as late as the reign of al-Ḥakam II (961–76), their military and political importance was in full decline. The tenth-century traveller Ibn Ḥawqal, coming from the eastern Islamic world, had a very low opinion of the fighting qualities of the Andalusis and especially of their horsemanship. He adds that 'Abd al-Raḥmān could never find more than 5,000 horsemen to enrol in the *dīwān* and accept *rizq* (salaries).[14]

The years of expansion, 912–29

The chronological history of 'Abd al-Raḥmān's reign can be divided into three phases. The first may be described as the years of expansion between his accession in 912 and his proclamation as Caliph in 929. There then followed ten years in which the new caliph's power was at its apogee (929–39). This was brought to an abrupt end by the defeat at Alhandega, which not only brought an end to major expeditions against the Christian north but also had serious internal repercussions.

The young Amir's campaigns against the rebel lords of Andalucia

13. E. Manzano Moreno, *La Frontera de Al-Andalus en epoca de los Omeyas* (Madrid, 1991), pp. 355–7.

14. Ibn Ḥawqal, *Ṣūrat al-arḍ*, ed. J.H. Kramers (Leiden, 1939), pp. 108–9, 113. For the army in general see Lévi-Provençal, *HEM*, iii, pp. 66–80; Vallvé Bermejo, *El Califato de Cordoba*, pp. 115–20.

began immediately after his accession. In the winter of 912/13 he dispatched an expedition to recover the Calatrava area to the north of Cordoba and Badr b. Aḥmad took Ecija, on the lowland fringes of Ibn Ḥafṣūn's territory. Early the next summer he led a three-month sweep which took him along the northern flanks of the Sierra Nevada through Guadix to Fiñana and then south over the mountains to Juviles, west along the Mediterranean coast to Salobreña and then over the mountains to Cordoba. All along the route castellans pledged allegiance to him and surrendered their strongholds, and many Muslims showed that they preferred his rule to that of the now Christian Ibn Ḥafṣūn. Before the end of the year there was more good news from Seville. The tough old ruler Ibn al-Ḥajjāj had died shortly before 'Abd al-Raḥmān's accession and his domains had been disputed between his son Muḥammad, based in Carmona, and his nephew Aḥmad b. Maslama in Seville itself. Predictably there were family quarrels and Muḥammad sought the help of Cordoba to drive his brother out. In December 913 Badr b. Aḥmad entered Seville. Needless to say, Muḥammad was disappointed in his hopes, and while he managed to maintain himself in Carmona for a couple of years, Seville was now permanently under Umayyad rule.[15]

In May 914 'Abd al-Raḥmān set off again, south this time to Malaga and then west along the coast, cutting off Ibn Ḥafṣūn's contacts with North Africa and then through Sidonia to Carmona and home. Only two years after his accession, 'Abd al-Raḥmān had recovered all the most populous areas of Andalucia and Ibn Ḥafṣūn was confined to the mountainous areas around Bobastro where his revolt had begun. It was now only a matter of time before his rebellion was crushed.

In the event, a major famine delayed 'Abd al-Raḥmān's assault, and in September 917 'Umar b. Ḥafṣūn died of natural causes and was given a Christian burial in the rock-cut church at Bobastro. It was not the end of the rebellion, but without its charismatic if unpredictable leader, the rebels were very much on the defensive. Ibn Ḥafṣūn's four sons continued resistance, and systematic warfare was needed to reduce their strongholds, but in January 928 the last surviving son Ḥafṣ surrendered and Cordovan troops led by the *wazīr* Aḥmad b. Muḥammad b. Ḥudayr entered Bobastro. It was half a century since Ibn Ḥafṣūn had first launched his resistance movement in the reign of the Amir Muḥammad and for the whole of

15. Ibn Ḥayyān, *Al-Muqtabis V*, pp. 32–55; trans., pp. 51–75.

that period it had sapped the financial and military strength of the amirate in its heartland. It was a great victory; poems were composed in honour of ʿAbd al-Raḥmān and a grandiose letter announcing his victory was circulated.[16]

Growing success in the south enabled ʿAbd al-Raḥmān to lead his first expeditions against the Christian north. During the reign of ʿAbd Allāh, the Christians in the western half of the peninsula had advanced to the Duero river, settling the plains to the north. Leon had become the effective capital and Zamora, on the north bank of the river, an important outpost. They began to launch audacious raids: in 913 King Ordoño II had raided far to the south and brutally sacked Evora, killing the garrison and taking 4,000 women and children captive. ʿAbd al-Raḥmān's first attempt to redress the balance was not a success. The veteran commander Aḥmad b. Abī ʿAbda was killed and his troops routed on the Upper Duero at San Esteban de Gormaz in September 917. In the summer of 920 ʿAbd al-Raḥmān decided to revenge this defeat and led the Muslims in person for the first time. He went north via Toledo, where he received the homage of the still independent ruler, Lubb b. Ṭarbīsha, and then to Madinaceli, over the mountains to the Upper Duero where he took San Esteban de Gormaz and sacked the now deserted city of Clunia. He then struck north-east through the unpopulated mountains to the Upper Duero at Tudela. He gathered support in the Upper March before heading north to strike at the heart of Navarrese power. In July 920 he defeated the Basques and their Leonese allies at Junquera, between Pamplona and Estella. Having achieved this show of force he returned south to Cordoba.[17] It was a major step in asserting his authority and gave clear indication to both Christians and the lords of the Marches that things in Cordoba had changed.

His next campaign, in the summer of 924, was still more ambitious.[18] He marched up the east coast, receiving the submission of dissident lords at Lorca and Murcia, to the Ebro valley and began systematically reducing the fortresses which protected Pamplona from the south. This time the capital itself, deserted by its inhabitants, was sacked, the cathedral burnt and the city ruined. It was a show of power but, as before, no new territory was taken and colonised. The Basques soon came down from the hills where they

16. Ibid., pp. 134–56; trans., pp. 161–81.
17. Ibid., pp. 103–10; trans., pp. 126–33.
18. Ibid., pp. 121–7; trans., pp. 146–51.

had taken refuge and rebuilt their ruined city. It was never entered by a Muslim army again.

By 929 ʿAbd al-Raḥmān had restored Umayyad power to the peak it had reached under his great-grandfather ʿAbd al-Raḥmān II. The south was under the direct control of Cordoba and he had convincingly shown himself as a leader of the Muslims against the infidels. It was against the background of this achievement that he decided to take the title of Commander of the Faithful, or Caliph, and the regnal title of al-Nāṣir (the Victorious).

There were a number of reasons for this important move. The Umayyads of Spain were fully aware that they were the descendants of the Umayyad caliphs of Damascus and they often used the honorific 'Sons of the Caliphs'. They could not be accused of being upstarts. They had probably been restrained from claiming the title before by the general feeling that there could only be one caliph in Islam at a time and the ʿAbbasids held on to this honour. In the early tenth century, however, this had changed. During ʿAbd al-Raḥmān's reign the ʿAbbasid caliphate slid into chaos and the caliphs themselves lost all effective power. Cordoba was very well informed about events in the east and everyone would have been aware of the complete débâcle of ʿAbbasid power, which made a mockery of their claims to lead the entire Muslim world.

Events nearer home also had their effect. In 909 the Fatimids, who claimed descent from the Umayyads' arch-rival, ʿAlī b. Abī Ṭālib, cousin and son-in-law to the Prophet, had captured Qayrawān, the then capital of Tunisia, and proclaimed themselves caliphs. This suggested that there could indeed be two caliphs at the same time, though the Fatimids, unlike the Umayyads of Spain, did have universal pretensions. If their old enemies could claim the title, should not the Umayyads do so too? The matter was made pressing by the growing influence of the Fatimids in the Maghreb: if the Umayyads were to counter this expansion, they too would have to boast an equal title.

So it was that early in 929 ʿAbd al Raḥmān caused the *khuṭba*, the formal Friday sermon in the mosque when the ruler was publicly acknowledged, to be given by the *qāḍī*, Aḥmad b. Bāqī, in his name as Commander of the Faithful.[19] A letter was dispatched to all the provinces announcing his new title. At the same time he caused gold *dīnār*s to be minted for the first time for two centuries,

19. Ibid., pp. 159–60; trans., pp. 184–5; Lévi-Provençal, *HEM*, ii, pp. 110–17, discusses the move.

a clear indication of his wealth but also of his status and so, as al-Rāzī put it, 'benefitting the people and completing the attributes of his sovreignty'. The chronicler goes on to comment on the excellent quality of the coins:[20] it was to be another 300 years before any northern European monarch minted gold. The gold itself almost certainly came from sub-Saharan Africa via Morocco and its appearance in coinage at this time is a sign of the growing links between Spain and North Africa.

Assuming the title of Commander of the Faithful was the prelude to a further expansion of power. Fortified by the legitimacy his new title conferred, he was determined to extend his authority beyond the areas of southern Spain traditionally ruled from Cordoba to the Marches in the north and the Maghreb in the south. His first objective was Merida, held by the Berber leader Mas'ūd b. Tajīt. He sent a military expedition which persuaded Mas'ūd to negotiate. The intermediary was a Berber legal scholar (*faqīh*) from Merida called Ibn Mundhir who arranged terms: the old ruler and his family were settled with honour and a pension in Cordoba and the inhabitants were promised freedom from extra taxes (*waẓā'if*) and security for their property. The new governor was a member of the Umayyad family, the Caliph's second cousin 'Abd al-Malik b. al-'Āṣī, who was installed in the Alcazaba built in the time of 'Abd al-Raḥmān II with a garrison of 3,000, including 1,000 Tangier Berbers. Ibn Mundhir was rewarded by being made *qāḍī* of the city. This combination of force and negotiation was typical of the way the Caliph extended his power in al-Andalus.[21]

His next target was Badajoz, still ruled by descendants of Ibn Marwān al-Jillīqī, and he led an expedition against it in person in the summer of 929 immediately after assuming his new title.[22] Badajoz was besieged and its orchards ravaged, but resistance was obstinate and the Caliph moved on to receive the submission of Beja. Here the local leader 'Abd al-Raḥmān b. Sa'īd b. Mālik was soon obliged to seek for terms. As usual he and his family were given safe conduct but were obliged to leave the city for Cordoba, where they were enrolled in the army (*ḥashm*) which meant they received salaries. The people's grievances were addressed and a governor appointed. He was to live in an alcazaba specially constructed

20. Ibn Ḥayyān, *Al-Muqtabis V*, pp. 160–1; trans., pp. 185–6. See also M. Barcelo, 'El hiato en las acuñaciones de oro en al-Andalus, 127–317/744(5)–929', in *Moneda y Credito* 132 (1975), 33–71.

21. Ibn Ḥayyān, *Al-Muqtabis V*, pp. 157–9; trans., pp. 182–5.

22. Ibid., pp. 161–4; trans., pp. 186–9.

for him and his men, suggesting that they remained a small group of outsiders. The Caliph then went on to Osconoba where he accepted the submission of Khalaf b. Yaḥyā b. Bakr. It was not until the next year that the deputy he had left to continue the siege of Badajoz, the Umayyad Aḥmad b. Isḥāq al-Qurashī, later executed for treason, negotiated the surrender of the city. The rebel leader ʿAbd Allāh b. Muḥammad and his men went with honour to Cordoba, but Badajoz and Merida were ruled by governors sent from the capital and garrisoned by the Caliph's troops.

No sooner had Badajoz fallen than the Caliph turned his attention to Toledo. True, the local ruler Lubb b. Ṭarbīsha had pledged his loyalty in the campaign of 920, but the Caliph wanted real authority. In the spring of 930 the Umayyad Saʿīd b. al-Mundhir al-Qurashī led the armies of Cordoba north and established a permanent siege camp overlooking the city on the hills to the south. The Toledans were determined and tenaciously attached to their ancient independence and for two whole years they held out until, in the summer of 932, famine forced them to seek terms. There seem to have been no reprisals against the people, but the Caliph took no chances and the city was heavily garrisoned.[23]

Characteristically, al-Nāṣir sought to follow up his success with campaigns against the Christian kingdoms, but he also had a more ambitious project: he was determined to reduce the turbulent lords of the Upper March to obedience.[24] In the mountains around Santaver, Ucles and Huete, the power of the Banū'l-Dhī'l-Nūn was effectively unchallenged, although it seems they were losing their influence in the plains of the Levante. Further north the Tujībīs held sway over Zaragoza, Calatayud and Daroca as well as many other areas of the Ebro valley. The Banū Qasī were no longer rivals for power in the area and they were effectively unchallenged by the Caliph. Only the Banū Shabrīṭ in Huesca and surrounding areas held out against them. There were rivalries within the Tujībī family, and the Calatayud and Daroca branches sometimes sided with the Caliph against their relatives in Zaragoza, though whether this was the result of real hostility or a sort of family insurance policy is difficult to say.

In 930 Hāshim al-Tujībī of Zaragoza died and was succeeded by his son Muḥammad, who became effective leader of the family. Al-Nāṣir tried to take advantage of the change and the jealousies of

23. Ibid., pp. 180–9; trans., pp. 205–15.

24. For a detailed analysis of his policy in this area see Manzano Moreno, *Frontera*, pp. 351–61.

other members of the family to extend his authority. His demands were modest. He asked for participation in raids against the Christian kingdoms (effectively acknowledging his military leadership of the Muslim community and preventing them from making independent alliances with the Christian powers) and for a tribute or *jibāya*. The amount of this tribute was never specified and its payment was probably more symbolic than a real contribution to Umayyad finances, but it was more than had been paid before. For two years the agreement held, but in 933 the Tujībīs of Zaragoza and the Banū Shabrīṭ of Huesca refused to join al-Nāṣir's ill-fated campaign against Osma. Worse was to come: a punitive expedition against Zaragoza in the summer of 935 failed to take the city and a general insurrection broke out, not only among the lords of the Upper March but the Banū'l-Dhī'l-Nūn to the south as well. It is possible that this was connected with the attempt by the Umayyad Aḥmad b. Isḥāq al-Qurashī to seize the throne at this time, and it was not until after he was executed in 936 that the Caliph could take the offensive again. In 937 a military expedition, led by the *fatā* Durrī and supported by Christian troops from Alava, forced Muḥammad al-Tujībī to make an agreement. Even now the terms were easy: Muḥammad was to surrender his city to the Caliph's forces and go to Cordoba, but only for a limited period. On his return he was to be governor for life in exchange for an oath of allegiance (*bay'a*), tribute and a promise not to make private treaties with the Christians. Similar agreements were reached with the other lords. Al-Nāṣir effectively acknowledged that he could not achieve control of the Dhū'l-Nūnid lands and the Ebro valley as he had of Badajoz and Toledo.

Despite the lack of complete success in the Ebro lands, the decade from 929 had on the whole been a period of success for the new caliphate. All this was to change in 939. In this year the Caliph decided on an expedition against the lands of King Ramiro II of Leon. The army set out via Toledo, where the Tujībī, Shabrīṭī and Dhū'l-Nūnid leaders joined it in accordance with their new treaty obligations. They turned north across the mountains and began to encounter Christian troops; in one of these skirmishes, Muḥammad b. Hāshim al-Tujībī was captured. The army invested Simancas, but after a fruitless and demoralising siege they moved on up the Duero. They then turned off south into mountainous country, apparently to suppress local guerilla activity, but were caught in broken terrain at an unidentified place referred to by the Arab sources as Al-Khandaq (the ditch, Hispanised as Alhandega). Here they were totally defeated, the Caliph and the shattered remnants of his army escaping over the hills to Guadalajara.

The main cause of the defeat seems to have been deep rifts within the Muslim army. Many of the frontier lords, most notably Fortūn b. Muḥammad of Huesca, were seething with anger at the terms of the agreement which had bound them to serve in the army. To make matters worse, the Caliph had entrusted command to one of his Slav soldiers, Najā. The role of this 'upstart' was deeply resented, not only by the frontier lords but also by the *jund* of Cordoba. Bitter words between Fortūn and Najā at the height of the battle are said to have begun the flight. There is also evidence that old-established Arab families who were leaders of the *jund*s of the south of al-Andalus were also fearful that they were being displaced by the new professionals and half-hearted in their support for the campaign.[25]

In the immediate aftermath of the catastrophe, the Caliph was determined to find a scapegoat and he executed Fortūn together with ten of his followers, but in the long run he seems to have taken a more realistic view. The desparate flight from Alhandega had quenched his thirst for adventure and he never visited the north again. The frontier lords were allowed to return to their previous independence in exchange for defending the Muslims against the Christians; the Dhū'l-Nūnids of Santaver played an important role in this. Muḥammad al-Tujībī was ransomed by the Caliph and re-established at Zaragoza, where his son Yaḥyā was allowed to succeed him on his death in 950 with the full approval of the Caliph. Even the Banū Shabrīṭ were allowed to continue as lords of Huesca despite Fortūn's treachery. And there were newcomers, the Berber Banū Razīn of Albarracin, who appear for the first time in this period and who were to survive longer than all the other dynasties in their little upland principality.

Toledo and the Middle March, in contrast, were mostly ruled and defended by the agents of Cordoba, old-established *mawālī* like Aḥmad b. Ya'la or more recently arrived Slavs like Qand (the name is Persian for sugar or candy). The most important move in this period was not a military expedition but the recolonisation and refortification of Medinaceli by the *ṣiqlabī fatā* Ghālib (sometimes called Ghālib b. 'Abd al-Raḥmān, to show his close connection with his master al-Nāṣir) in 946/7, which represented a signifi-

25. See P. Chalmeta, 'Simancas y Alhandega', in *Hispania* xxxvi (1976), 359–444, for the classic discussion of the campaign and its implications; also Manzano Moreno, *Frontera*, pp. 361–70.

cant strengthening of the frontier on the way to the Upper Duero valley.

Umayyad intervention in North Africa

The caliphate of al-Nāṣir saw the first sustained involvement by the Umayyads in North African politics.[26] Morocco at this stage was, compared with Muslim Spain, a very underdeveloped country. There had been very little Arab settlement and the country remained overwhelmingly Berber and largely rural, the inhabitants living either as pastoral nomads or settled farmers. Tribal allegiances and rivalries remained the basis of political activity. Only Fes, settled in the ninth century by colonists from Qayrawān and Cordoba, was a really urban community, although Sijilmāssa, the great entrepôt for Saharan trade far to the south, was a large oasis settlement. In theory much of the area was under the authority of the Idrisids, based in Fes. The Idrisids were descendants of ʿAlī, who had fled west in 786 after a failed rebellion against the ʿAbbasids.[27] They did not rule a state in the conventional sense but, somewhat like the traditional Zaydi Imams of Yemen, enjoyed a certain prestige among the tribal leaders because of their religious status and were acknowledged as mediators if not rulers. They seem to have had no organised administration or government apparatus. By the beginning of the tenth century, the Idrisid family had split into many different branches which vied ineffectually for such authority as the family name could still command.

Smaller but more coherent were the political units based on Sijilmāssa and Nakur. Sijilmāssa on the fringes of the Sahara was ruled by the Midrarids, a Berber dynasty of Kharijite persuasions. Nakur on the Mediterranean coast was a small city-state ruled by a popular Sunni dynasty, the Banū Ṣāliḥ, who had had contacts with the Umayyads in the previous century.

There had certainly been commercial and personal contacts between al-Andalus and North Africa in the ninth century, especially with the Rustamid dynasty of Tahert in central Algeria. Members of the Rustamid family had served in the armies of ʿAbd al-Raḥmān II, while Ibn Ḥafṣūn had sheltered in Rustamid territory

26. This policy is discussed in detail in Lévi-Provençal, *HEM*, ii, pp. 78–110.
27. H. Kennedy, *The Early Abbasid Caliphate: A Political History* (London, 1981), pp. 204–7.

before beginning his rebellion. The prosperity of the sailors' commune at Pechina is evidence of the importance of trade. Yet none of these contacts had led to serious political involvement; divided North Africa was not a threat to al-Andalus, nor was it prosperous enough to tempt an invasion.

This changed rather suddenly as a result of a political revolution of major importance. In 909, just before the accession of al-Nāṣir, the Aghlabids of Tunisia and the Rustamids of Tahert were swept away by the power of the Fatimids and their Kutāmā Berber supporters. From this time Tunisia was ruled by a dynasty which claimed descent from Muḥammad and which was determined to extend its control over the whole Muslim world. They soon began to assert themselves on land and sea, building a new naval base at al-Mahdīya and sending one of their Berber allies to take over Tahert. The nature of the new threat must have been vividly brought home to al-Nāṣir when Ibn Ḥafṣūn caused the Fatimids to be proclaimed in all the mosques under his control. The direct threat came much nearer in 917 when Fatimids attacked the Umayyads' allies at Nakur, just across the water. Despite the fact that the town was captured, the Fatimids could not sustain themselves and al-Nāṣir aided the Salihids to recover their city. This was not the end of the menace. In 922 a Fatimid army sacked Sijilmāssa and Fes, where the last Idrisids were driven out and a pro-Fatimid Berber chief, Mūsā b. Abī'l-'Āfīya of Miknāsa, took over.

The Umayyad response was cautious. The fortifications of al-Andalus were improved (it is probably at this time that the splendid surviving castle at Fuengirola on the Costa del Sol was constructed) and al-Nāṣir sought allies among rival Berber chiefs, notably Muḥammad b. Khazar of Zanāta. The Caliph also established bases on the coast: Melilla was taken in 927 and, more importantly, Ceuta in March 931 and Tangier in 951. (It is interesting to reflect that Melilla and Ceuta are, of course, the two cities Spain still holds on the North African coast to this day.)

The taking of these coastal outposts was not the prelude to a more general conquest. Al-Nāṣir wanted two things from his policy, a network of alliances which would prevent the Fatimids from threatening Spain and the opportunity to recruit Berber soldiers for his armies. The Fatimid menace continued: in 935 the Fatimid *fatā* Sandal led an army which took Fes (where Mūsā b. Abī'l-'Āfīya had been won over to the Umayyad side) and Nakur, but again the Fatimids could not sustain their power and in 945 they were severely weakened by a Kharijite rebellion in their own territory led by Abū Yazīd, called 'the Man on the Donkey'. After his accession in 953 the new Fatimid ruler al-Mu'izz began a new policy of aggression and by 958/9 his brilliant general Jawhar, later to be famous as the conqueror of Egypt, had subdued the whole of Morocco except for Ceuta and Tangier. There was also naval warfare: in 955 a Fatimid fleet from Sicily burned Almeria and the Umayyad general Ghālib was sent with some 70 ships to take his revenge on the Tunisian coast.

Despite these Fatimid successes in the final years, al-Nāṣir's North African policy had been extremely successful. He had preserved his country from invasion at very little cost or difficulty to himself and he had established a network of alliances which his son al-Ḥakam was to use to establish a widespread dominance over Morocco.

The later years of 'Abd al-Raḥmān III, 939–61

The Caliph's prestige led to exchanges of embassies with more distant powers. In about 950 there began an exchange of ambassadors with the German emperor Otto I (938–73). Otto wanted al-Nāṣir's cooperation in the suppression of the Muslim pirates who had occupied Fraxinetum, near Fréjus in Provence, since the end of the ninth century and had raided far up the Rhône valley. We only know of these contacts from Latin sources, notably the surviving fragment of the life of John, abbot of Gorze, who was sent as ambassador in about 950. His intransigence meant that progress was very slow. Eventually al-Nāṣir sent a Mozarab, Recemundo, or Rabī' b. Zayd, to Otto and John was allowed to soften his attitude and was finally granted an audience by the Caliph in 956. His description of the Umayyad court survives, but unfortunately the manuscript breaks off at this point and we have no knowledge of the results, if any, that were achieved. There is no record of further contacts.[28]

Al-Nāṣir also entered into diplomatic relations with the Byzantine empire, then at the height of its power. In 840 the Emperor Theophilos had tried to interest 'Abd al-Raḥmān II in an alliance against the Arabs who had taken Crete, but without success. In the summer of 949 an embassy from Constantinople was received in Cordoba, and in October of the same year a delegation from al-Andalus, again led by the Mozarab Rabī' b. Zayd, was in Byzantium.

28. Lévi-Provençal, *HEM*, ii, pp. 153–63.

Although both parties came to share a common enemy in the Fatimids, this diplomacy seems to have been more about display and prestige than political alliances. Byzantine mosaicists came to work in Cordoba, Greek manuscripts were sent and in 951 a Greek monk called Nicolas was dispatched to Cordoba to work on a text of Dioscorides since, apparently, no-one in al-Andalus knew the Greek language at this time. All this was very edifying and served a certain political purpose. The Byzantine emperors were the traditional rivals of the caliphs, worthy opponents acknowledged to be on the same cultural level. In the early tenth century the 'Abbasid caliphs of Baghdad, keen to bolster their falling prestige at home, put on elaborate receptions for Byzantine ambassadors. No doubt the new Caliph in the west felt that Byzantine diplomacy, like minting gold coins, was one of the attributes of his new office.[29]

As befitted a caliph, al-Nāṣir lived and governed in surroundings of increasing luxury and grandeur. The Umayyad amirs used the old palace in Cordoba not only as their residence but also as their government offices. The palace was situated, like many Muslim palaces, beside the mosque. Al-Nāṣir may have found this site too cramped for his expanding administration and for housing the increased numbers of *ṣiqlabī* soldiers in his army. As the tensions which caused the defeat at Alhandega showed, relations between the *ṣaqāliba* and the old elite were often strained and he may have wished to separate the two. Whatever the reason, in November 936 he began work on a new palace/city some 5 kilometres north-west of Cordoba on the lower slopes of the wooded hills which overlook the Guadalquivir valley. This city was, apparently, named after a favourite concubine of his, Madīnat (city of) al-Zahrā, and substantial remains survive to the present day. The city itself was violently destroyed by Berber soldiers in 1013, but excavation and painstaking reconstruction give us a vivid idea of its splendours. The centrepiece was an audience hall where the Caliph received ambassadors and other deputations in the solemn assemblies which Ibn Ḥayyān describes. Around it were pools and gardens, a mosque and luxurious accommodation for courtiers. We are left in no doubt that this was a highly developed and ordered court culture. It certainly had no equal in western Europe and we would probably have to look to Baghdad or Constantinople to find anything to compare

29. Ibid., pp. 143–53, gives details and discusses the problems of chronology. For Byzantine–Muslim dipomacy in the East see H. Kennedy, 'Byzantine–Arab diplomacy in the Near East', in *Byzantine Diplomacy*, ed. J. Shepard and S. Franklin (Aldershot, 1992), pp. 133–43.

it with. Madīnat al-Zahrā was also exceptional in the political culture of al-Andalus. Purpose-built palace-cities were common in the Muslim east – Baghdad, Samarra, Mahdiya and Cairo are the classic examples from the eighth to the tenth centuries – but in al-Andalus only the fourteenth-century palace-city of the Alhambra in Granada offers a real parallel. On the whole, rulers made their capitals at existing centres rather than founding new ones.[30]

In the years after the defeat at Alhandega in 939, it seems that al-Nāṣir seldom left the Cordoba area. Our sources for this period are very thin. The surviving portion of Ibn Ḥayyān's great work, which is the foundation for our understanding of the first part of the reign, breaks off after the year 941 and the information given by later compilers like Ibn Idhārī for this later period is very sketchy. The impression given, however, is that he retained absolute authority while using trusted agents to pursue his policies on the Christian frontier and in North Africa. There seems to have been no serious internal dissent.

The reign of al-Ḥakam II al-Mustanṣir, 961–76

The Caliph died on 15 October 961 and was buried with his predecessors in the Alcazar at Cordoba. There was no dispute about the succession. His chosen heir, al-Ḥakam, born in 915, had long been acknowledged and given the regnal title of al-Mustanṣir. As early as 919 his father had taken to leaving him in the palace at Cordoba with a senior *wazīr* as his guardian when he himself left on campaign. At the age of 12 in 927 he accompanied his father on campaign for the first time. This early experience meant that he was well versed in his father's methods and indeed he may have played an important part in formulating policy in the later years of al-Nāṣir's reign. Not surprisingly, his accession was marked by a continuity of policy and personnel.

Our understanding of al-Ḥakam's reign is heavily influenced by the nature of the sources. For the period 971 to 975 we have the text of Ibn Ḥayyān's chronicle.[31] This section is in turn heavily

30. The literature on Madīnat al-Zahrā is considerable. See F. Hernandez Gimenez, *Madinat al-Zahra* (Granada, 1985), and A. Vallejo Triano, *El Salon de Abd al-Rahman III* (Cordoba, 1995). See also the three volumes of *Cuadernos de Madinat al-Zahra* (3 vols, Cordoba, 1987, 1988–90, 1991).

31. *Al-Muqtabis fi akhbār balad al-Andalus (al-Hakam II) (Al-Muqtabis VII)*, ed. A.A. al-Hajji (Beirut, 1965); Spanish trans., *Anales Palatinos del Califa de Cordoba al-Hakam II* by E. Garcia Gomez (Madrid, 1967).

dependent on the court chronicle of 'Īsā al-Rāzī. This chronicle has no parallel in the historiography of Umayyad Spain and is very different from the earlier sections of Ibn Ḥayyān's work. It is essentially a court diary, recording in minute detail affairs at Madīnat al-Zahrā. It is concerned almost exclusively with palace affairs, giving detailed accounts of court ceremonies, the movements of the Caliph and the comings and goings of numerous ambassadors, but it provides virtually no information about events elsewhere; for example, the lists of provincial governors which are a regular and useful feature of Ibn Ḥayyān's account of al-Nāṣir's reign are completely lacking here. Despite these limitations, other later sources confirm the general picture of peace and prosperity.

Al-Ḥakam came to rely on two individuals. Ghālib b. 'Abd al-Raḥmān was a *ṣiqlabī* soldier who had become important in the latter years of his father's reign. He had established a firm base in the most strategic area of the frontier around Medinaceli which he had rebuilt. This commanded the main route to the Upper March and the Ebro valley and the main road north over the mountains to the Upper Duero and thence to the frontier fortresses of Castile. Ghālib was a central figure in frontier defence but was also active elsewhere: in 956 he had led a naval expedition to ravage the shores of Fatimid Tunisia. When in 962 King Ordoño IV of Leon fled from his enemies in Castile, it was to Ghālib in Medinaceli that he went, and Ghālib sent him onwards to plead his cause in Cordoba. Though we have no direct evidence, it is likely that Ghālib established his *ṣaqāliba* followers in the area to form a little enclave of territory loyal to him and to his master in a crucial area. In 974 new diplomas of authority (*sijilāt*) were given to the minor lords of the Middle March, giving them authority over their lands and castles as was the custom and according to the decision of Ghālib, who is described as their *za'īm* (leader), a clear indication of his authority in this area.[32]

He was, however, too useful to be allowed to remain on the frontier all the time. When al-Ḥakam decided on a major expedition to Morocco in 973 against the most difficult of the Idrisid opponents of Cordoba, al-Ḥasan b. Gannūn, Ghālib was chosen to lead it. After his triumphal return to Cordoba in early September 974 the emphasis shifted to the Christian frontier again and Ghālib was sent north to relieve the hard-pressed Muslim garrison at Gormaz on the Upper Duero, which he successfully did in the summer of

32. Ibn Ḥayyān, *Al-Muqtabis VII*, ed. Hajji, p. 203; trans., p. 234.

975. He went on to pursue Count Garci Fernandez of Castile into his own territory.[33]

His loyalty and undoubted military abilities brought him gifts and honours. In 972 he was appointed chief general (*al-qā'id al-a'lā*), the first time any individual had been singled out for such distinction.[34] Three years later, after his triumphs in North Africa (975), he was decorated with two gilded swords and given the honorific Dhū'l-Sayfayn (Lord of the Two Swords); Ibn Ḥayyān allows himself a small scholarly digression to explain how this was an honorific originally awarded by the 'Abbasid regent al-Muwaffaq to his *mawlā* Isḥāq b. Kundāj, another illustration of how closely people in Cordoba followed affairs in the east.[35] Official honours were followed by popular acclaim and many volunteers left Cordoba to join the relief of Gormaz, somewhat to the amazement of the authorities.[36]

Al-Ḥakam's other lieutenant was Ja'far b. 'Uthmān al-Muṣḥafī. He came from an obscure Berber family from the Valencia area. His father, described as a teacher of literature (*mu'addib*) from Cordoba,[37] was appointed as tutor to the young al-Ḥakam, and his son Ja'far became firm friends with the young prince, who took him as his secretary and made him governor of Majorca. When he became Caliph, Ja'far became his secretary and also held the office of *ṣāḥib al-madīna* (prefect of the city) of Cordoba. He was present on the Caliph's left hand at almost all the formal receptions which formed such an important part of court life and he was an expert at managing ceremonial occasions.[38] He was also skilled at preparing legal documents such as investitures.[39] He had close relations with Ghālib and he, the Caliph and the heir apparent were the only people present when Ghālib was awarded his title of Dhū'l-Sayfayn. Unlike Ghālib he had a family to support him and one of them, his nephew Hishām b. Muḥammad, was an influential soldier, commanding the *ṣā'ifa* on occasion.[40] Interestingly, he is described as *qā'id* (military commander) of al-Muṣḥafī's home

33. Ibid., pp. 218–37; trans., pp. 256–79. 34. Ibid., p. 69; trans., p. 91.
35. Ibid., pp. 219–22; trans., pp. 259–62. 36. Ibid., p. 226; trans., p. 266.
37. Ibn al-Faraḍi, *Ta'rīkh 'ulamā' al-Andalus*, ed. F. Codera (Madrid, 1890), p. 896; Ibn al-Abbār, *Al-Ḥulla al-siyarā'*, ed. H. Mu'nis (2 vols, Cairo, 1963), i, no. 100.
38. See Ibn Ḥayyān, *Al-Muqtabis VII*, p. 109; trans., p. 140, for his organisation of the ceremonies marking the circumcision of the sons of the Idrisids who had submitted to Cordoba in 973.
39. See for example ibid., pp. 111–14; trans., pp. 142–5, for the complicated provisions under which Abū'l-'Aysh b. Ayyūb was given authority over those Kutāma Berbers who were loyal to Cordoba in 973.
40. In 972 against the Normans: see ibid., p. 77; trans., pp. 101–2.

province, Valencia,[41] and Tortosa, perhaps suggesting that the family was building up a provincial power base.

In addition to these two, al-Ḥakam continued to rely on the cadres who had supported his father, but there were changes. After the débâcle at Alhandega, al-Nāṣir had been content to leave the lords of the Upper March alone, but al-Ḥakam tried to integrate them more firmly in the Umayyad state.[42] When the surviving section of Ibn Ḥayyān's chronicle opens, we find the Tujībīs of the Ebro valley, led by their *za'īm*, Yaḥyā b. Muḥammad b. Hāshim, attending the celebrations to mark the end of Ramadan at Madīnat al-Zahrā.[43] It seems that they remained at court in honoured positions. When al-'Āṣī b. al-Ḥakam al-Tujībī of Calatayud died in 972, his sons came to court and were confirmed in their positions.[44] In August 973 Yaḥyā b. al-Hāshim al-Tujībī was sent with a large army to reinforce Ghālib in Morocco. He took with him many members of his family who had been in disgrace for reasons we do not know, and he was also given command of units of the regular army (*jund al-mamlaka*).[45] When Ghālib was ordered to return to Cordoba in August 974, Yaḥyā was appointed to take over command of the whole army.[46] In their absence, the Caliph appointed his own agent as governor of Zaragoza. Members of the family were still active in the Ebro valley, and towards the end of the reign, in the summer of 975, while Ghālib was fighting the Castilians, 'Abd al-Raḥmān b. Yaḥyā al-Tujībī, who held the senior military office of *ṣāḥib al-shurṭa al-'ulyā* (the *shurṭa*, police, had been divided into upper, middle and lower, presumably with different functions, though this is not clear: 'Abd al-Raḥmān was chief of the upper *shurṭa*), led the Muslims who defeated Ramiro Sanchez of Navarre near Tudela. By the time of al-Ḥakam's death, Yaḥyā too had returned to his home territory.[47]

The details provided by 'Īsā al-Rāzī allow us to see al-Ḥakam's policy at work. He was not attempting to destroy the power of the Tujībīs but to incorporate them in the ruling class of the caliphate of Cordoba. The fact too that such prominent members of the Andalusi aristocracy could have such important military posts gives the lie to the idea that the caliphate had come to depend entirely on slave soldiers and foreign mercenaries.

41. Ibid., p. 46; trans., p. 65.
42. For his policy see Manzano Moreno, *Frontera*, pp. 370–80.
43. *Al-Muqtabis VII*, p. 29; trans., p. 52.
44. Ibid., p. 75; trans., p. 97.
45. Ibid., pp. 128–30; trans., pp. 162–4.
46. Ibid., p. 177; trans., pp. 215–16.
47. Lévi-Provençal, *HEM*, ii, p. 195, suggests that he was allowed to return by al-Muṣḥafī during al-Ḥakam's last illness.

We know much less about the minor lords of the Marches but it is clear that they were able to continue as before as long as they received their *sijil* or diploma from the Caliph. The cases of the lesser lords of the Middle March and the Tujībīs of Calatayud have been noted; the newly acquired status of the Banū Razīn of Albarracin was confirmed in 972 when, after his death, the possessions of Marwān b. Hudhayl were divided among his sons, each one being given a *sijil* for his area. They were entertained lavishly and sent on their way happy.[48] Early in 974 the position of the Dhū'l-Nūnids was consolidated when al-Muṭarrif b. Ismā'īl was given a *sijil* for the castle of Huete to which were added most of the other castles of the Santaver region.[49] As far as we can tell, the city of Toledo and the Lower March were entirely without local leadership at this stage. We are told, with the implication that it was something quite unusual, that 1,700 Toledans, well-equipped and armed with Frankish swords, were sent to Cordoba by the governor, Sa'āda (certainly a *fatā* or slave soldier). They were reviewed, paid and sent on to join the army in Morocco.[50]

The internal policies of al-Ḥakam can be seen as maintaining a balance between the *ṣaqāliba* slave soldiers and old-established elements like the *junds* of Andalucia and the lords of the Marches. This balance was tested and to an extent disrupted by events in North Africa.

Al-Ḥakam was faced with a quite different position from his father. In 969 the Fatimid general Jawhar, who had previously reduced Morocco except for Tangier and Ceuta for his masters, conquered Egypt. Soon after the Fatimid court followed him east and they abandoned any attempt to control Morocco and ceased to pose any threat to al-Andalus. The Fatimid Caliph al-Mu'izz (953–77) left a deputy in Tunisia, the Ṣanhāja Berber chief, Zīrī b. Manād, whose family were to play an important role in Andalusi politics. He represented the Fatimid cause, but he also built up the Ṣanhāja tribal federation as a major political grouping in opposition to the Zanāta who more usually looked to Cordoba for support. The rivalry between these two groups became an important factor in the politics of both the Maghreb and al-Andalus. Zīrī began to take the offensive against the rival Zanāta, but after some successes he was defeated and killed by the Zanāta and an adventurer of Spanish origin known as Ibn al-Andalusī in 971. Zīrī's son Buluggīn set out on the warpath against the nomad Zanāta and

48. Ibn Ḥayyān, *Al-Muqtabis VII*, p. 150; trans., p. 190.
49. Ibid., p. 150; trans., p. 190. 50. Ibid., p. 117; trans., p. 150.

harried them, driving them west to Tlemcen before being recalled by the Fatimids.

The Zirid retreat left the Umayyads a free hand in Morocco, but they soon encountered serious opposition from the resurgent Idrisids. In 972 al-Ḥakam began to assemble a large army, commanded by Muḥammad b. Qāsim b. Ṭumlus, in Ceuta.[51] The object of their attack was the Idrisid prince, al-Ḥasan b. Gannūn. He had taken over all of north-western Morocco, including Tangier, and the threat he posed could not be ignored. The struggle was a hard one; after some initial success, Ibn Ṭumlus was defeated and killed. In 973 Ghālib was sent and finally took the Idrisids' mountain fortress of Ḥajar al-Naṣr. The Idrisids were brought in triumph to Cordoba, but that was not the end of the problem. Maintaining the army in Morocco was extremely expensive and al-Muṣḥafī began to look for a local agent whom the Umayyads could rely on to further their interests without incurring massive expenditure. In the end he sent Ibn al-Andalusī, who was generally supported by the Zanāta and others. The Idrisids were deported to Egypt where they took refuge with the Fatimid court. Massive sums had been spent on armies and on diplomacy, but the end results were far from spectacular.

Once again the Umayyads had found that Morocco was an unrewarding area of occupation. However, the campaigns greatly increased contacts between Cordoba and the Berber chiefs. ʿIsa al-Rāzī's court diary of the reign is full of accounts of receptions given to Berber chiefs at Madīnat al-Zahrā, and it is clear that the Cordoba government, like the Byzantine government, sought to overawe by wealth and splendour those it could not subdue by force.

The Berbers were greatly respected as soldiers, especially as horsemen, and al-Ḥakam was keen to recruit more into his army. There were cultural strains, however. The Berbers found it difficult to adjust to urban life and the discipline of living under settled government. There must have been many like Zīrī b. ʿAṭīya al-Maghrāwī (no relation of the Zirids) who rapidly wearied of the court life and returned to his native North Africa, winding his familiar turban round his head once again and shouting, 'O my head! I know that you are mine from now on!'[52] Among the Berbers recruited at this time were the Banū Birzāl. Described as 'superior

51. See M. Meouak, 'Les Banū Rumāhis et les Banū Ṭumlus, fonctionnaires au service de l'état Hispano-Umayyade', in M. Marin *et al.* (eds), *Estudios Onomastico-Biograficos de Al-Andalus* (5 vols, Madrid, 1988–92), v, pp. 273–88.

52. Quoted in Lévi-Provençal, *HEM*, ii, p. 265.

to all others in courage and bravery', they were Kharijites who had rebelled against Zīrī b. Manād and had been responsible for his death. This had brought them widespread fame but meant that they could no longer remain in their homelands for fear of the vengeance of Zīrī's son Buluggīn. They were invited to al-Andalus by al-Ḥakam, given a warm welcome and assigned generous salaries. Despite the fact that they were Kharijis, they were allowed to practise their own religious faith.[53] It was significant for the future that they came across as a group with their tribal solidarity intact, unlike the *ṣaqāliba* who seem to have been isolated individuals who had preserved no family or kinship ties from their lives before they came to al-Andalus. The Banū Birzāl, like other similar groups, had no prospect of return to their native lands: they had to secure a permanent place for themselves in al-Andalus. This small group, perhaps only 300 strong, were an important source of military support for al-Manṣūr during his rise to power. After the disintegration of the Cordovan state, they took over Carmona where they established a short-lived Taifa kingdom.[54]

By the end of his reign al-Ḥakam had recruited some 700 Berber horsemen. Apart from Ibn al-Andalusī, his main intermediary with the Berber chiefs was Muḥammad b. Abī 'Āmir. In 971 it had been he who was sent to greet Ja'far b. al-Andalusī on his arrival in Spain and hand over the Caliph's presents to him. In July 973 he was appointed *qāḍī* of Morocco and sent with large sums of money to distribute to Berber chiefs,[55] and in September, at a great gathering of Berber chiefs for the 'Īd al-Aḍḥā, he preached to them about the power, orthodoxy and generosity of the Umayyad caliph.[56] He remained there until September 974, when illness obliged him to return to Cordoba.

Al-Ḥakam died on 1 October 976. His reign had been one of unrivalled political stability. It was also a period of great cultural efflorescence. The Caliph himself was a genuinely cultivated man, a great book collector and literary patron. He continued with the construction of the palace-city at Madīnat al-Zahrā. He also made an addition to the mosque in Cordoba itself. His work still survives in its full glory in the area around the *mihrab* (the niche showing the direction of Mecca) at the south end of the building. In contrast to the simple arched naves of 'Abd al-Raḥmān I and 'Abd

53. Ibn Ḥayyān, *Al-Muqtabis VII*, p. 192; trans., pp. 230–1.
54. See below, pp. 142–3.
55. Ibn Ḥayyān, *Al-Muqtabis VII*, p. 123; trans., p. 156.
56. Ibid., p. 138; trans., p. 173.

al-Raḥmān II, al-Ḥakam's work is richly decorated in carved stone, stucco and mosaic, produced by Byzantine craftsmen. With its rich textures and the superb architectural geometry of its domes, the mosque at Cordoba still breathes the spirit of this sophisticated and luxuriant court culture.

The government of al-Andalus had become highly centralised. In the early years of al-Nāṣir's reign the monarchy had been proactive: the Caliph had led campaigns and traversed the country on the way to the *ṣā'ifa*, meeting local leaders and consolidating his influence. Under al-Ḥakam all this seemed unnecessary. Cordoba was the centre of power and patronage. Local leaders came to the Caliph to receive commands, investitures and presents. The dazzling ceremonies which marked the great festivals of the Muslim year, the 'Īd al-Aḍḥā and the 'Īd al-Fiṭr, were occasions when the Caliph could entertain and dispense patronage. This style of attractive monarchy, unique in western Europe, was a product of wealth and stability and of a government in which a literate and numerate bureaucracy could collect taxation on a regular and systematic basis. But there were potential problems. The Caliph had become very isolated. Access to the royal court, the only source of political power, could be controlled by a small number of palace officials. Under a strong and experienced ruler like al-Ḥakam, this caused no problems, but a youthful and uncertain caliph could easily be manipulated and managed. This was to be the fate of al-Ḥakam's successor.

The caliphate in Mediterranean society

The prestige of the caliphate extended beyond its frontiers. Despite the defeat at Alhandega, the caliphate overshadowed the Christian states to the north both militarily and economically. In the early part of his reign, 'Abd al-Raḥmān III was confronted by powerful monarchs, notably Ramiro II (930–51), the victor of Alhandega. After Ramiro's death, however, the kingdom was beset by succession disputes, in which the Muslims intervened to their own advantage, and rivalry with the growing power of Castile under its dynamic Count Fernan Gonzalez (923–70), hero of history and legend. Neither the late-tenth-century kings of Leon, nor their contemporaries in Navarre and Catalonia, were able to take the initiative against the Muslims.

There is no doubt that al-Andalus was extremely wealthy during this period. The evidence for this is essentially anecdotal rather than statistical, but the general impression is clear. The wealth was based on agriculture. Two trends had led to the development of farming techniques in this period. The first was the introduction of new crops in what has been described as a 'green revolution'.[57] These included rice, hard wheat, sugar cane and citrus fruits, and the use of rice and hard wheat (from which pasta is made) greatly increased the quantity and variety of staples available. The second innovation was the more extensive use of irrigation techniques, which were especially useful in the Guadalquivir valley. These may have originated in Yemen, original homeland of many of the early settlers, or the oasis of Damascus, familiar to later Syrian immigrants, but they were easily adapted to Andalusi conditions.

The development of a prosperous and intensive agriculture both allowed and benefited from the development of a large capital city at Cordoba.[58] It is probable that the population of the capital was over 100,000 in the tenth century, making it, along with Constantinople, the largest city in Europe. While the city had an important role as the official capital, the court attracted industries, most notably textiles but also ceramics, glass and metal and leather work. Both in terms of population, the industry it supported and the level of civic amenity, Cordoba was vastly more developed than any of the muddy market towns of northern Europe. However, it was also vulnerable to disruption of revenues and supplies. Like contemporary Baghdad, it was dependent on peace and orderly government for its survival. When these conditions disappeared in the early eleventh century, the city itself was ruined. Cordoba at its height was a product of a particular set of economic and political factors. Other Andalusi cities were probably much smaller, and some areas which were later to be important economic centres, like the city and huerta of Valencia, had hardly begun to develop.

Al-Andalus was also linked with international commercial networks. Until the twelfth century, most of these contacts seem to have been with the other Muslim states of North Africa and the eastern Mediterranean. Textiles and dyestuffs were probably the most important exports. Andalusi merchants were to be found in all these areas and must have returned with information about cultural and intellectual trends in the rest of the Muslim world. Economically as well as culturally, al-Andalus was closely integrated into the Dar al-Islam. In contrast, apart from the trade in *ṣaqāliba* there

57. On which see A.M. Watson, *Agricultural Innovation in the Early Islamic World* (Cambridge, 1983).

58. Cordoba in this period is described in Lévi-Provençal, *HEM*, iii, pp. 356–95.

was little commercial contact with the Christian north, and Andalusi merchants were unknown in the Mediterranean ports of France and Italy. All this was to change after the great expansion of Frankish maritime trade in the twelfth and thirteenth centuries, when al-Andalus became an important destination for Latin merchants but lost its commercial contacts with the eastern Islamic world.[59]

59. For these changes see O.R. Constable, *The Commercial Realignment of the Iberian Peninsula, 900–1500* (Cambridge, 1994).

CHAPTER FIVE

The 'Amirids and the Collapse of the Caliphate of Cordoba[1]

The rise of al-Manṣūr, 976–81

In this rather closed, even claustrophobic, political society where access to the ruler was tightly controlled, it was easy for a few individuals to wield enormous power quite unrelated to their origins or their wider political support. The most successful of these political operators in the later years of al-Ḥakam's reign was Muḥammad b. Abī 'Āmir.[2] He claimed Arab origin and that one of his ancestors had participated in the original conquest of al-Andalus in 711, meaning, amongst other things, that his family could claim to have been in al-Andalus longer than the Umayyads themselves. They settled in Algeciras where they maintained a modest and undistinguished prosperity, ignored by the chroniclers, until the time of the young Muḥammad, born in 938. According to the Arab sources, he determined early on to make himself the most powerful figure in al-Andalus and since opportunities for Arabs in the military were very limited, he went to Cordoba and acquired a firm grounding in religious law. In circumstances which are not entirely clear but gave rise to gossip among his enemies, he established close relations with members of al-Ḥakam's harem, notably Ṣubḥ, a Basque who was mother of the heir apparent Hishām; he became manager of her considerable wealth and that of the young prince. This patronage led to further promotion and in 973 he was appointed *qāḍī* of the areas of Morocco which the Umayyads held, in effect to act as a political officer alongside the military commander Ghālib and

1. The best general account of this period remains Lévi-Provençal, *HEM*, ii, pp. 196–345. See also the important reassessment in P.C. Scales, *The Fall of the Caliphate of Cordoba* (Leiden, 1994), with a full bibliography.
2. For his origins and rise to power see Lévi-Provençal, *HEM*, ii, pp. 196–205.

his successors. Ibn Abī ʿĀmir became the main link between the Berber chiefs of the area and Cordoba.

The Caliph al-Ḥakam al-Mustanṣir died on the night of 1 October 976. Affection for his only son and heir, Hishām, had induced al-Ḥakam to appoint him as heir apparent in 970, even though he was only eight at the time, but he seems to have given him none of the political and military experience he himself had had from his own father when young. On his father's death Hishām was fourteen or fifteen years old but had no political personality of his own.[3] In these circumstances, it was only natural that ambitious figures at court would attempt to control the young sovereign for their own advantage.

The eventual victor in the power struggle which followed was Muḥammad b. Abī ʿĀmir, who took the title of al-Manṣūr (the victorious) and became effective ruler of al-Andalus until his death in 1002. The Arabic chronicles on which we depend for our understanding of his personality and policies have an ambiguous attitude to him.[4] On the one hand, his rule saw the apogee of the power of Muslim Spain, and later writers could not fail to be impressed by the way in which he defeated the Christians time after time, especially when they were aware how quickly these same Christians were able to take advantage of the dissension which followed his death. In some anecdotes he also appears as the stern, just and omniscient ruler, a favourite type in Islamic historiography. But this admiration was not unqualified. For a start, it had to be admitted that al-Manṣūr's rule seriously undermined the prestige and influence of the Umayyad family who had for so long been the real focus of unity in the country. On top of this was his patronage of the Berbers, large numbers of whom he brought across to serve in his armies. The great eleventh-century compiler, Ibn Ḥayyān, held the Berbers responsible for the calamities which had struck his country, and al-Manṣūr had to take a share of the blame. What is characteristic of all the surviving narrative sources is that al-Manṣūr himself monopolises the limelight: the account of his rise to power and his subsequent rule completely eclipses other events and personalities. We have, for example, virtually no information about provincial governors. Presumably they continued to be appointed and dismissed as they had been under al-Nāṣir and al-Ḥakam, but their

3. On Hishām's proclamation as Caliph see M.L. Avila, 'La proclamacion (bay'a) de Hišam II, ano 976 d.C.', in *Al-Qantara* i (1980), 79–114.

4. There is an excellent discussion of the Arabic sources for this period in Scales, *Caliphate*, pp. 10–35.

names and deeds are not recorded. This is no accident but rather a consequence of al-Manṣūr's effective monopoly of the media along with his monopoly of other sources of power.

We are told that he had a very clear idea of what he wanted to do and a single-minded ambition to become effective ruler of al-Andalus. In this aim he is said to have been inspired by the example of the Buyids,[5] a family from northern Iran who had taken over the 'Abbasid caliphate in 945 and, while keeping the caliphs in luxurious confinement, had established themselves as hereditary rulers and retained the caliphs only as powerless figureheads. The Buyids were then at the height of their power and they were a very attractive model for an extremely ambitious man who realised that he was excluded by the accident of birth from ever being able to claim the caliphate in his own right.

We have a shrewd analysis of his political methods as they were remembered in the second half of the eleventh century by the last Zirid prince of Granada, 'Abd Allāh, whose family were among the Berbers brought over to al-Andalus by al-Manṣūr. It is worth quoting at some length:

> Despite his humble antecedents and the fact that he was not of the royal house – for he had no right to inherit the kingdom from his ancestors – and since he was not all that powerful, al-Manṣūr b. Abī 'Āmir achieved great things thanks only to his shrewdness and his courting of the common people . . . Had he not proclaimed allegiance to the Caliph, had he not appeared to submit to him in all his actions and obey him and meet all his needs, had he not assumed the posts of *ḥājib* and *wazīr*, had he not reduced to obscurity the men who had been prominent in the Caliphate of al-Ḥakam and had he not ruthlessly eliminated them, on the pretext that only through such a measure could his power be maintained and enhanced and that their survival would have led to much discord and dissension and culminated in the ruin of the Muslims, al-Manṣūr would not have achieved what he aspired to, nor would he have reached in all this the highest goal . . .
>
> Since all his troops were of one race, al-Manṣūr anticipated that they might engage in conspiracies calculated to undermine his power and join forces in revolt against his authority irrespective of whether his commands were to their liking or not. He therefore paid close attention to the problem and allowed himself to be guided by the view that his troops should be drawn from various tribes and diverse

5. Ibn Idhārī al-Marrākushi, *Al-Bayān al-mughrib fi akhbār al-Andalus wa'l-Maghrib*, vols I–II ed. E. Lévi-Provençal and G.S. Colin (Paris, 1948), ii, pp. 272–3, gives another example of the awareness in al-Andalus of political events in the Near East.

> elements so that, should any one group think of defecting, he might subdue it with the help of other detachments. Moreover, al-Manṣūr needed to strengthen his army and increase the number of his troops so that he might be able to make repeated descents on enemy territory and subjugate it at will. He therefore imported such Berber chieftains, champions and redoubtable warriors as were known to him for their horsemanship and skill in the arts of war. The call to *jihād* spread abroad, and men famed for their exploits, qualities and valour in the face of the Christians rallied to the call from the eastern Maghreb. With these forces Ibn Abī ʿĀmir launched his attacks on the enemy. It was they who were the mainstay of his army and it was in them that all trust was placed in combat and on the battlefield. My paternal uncle, Zāwī b. Zīrī, and then his brother's son, Ḥabūs b. Māksan, were among the shrewdest and most zealous of them, so it was they whose opinions and counsel were sought, and it was upon them that command over lesser troops devolved.[6]

ʿAbd Allāh b. Buluggīn may not have been a successful practical politician in his own right, but he clearly had a good grasp of the theory: he puts his finger on the elimination of rivals in the elite, winning the favour of the populace, using Berber troops to balance the other elements and developing the appeal of the *jihād*, all central elements in al-Manṣūr's strategy.

Ibn Abī ʿĀmir returned from his North African posting immediately before the old Caliph's death. He did not have to wait long to make his mark. When al-Ḥakam passed away, two leading *ṣiqlabī* officials, Fā'iq al-Niẓāmī, in charge of the *tirāz* (official textile factory) and the post, and his colleague, Jaw'dhar, responsible for the jewels and falcons, decided to take the initiative. They were the chiefs of some 1,000 *ṣaqāliba* who worked in the palace as well as being in charge of the palace guard. They were a powerful interest and they determined to order the succession as they wished. They were with the Caliph when he died and were able to keep the Caliph's death a secret while they made their plans. They wanted to remove Hishām from the succession and replace him with an adult brother of al-Ḥakam's, al-Mughīra b. al-Nāṣir. Their first move was to summon the *ḥājib*, al-Muṣḥafī. The ruthless Fā'iq advised, rightly, that al-Muṣḥafī should be murdered immediately, but Jaw'dhar, more scrupulous, urged that they try to win him over. Al-Muṣḥafī readily agreed to follow their plan, but as soon as he had left them he alerted Hishām's supporters, among them Ibn Abī

6. ʿAbd Allāh b. Buluggīn al-Ziri al-Ṣanhāji, *Al-Tibyān*, trans. A.T. Tibi (Leiden, 1986), p. 44.

ʿĀmir. He seized the initiative, mobilising the Berber Banū Birzāl and other troops and urging that al-Mughīra, who was still unaware of the turn of events, should be executed. It was Ibn Abī ʿĀmir who led 100 *ghilmān* to meet the unfortunate prince. Al-Mughīra seemed innocent of any political aspirations, readily agreeing to acknowledge Hishām, and Ibn Abī ʿĀmir would have relented and spared his life had not al-Muṣḥafī insisted on his immediate execution. He was strangled in his own house in front of his family.[7]

Ibn Abī ʿĀmir's speed of action, and his military contacts, meant that not only were the ambitions of the *ṣiqlabī* leaders foiled, but that he had emerged alongside al-Muṣḥafī as one of Hishām's leading supporters. The *ṣaqāliba* were forced to witness the investiture of Hishām as Caliph. Jaw'dhar was murdered shortly afterwards and Fā'iq sent into exile in the Balearic Islands, where he died. Only those *ṣaqāliba* who agreed to submit to Ibn Abī ʿĀmir's leadership were allowed to remain in the palace, and their political power was destroyed for a generation.

When the formal oath of allegiance was taken to Hishām, who was given the regnal title of al-Mu'ayyad, at the end of September 976, it was Ibn Abī ʿĀmir who supervised the process. His next move was equally bold. The Christians had taken advantage of the succession to begin raids on Muslim territory and the new administration had to make a response. While others hesitated, Ibn Abī ʿĀmir volunteered to lead the army, despite his lack of military connections and experience. He was given large funds from the state coffers to equip his army and reward the troops and in February 977 he set out for the frontier. He was already well on his way to building up a military following. The expedition was a success and was the first of many.

The next stage in Ibn Abī ʿĀmir's plan was the elimination of al-Muṣḥafī. Al-Muṣḥafī's power had depended on the patronage of al-Ḥakam II and, despite the fact that he had given military and civil posts to his family, including the position of *ṣāḥib al-madīna* (prefect of the city) in Cordoba to his son Muḥammad, he had no power base of his own. The rise of this obscure, if well-educated, Berber to the highest office had alienated the traditional leaders of the Cordoba bureaucracy like the Banū Abī ʿAbda, the Banū Shuhayd and the Banū Futays,[8] whose families had served the caliphs for generations, so that there was no solidarity among the administrators and they were happy to allow al-Manṣūr a free hand.

7. Ibn Idhārī, *Al-Bayān*, ii, pp. 259–62. 8. Ibid., p. 272.

His military expeditions also allowed him to make another alliance with the veteran commander Ghālib. Ghālib was an old man by now (he is said to have been 80). He belonged to a previous generation of officials, having been promoted by al-Nāṣir, and he seems to have regarded al-Muṣḥafī as something of an upstart. Ibn Abī ʿĀmir treated him with deference and respect, following his advice in military matters, and he may have reached an understanding whereby Ghālib would retain independent command of the frontier armies from his base at Medinaceli while Ibn Abī ʿĀmir would command the army at the capital. On his return from campaign, Ibn Abī ʿĀmir turned the pressure on al-Muṣḥafī, aided by the popularity he had acquired among the people by his successful campaign on the frontier. Seriously worried, al-Muṣḥafī proposed a marriage alliance between Ghālib's daughter al-Asma and one of his sons, only to be outmanoeuvred again when Ghālib broke off the engagement and promised Asma to Ibn Abī ʿĀmir himself. In March 978 the *ḥājib* was arrested and interrogated before being flung into prison, where he died five years later.

Ibn Abī ʿĀmir now began to consolidate his power in the capital by building a massive new palace and administrative headquarters on the eastern outskirts of the city at a place he called Madīnat al-Zāhira (not to be confused with al-Nāṣir's palace-city of Madīnat al-Zahrā, which lay to the west of the old city and which seems to have fallen into disuse at this time). He began work in 979 and ordered that all the administrative offices be moved there, leaving the Caliph isolated with his private household and Ibn Abī ʿĀmir's spies behind the heightened and strengthened walls of the old Alcazar. Although the Caliph was no longer a minor, it was given out that he wished to devote himself entirely to religion and was entrusting the exercise of power to Ibn Abī ʿĀmir.[9]

Having achieved absolute authority in the capital, Ibn Abī ʿĀmir felt himself strong enough for a showdown with Ghālib. In the summer of 981 he assembled an army and marched north for a trial of strength. He called on an old friend from his days in North Africa during the previous reign, Jaʿfar b. ʿAlī b. Ḥamdūn, known as Ibn al-Andalusī, who came with a force of some 600 Berbers. In addition he had a body of Christian mercenaries, and he recruited troops from the Upper March, led by Maʿn b. ʿAbd al-ʿAzīz al-Tujībī. Against these Ghālib could only muster his loyal followers from the Middle March and a large Castilian contingent, led by his old

9. Ibid., pp. 275–6; Lévi-Provençal, *HEM*, ii, pp. 220–5.

adversary, Garci Fernandez, Count of Castile: civil war on either side soon blurred religious dividing lines. When the two armies met in July near Atienza, there was a confused conflict, but Ghālib was killed in the mêlée and his army broke up in disorder.[10] Once again Ibn Abī ʿĀmir had showed his skill at putting together coalitions of unlikely allies and so isolating his enemies, and again the Berbers had played an important part at a crucial moment in his rise to power. Soon after, he turned on both his main supporters: first Ibn al-Andalusī and then Maʿn al-Tujībī were taken by treachery and murdered, leaving Ibn Abī ʿĀmir, as Ibn Idhārī says, 'unique and unrivalled'.[11]

Al-Manṣūr in power, 981–1002

This victory meant that Ibn Abī ʿĀmir's power was now unchallenged, and to celebrate this he took a regnal title, that of al-Manṣūr, a title which had been held by one of the greatest of the ʿAbbasid caliphs (Abū Jaʿfar al-Manṣūr, 754–75). For the next twenty years he was to be undisputed ruler of al-Andalus, a period which in some ways saw the apogee of Muslim Spain in terms of territorial security and internal peace and prosperity. Al-Manṣūr was careful to respect the theoretical rights of the Caliph, but this effective usurpation did not go entirely unchallenged. In 989 there was an abortive conspiracy led by a descendant of al-Ḥakam I called ʿAbd Allāh b. ʿAbd al-ʿAzīz, known as al-Ḥajar (Dry Stone, because of his avarice). He was supported by ʿAbd al-Raḥmān b. al-Muṭarrif al-Tujībī, lord of Zaragoza and the Upper March, and al-Manṣūr's own son, also called ʿAbd Allāh, who had been staying with the Tujībīs in Zaragoza. ʿAbd al-Raḥmān persuaded him that he was much braver and more intelligent than his brother ʿAbd al-Malik (later to succeed as al-Muẓaffar), who was being favoured by his father. They agreed that al-Andalus should be divided, with ʿAbd Allāh b. al-Manṣūr taking Cordoba and the *ḥaḍra* and the Tujībī taking the Marches. They are said to have been supported by a group of leading solders and palace servants in Cordoba, but the plot was discovered while al-Manṣūr was on the *ṣāʾifa*. ʿAbd al-Raḥmān was accused of embezzling his troops' pay and executed, while ʿAbd Allāh al-Ḥajar and ʿAbd Allāh son of al-Manṣūr took refuge with the

10. Ibn Idhārī, *Al-Bayān*, ii, pp. 278–9; Ibn al-Khaṭīb, *Aʿmāl al-aʿlām fī man buyiʿa qabla ʾl-iḥtilām min mulūk al-Islām*, ed. E. Lévi-Provençal (Beirut, 1956), pp. 71–4; Lévi-Provençal, *HEM*, ii, pp. 224–8.

11. *Al-Bayān*, ii, p. 279.

Christians. Al-Manṣūr's son was surrendered to his father by Garci Fernandez, Count of Castile, and executed, and al-Ḥajar remained in prison for the rest of the reign.[12] In 996 Hishām's mother Ṣubḥ, now completely alienated from her ex-favourite, attempted to secure her son's liberation and restoration to power, but her attempts were immediately uncovered by al-Manṣūr's agents.[13] Apart from this there was little internal dissidence and the Umayyad family were obliged to accept their effective exclusion from power.

Away from the capital, some local magnates managed to retain their influence. As usual, this was particularly marked in the Upper March where the Tujībīs managed to maintain their power throughout al-Manṣūr's reign. Ma'n b. 'Abd al-'Azīz, who had been in rebellion against Cordoba in al-Ḥakam's reign, returned to favour through his services to al-Manṣūr. He is described as '*fāris al-'arab*' (knight of the Arabs), a title full of poetic and chivalric resonances, suggesting that he was acknowledged as the leading Arab military leader of the time.[14] Ma'n was instrumental in the assassination of Ibn al-Andalusī before being himself murdered shortly afterwards on al-Manṣūr's orders. The main branch of the family successfully maintained their independence against al-Manṣūr's centralising policies, and an interesting illustration of this can be seen at the time of the conspiracy of 'Abd Allāh al-Ḥajar mentioned above. 'Abd al-Raḥmān b. Muṭarrif al-Tujībī, the governor of Zaragoza and a veteran of al-Ḥakam's reign, joined the conspiracy because he had become increasingly apprehensive, quite understandably, about his position since he alone was left of all the great men who had held office before al-Manṣūr came to power. After the collapse of the conspiracy and 'Abd al-Raḥmān's execution, al-Manṣūr was obliged to nominate his nephew 'Abd al-Raḥmān b. Yaḥyā al-Tujībī in his place to retain the loyalty of the lords of the Upper March.[15] Individual members of the family might fall, but the dynasty itself survived. We hear nothing about such Berber chiefs as the Banū Dhī'l-Nūn and the Banū Razīn, but their influence continued undiminished into the eleventh century and it is likely they retained a degree of autonomy throughout al-Manṣūr's reign.

Al-Manṣūr devoted great care to the building up and rewarding of the army of al-Andalus. In this, he was continuing policies

12. Ibid., pp. 282–4; Scales, *Caliphate*, pp. 128–9.
13. Lévi-Provençal, *HEM*, ii, pp. 230–1.
14. Ibn Idhārī, *Al-Bayān*, ii, p. 279; cf. Lévi-Provençal, *HEM*, ii, p. 226 n. 1.
15. Ibn Idhārī, *Al-Bayān*, ii, pp. 282–4.

which had been developing since the accession of ʿAbd al-Raḥmān al-Nāṣir in 912. Basically, this meant the dismantling of the remains of the *jund* system and its replacement by a fully professional army, largely recruited from *ṣaqāliba* and Berbers. The Umayyads had employed *ṣaqāliba* from the time of al-Ḥakam I (796–822), but only in the tenth century did they become a large professional military force as well as forming the most influential group among the palace servants. Increasingly too they were recruited from the Christian areas of Spain rather than from eastern Europe, the best ones being said to come from Jilliqīya (= Galicia, though the term is used for the whole of the Kingdom of Leon). They were commanded by *fityān* (sing. *fatā*) who could acquire estates and recruit their own followings among the *ṣaqāliba.* Al-Manṣūr may have disposed of their leaders, Ghālib and others, but the *ṣaqāliba* as a group remained influential and were still important, and towards the end of al-Manṣūr's reign we see the emergence of a new leader, Wāḍiḥ, whose power was based on the Middle March and Ghālib's old centre at Medinaceli.[16]

Berbers had also been employed by the Umayyads since early in Umayyad rule and ʿAbd al-Raḥmān II recruited Rustamid princes and their followers into his army,[17] but in the reign of al-Ḥakam II we find new groups of Berbers being recruited. This process was speeded up by al-Manṣūr who used them as a balance to the *ṣaqāliba* and the remaining Andalusi elements in the army.

These developments made heavy demands on the fiscal system, and the payment of these troops seems to have caused genuine distress. As so often, our information about taxation in al-Andalus is meagre, vague and contradictory, but we can make some tentative conclusions.[18] Naturally, different groups had different opinions about the changes, depending on whether they were beneficiaries or victims of the new system. Abu Bakr al-Turṭūshī, writing a century later but reflecting the views of the old-established *jundis*, explains:

> According to some old Andalusis, some of whom had formed part of the *jund* and others not, the Muslims were superior to their enemies who remained weak and divided as long as the lands were distributed as fiefs [*muqaṭṭaʿa*] to the soldiers. They worked them in partnership with the peasants whom they cared for as the merchant cares

16. For a full discussion see Scales, *Caliphate*, pp. 132–41.
17. See above, p. 45.
18. For the best discussion of this see P. Chalmeta, 'Concesiones territoriales en al-Andalus hasta la llegada de los almoravides', in *Cuardernos de Historia. Anexos a la revista Hispania* vi (1975), 66–73.

for his business. With this system the lands were cultivated, resources were abundant and the troops were numerous and had more arms and mounts than they needed. This situation lasted until the last years of Ibn Abī ʿĀmir who established monthly stipends [*ʿaṭā'*] for the troops, which were collected in cash through the imposition of a tribute [*jibāya*] on the land which was collected by the army. The troops ruined the people and devastated their agriculture. The population fled and agriculture became impoverished, with the result that the revenues collected by the state declined, the army was enfeebled, so that the enemy could conquer Muslim territory, taking most of it. The decadence of the Muslims, and the superiority of the enemy, continued until the arrival of the Almoravids who established the concessions [*iqṭāʿat*] as they had been in the past.[19]

The Berber beneficiaries saw it very differently. ʿAbd Allāh b. Buluggīn saw only advantages in the reforms:

Ibn Abī ʿĀmir asserted the prestige of the Caliphate, subdued the Christians and exhorted all Muslims to launch expeditionary incursions against the enemy. The peasantry of al-Andalus were unequal to such a task and complained to him of their inability to fight and of the fact that expeditions would prevent them from farming their land. Moreover, they were not a warlike people. Al-Manṣūr therefore conceded to them the right to concentrate on the cultivation of their land while in turn they willingly agreed to make annual contributions to support troops to act in their stead. And so he imposed taxes on them and had assessments of all their property entered into the registers. Dividing the taxes among them, he fixed a collective sum that was to be paid for the upkeep of the army . . .

It was left to people's own honesty to pay the alms-tax [*zakāt*] due on their property in cash, produce or livestock and to distribute such alms among the poor in each town. This matter did not come within the competence of the ruler who was merely concerned with funds for maintaining the army and the government on which all else depended – for were it not for the protection afforded by rulers to their subjects, were it not for the might of their government and its defensive capacity, subjects would have enjoyed neither peace nor prosperity. The whole of this policy was pursued on the basis of sound and righteous government and benevolent administration.[20]

Despite these radically different perspectives, it is clear that Andalusi *jundi*s, whose ancestors had come from Syria in the eighth

19. Al-Turṭūshī, ii, p. 92, quoted in Chalmeta, 'Concesiones territoriales', 66–7; see also Scales, *Caliphate*, pp. 129–30.

20. ʿAbd Allāh b. Buluggīn, *Al-Tibyān*, ed. Lévi-Provençal, pp. 17–18; annotated trans., A.T. Tibi, pp. 44–5.

century, were reduced to tax-paying subjects and the lands they had been given for their support were exploited for the benefit of others. Despite the fact that both commentators attribute the changes to al-Manṣūr, it is clear that these were the culmination of developments which had occurred throughout the tenth century. The result was that Andalusi society was divided into a small military caste recruited from outsiders, and the bulk of demilitarised taxpayers. Perhaps more than any other factor, this accounts for the inability of the Andalusis to resist Christian advances more effectively.

The new regime undoubtedly enjoyed some popular support, partly because of the prosperity and stability it brought but also because of a strong commitment to rigorist Islam. Al-Manṣūr himself made his personal devotion clear: on campaign against the infidel he carried with him a Qur'an, copied by himself, and, in case of his death, a linen winding sheet, made of flax grown on the land he inherited from his father and woven by his daughters. On each of his expeditions, dust was collected from enemy territory to be mixed with the perfumes when his body was washed: we can be sure that news of these private austerities was not kept from the wider Cordovan public, any more than it has been kept from us. On a larger scale, he built a massive final extension to the mosque in Cordoba for the Berber immigrants and others. It still stands today, an austere and dignified contrast to the luxuriant decoration of al-Ḥakam II's work in the same building. He also took strong measures against any sign of heterodoxy, purging al-Ḥakam's great library of any works which might upset orthodox opinion and publicly crucifying a scholar accused of Mu'tazilite thought.[21]

The most important part of this populist commitment to Islam, however, was his systematic pursuit of the *jihād* against the Christians. Previous rulers, notably 'Abd al-Raḥmān II and al-Nāṣir in the first part of his reign, had used leadership of the Holy War to legitimise their rule and keep them in touch with outlying areas of al-Andalus, but none had developed this as a policy to the same extent as al-Manṣūr. The Arabic sources mention more than 50 raids, from small-scale expeditions to major campaigns like the 985 sack of Barcelona and the 997 sack of Santiago de Compostella.[22] Despite the fact that he seems to have had no military background

21. Ibn Idhārī, *Al-Bayān*, ii, pp. 286–8; Lévi-Provençal, *HEM*, ii, pp. 214–15.
22. For a detailed account of the campaigns see Lévi-Provençal, *HEM*, ii, pp. 233–58.

or training, his expeditions were usually successful, suggesting that he was a competent organiser and had a good relationship with the military. Very striking is the way in which al-Manṣūr made certain that news of his triumphs, real, exaggerated or imagined, was spread in Cordoba, the clearest example of this being after the fall of Santiago when the bells of the cathedral were carried south to Cordoba by prisoners of war.

The propaganda effect of these triumphs was immense, both inside al-Andalus and among the Christians of the north, where the constant raids and continuous destruction caused real fear. In the end, however, they achieved little in military terms. Christian resistance was strong and remained so right up to the end of al-Manṣūr's life when in the summer of 1000 Sancho Garcia, Count of Castile, inflicted major losses on the Muslims and nearly clinched a remarkable victory. Cities were sacked but, apart from a brief and abortive attempt to establish a Muslim garrison at Zamora in 999, no effort seems to have been made to advance the frontiers of Muslim settlement. The military activity against the Christians was a central part of al-Manṣūr's political programme, justifying to Muslim popular opinion both his take-over of power and his development of new military forces with the taxation that went with them. It was difficult for anyone to challenge his policies, when they were so publicly and insistently directed towards the prosecution of the *jihād*.

Paradoxically, this policy of aggression went along with the development of kinship ties across the frontier. As has already been noted, Ṣubḥ, mother of the titular Caliph Hishām, was a Basque and al-Manṣūr continued the connection by marrying ʿAbda, daughter of King Sancho Abarca of Navarre, who was the mother of his son ʿAbd al-Raḥmān, known as Sanchuelo, born around 983. In 993 he is said to have taken a daughter of King Vermudo II of Leon as a concubine whom he subsequently liberated and married.

Al-Manṣūr also pursued an active policy in North Africa.[23] As before, Cordovan policy was concerned with finding local tribal leaders who would be strong enough to defend Cordovan interests and yet be prepared to accept its overall authority. There was no longer any third power, as the Fatimids had been until 969, seeking to exploit the situation, but this did not make it easier to find reliable allies. From 988 the head of the Maghrāwa tribal confederation, Zīrī b. ʿAṭīya, seemed the best agent Cordoba could find and he founded a new centre at Wajda to base himself in. He was

23. For the details see ibid., pp. 259–73.

invited to the capital and established in a luxurious palace, but the Berber chiefs always seem to have found this sumptuous environment constraining and he was soon back on his native territory. In 997 he rejected the authority of al-Manṣūr who then decided on a more active policy. Up to this point, Cordovan forces had only occupied Ceuta, but in 998 al-Manṣūr sent his leading *ṣiqlabī* commander, Wāḍiḥ, with a large force. Fes was occupied and an Andalusi administration installed which survived until al-Manṣūr's death.

The expense was considerable and the conquests ephemeral, but the most important legacy in al-Andalus was the large number of new Berber troops. These new troops were usually recruited not as individuals but in tribal groups under their own chiefs who continued to command and lead them. This meant that they retained much of their tribal group spirit (called *ʿaṣabīya* in the Arabic sources). Combined with the fact that few of them spoke Arabic and that they were wholly unused to an urban environment such as the great city of Cordoba, it meant that they remained a very alien presence, uncomprehending and uncomprehended at the heart of Andalucian society.

The most important group came not from Morocco but from Zirid Tunisia. The Zirids were chiefs of the Ṣanhāja tribal confederation and they had been left in charge of Ifrīqīya when the Fatimids had moved east to Egypt in 969. With Fatimid support Zīrī (d. 971) and his son Buluggīn (d. 984) attempted to extend their authority over the central Maghreb (modern Algeria) in a series of campaigns. One result of this was to polarise the Berbers into two major tribal groups, the Ṣanhāja, in effect the allies of the Zirids, and the Zanāta, their opponents, who often looked to al-Andalus for support. After the death of the Zirid ruler al-Manṣūr b. Buluggīn in 996, his son Bādīs was challenged by two of his great-uncles, Zāwī and Māksan, who revolted in Tlemcen and acknowledged Cordovan overlordship. However, they seem to have been unable to sustain their independence and either al-Manṣūr or his son al-Muẓaffar invited them and their Ṣanhāja followers to join his army in Cordoba. Not only were they militarily a very formidable group of horsemen, but they were also exiles, unable to return to their native lands. Having crossed to al-Andalus, they had to make their home there.

Al-Manṣūr's reign was in many ways a culmination of trends which had been evident in al-Andalus throughout the tenth century, especially the growing professionalisation of military and civil hierarchies and the concentration of military power in the hands of non-native groups. At the same time there were a number of new factors, not all of them beneficial. Al-Manṣūr had significantly undermined the prestige of the Umayyad dynasty which had been the focus of unity in Muslim Spain for so long. Not only was the Caliph a feeble recluse, but other members of the family were completely excluded from power and influence. He had systematically destroyed the authority of anyone who could command a following in the state and his subordinates were often people of little independent standing. While he remained in charge, the system worked, despite the cruelty it exhibited at the highest level; under less competent management, its future was less assured.

The rule of al-Muẓaffar, 1002–8

Al-Manṣūr was succeeded by his adult son, ʿAbd al-Malik al-Muẓaffar,[24] who had extensive experience of frontier warfare and of managing the military. He stepped into his father's shoes to become effective ruler of Andalus from 1002 to 1008. For later Arab commentators writing after the collapse of the caliphate the reign was a sort of Edwardian summer, when al-Andalus was peaceful, strong and prosperous, in marked contrast to the chaos of the years that followed. Reading between the lines, it is clear that things were not quite so settled and discontent surfaced repeatedly. Part of the problem was the personality of the ruler himself. ʿAbd al-Malik was a competent soldier but he had little time or enthusiasm for day-to-day administration, a problem which was aggravated by the fact that he drank wine, heavily and often, and abandoned himself to his pleasures. This in turn meant that ambitious and unscrupulous men could take advantage of the situation to assume absolute power in the administration. The sources also report that the administration was generally unpopular among the people of Cordoba, who resented high taxation and the pretensions of the ʿAmirids and their followers.

The new generation of leaders who had risen in al-Manṣūr's years had now reached political maturity and had acquired followings and ambitions of their own. This was particularly apparent among the *ṣaqāliba.* They had been left largely leaderless by al-Manṣūr's purges, but now a new generation of leaders had emerged, Ṭarafa, Mujāhid and above all Wāḍiḥ. These new leaders now formed a powerful bloc opposed to the Berber tribal chiefs.

Two senior officials attempted to use their position to take

24. For his 'reign' see ibid., pp. 273–90.

control of the government into their own hands. The first of these was Ṭarafa in 1003 who was denounced, arrested and executed after having been entrusted with the most important offices. In 1006 it was the turn of the chief *wazīr*, ʿĪsā b. Saʿīd al-Yaḥṣubī. Although himself of modest origins, al-Muẓaffar's negligence in ordinary administrative affairs had allowed ʿĪsa to assume almost absolute authority and he had developed close links with old-established families in the civil administration like the Banū Ḥudayr and the Banū Futays. He planned a *coup* to restore the Umayyads to real power, under his tutelage, of course, but the plan was denounced and both ʿĪsa and his candidate for the throne, a grandson of al-Nāṣir, were put to death. It is said that after this al-Muẓaffar determined to take a serious interest in administration, but he died before this could bear any fruit. Both incidents showed serious instability among the ruling elite.

Al-Muẓaffar's way of dealing with, and perhaps escaping from, these problems was to devote himself to the Holy War, and he launched annual raids against the Christians. Here again the Arab chroniclers portray this as a stream of victories, but in truth the results were pretty meagre and amounted to the sack of a few frontier forts. Unusually, al-Muẓaffar did try to encourage settlement of a castle near Lleida by offering fiscal inducements to anyone who would live there. Ibn Idhārī explains: 'He summoned those Muslims who wanted to be entered in the *dīwān* at two *dīnār*s per month on condition that they made their homes in this castle. In addition they were given a house and arable land. Many people wanted this and settled the place immediately.'[25] This shows that there could on occasion be incentives to settle frontier lands but, as with other examples, it is not clear that this came to anything. This must have been in part because the settlement was dependent on an injection of cash from the government to pay salaries. If disturbances or lack of cash should interrupt this, then the settlers would abandon the fortress.

An ominous sign for the future was that Christian resistance to these campaigns was fierce, and Count Sancho Garcia of Castile especially showed himself to be an opponent who could take on the Muslims on equal terms. The most noticeable feature of these campaigns was the care with which al-Muẓaffar publicised his achievements in Cordoba, writing letters which were to be read out in the mosque at Friday prayers (letters which may form the basis of our

25. Ibn Idhārī, *Al-Bayān*, iii (ed. E. Lévi-Provençal, Paris, 1930), p. 7.

literary accounts) and organising victory parades. But even then, people complained that he did not send as many new slaves as his father had done.

Only against the background of subsequent disaster did al-Muẓaffar's reign acquire a golden glow. In reality, the instability of the 'Amirid state was increasingly apparent.

The collapse of the Cordovan state, 1008–31

On the death of al-Muẓaffar, his brother 'Abd al-Raḥmān, known as Sanchuelo (little Sancho after his maternal grandfather, Sancho Abarca of Navarre), succeeded to his position. 'Abd al-Raḥmān had been his brother's right-hand man but his extensive experience did not bring political wisdom. He immediately decided to break with the policies of his father and his brother in two distinct ways. In November 1008 he obliged the Caliph Hishām to appoint him heir apparent: both the two previous 'Amirids had been careful to maintain a screen of constitutional legality to justify their absolute power, but this was now swept away. In his public letter announcing the appointment, Hishām was made to claim that he had examined all the possible successors from Quraysh (the Prophet's tribe to which the Umayyads, but not the 'Amirids, belonged) and other groups, and had decided that 'Abd al-Raḥmān was the best possible candidate in terms of ability and moral qualities.[26] Sunni Muslims were agreed that the caliph should be chosen from Quraysh, and a rather feeble attempt was made to overcome this problem by referring to an alleged tradition of the Prophet that a Qaḥṭānī (i.e. a man from the Yemeni tribe of Ma'āfir) should rule the Muslims. In making this arrangement, 'Abd al-Raḥmān totally alienated the numerous members of the Umayyad family who realised that their remaining status would be destroyed.

His second move was to demonstrate openly his reliance on the Berbers, most obviously by ordering his court to appear on 3 February 1009 dressed in turbans, a typically Berber headgear.[27] Al-Manṣūr's system had depended on balancing different elements

26. The letter is translated into English with a commentary in Scales, *Caliphate*, pp. 43–51.

27. Ibn Idhārī, *Al-Bayān*, iii, p. 48. Scales, *Caliphate*, pp. 51–2, discusses the incident, suggesting that the anecdote may be Ibn Idhārī's invention. Whatever the truth, it is clear that Sanchuelo alienated the political elite extremely quickly, which suggests real incompetence and insensitivity.

within the military, notably the *ṣaqāliba* and the Berbers but also the Arabs from the Upper March led by the Tujībīs. By relying on one group, 'Abd al-Raḥmān inevitably alienated the others.

He attempted to surmount the obvious opposition in the traditional 'Amirid way and, even though it was mid-winter, he immediately set out on an expedition against the Christians, hoping to win a victory and justify his title. The opposition realised that his absence gave them their opportunity, and as soon as they knew he had entered Christian territory, they struck. The leadership seems to have come from the Umayyad family headed by Muḥammad b. Hishām b. 'Abd al-Jabbār b. 'Abd al-Raḥmān al-Nāṣir. His father had been executed by al-Manṣūr for conspiring with 'Īsā b. Sa'īd in 1006 and he himself had led a fugitive existence since. At the same time, he had attracted a considerable following among the people of Cordoba.

The news of Sanchuelo's entering Christian lands arrived on 15 February and the conspirators struck that night,[28] attacking first the Alcazar, where they obliged the Caliph Hishām to abdicate in favour of Muḥammad, and then Madīnat al-Zāhira, the 'Amirid stronghold, which was thoroughly pillaged. The new Caliph took the title of al-Mahdī, a title with messianic overtones which implied that he would restore true and legitimate Muslim government. His first appointments showed that he intended the Umayyad family to play a major role and he appointed his cousins as both *ḥājib* and the *ṣāḥib al-shurṭa* (commander of the security police). He also began to recruit a militia from the people of Cordoba, entering their names in a *dīwān* and promising them salaries (*'aṭā'*). It was a deliberate attempt to break the stranglehold of Berbers and *ṣaqāliba* over the military and to arm the people of the city. The chroniclers tend to be very disapproving of this,[29] criticising him for employing tradesmen and the riff-raff of the *ṣūq* in his army (*sufla, ghawghā, awbāsh,* all meaning mob, plebs, etc., are among the disparaging terms used), but it is clear that many of his supporters were substantial tradespeople and merchants, perhaps alienated by the 'Amirids' imposition of taxes on city trades. In its initial stages, this was a movement which incorporated all classes of the population of the city. Al-Mahdī's enrolment of them in a *dīwān* was a bold attempt to develop a new power base among the Andalusis

28. For al-Mahdī's *coup* see Ibn Idhārī, *Al-Bayān*, iii, pp. 52–9; Ibn al-Khaṭīb, *A'mal*, pp. 127–30; Lévi-Provençal, *HEM*, ii, pp. 297–303. His short reign is fully discussed in Scales, *Caliphate*, pp. 56–78.

29. Scales, *Caliphate*, pp. 67–8, 74–5.

which would enable him and them to dispense with the hated Berbers.[30]

Muḥammad al-Mahdī managed to cling on to power in Cordoba for nine months, until November 1009, but while the new regime may have been popular in the streets of the capital, it faced formidable opponents. The least of these was Sanchuelo who, despite all advice, determined to return to the capital. His troops melted away and he was arrested and executed at a monastery near Cordoba where he had stopped for the night, the Christian Count Garcia his only companion. He was the last of the 'Amirids and no attempt was subsequently made to revive their fortunes in Cordoba.

More serious was the fact that the established military groups rightly saw al-Mahdī and his new army as a threat to their position. The *ṣiqlabī* leader Wāḍiḥ at Medinaceli threw in his lot with the new regime, which he no doubt preferred to a Berber-dominated government, but many of the *ṣaqāliba* left Cordoba and established themselves in the Levante, so depriving al-Mahdī of a military force to balance the Berbers. The Berbers themselves were not so accommodating. Hostility between them and the citizens of Cordoba was a continuous problem that ran through all the chaotic events of the period. Without a friendly government in Cordoba the Berbers could not survive, but al-Mahdī had his own constituency to satisfy and they demanded the humiliation of these alien soldiers. He introduced a series of measures like forbidding them to carry arms in the city which left them vulnerable to any attack. Zāwī b. Zīrī, the most prominent leader, was refused access to the palace, and the quarter where most of them had their homes was pillaged. This culminated in their expulsion from the city after an abortive *coup* attempt at the beginning of June 1009.[31]

In order to press their claims, the Berbers, who had now withdrawn north to Calatrava, adopted a member of the Umayyad family, Sulaymān b. al-Ḥakam b. Sulaymān, as their candidate for the throne. They moved north where their advances were rejected by the *ṣiqlabī* commander Wāḍiḥ at Medinaceli but where they negotiated the support of Sancho Garcia of Castile, who supplied them with 1,000 wagons of flour and food, 1,000 oxen and 15,000 sheep.[32] Then the joint Berber–Castilian army attacked the capital.

30. Scales, pp. 59–61, sees this as a protest of the Marwanids against the *'aṭā* system introduced by the 'Amirids, whereas I would argue that al-Mahdī and his supporters were trying to take over the system to benefit themselves and the Andalusis in general rather than the Berbers.

31. Ibid., *Caliphate*, pp. 69–71. 32. Ibn Idhārī, *Al-Bayān*, p. 71.

The hostile accounts we have of the Cordovan army show clearly that this was a town militia of tradesmen with little equipment and less experience in warfare. Not surprisingly, they were severely defeated by their professional opponents. Muḥammad al-Mahdī fled to Toledo, and on 8 November 1009 Sulaymān entered the city and was proclaimed Caliph with the title of al-Mustaʿīn. Amid a sullen populace he was acclaimed by the Berbers and gave his ally Sancho Garcia a formal reception.

Inevitably there was a reaction. Al-Mahdī escaped to Toledo and Wāḍiḥ negotiated with the Counts of Barcelona and Urgel who contracted to supply 9,000 troops at the exorbitant pay of 2 *dīnār*s a day, in addition to supplies, while the Counts were each to receive 200. The army marched on Cordoba and Sulaymān al-Mustaʿīn, knowing that he was unpopular in the city, marched north to meet them at ʿAqabat al-Baqar where, on 22 May 1010, the Berbers were defeated. Despite this setback, the Berbers were able to retreat southwards and maintain themselves in the southern mountains of Andalucia while Muḥammad al-Mahdī and Wāḍiḥ attempted to establish a government in the capital. Now, however, his regime was based on the support of the *ṣaqāliba* soldiers led by Wāḍiḥ rather than the populace, and they tired of him rapidly. On 23 June 1010 he was arrested and executed after a summary trial and replaced by the useless Hishām II once again.[33]

These events took place against the background of a siege by the Berbers which lasted from late 1010 to 1013 and resulted in terrible hardship among the inhabitants. Wāḍiḥ attempted to negotiate with the Berbers, but his messenger was intercepted, and Wāḍiḥ himself was executed trying to escape from the doomed city in November 1011. By May 1013 the citizens had had enough, the hardships of siege were exacerbated by floods and fires. A last desperate sortie on 11 May failed and the citizens deputed the *qāḍī*, Ibn Dhakwān, to ask for terms. Although a safe conduct was granted, the Berber troops were unrestrained in their pillage and destruction of the city. Many citizens perished, among them numerous learned men including the historian Ibn al-Faraḍī, author of the earliest surviving biographical dictionary of Andalusi learned men.[34] The Caliph Hishām II disappeared soon after and was probably murdered, though a variety of pretenders later appeared, claiming to be him.[35] Sulaymān maintained a shadowy rule in the ruined city,

33. Scales, *Caliphate*, pp. 77–8. 34. Ibid., pp. 88–9.
35. Lévi-Provençal, *HEM*, ii, pp. 320–2.

but his Berber backers had withdrawn to richer and more secure bases in the southern mountains.[36] In many ways, the sack of Cordoba marks the end of its role as a capital; from this time on it was an important city, but it had lost the preponderance which it had enjoyed in the tenth century. From May 1013 other centres of power in al-Andalus were possible.

Another important consequence of the confusion in Cordoba was the immediate shift in the balance of power between Muslims and Christians in the peninsula. This probably did no more than bring into the open a shift which had been occurring since the débâcle of al-Nāṣir's defeat at Alhandega in 939. Al-Manṣūr's determination meant that the Christians were on the defensive in the 'Amirid period, but resistance was stiff and when political troubles erupted in the capital, the Christians were able to take advantage immediately and effectively. A Christian count, possibly Garcia Ramirez of Viguera,[37] was Sanchuelo's main supporter in his attempt to regain his position after al-Mahdī's coup in 1009. Both Muḥammad al-Mahdī and Sulaymān al-Musta'īn had sought the support of Sancho Garcia of Castile, and Sulaymān, who secured it, had to hand over strategic castles in payment. Al-Mahdī and Wāḍiḥ were prepared to pay extortionately for Catalan help against the Berbers. Christian military superiority over the Andalusis, which became so painfully apparent as the eleventh century wore on, was already becoming obvious.

Attempts to restore central authority continued to be made.[38] The most sustained of these was made not by the Umayyads but by the Ḥammūdī brothers, Berbers who claimed Arab descent. The Ḥammūdīs were late arrivals on the Andalucian scene. It was not until the second reign of Sulaymān from 1013 that 'Alī was given the governorate of Ceuta and his brother al-Qāsim, Algeciras and Tangier. The family did have one advantage over other Berber leaders, their ancestry. Much of the original success of the Umayyads in establishing themselves in al-Andalus had been due to their descent from the caliphs of Damascus and their consequent prestige and ability to stand apart from and above local feuds and jealousies and so attract loyalty from a wide cross-section of society. The Ḥammūdīs were Idrisids and so ultimately descended from the fourth Caliph, 'Alī b. Abī Ṭālib; they belonged to the house

36. See below, pp. 141–3.
37. For this identification see Scales, *Caliphate*, pp. 55–6.
38. The last, confused, years of the caliphate of Cordoba are covered in detail in Lévi-Provençal, *HEM*, ii, pp. 320–41.

of the Prophet himself. They were of Quraysh descent and they had more chance of attracting widespread support than even the most powerful Berber chiefs.

In 1016 'Alī b. Ḥammūd took advantage of growing Berber disenchantment with their Caliph Sulaymān and, claiming to be the legitimate heir and avenger of Hishām II, he marched on Cordoba. For a while he made a serious attempt to build up a broad-based coalition of Cordovan people and Berbers, but their mutual hostility meant that he had more and more to depend on Berber military force and in 1018 he was assassinated by some domestic slaves.

His disconcerted supporters then sent for his brother al-Qāsim who was, for a time, more successful. He conciliated the Cordovans and had good relations with the *ṣaqāliba* leaders, confirming Khayrān in Almeria and Zuhayr in Jaen. In an attempt to free himself from total dependence on the Berbers, he began to build up a bodyguard of Negro troops. As always, the Berbers felt their position threatened, so they joined 'Alī's son Yaḥyā in rebellion in 1021 in Malaga. The resulting civil war destroyed the Ḥammudid attempt to restore the caliphate. Its fate serves to illustrate the almost insuperable problems faced by anyone who tried to restore a state which would be acceptable to all Andalusis, rather than be dominated by Berbers, *ṣaqāliba* or any other group.

Other Umayyads were chosen by the Cordovans to occupy the Alcazar of their ancestors, but none of them was able to sustain their power, having neither reliable troops nor a regular income to call upon. For most of al-Andalus, the caliphate was now an irrelevance. In 1031 a leading local notable, Abū'l-Ḥazm b. Jahwar, persuaded the Cordovans that it was more trouble than it was worth and the Umayyad caliphate of Andalus was definitively and finally abolished. Such had been the bitter experience of the last quarter of a century, that no serious effort was ever made to revive it.

CHAPTER SIX

The Taifa Kingdoms

The emergence of the Taifa kingdoms

In the years between the death of al-Muẓaffar in 1008 and the final abolition of the caliphate of Cordoba in 1031, al-Andalus disintegrated into a variety of small states, each independent from the other and often in direct competition. The rulers of these small kingdoms were known to the Arabic historians of al-Andalus as the *mulūk al-ṭawā'if* (kings of factions or groups). This term was Hispanised into Reyes de Taifas (from *ṭā'ifa*, singular of *ṭawā'if*), hence Taifa kingdoms. Like many terms in the historiography of al-Andalus, this is an echo of eastern history, the original *mulūk al-ṭawā'if* being the name given to the successors of Alexander the Great and the Parthian rulers of Iran.

The phrase *mulūk al-ṭawā'if* also reflects a fundamental problem about the legitimacy of these monarchs. They could claim no justification for styling themselves caliphs or leaders of the whole Muslim community. The ignominious failure of 'Abd al-Raḥmān Sanchuelo to appropriate the caliphal title had shown that this could not be done lightly. Several of the Taifa dynasties could claim Arab origins, but none of them were from the Prophet's tribe, Quraysh, as the Umayyads and even the Berberised Ḥammudis were. This meant that they had to claim to be acting for a caliph, but who could this caliph be? There seems to have been no attempt to acknowledge the distant 'Abbasids of Baghdad, still considered legitimate caliphs by much of the Muslim world. The simplest solution was to continue the precedent set by al-Manṣūr and claim to be ruling in the name of an Umayyad.

The most obvious candidate for the role of titular caliph was the unfortunate Hishām II. It is generally assumed that he perished in the Berber sack of Cordoba in 1013, but his body was never displayed and his death never publicised. It was possible therefore to claim that he was still alive. In about 1035 the ruler of Seville, Muḥammad b. ʿAbbād, announced the reappearance of Hishām II and acknowledged him as his Caliph. He was followed by the rulers of other states who wished to keep on good terms with Seville, or for whom this was a convenient fiction: the *ṣiqlabī* rulers of Denia, Valencia and Tortosa acknowledged him, as did Cordoba, where there was considerable popular enthusiasm for the Umayyad restoration. With the exception of the Birzalids of Carmona, the Berber monarchs rejected the new sovereign. Under the expansionist rule of al-Muʿtaḍid (1042–69), acknowledgement of the Umayyad meant acknowledgement of the leadership of the king of Seville. As time went on, however, this story became increasingly difficult to maintain and in 1060, when Hishām would have been about 100 years old, al-Muʿtaḍid announced that the Caliph had in fact died in 1044 and would not be replaced. Nonetheless, a convenient fiction does not die easily, and as late as 1082/3 Hishām II was still being mentioned on the coinage of the Hudids of Zaragoza, when he would have been over 120.[1]

Since they could not aspire to be caliphs, and the word *malik* (king) was not normally used as a title by Muslim rulers at this time, the Taifa kings looked to al-Manṣūr as a model for their titulature. Many of them styled themselves *ḥājib* to some real or imaginary monarch and then added a personal regnal title. The more pretentious rulers, those of Seville, Badajoz or Zaragoza, for example, followed al-Manṣūr's example and took titles which had been associated with the ʿAbbasid caliphs, so we have al-Muʾtaḍid of Seville (1041/2–68/9), al-Mutawwakil of Badajoz (1068–94) or al-Muqtadir of Zaragoza (1049/50–82/3). Lesser rulers often took titles like ʿIzz al-Dawla (Moron, c. 1041–45) or Niẓām al-Dawla (Alpuente, 1009–30). These titles are based on those used by the Buyid rulers of Iraq and western Iran from 945 onwards. In these titles, the first element usually means strength or glory or some similar abstract noun, while the 'al-Dawla' element refers to the sovereign dynasty, either the impotent ʿAbbasids or the vanished Umayyads of al-Andalus. These extravagant titles reflect a striving for legitimacy among dynasts whose rise to power was accomplished by opportunism and force and who were, in many cases, no more than small-town

1. M.J. Viguera Molins, *Los Reinos de Taifas y las Invasiones Magrebies* (Madrid, 1992), pp. 76, 110–11.

war-lords: no wonder their subjects sometimes regarded them with derision and contempt.

The period is a difficult one to assess. In some ways it was an era of great achievements, notably in poetry and other forms of literary activity, and the recent restoration of the Aljaferia palace in Zaragoza has enabled us to see how accomplished architecture and architectural decoration could be at these minor courts. At the political level, however, it was a period of weakness and conflict when the Andalusis proved incapable of finding a structure of government which would enable them to resist the increasingly aggressive Christians from the north. It is interesting to observe how acutely contemporaries noticed this failure. Both the writer Ibn Ḥazm (d. 1064) and the historian Ibn Ḥayyān (d. 1076) were painfully aware that Andalusi political society was fundamentally sick, but they, and those who felt like them, were unable to resolve the tensions which were tearing it apart.[2]

Since the earliest years of the Muslim conquest, Cordoba had been the centre of unity of al-Andalus. It had always been the capital of the amirs and caliphs: provinces may have sought to assert their independence from Cordoba, but there was no attempt to establish an alternative capital. The only figures we have suggest that the fertile Campiña around Cordoba was the source of a large part of the revenue of the amirs of the ninth century, and this probably continued to be true of the caliphs of the tenth century. There is evidence that the civil wars of the early eleventh century were extremely destructive in this area and that the prosperity of the countryside never really recovered. We know that the palace-city of Madīnat al-Zahrā was destroyed in around 1013 and the site was deserted and ruinous after that. We have Ibn Ḥazm's lament for his family's ruined and desolate country estate at Balāṭ Mughīth, outside Cordoba. The geographer al-Bakrī, who details the revenues previously yielded by this area, contrasts past prosperity with present desolation: 'The civil war which broke out at the beginning of the fifth century of the *hijra* [1009] and has continued to the present day, that is the year 460 [1067/8] has wiped out all vestiges of these villages and obliterated the traces of that agricultural prosperity and it has mostly been deserted.'[3] This impression is reinforced by evidence that lack of money was a main reason for the failure

2. For the attitudes of Ibn Ḥayyān and Ibn Ḥazm see P.C. Scales, *The Fall of the Caliphate of Cordoba* (Leiden, 1994), pp. 10–31.

3. See Ibn 'Abd al-Mun'im al-Ḥimyarī, *Rawḍ al-Miṭār fi akhbār al-aqṭār,* trans. E. Lévi-Provençal, *La Péninsule Ibérique au Moyen-Age* (Leiden, 1938), pp. 250–1.

of the last attempts to restore the Umayyad caliphate: in 1024, for example, the young and talented Umayyad ʿAbd al-Raḥmān b. Hishām was chosen as Caliph by the people of Cordoba in the great mosque. He surrounded himself with distinguished counsellors, including the writer Ibn Ḥazm, but absolute lack of resources to pay them or anyone else meant that he had to extort money from the townspeople whose support he consequently lost. Worse, lack of resources to pay troops led him to accept the services of a party of Berbers, which inevitably provoked outrage in the capital and led to a *coup* resulting in the deposition and death of the young claimant.[4] There is some evidence, then, to suggest that the caliphate could not be revived because the resource base which had sustained it no longer existed.[5]

While the Cordoba area remained desolate, other areas maintained or increased their prosperity. The most obvious of these was Valencia, where urban and agricultural growth, probably beginning in the second half of the tenth century but certainly continuing in the eleventh, meant that the area became an important power base for the first time since the Muslim conquest. Seville almost certainly became the largest city in al-Andalus and came to eclipse Cordoba as a centre of regional power in the Guadalquivir area. Granada, founded by the Zirids when the old settlement of Elvira was abandoned, became a major city, and the rulers of Zaragoza were able to defend their kingdom from the Christians and build themselves a sumptuous new palace. It seems likely that other regional centres also prospered when money was no longer extracted from the local economies by a demanding government in Cordoba, but we have no figures to support this hypothesis. Culture followed political independence. Even a Taifa of modest size like Denia on the east coast maintained a bureaucracy, and it was among the *kuttāb* who serviced this bureaucracy that Arabic letters and poetry flourished.[6]

The abolition of the caliphate in 1031 had little impact beyond Cordoba itself. The real change had come much earlier, during the long siege of the capital between 1010 and 1013 when central government had been paralysed. In the absence of control and

4. Lévi-Provençal, *HEM*, ii, pp. 334–5.

5. See M. Barcelo, 'Un estudio sobre la estructura fiscal y procedimientos contables del emirato omeya de Cordoba (130–300/755–912) y del califato (300–366/912/976)', in *Acta Medievalia* v–vi (1984–85), 66–70.

6. For the prosperity of the Levante in general see P. Guichard, *Les Musulmans de Valence et la reconquête* (2 vols, Damascus, 1990–91), i, pp. 57–62. For the link between political independence and culture see the excellent study by M.J. Rubiera Mata, *La Taifa de Denia* (Alicante, 1985).

direction from Cordoba, locally based lords assumed control without formal renunciation of allegiance or active rebellion. In many areas this simply meant that long-established local magnates, like the Tujībīs in Zaragoza, assumed power, formalising a position they had long held in the area and providing a broad degree of continuity. In other areas, like the Berber kingdoms of the south, there was a fundamental rupture of traditional power structures as an entirely new ruling group imposed itself on the area.

The processes by which they took over were quite simple. ʿAbd Allāh b. Buluggīn gives a clear and concise account:

> When the ʿAmirid dynasty came to an end and the people were left without an *imām* [leader of the Muslim community], every military commander rose up in his own town and entrenched himself behind the walls of his own fortress, having first secured his own position, created his own army and amassed his own resources. These persons vied with one another for worldly power, and each sought to subdue the other.[7]

The rulers who emerged in the 1010s and 1020s can be divided, roughly speaking, into four groups: local Arab patrician families, old-established Berber chiefs, *ṣaqāliba* leaders and newly arrived Berber soldiers.

Arab patrician Taifas: Seville, Zaragoza and Cordoba

The Arab patrician families took over major urban centres like Seville and Zaragoza but also smaller towns like Niebla and Murcia. In Seville[8] the power of the Banū'l-Ḥajjāj, who had ruled during the reign of the Amir ʿAbd Allāh (888–912), and their partners the Banū Khaldūn had declined.[9] In 974 there was a disturbance in

7. ʿAbd Allāh b. Buluggīn al-Ziri al-Ṣanhāji, *Al-Tibyān*, ed. E. Lévi-Provençal (Cairo, 1963), p. 18; annotated trans., A.T. Tibi (Leiden, 1986), p. 45.

8. The main sources for the rise of the ʿAbbadids are Ibn al-Khaṭīb, *Aʿmāl al-aʿlām fī man buyiʿa qabla 'l-iḥtilām min mulūk al-Islām*, ed. E. Lévi-Provençal (Beirut, 1956), pp. 177–83, and Ibn Idhārī, *Al-Bayān al-mughrib fi akhbār al-Andalus wa'l-Maghrib*, vol. III ed. E. Lévi-Provençal (Paris, 1930), pp. 193–203, both dependent in part on Ibn Ḥayyān; see also J. Bosch Vila, *La Sevilla Islamica* (Seville, 1984), pp. 92–106; D. Wasserstein, *The Rise and Fall of the Party Kings* (Princeton, 1985), esp. pp. 119–21.

9. The Banū Khaldūn soon regained something of their previous status and are described as one of the leading families of Seville in the mid-eleventh century. They remained so until the fall of the city to the Christians in 1248: see P. Guichard, *Structures sociales 'orientales' et 'occidentales' dans l'Espagne musulmane* (Paris, 1977), pp. 150–1; for the later Banū'l-Ḥajjāj see Viguera Molins, *Los Reinos de Taifas*, pp. 330–1.

the city, probably a protest against the government of al-Ḥakam II. The leading figures seem to have been ʿUmar b. Khālid b. Khaldūn and Ḥabīb b. Sulaymān b. al-Ḥajjāj. A military expedition led by the *ṣāḥib al-shurṭa* Ibn Ṭumlus was sent from Cordoba and the uprising was crushed. This seems to have broken the influence of these two leading families in the city and when the power of the caliphate collapsed, there was a new leading family, the ʿAbbadis. Like their predecessors, the Banū ʿAbbād claimed to be from the Yemeni Arab tribe of Lakhm and to have arrived with the *jundi*s of Hims in 741. The family lived in complete obscurity in Seville until the time of Ismāʿīl b. ʿAbbād, who was appointed *qāḍī* of Seville by al-Manṣūr. 'He was', said Ibn Ḥayyān, 'a man unique in learning, culture and administrative ability and he protected Seville against the Berbers who had overrun the surrounding area and surrounded it by his good organisation and intelligence and care for the affairs of government.'[10] He also amassed a huge property, said to have amounted to a third of all the land of the city. It is not surprising to find the *qāḍī* acting as political leader of a city in the absence of any effective military command. This phenomenon became quite common in the Near East in the eleventh century[11] and the *qāḍī*s increasingly emerged as leaders of the civilian, as opposed to the military, elite in the cities. Usually drawn from one of the most prominent landowning and merchant families, the inhabitants would naturally turn to them in times of crisis. We have already seen how the *qāḍī* Ibn Dhakwān led the delegation of Cordovans who surrendered to the Berbers in 1013.[12] The first ruler of the Taifa kingdom of Toledo was the *qāḍī* Yaʿīsh, and the Muzayni dynasty who ruled the kingdom of Silves in the Algarve were *qāḍī*s of the city.

Ismāʿīl died in 1019 and his position was inherited by his son Muḥammad, who was appointed *qāḍī* by the Ḥammudi claimant to the caliphate, al-Qāsim. In September 1023 he ordered that the gates of the city should be shut against al-Qāsim, who was then fleeing from Cordoba with his Berber supporters. This marks the effective independence of Seville, though the Ḥammudis tried to take the city as late as 1035. At first, Ibn ʿAbbād ruled as part of a triumvirate which also included the *faqīh* al-Zubaydī and the *wazīr* ʿAbd Allāh b. Maryam, but he soon removed his partners,

10. Quoted in Ibn al-Khaṭīb, *Aʿmāl*, p. 177.

11. In Tyre, Tripoli and Amid (Diarbakr), for example. There is a good discussion of this phenomenon in M. Fierro, 'The Qadi as Ruler', in *Saber Religioso y Poder Politico en el Islam*, ed. M. Marin and M. Garcia-Arenal (Madrid, 1994), pp. 71–116.

12. On the Banū Dhakwān see Viguera Molins, *Los Reinos de Taifas*, pp. 305–6.

establishing himself as sole ruler. He contented himself with the title of *ḥājib*, which had, of course, been borne by the great al-Manṣūr, maintaining a fiction that he was the representative of the vanished Umayyad, Hishām II. By the time of his death in 1042, he left a securely established kingdom which included Seville and much of the Alemtejo to the west but not, as yet, the Algarve or Carmona and Arcos to the south-east. His son Muḥammad inherited his position without real opposition.

In Zaragoza, there was already a well-established local dynasty, the Tujībīs, who had been effectively lords of the city since the beginning of the tenth century and had survived the centralising policies of both al-Nāṣir and al-Manṣūr. However, it was not the main branch of the Tujībīs which took power in Zaragoza but a junior branch who had been lords of Daroca. The leader of these, al-Mundhir b. Yaḥyā, had been promoted by al-Manṣūr and al-Muẓaffar. In 1013 he acknowledged the caliph of the Berber party, Sulaymān al-Mustaʿīn, in exchange for which he was formally granted Zaragoza. In 1018 he joined the supporters of the Umayyad claimant to the caliphate, al-Murtaḍā, on the expedition against the Zirids of Granada, but after this ended in defeat he retired to the Upper March and consolidated his power there, taking the title of *ḥājib*. On his death in 1021/2, he was succeeded by his son Yaḥyā and the kingdom became effectively hereditary.

In 1038/9, disputes within the Tujībī family led to the collapse of the dynasty. Al-Mundhir b. Yaḥyā b. al-Mundhir was assassinated by his distant cousin ʿAbd Allāh b. al-Ḥakam, who was a member of the senior branch of the family and a grandson of the ʿAbd al-Raḥmān who had been executed after conspiring against al-Manṣūr in 989. ʿAbd Allāh gathered the notables of the city to approve his usurpation of power but, for reasons we do not know, he was not accepted and was driven out by a popular rebellion.

In the chaos, power was seized by Sulaymān b. Hūd. Sulaymān came from a family which claimed descent from the Arab tribe of Judhām. Like al-Mundhir al-Tujībī, he had risen in the army of al-Manṣūr, and when the caliphate collapsed, he took over Tudela and Lleida. He had also acquired a reputation as a warrior against Sancho the Great of Navarre and when he arrived in Zaragoza, ostensibly to avenge the assassinated al-Mundhir al-Tujībī, he was widely welcomed. He and his family soon acquired a firm grip on the Taifa, and he installed his sons as governors in Zaragoza, Calatayud, Huesca, Tudela and Lleida. The Tujībīs disappeared from the scene and it was the Hudids who were to rule the Taifa until its annexation by the Almoravids in 1110.[13]

In other, smaller towns, especially in the Algarve area, local Arab elites also took over. Such were the Bakrīs of Huelva and Saltes[14] and the Banū Muzayn of Silves. The Yaḥṣubīs, who ruled Niebla until it was taken by Seville in 1053/4, came from a tribe which had been established in the area since the mid-eighth century.[15]

After the abolition of the caliphate, Cordoba itself was ruled by a consortium of local notables, the *jumā'a*. They were headed by one Ibn Jahwar, who took the title of *shaykh al-jumā'a*. Ibn Jahwar was a member of the Banū Abī 'Abda, Umayyad *mawālī*, who had supplied numerous military commanders and administrators for the dynasty and had himself been secretary to 'Abd al-Raḥmān Sanchuelo. After the suppression of the caliphate, he was careful to maintain the show of a 'republican' government, somewhat like Florence under the Medici, but in fact he seems to have been in effective control. He set about restoring order in the city and largely dispensed with Berber soldiers, recruiting instead the citizens of the town into a local militia as al-Mahdī had attempted to do after the *coup* of 1009. On his death in 1043 he was succeeded by his son Muḥammad al-Rashīd, who 'reigned' until his assassination in 1062. The Banū Jahwar received a good press from the historians, not least because Ibn Ḥayyān was secretary to al-Rashīd, but also because they represented a sort of continuity with the golden age of the caliphate and because they pursued an essentially peaceful policy towards other states, patching up peace treaties between different Taifas and providing a refuge for exiled rulers like the Bakris of Huelva and the Yaḥṣubīs of Niebla, whose territories had been swallowed up by Seville. Cordoba under the Banū Jahwar offered an alternative political model for a Taifa state and in many ways this seems to have been successful, but in the end it was unable to withstand the expansionist designs of Seville.[16]

13. Ibn al-Khaṭīb, *A'māl*, pp. 198–204; Ibn Idhārī, *Al-Bayān*, iii, pp. 175–81, 221–5; A. Turk, 'El reino de Zaragoza en el siglo XI de Cristo', in *Revista del Instituto de Estudios Islamicos en Madrid* 17(1972–73), 7–122, and 18 (1974–75), 7–74; Wasserstein, *Party Kings*, pp. 93–4; Viguera Molins, *Los Reinos de Taifas*, pp. 72–80.

14. Wasserstein, *Party Kings*, pp. 88, 101. The last of the Bakrīd princes wrote an important work of geography after he was forced into retirement when the 'Abbadids of Seville took over his principality in 1051/2.

15. Wasserstein, *Party Kings*, p. 92; Viguera Molins, *Los Reinos de Taifas*, pp. 101–3.

16. Ibn al-Khaṭīb, *A'māl*, pp. 168–77; Ibn Idhārī, *Al-Bayān*, iii, pp. 185–8; Wasserstein, *Party Kings*, pp. 87, 139.

The 'old' Berber Taifas: Badajoz, Toledo and Albarracin

There were also long-established Berber groups who secured their independence. The Berbers had tended to settle in the upland areas of the central southern Meseta and it was here that tribal loyalties lingered longest, so it is not surprising to find Berber families emerging as independent rulers in this area. In 1012/13, while Berbers encircled Cordoba and paralysed the administration, Badajoz was taken over by a *ṣiqlabī* commander, Sābūr. Among his soldiers was 'Abd Allāh b. Muḥammad b. Maslama, known as Ibn al-Aftas, a Berber from the Miknāsa tribe. In 1022 Sābūr died, leaving two young children, and his position was taken over by Ibn al-Aftas. Unfortunately for historians, the Aftasids 'rose without trace' and we know nothing of their history before they became independent rulers. Ibn Ḥayyān says that Ibn al-Aftas came from a family with no social status (*nubāha*) but that he was strong, shrewd and cunning.[17] Whether he had any connections in the area before this period is not clear, but the Miknāsa were among the most important of the Berber tribes in the area and his success probably owed something to his Berber origins.

Once established, 'Abd Allāh b. al-Aftas, supported by the Berber tribes of the area,[18] struggled to defend his position against the 'Abbadids of Seville. In 1030 there was a truce and Ibn al-Aftas devoted himself to the rebuilding of the walls of his capital Badajoz, by now well established as the largest city in the area. He was taking no chances. In 1034 Ismā'īl b. 'Abbād of Seville sought to revive the tradition of raids against the Christians, but the forces he sent to attack Leon were attacked and destroyed, and he himself was forced to flee to Lisbon. We know nothing of the last years of Ibn al-Aftas's reign, but by the time he died in 1045[19] his kingdom was well established and his son Muḥammad succeeded without opposition. Muḥammad, who took the title of al-Muẓaffar, was a poet of note

17. Ibn al-Khaṭīb, *A'māl*, p. 211; for the history of the dynasty see also H.R. Idris, 'Les Aftasides de Badajoz', in *Al-Andalus* 30 (1965), 277–90; Wasserstein, *Party Kings*, pp. 84–5; Viguera Molins, *Los Reinos de Taifas*, pp. 84–6; for the Berbers of this area see E. Manzano Moreno, *La Frontera de Al-Andalus en epoca de los Omeyas* (Madrid, 1991), pp. 233–57.

18. Ibn Idhārī, *Al-Bayān*, iii, p. 203.

19. Two inscriptions recording his death, one now lost, are given in E. Lévi-Provençal, *Inscriptions Arabes d'Espagne* (Leiden/Paris, 1931), pp. 54–5.

and, with his secretary Sa'īd b. Khayra, the author of a 40-volume encyclopaedia called *Al-Muẓaffarī*, now lost.

We know much more about the early history of the Dhu'l-Nunids of Toledo.[20] Originally from the Hawwāra Berber tribe, they first appear as independent lords in Santaver (roughly the modern province of Cuenca) in the ninth century, taking advantage of the breakdown of government under the Amir 'Abd Allāh (888–912). They rose to power as leaders of the transhumant Berber tribes who migrated between the uplands and the plains around Valencia, very much as their contemporaries, the Hasanuyids, Rawwadids and Marwanids, did with the transhumant Kurds in the Zagros Mountains and northern Mesopotamia.[21] Neither al-Nāṣir nor al-Manṣūr had been willing to destroy their power, so the breakdown of the caliphate after 1010 saw them securely in control of their homelands but without any major urban centre. Meanwhile, Toledo was the scene of a power struggle between the *qāḍī* of the city, one Ya'īsh b. Muḥammad al-Asadī, and the 'Amirid governor. When the *qāḍī* was driven out, a group within the city invited Ismā'īl b. 'Abd al-Raḥmān b. Dhī'l-Nūn, lord of Ucles, to take over and by 1018/19 he was established as ruler. So began one of the most famous of the Taifa dynasties, legendary for their luxurious living. Their name is always associated with Toledo and, of course, with its fall to Alfonso VI in 1085, but the roots of their power lay in the wild steppe land to the south-east and many in Toledo may have resented them as incomers.

Also from the Hawwāra Berbers were the Banū Razīn, who gave their name to their capital city, the small mountain town of Albarracin. Their kingdom maintained its independence into the early twelfth century, largely because of its remoteness and the skill of its leaders, notably 'Abd al-Malik b. Razīn (1044/5–1103), the longest reigning of any Taifa king. It was not until 1104 that it was finally taken by the Almoravids and absorbed into their empire.[22]

20. See D.M. Dunlop, 'The Dhunnunids of Toledo', *Journal of the Royal Asiatic Society* (1942–43), 77–96; Viguera Molins, *Los Reinos de Taifas*, pp. 86–91; and the comments in Guichard, *Structures*, pp. 321–3. The name is probably an Arabisation of the Berber name Zannun, Dhū'l-Nūn being the name of the sword carried by the pre-Islamic hero Malik b. Zuhayr, on which see Dunlop, 77–8, where the significance of the name is discussed.

21. For these Kurdish dynasties see H. Kennedy, *The Prophet and the Age of the Caliphates* (London, 1986), pp. 250–66.

22. J. Bosch Vila, *Albarracin Musulman* (Teruel, 1959), parte I, 'El reino de taifas de los Bani Razin'; Guichard, *Structures*, pp. 317–18; Viguera Molins, *Los Reinos de Taifas*, pp. 81–3. Wasserstein, *Party Kings*, p. 101, numbers the Banū Razīn among the Arabs.

Interestingly, Albarracin became independent again around 1166 when it was taken over by the Christian Azagra family, in theory as vassals of Ibn Mardanīsh of Valencia, and after the Reconquista they made the city the base of a great feudal lordship.[23] A similar small Taifa was established further south at Alpuente by the Banū Qāsim, Kutāma Berbers who claimed Arab origin.[24]

The ṣaqāliba *Taifas of the Levante*

Not all those who founded Taifa kingdoms had deep roots in al-Andalus. With the collapse of the caliphate, some of the leading *ṣaqāliba* attempted to set up independent lordships.[25] When they fled Cordoba after the fall of ʿAbd al-Raḥmān Sanchuelo in 1019, most of them headed for the Levante. It is not entirely clear why this should have been, but it seems that some of them had been appointed as governors in these areas by al-Manṣūr and his sons. It is also possible that they were attracted to the area because there were no powerful local leaders, as at Zaragoza or Seville, who would have prevented them dominating the district. By the time Cordoba fell to the Berbers in 1013, Mujāhid had established himself in Denia and the Balearic Islands, Khayrān in Almeria, Mubārak and Muẓaffar in Valencia and, shortly afterwards, Muqatil in Tortosa.

The *ṣaqāliba* had difficulty maintaining their position, perhaps because many of them were eunuchs and, after the collapse of the caliphate, because no further *ṣaqāliba* were purchased to swell their numbers. Valencia was the first to go, in about 1021, when it was taken over by ʿAbd al-ʿAzīz, son of ʿAbd al-Raḥmān Sanchuelo and hence grandson of the great al-Manṣūr. He was the only member of his family to make a successful career for himself in the new political environment of the eleventh century and governed for almost 40 years until his death in 1060/1. Murcia came under the control of the Banū Ṭāhir, a family of Andalusi-Arab origin, from 1038 and Almeria was taken over by Ibn Ṣumādiḥ, a member of the Tujībī family of Zaragoza, in 1041/2. Tortosa was taken by Zaragoza in 1060 and Denia followed suit in 1075/6.

23. J.L. Shneidman, *The Rise of the Aragonese-Catalan Empire* (2 vols, New York, 1970), i, pp. 112–13.
24. Viguera Molins, *Los Reinos de Taifas*, p. 83.
25. The *ṣiqlabī* Taifas are discussed in ibid., pp. 54–70.

The Zirids of Granada and other 'new' Berber Taifas

The last group of Taifa kings came from the newly arrived Berber troops recruited by al-Ḥakam II and al-Manṣūr. Zāwī b. Zīrī and his war-band of Ṣanhāja Berbers were much the most formidable of these new groups. They were also among the most recent arrivals: al-Manṣūr had refused to let Zāwī in because of his reputation as a trouble-maker and it was not until the rule of his son al-Muẓaffar (1002–8) that they crossed the Straits. Al-Manṣūr's apprehensions were fully justified and Zāwī was a leading figure in the election of the anti-Caliph Sulaymān al-Mustaʿīn and the Berber assault on the old capital.[26] After their expulsion from Cordoba in 1010, the Berbers had besieged the city for three years and finally succeeded in installing their candidate, Sulaymān al-Mustaʿīn, as Caliph. By 1013, however, their priorities had changed. Whereas at the outbreak of the civil war they wanted to establish a government which would continue to pay and support them as the 'Amirids had done, they now seem to have realised that the old system could not be revived and instead sought areas of al-Andalus where they could establish themselves and whose revenues they could live off. Their puppet Caliph Sulaymān obliged and the Zirids were given Elvira.

We know much more about the Zirid kingdom of Granada than any other Taifa state because the last Amir, 'Abd Allāh b. Buluggīn, wrote his memoirs (the *Tibyān*), which also included a history of his dynasty and interesting reflections on the political practice of the day.[27] These memoirs were written after his deposition by the Almoravids in 1090 when he was in exile at Aghmāt by Marrakesh. Like most political memoirs, these were written to justify his conduct, and in 'Abd Allāh's case he was particularly concerned to persuade his new, strictly Muslim masters that he had not at any time co-operated or thought of co-operating with the Christians. He had every interest then in claiming that his family had not encouraged civil war among the Muslims and had rather exerted themselves to protect the Andalusis and that he himself was the powerless but virtuous victim of circumstances.

26. See 'Abd Allāh b. Buluggīn al-Ziri al-Ṣanhāji, *Al-Tibyān*, ed. E. Lévi-Provençal (Cairo, 1963), p. 196, n. 51.

27. These memoirs have been translated into English with excellent notes by A.T. Tibi (Leiden, 1986). See also A. Handler, *The Zirids of Granada* (Coral Gables, Florida, 1974).

When he came to explain the rise of the Zirids, he tells a very different story from Andalusis like Ibn Ḥayyān. He explains how Zāwī b. Zīrī and his Ṣanhāja Berber followers, about 1,000 in number, were considering returning from North Africa when they answered an appeal from the people of Elvira who were fearful of conquest by outsiders but incapable of co-operating among themselves: 'such was their dislike of one another that each would build by his home a mosque and a bath-house to escape any contact with his neighbour. They showed neither obedience nor submission to any ruler.' In return for protection, the people of Elvira offered sovereignty and taxation and, with some misgivings, Zāwī accepted and obliged the inhabitants to move to the more defensible site of Granada. In 1018 the Ṣanhāja were able to defeat an Andalusi army of some 4,000, led by the Umayyad claimant al-Murtaḍā and his supporters. In fact, this picture of an invitation from the people is not as unlikely as it sounds. There are other examples of citizens appealing to neighbouring princes to come and take over. It was an appeal from at least some of the citizens of Toledo that led to the take-over of the city by Ismā'īl b. Dhī'l-Nūn in 1018/19. When the *ṣiqlabī* ruler of Almeria, Zuhayr, died in 1038, the people wrote to 'Abd al-'Azīz of Valencia offering him the lordship of their city, and it was the people of Zaragoza who approached Sulaymān b. Hūd to take control after the collapse of the Tujībī regime. Local civil elites could sometimes choose their rulers but, once installed, these usually tried to make their authority hereditary.[28] No formal procedures of election or contract were ever developed.

In 1019/20 Zāwī decided to return to North Africa and try his fortune there. He was succeeded by his nephew Ḥabūs, who was invited from Jaen by the *qāḍī* of Granada, Abū 'Abd Allāh b. Abī Zamanīn, to take over instead of Zāwī's sons. It was in his reign (he died in 1038) that the Zirid kingdom of Granada was established as a major political force in al-Andalus.

Less powerful and numerous groups also founded small states in Andalucia at the same time. The Birzalids had come over in the days of al-Ḥakam II and though only 300 in number had played an important role in al-Manṣūr's rise to power. He had established them in Carmona. In 1013 the Caliph Sulaymān al-Musta'īn gave Carmona to the Birzalid chiefs and a small Taifa, based on this strong natural fortress, came into being. Ruled by the Birzalid chiefs, it always struggled to survive the onslaughts of Seville. A

28. The influence of local elites is discussed in Wasserstein, *Party Kings*, pp. 140–4.

Zanāta Berber clan, the Dammarīs, who had been brought over to al-Andalus by al-Manṣūr, were given Moron at the same time. Another Zanāta group, the Khizrūnīs, took over Arcos and the Īfranīs, also Zanāta, controlled Ronda.[29] Small Taifas were also established by the Ḥammūdīs, who had contested the title of caliph with the Umayyads from 1016 to 1026 in Malaga and Algeciras, but their efforts were continuously undermined by family quarrels and by 1065 their power was finally extinguished by the Zirids of Granada.[30]

Taifa politics

There are some surprising gaps in the list of groups who founded Taifas. The most obvious of these is that there were no Umayyad Taifas. Despite the vast numbers of children attributed to Umayyad rulers, there seems to have been a dearth of talented princes in the family. It may be that all the ambitious Umayyads tried to assert their claims to the caliphate and the rule of Cordoba and perished in the attempt, but the complete disappearance of the ruling family is nonetheless most remarkable: as Ibn Idhārī put it: 'The Marwanid wind was motionless from that time and their offspring from the outermost parts of the land were killed. The people despaired of their government, apathy turning many of them away. They were scattered throughout the land and were submerged in the flood of people, despised and disdained.'[31]

It is also curious that there were no *muwallad* Taifas, that is, Taifas ruled by families of local origin. In the previous period of political disintegration, at the end of the ninth and beginning of the tenth centuries, both Badajoz (certainly) and Toledo (probably) were governed by people of *muwallad* descent and *muwallads* were prominent in the political struggles in Seville, to say nothing of the long revolt of the *muwallad* Ibn Ḥafṣūn. By contrast, there are no *muwallads* active in the politics of the Taifa period. It is difficult to know whether this is because they had lost political influence or because people stopped describing themselves as *muwallads* and politically ambitious groups adopted Arab or Berber genealogies to secure their place in the elite.

29. For these small Berber states see Viguera Molins, *Los Reinos de Taifas*, pp. 50–4.
30. Ibid., pp. 41–2.
31. Quoted in Ibn Idhārī, *Al-Bayān*, iii, p. 128, and translated in Scales, *Caliphate*, p. 100. There is a full discussion of the disappearance of the Marwanids (Umayyads) in Scales, *Caliphate*, pp. 110–31.

The origins of the Taifa kingdoms were very varied. Sometimes they represented a complete break with the old power structures, like the *ṣaqāliba* in the Levante and the Berbers in Andalucia, in other places they were merely a development and extension of existing powers. But once they were established, they acquired a political dynamic of their own. Attempts have been made to see ethnic tensions as a motivating force in the conflicts between Taifas – an Andalusi bloc headed by Seville against a Berber bloc led by the Zirids of Granada – but these are not entirely convincing. There was certainly widespread hostility to the newly arrived Berbers in the first quarter of the eleventh century, but in the second and third generations the Berber rulers became increasingly Arabised and acculturated to Andalusi civilisation. Even within their own ranks, the newly arrived Berbers did not form a cohesive group, the Ṣanhāja Zirids coming from a different tribal group than the Zanāta Berbers further to the west, and they never united against their enemies.

The politics of the Taifa kingdoms were driven not by ethnic rivalries but by the desire, even the need, of powerful kingdoms to take over their neighbours and so capture more resources. Until the middle of the eleventh century, most of the states which had been established after 1010 maintained their separate identities. Thereafter there was a spate of take-overs and mergers which meant that by 1085 there was a much smaller number of big players.

The most expansionist of the kingdoms was Seville. The main phase of this expansion took place in the reign of al-Muʿtaḍid (1042–69). It began in the Algarve, where Mertola was taken in 1044/5, Niebla in 1051, Huelva and Saltes in 1051–53 and Silves in 1063, which brought the whole area under ʿAbbadid rule. At the same time, Seville took over the small Zanāta kingdoms to the east and south of the city, Algeciras in 1054/5, Ronda in 1064–66, Moron in 1056–66, Carmona in 1066/7 and Arcos in 1068/9. In 1069/70 ʿAbbadid troops took over the ancient capital of Cordoba from the last of the Banū Jahwar, ʿAbd al-Malik, who had assumed grandiose royal titles and tried to make it into a more conventional Taifa kingdom. Cordoba was subsequently lost to Toledo in 1075 and regained in 1076/7. By 1070 Seville had come to dominate western Andalucia and the Algarve. Its eastern frontiers now marched with those of the Zirids of Granada and the Dhū'l-Nūnids of Toledo, while to the north lay the Aftasids of Badajoz, with whom relations had long been bad. A series of ancient and deeply felt rivalries between these surviving powers meant that co-operation on any issue of importance was virtually impossible.

The Zirids of Granada were less ambitious in their expansion. In 1056 they took over Malaga from the last of the Ḥammūdī rulers and it became a sort of second capital for the kingdom, entrusted to cadet members of the ruling dynasty. However, the Zirids failed to take over the small Berber Taifas to the west of Granada which fell into the hands of the rulers of Seville. Granada itself was the subject of an attempted take-over in 1066 when Joseph, son of the Jewish *wazīr* Samuel b. Naghrīla, appealed to al-Muʿtaṣim, ruler of Almeria, to come and rule. The attempt was defeated by the Ṣanhāja and it gave rise to a fierce pogrom against the Jews in the city.

The Dhū'l-Nūnids of Toledo also expanded their domains in the Levante, an area where the dynasty had always had interests and contacts. During the reign of Yaḥyā al-Ma'mūn (1043/4–75) they took Valencia (1065). The high point of Toledan power came in 1075 when they briefly took Cordoba itself from Seville. But the influence of the Dhū'l-Nūnids in the Levante was curtailed by the power of the Hudids of Zaragoza. Aḥmad al-Muqtadir (1049/50–83/4) occupied Tortosa in 1060/1 when its people rose against the *ṣiqlabī* ruler Nabīl, and he took over Denia in 1076, apparently as a result of an intrigue by the *wazīr* Ibn al-Royolo. The Balearic Islands, which had been attached to Denia, remained as an independent Taifa until the Almoravid conquest in 1115.

The process of consolidation meant that by 1080 only nine Taifas, out of around 30 recorded, still retained their independence – Albarracin, Almeria, Alpuente, Badajoz, Granada, Majorca, Zaragoza, Seville and Toledo.[32] This consolidation did not bring strength. From the break-up of the caliphate after 1009, the people of al-Andalus were increasingly harassed, both militarily and financially, by the Christian powers to the north, and their rulers seem to have been powerless to respond except by paying large sums of money, usually called 'parias', to their tormentors.

The process had begun when both the people of Cordoba and the Berbers sought Christian allies in the struggles for the city between 1010 and 1013 and armed Christian horsemen were able to parade through the streets of the capital. Thereafter, al-Andalus enjoyed a short respite, but rivalries and conflicts among the Muslims soon led rival factions to appeal for help. During the border warfare between the kingdoms of Zaragoza and Toledo over the control of the city of Guadalajara in the years 1043/4–47, the Dhū'l-Nūnids of Toledo, being driven back by the enemy, made an alliance with Garcia Sanchez of Navarre.

32. Figures calculated from the list in Wasserstein, *Party Kings*, pp. 83–98.

> He showered them [the Christians] with money and supplies and sent them against the lands of Sulaymān b. Hūd . . . The Christians spread out in complete safety and their horsemen roamed unchallenged where they wanted in the lands of the Muslims. Ibn Hūd and his sons took refuge from them in their castles . . . It was harvest time and the polytheists settled on the plains and summoned their peasants (*'ulūj*) to reap and transport the harvest for two whole months until they had gathered the crops and threshed them and taken them away to their lands. The Muslims looked on, unable to defend themselves.[33]

In response, Ibn Hūd invited the help of Fernando I of Leon-Castile:

> he sent him a large sum of money and superb gifts and asked him to attack the land of Ibn Dhī'l-Nūn, so he invaded the frontier regions of Toledo with a large army and annihilated its defenders and ravaged their lands. God most high struck the people of the frontier with unparalleled cowardice towards the enemy and none of them could meet him in open conflict . . . Much of the wealth of Toledo vanished with these repeated raids, disasters multiplied and many of the people from their villages and countryside emigrated to the capital.[34]

The people of Toledo then sent emissaries to Fernando. They did not have an easy time. According to the account in Ibn Idhārī,[35] the King made financial demands which they could not possibly meet. They told him so and added that if they had that sort of money they would have paid it to the Berbers to come and put an end to this disgraceful state of affairs. Fernando was unconvinced, saying that they could find the money and anyway they could not call on the Berbers because they were so hostile to them. He went on to suggest that the only solution was for the Muslims to migrate to North Africa and leave the Christians in control of the land which had once been theirs. Negotiations broke down and the destructive warfare continued until the death of Sulaymān b. Hūd in 1047.

The affair sheds interesting light on the weaknesses of al-Andalus, which were already glaringly apparent by the 1040s. Most obvious was the way in which rivalries between Muslim rulers meant Muslims actually paid the Christians to invade other Muslims' lands. Equally striking is the complete failure of either the Banū Hūd of Zaragoza or the Banū'l-Dhī'l-Nūn of Toledo to defend their lands

33. Ibn Idhārī, *Al-Bayān*, iii, p. 278; trans., pp. 230–1.
34. Ibid., iii, pp. 279–80; trans., p. 232.
35. Ibid., iii, p. 282; trans., p. 233.

effectively, leaving the Christian armies to rampage unchecked. The economic damage was obviously considerable, not just in terms of the tribute paid but also of ravaged lands and deserted villages.

The death of Sulaymān b. Hūd did not relieve the pressure for long. In 1051 Yūsuf b. Hūd, ruler of Lleida, was paying money to the Catalans to protect him against his family in Zaragoza. From 1060 onwards Fernando I was collecting annual parias from Zaragoza.[36] Other Taifa kingdoms were forced to enter into tributary arrangements with the Christians. In around 1058 Fernando invaded the territories of the Aftasids of Badajoz and attacked Santarem. The king, al-Muẓaffar, had no choice but to negotiate to save this strategic city, key to the lower Tagus valley. 'They met', an eyewitness reported, 'in the middle of the river of Santarem, Ibn al-Aftas in a boat and the Christian [*'ilj*, a pejorative term often used in al-Andalus to describe Christians] mounted on his horse so that the water reached up to its belly. They had a long discussion about peace and tribute and al-Muẓaffar refused until after much argument and debate it was agreed that he would pay him 5,000 *dīnār*s per year as long as the truce lasted.'[37]

Lack of a common frontier with the Christians did not protect the Taifa rulers: in about 1063 al-Mu'taḍid of Seville, the richest and most powerful of them, felt obliged to pay.[38] Parias became an established system of raising revenue for the Christian rulers: when Fernando I of Castile-Leon died in 1065, he divided up his assets among his sons, Sancho (1065–72), who became King of Castile, Alfonso VI (1065–1109) of Leon, and Garcia, who was given the independent kingdom of Galicia. Along with lands went parias: Sancho was given the parias of Zaragoza, Alfonso those of Toledo and Garcia those of Seville and Badajoz. These revenues went far beyond the Pyrenees: the 2,000 gold pieces per year which Alfonso VI paid to the monastery of Cluny helped to finance the construction of the church of Cluny III, the most magnificent building of its age.

The most vivid account of the extraction of parias comes from the memoirs of 'Abd Allāh b. Buluggīn of Granada. Immediately after 'Abd Allāh's accession in 1073, Alfonso

> recognised that he couldn't be luckier or have any greater opportunity for demanding money. He therefore sent us his envoy. This

36. Viguera Molins, *Los Reinos de Taifas*, p. 77.
37. Ibn Idhārī, *Al-Bayān*, iii, p. 238; trans., p. 198.
38. Viguera Molins, *Los Reinos de Taifas*, p. 112.

was the first time we had entered into negotiations. Pedro Ansurez came to demand that we should pay his tribute. This we unanimously agreed not to do as he asked in the belief that Alfonso could do us no possible harm and as long as someone stood between us – by which I mean Ibn Dhī'l-Nūn [of Toledo]. I did not think that anyone would conclude a treaty with him against a Muslim. The envoy left me with nothing to show for his efforts.

Ibn 'Ammār [*wazīr* of al-Mu'tamid of Seville, d. 1084] seized this opportunity. He had been waiting for the envoy at Priego, anxious to know the outcome of his mission. Perceiving that the envoy had achieved nothing, Ibn 'Ammār immediately offered to strike a bargain with him and said, 'If you've been refused 20,000 *dīnār*s – which was the amount he had demanded as tribute – well, we are ready to give you 50,000 on condition that we conclude an arrangement with you over Granada whereby you will give us the capital in exchange for the riches it contains.' So on these terms they concluded an agreement. They unanimously agreed to build a stronghold from which Granada could be harassed into surrender . . . Ibn 'Ammār engaged some of Alfonso's soldiers with whose help he was able to complete the building [of the fortress of Belillos, north-west of Granada] at a very considerable cost . . . On the departure of al-Mu'tamid and the Christian troops from the fortress, I prepared a large army and marched against it but was unable to achieve anything there. My people, therefore, despaired of our dynasty because those who had covetous eyes on it now joined forces with the Christian. I regretted not having concluded a treaty with him in the first place as he had asked.

The garrison of Belillos had ravaged and harassed the Vega of Granada and, as if I had not suffered enough from it, Alfonso made me disburse what I had failed to pay him in the past as a punishment for my having refused to conclude a treaty with him . . . The intermediary in this business was Ibn Dhī'l-Nūn [of Toledo] who did his best to obtain money for the Christian in order to please him, on the one hand, and on the other in the expectation of ruining my kingdom so that he might either seize it or get his share of it.[39]

Later, 'Abd Allāh imagines how Alfonso would have viewed the situation:

'This is a gamble which I cannot fail to win, even if the city [Granada] is not taken. What benefit do I get from giving the city of one to the other except strengthening him against me? The more rebels there are, and the more rivalry there is among them, the better it is for me.' He therefore came with the intention of taking money from

39. 'Abd Allāh b. Buluggīn, *Al-Tibyān,* trans. Tibi, pp. 87–8.

> both sides and crushing their heads against one another. It was not his hope to seize the country for himself, for he had pondered the matter and said to himself, 'I am not of their faith and the inhabitants hate me. On what basis shall I aspire to take it? By submission? No, that's impossible. By combat? No, my men will perish, my money will disappear and my losses will be greater than any benefit I could hope to derive should the city fall into my hands. Even if it does fall to me, it cannot be held without the co-operation of its inhabitants – but then, they are not to be trusted. Nor is it possible to massacre the inhabitants and settle some of my co-religionists in it. The best plan, indeed the only plan, is to threaten one with the other and to take their money all the time until their cities are impoverished and weakened. When they are weakened, they will surrender and become mine of their own accord.' This is what actually happened in the case of Toledo. The city fell to him without much difficulty since the population was impoverished and split up, coupled with the weakness and decline in fortune of its Prince.[40]

As before, we can see the destructive nature of the feuds between the Taifa kings, the apparent inability of their armies to resist the Christians militarily and the debilitating effect of economic warfare on the Taifas.

The effects of the payment of parias were bad enough in themselves, but, as 'Abd Allāh recognised, they were also the prelude to complete domination. According to him, this was spelled out by the Mozarab count Sisnando Davidiz, who often acted as Alfonso VI's intermediary with the Muslims, who said, 'Al-Andalus originally belonged to the Christians. Then they were defeated by the Arabs and driven into the most inhospitable region, Galicia. Now that they are strong and capable, the Christians desire to recover what they have lost by force. This can only be achieved by weakness and encroachment. In the long run, when al-Andalus has neither men nor money, we'll be able to recover it without any difficulty.'[41]

The Christian advance, 1057–86

In fact, the Christians were slow to begin territorial expansion into al-Andalus. The Christian states of the north went through a period of fundamental change in the early eleventh century. Sancho the Great of Navarre (1000–35) led a rapid expansion of his mountain kingdom to the west and in doing so took over the County of Castile

40. Ibid., pp. 89–90. 41. Ibid., p. 90.

and most of the Kingdom of Leon, putting an end to the power of local dynasties there. On his death he had divided up his lands among his sons: Garcia inherited his ancestral kingdom of Navarre, Fernando Castile and the conquered parts of Leon, while his illegitimate son Ramiro was given the tiny mountain county of Aragon which was elevated into a Kingdom for the first time. Fernando's inheritance was much the largest and he soon consolidated it by taking over the rest of Leon on the death of the last king of the old dynasty, Vermudo III in 1037, and marrying into the old royal line. A new and powerful Christian power had emerged, the Kingdom of Leon-Castile.

Fernando I of Leon-Castile (1035–65) was largely preoccupied by consolidating his authority in his new realms and was content to collect parias from the Muslims. Only in the west did the Christians advance, at the expense of the Aftasids of Badajoz. Here Lamego and Viseu fell in 1057/8 and, more important, Coimbra in 1064 and Coria in 1076, but these were all small towns, remote from the centres of power, and their loss does not seem to have caused great alarm. In Aragon, Barbastro was lost in 1064 and recovered in 1065, but Alquezar was lost forever in 1065.

The reasons for the failure of Muslim arms in this period are not entirely clear; after all, it was only half a century since al-Manṣūr had led a triumphant *ṣā'ifa* to take Santiago in 997. Much of the blame must be laid on divisions among the Muslims. The small armies the Taifa kings did gather seem to have been largely directed against fellow Muslims. There was probably an absolute shortage of men as well. We have very few numbers for the armies of Taifa kingdoms, but those we do have seem very small.[42] When al-Mu'taḍid attacked al-Qāsim b. Muḥammad al-Ḥammūdī in Algeciras, he only had 200 horsemen. The army from Seville which conquered Cordoba in 1069/70 consisted of an advance guard of 300 horse followed by a main body of 1,000; it must be noted that this was a major expedition by the largest and most powerful of the Taifa states. By contrast, Ibn Idhārī says that Fernando I led 10,000 knights and more than 20,000 foot when he raided the kingdom of Badajoz in the late 1050s.[43] While this is almost certainly an exaggerated estimate, the impression remains, nonetheless, that Christian armies were on occasion very much larger than Muslim ones.

It seems as if the demilitarisation of the native Muslim population of al-Andalus which had characterised the caliphate of the

42. Viguera Molins, *Los Reinos de Taifas,* pp. 202–3.
43. Ibn Idhārī, *Al-Bayān,* iii, p. 238; trans., p. 198.

tenth century had made it very difficult to find suitable recruits. The only significant attempt we know of was the move of the Banū Jahwar of Cordoba in the 1030s to recruit the 'people of the markets' into his army and to provide them with arms. This was considered unusual enough to be commented on by a later chronicler,[44] but this army was unable to save the city from the ambitions of Seville. As Fernando I had observed, the Andalusis were very reluctant to engage the services of any more Berbers, and the supply of *ṣaqāliba* had entirely dried up.

There were few attempts to mobilise volunteers for the *jihād* as the Umayyads had done. In 1034, when Ismā'īl b. 'Abbād of Seville wanted to lead a raid in the traditional way against the Christians of Leon, his attempt was sabotaged by the ruler of Badajoz through whose territory he had to pass. The most striking attempt to mobilise Muslim popular opinion came after the fall of Barbastro to the Franks in 1064. Al-Muqtadir of Zaragoza was determined to recover the city and his secretary sent out an emotive appeal to his fellow Muslims. Ibn Ḥayyān, writing in Cordoba at this time, records a vivid account of the conquest and the sufferings of the Muslims which is probably part of this propaganda.[45] It was successful. Many volunteers appeared from the Marches and even al-Mu'taḍid of Seville sent 50 horsemen. There were said to have been 6,000 archers in the Muslim force which retook the city, though all the numbers in these accounts must be treated with caution.[46] The episode showed that enthusiasm for the *jihād* could still bring results, but it remained an isolated incident.

With the death of Fernando I in 1065, the Kingdom of Leon-Castile underwent another convulsion when he divided his lands among his sons. As mentioned above, the eldest, Sancho, received Castile, now an independent kingdom for the first time, and larger and more powerful than Leon. His second son, Alfonso, became King of Leon and a third son, Garcia, was given Galicia. Sancho and Alfonso soon combined to deprive Garcia of his meagre inheritance and imprison him for the rest of his life, but soon after they began to dispute the inheritance. Sancho succeeded in driving Alfonso out in 1071 and forcing him to take refuge with the Dhū'l-Nūnid King of Toledo.

Sancho's triumph was short-lived. The next year, 1072, while he

44. Viguera Molins, *Los Reinos de Taifas*, p. 105, quoting 'Abd al-Wāḥid al-Marrākushī, *Al-Mu'jib*, ed. M. al 'Uryan (Cairo, 1963), pp. 42–3.

45. Preserved in al-Maqqarī, *History of the Mohammaden Dynasties in Spain*, trans. P. de Gayangos (2 vols, London, 1840–41), ii, pp. 265–70.

46. See M.J. Viguera Molins, *Aragon Musulman* (Zaragoza, 1981), pp. 191–4.

was besieging Alfonso's supporters at Zamora on the Duero, he was assassinated. It was widely suspected that Alfonso's partisans were responsible for the deed. Nonetheless, Alfonso was clearly Sancho's heir and he was allowed to assume his dead brother's kingdom of Leon-Castile, but only after Sancho's Castilian supporters, including El Cid, had obliged him to swear in public that he was not responsible for his brother's death. It was not for some time after he had entered into his troubled inheritance that Alfonso was in a position to take the initiative against the Muslims and to seek to expand his lands to the south. Even when he did move, it was more as a response to the internal problems in the Taifa kingdom of Toledo than the result of long-term strategy.

At the beginning of the 1080s al-Andalus slid rapidly towards a crisis which looked as if it would be terminal. In part this was simply an intensification of the existing pressures on the Taifas and the demand for ever higher parias. In 1082, for example, al-Muʿtamid of Seville tried to pay Alfonso in debased coinage and crucified his envoy, the Jew Ibn Salib, when he protested. Alfonso's revenge showed just how wide-ranging Christian power had become: he raided deep into the lands of Seville until he reached Tarifa at the extreme south, overlooking the Straits of Gibraltar.

This restriction of Christian activity to tribute gathering was changed by a political crisis in Toledo. As has been pointed out, the Dhū'l-Nūnids were not native to the city and had only established themselves there some 60 years before. It may well be that powerful elements in the city resented their rule. During the reigns of two effective sovereigns, Ismāʿīl al-Ẓāfir (1018/19–43/4) and his son Yaḥyā al-Ma'mūn (1043/4–75), these divisions remained hidden. They paid parias to Leon-Castile and it was with the support of Castilian troops that al-Ma'mūn was able to take Cordoba in the spring of 1075. Their control in the kingdom was effectively unchallenged and al-Ma'mūn was in a position to offer Alfonso VI a refuge when he was temporarily driven from his throne in 1071.

In 1075 al-Ma'mūn was assassinated and his throne passed to his feeble young son al-Qādir. Al-Muʿtamid of Seville, now at the height of his power, soon began to take advantage of his weakness. He recovered Cordoba in 1076/7 and then, in 1078, took Valencia from al-Qādir, so establishing a bloc of territory from Seville to the Levante. As a result of this débâcle, a group in Toledo staged a *coup* in 1078/9 and al-Qādir was forced to flee to the homelands of the Dhū'l-Nūnids around Cuenca. From here he appealed to his ally Alfonso VI.

Al-Qādir's opponents in Toledo had acknowledged al-Mutawwakil of Badajoz as their new ruler. Alfonso set about opposing him by allying with al-Mu'tamid of Seville and attacking the city of Coria on the northern frontiers of the kingdom of Badajoz. Al-Mutawwakil was obliged to give up Toledo and al-Qādir was reinstated. At this time, Alfonso seems to have wanted a quiet and compliant Toledo which would continue to pay good parias. Al-Qādir was obliged to allow Leonese garrisons to be established at Zorita, east of Toledo, and Cantuarias to the west, but he still remained king. The situation might have continued if al-Qādir had been able to assert his authority effectively, but he was not, and in 1082 there was another rebellion which must have convinced Alfonso that he had to act. Also in 1082, the wily and experienced al-Muqtadir of Zaragoza died and the disputes over the succession meant that Alfonso had nothing to fear from that direction.

In the autumn of 1084 Alfonso set up a loose siege of Toledo, but he himself did not appear until March 1085. There was little serious resistance. Alfonso promised al-Qādir that he would be installed as King of Valencia and the people of the city were assured that they could keep their lives, their property and their mosques. On 25 May 1085 Alfonso entered the city and took possession without any serious resistance. He soon took control of most of the kingdom and established a far south-eastern outpost at Aledo, where the castle could dominate the important road from the Muslim south to the Muslim Levante.

The fall of Toledo marked a turning point in the fortunes of al-Andalus, especially as military victory was backed up by expanding Christian settlement in the Tagus valley. It meant that al-Andalus lost its geographical heart and that its kingdoms were now scattered on the southern and eastern frontiers of the vast domains of the king of Leon-Castile. No part of the country could be wholly secure from Christian raids, and no Muslim force was ever again to penetrate north of the Cordillera Central. It is probably true to say that from 1085, al-Andalus was no longer a viable and self-sustaining political entity.

It soon became clear that the conquest of Toledo was not the end of Alfonso's ambitions. In the spring of 1086 he began to besiege Zaragoza while the troops of one of his nobles, Alvar Fañez, installed the deposed al-Qādir in Valencia. It was in response to these catastrophes that a group of the surviving Taifa kings swallowed their misgivings and their pride and turned again to seek military help from the Berbers of North Africa.

CHAPTER SEVEN

The Empire of the Almoravids[1]

The origins of the Almoravid movement, c. 1050–86

The Almoravid movement, which was to save al-Andalus from a slow death at the hands of Alfonso VI, was born far to the south. The immense trackless wastes which lie between the most southerly cultivated areas of Morocco and the settled plains around the Senegal and Niger rivers were inhabited only by groups of Berber tribesmen. The landscape is extremely inhospitable, endless plains of gravel and sand, scorching and windswept, with a few widely scattered wells and, discernible only to the experienced eye, patches of sparse grazing. These Berbers lived a completely nomad life: 'they know nothing', writes the contemporary Andalusi geographer al-Bakrī, 'about tilling the land, nor cultivating crops, nor do they know bread. Their wealth consists only of herds and their food of meat and milk. One of them might spend his whole life without

1. The standard work on the Almoravid period in al-Andalus is J. Bosch Vila, *Los Almoravides*, originally published in Tetouan in 1956 but which should now be consulted in the new edition by E. Molina Lopez (Granada, 1990) with a good introduction which brings the work up to date. For the origins of the movement in North Africa and the arrival of the Almoravids in al-Andalus, V. Lagardère, *Les Almoravides* (Paris, 1989), is essential reading. He combines a shrewd critique of the sources with a political analysis and I have used his work extensively. Also by the same author is *Le Vendredi de Zallāqa: 23 Octobre 1086* (Paris, 1989) which covers much of the same ground in a more popular way but also contains more material on Almoravid rule in al-Andalus and their relations with the Andalusi *fuqahā*. For the latter stages of Almoravid rule, F. Codera y Zaidin, *Decadencia y desaparicion de los Almoravides en Espana* (Zaragoza, 1899), remains useful. A good general survey is M.J. Viguera Molins, *Los Reinos de Taifas y las Invasiones Magrebies* (Madrid, 1992). For the Reconquista and the politics of Christian Spain in this period see B.F. Reilly, *The Contest of Christian and Muslim Spain, 1031–1157* (London, 1992).

ever eating or seeing bread if the merchants who passed through their country from the land of Islam or the Sudan did not give him bread or present him with flour.'[2] They were remarkable, too, for their veils which they wore, like the Touareg of today, so that only their eyes were visible. It was said that they thought it indecent to expose the mouth and that none of them would recognise a comrade if they saw him unveiled. The veils, so practical in the dusty desert conditions, were very noticeable in the streets of Andalusi towns, and the Almoravids were frequently singled out and described as *al-mulathimūn,* the veiled ones (from Arabic *lithām,* a veil). It emphasised their separateness and their status as outsiders.

These Berbers are described as belonging to the Ṣanhāja group of tribes and so they were distant 'cousins' of the Zirids and other Ṣanhāja groups in the eastern Maghreb. This distinguished them from the more settled Maṣmūda of the Atlas Mountains and the Zanāta tribes of northern Morocco. These divisions purport to be based on lines of descent from common ancestors, but in reality the designations reflect cultural differences. These Ṣanhāja were in turn divided into many different tribes: in the Wādī Dar'a in the southern foothills of the Atlas Mountains were the Gazzūla and the Lamṭa; further south in the deep desert were the Massūfa, the Lamtūna, the Banū Wārith and, most distant and southerly of all, the Guddāla.

As Bakrī's comment shows, they were not completely isolated from the outside world. By the tenth century there was a thriving trade route from Morocco to Ghana, a journey of two months' continuous travelling in each direction.[3] Its northern terminus lay at the famed trading city of Sijilmāssa and at its southern end were the town of Awdaghast, a Muslim settlement, and beyond that Ghana itself. It was gold which enticed Muslim merchants through this desolate land and they brought with them textiles and other manufactured goods and, most important, salt, which they picked up from the mines of Awlīl on their way.

It was not just material goods these merchants brought to the Ṣanhāja, it was also their religion, and it seems that by the tenth century many of these tribes were at least nominally Muslim. Around 1035 a chief of the Guddāla tribe of the Ṣanhāja, Yaḥyā b. Ibrāhīm

2. Al-Bakrī's important description of West Africa is translated in N. Levtzion and J.F.P. Hopkins, *Corpus of Early Arabic Sources for West African History* (Cambridge, 1981), pp. 62–87. For this quote see p. 70.

3. This trade is described in E.W. Bovill, *The Golden Trade of the Moors* 2nd edn (Oxford, 1970), pp. 67–85.

(both good Muslim names), went on pilgrimage to Makka. On his return he visited the great centre of Muslim learning at Qayrawān in Tunisia and met Abū 'Imran al-Fāsī, a distinguished teacher originally from Fes. Yaḥyā was increasingly aware that his people had a very limited understanding of the Muslim religion and he asked if one of the great man's pupils could return with him to his tribe to instruct them. It is perhaps not surprising that none of them were prepared to abandon the city for a life in this harsh and desolate area. Abū 'Imrān did, however, give Yaḥyā an introduction to a teacher called Wajjāj b. Zalwī al-Lamṭī, who ran a school at Malkus in the Wādī Zīz in the extreme south of Morocco. It was here that Yaḥyā came into contact with 'Abd Allāh b. Yāsin, the effective founder of the Almoravid movement.[4]

'Abd Allāh came from the Gazzūla tribe of Ṣanhāja. He had visited al-Andalus where he had studied Islam, and he seems to have returned with a determination to spread true religion among his people and to unite them in a war of conquest. The example of the Prophet Muḥammad, whose *sīra* or biography he would certainly have studied, was a potent inspiration. So it was that 'Abd Allāh returned with Yaḥyā b. Ibrāhīm to his tribe.

When Ibn Yāsin arrived among the Guddāla under Yaḥyā's protection, he began to enforce a simple and rigorist view of Islam. Al-Bakrī stresses his greed and his violence: he decreed that he was entitled to a third of all 'unclean' property, that is, the possessions of all converts, and he instituted a regime of brutal floggings, not only for adultery, slander and drunkenness but for minor irregularities in the performance of prayer.[5] Not surprisingly, this made him numerous enemies in the tribe and after the death of his protector Yaḥyā b. Ibrāhīm, he was expelled and found himself once more at the school of his master al-Wajjāj b. Zalwī.

He had not, however, abandoned his vocation. His next mission was to the Lamtūna tribe, cousins and rivals of the Guddāla. Here he was received by the chief, Yaḥyā b. 'Umar b. Targūt, and his brother Abū Bakr, heads of a remarkable clan, the Banū Targūt, whose members were to form the core of the Almoravid elite. While Yaḥyā b. Ibrāhīm of the Guddāla had been rather in awe of Ibn Yāsin, the Lamtūna chiefs seem to have had a much more equal relationship with him and they formed a very successful partnership.

4. For the early years of the movement see Lagardère, *Les Almoravides*, pp. 45–66.
5. Levtzion and Hopkins, *Corpus*, pp. 71–2.

With Ibn Yāsin, Islamisation and conquest went together. Like the Prophet and the early Muslim leaders on whom he modelled himself, he sought to unite the tribes to conquer the outside world and to replace the tribal leadership with a religious one, breaking down inter-tribal rivalries. Once he had secured his position among the Lamtūna, he immediately launched military expeditions, as the Prophet had done against the Meccans after he had established himself at Madina in 622. It was probably in about 1054 that Ibn Yāsin and Yaḥyā b. 'Umar, leading a force of Lamtūna, Guddāla (now won over to the cause) and other associated tribes, launched their *jihād* against southern Morocco.

Their first conflict with the Berbers of the Dar'a valley was hard fought, and it seems that it was after this victory that Ibn Yāsin took to calling his followers Almoravids (*al-Murābiṭūn*), a designation already known in al-Bakrī's time. Later sources, notably the *Rawḍ al-Qirṭās* of Ibn Abī Zar' (d. c. 1315), explain the name by recounting how Ibn Yāsin and his followers were obliged at one stage to retire to a *ribāṭ* (an Islamic fortress monastery) and took their name from this.[6] Ibn Idhārī, probably based on the lost work of Ibn al-Ṣayrafī, provides a simpler and more plausible explanation: *murābiṭūn* is the active participle of a root which means to band together for fighting and it is used in this sense in the Qur'ān.[7] By adopting this title after a fierce but ultimately victorious struggle, Ibn Yāsin may indeed have been alluding to Qur'ān 3, 200: 'Believers, be faithful, be patient and endure. Persevere in fighting (*rābiṭū*) and fear God so that you may triumph.' By choosing this name, Ibn Yāsin was identifying his followers with the early Muslims and proclaiming that it was religion, not tribal solidarity, which bound his forces together, and, by extension, that anyone, regardless of their origin, could join as long as they were firm in their faith.

Under the joint leadership of Ibn Yāsin and Yaḥyā b. 'Umar, the Almoravids began to expand along the trade routes. In 446/1054/5 they took Sijilmāssa at the north end and Awdaghast at the south, though Sijilmāssa had to be conquered a second time after a rebellion. Not all this expansion was achieved by force. In 450/1058 Ibn Yāsin travelled among the Maṣmūda of the High Atlas, calling on

6. For an attempt to locate such a *ribāt* see P.F. Moraes Farias, 'The Almoravids: some questions concerning the character of the movement during the period of closest contact with the Western Sudan', *Bulletin de l'Institut fondamental d'Afrique noire* 29 (1967), 794–878.

7. Ibn Idhārī al-Marrākushī, *Al-Bayān al-mughrib fi akhbār al-Andalus wa'l-Maghrib*, vol. iv, ed. I. Abbas (Beirut, 1967), p. 12.

them to abandon their feuds and join the Almoravids, specifically appealing to the example of the Prophet himself; he met with a large measure of success. The next year, 451/1059, he set out to preach to the Barghwāṭa Berbers of the Atlantic coast of Morocco with less success. The Barghwāṭa were reckoned as heretics by orthodox Muslims, but they kept firmly to their faith and Ibn Yāsin was put to death: his grave had already become a shrine when al-Bakrī wrote.[8] As religious leader of the movement, he had no successor.

Yaḥyā b. 'Umar had been killed in 448/1056 and leadership of the movement had passed to his brother, Abū Bakr. With the death of Ibn Yāsin, Abū Bakr was now in sole charge and the Almoravids were led by the secular, tribal *shaykhs* of Lamtūna, not by a religious leader. The armies of the desert Ṣanhāja and mountain Maṣmūda are said to have numbered as many as 30,000, but they were usually smaller: in 450/1058 Abū Bakr led a force of 400 horsemen, 800 camel men and 2,000 foot soldiers. Most Almoravids fought on foot in ranks, the first with long spears and those behind with javelins. They were commanded by a man with a banner in front; when the banner was erect they would stand, when it was lowered they would kneel. While Almoravid field armies were often very successful, they had little or no experience of siege warfare. At the siege of Aledo in al-Andalus in 1088 they had to rely on the expertise of the people of Murcia to provide siege engines because they had none. This lack of technical expertise was to prove a devastating weakness when they attempted to regain Toledo and other towns in al-Andalus which had been taken by the Christians.[9]

The appeal of the Almoravids was simple: they summoned men with the slogan, 'The spreading of righteousness, the correction of injustice and the abolition of unlawful taxes', aims with which all pious Muslims could agree. An important part of the appeal of the Almoravids lay in their policy on taxation. They claimed that they would abolish the *maghārim*, the non-Quranic taxes in all the areas which became submitted to their rule. This meant that they would only be required to pay the *'ushr* (tithe). After the death of Ibn Yāsin, none of the Almoravid leaders claimed a religious authority and they did not style themselves as Caliph or Amir al-Mu'minīn, as the Umayyads of Cordoba had before and the Almohads were to do later. They modestly contented themselves with the title of

8. Levtzion and Hopkins, *Corpus*, p. 74.
9. Almoravid armies are discussed in Lagardère, *Les Almoravides*, pp. 187–207.

Amir al-Muslimīn (Prince of the Muslims). In 1098 Ibn Tāshfīn sent a delegation led by one of the leading citizens of Seville, ʿAbd Allāh b. al-ʿArabī, and his son Abū Bakr to the ʿAbbasid Caliph al-Mustaẓhir (1094–1118) in Baghdad. In exchange for an oath of allegiance, Ibn Tāshfīn was given a formal written investiture of the government of the Maghreb. This vague suzerainty was nonetheless important in conferring a clear legitimacy on the new regime.[10]

The establishment of the new regime was confirmed with the foundation of a new capital. Marrakesh was built on the plains of Morocco, just north of the High Atlas. It was clearly designed to be a base for expansion north while retaining close links with the desert to the south. It was an uninhabited site and Abū Bakr stressed that he needed a city in a desert region familiar to the Lamtūna and their flocks. He also needed a settlement which did not invade the territories of other, settled, tribes. The new city was begun in 463/1070: a headquarters, the *Dār al-Hajar* (stone house), was constructed and other dwellings soon sprang up around it. The Almoravid foundation, enlarged and developed by the Almohads, forms the old city of Marrakesh as it exists today.[11]

Soon after the construction of the city was begun, news came of a rebellion by the Guddāla, ancient rivals of the Lamtūna in the Sahara. This was a major threat to the Almoravids, for if they lost control of the Sahara they would lose not only their major source of new recruits but also the control of the salt and gold trades which provided so much wealth. Faced with this challenge, Abū Bakr decided to go south to meet it. He left in charge in Marrakesh his cousin Yūsuf b. Tāshfīn, who was given charge of the Almoravids north of the Atlas and, apparently, told to marry Abū Bakr's beautiful and shrewd wife Zaynab. Ibn Tāshfīn, slightly built with a sparse beard, black eyes and an aquiline nose, was probably half negro. He was also ascetic in his behaviour and highly intelligent, as can be seen from the skill with which he developed his desert polity in response to the challenges of taking over the more settled areas of Morocco and later of al-Andalus.

He soon made it clear that he intended to remain in control: when Abū Bakr returned the next year he was loaded with gifts and told, politely but firmly, to go away. Abū Bakr spent the years until

10. See E. Lévi-Provençal, 'Le titre souverain des Almoravides et sa légitimation par le califat Abbasside', *Arabica* iii (1955), 265–80, and the discussion in Lagardère, *Les Almoravides*, pp. 165–7.

11. For the early history of Marrakesh see G. Deverdun, *Marrakesh des origines à 1912* vol. 1 (Rabat, 1959).

his death in 1087 trying to secure Almoravid control over the desert and gold-producing Ghana beyond, but he never again challenged Yūsuf's control over the north.

Yūsuf b. Tāshfīn devoted himself to further conquests of the north of Morocco, mostly held by tribal leaders from the Zanāta group. In 466/1073 his cousin Mazdalī took Salé and Yaṭī b. Ismā'īl Meknes. In 467/1075 Yaḥyā b. Wasinū took Fes and in the same year Mazdalī took Tlemcen far to the east. The year 469/1076/7 saw the capture of the Rif and other areas of northern Morocco and in 471/1078 Tangier fell. Only Ceuta, whose amir had a fleet and which could be supplied by sea, still remained independent.[12]

These 'conquests' were largely achieved by peaceful means and the existing amirs were either allowed to remain in their home towns or were retired to Marrakesh. Though the sources are not full, there is no mention of the imposition of specifically Almoravid doctrines on an unwilling population, and the appeal to basic Islamic values was essentially uncontroversial.

Ibn Tāshfīn himself took no part in these conquests, but he kept command firmly in the hands of a small number of men, almost all of them from the Banū Turgūt of Lamtūna, like Mazdalī and Sīr, closely related to the leader. Other tribal groups were co-opted into the army, including many of the conquered Zanāta, but command remained with the *shaykhs* of Lamtūna. This early pattern remained the case until the end of Almoravid rule. In some ways it was a great source of strength: the Almoravid regime was singularly free of internecine feuds and civil wars. Potential crises, like the attempt of Abū Bakr's son Ibrāhīm to reclaim his father's position, were settled peaceably and Sīr b. Abī Bakr, who would seem at first sight to have had a good claim to leadership, remained Ibn Tāshfīn's loyal lieutenant. On the other hand, it meant that the Almoravid power base was very restricted: outsiders were not brought into the elite and in time this group became increasingly isolated and lacking in any basis of popular support.

Ibn Tāshfīn introduced administrative divisions into Morocco for the first time. Unlike al-Andalus, where provincial boundaries had long been established, Morocco had been tribal territory with few firm borders and the small cities that did exist (Fes, Tlemcen, Salé, Tangier) were in no sense capitals. The Atlantic coast from Salé to Ceuta and inland to Meknes was put under the command of Ibn Tāshfīn's cousin, Sīr b. Abī Bakr, who was to play a major

12. For the conquest of Morocco see Lagardère, *Les Almoravides*, pp. 80–101.

part in the conquest of al-Andalus. Fes and the surrounding area was under a chief of the Massūfa tribe, ʿUmar b. Sulaymān, Sijilmāssa and the Darʿa beyond the Atlas to Dāwud b. Āʾisha, another Ṣanhāja chief, while Marrakesh, the plains of Tadla and the High Atlas, the richest portion, were entrusted to the ruler's own son Tamīm. Ibn Tāshfīn also developed a rudimentary central government based on Marrakesh, where there was a *dīwān* of sorts. Like the Umayyads before him, he began the purchase of slave soldiers to form a *ḥashm* or guard, composed of 2,000 blacks and 500 *ʿulūj* (probably slaves of Frankish origin) from al-Andalus. The vast bulk of the armies, however, were recruited from the Ṣanhāja tribes, and Ibn Tāshfīn sent to the Lamtūna, Guddāla and Massūfa who remained in the Sahara, telling them of his successes and encouraging them to join him. To reward them, he used the gold of Ghana to start minting very fine Almoravid *dīnār*s in his capital.[13] Apart from the gold, it is not clear that the 'state' had any regular income: the tithes (*ʿushūr*) could be collected, but there is no evidence of a fiscal administration to do this. The other legitimate source of income was the *jizya*, which could be collected from the *dhimmi*s. We are told that Ibn Tāshfīn extorted a large lump sum from the Jews but, unlike al-Andalus, there were few if any Christians in Morocco and the *jizya* was necessarily limited. The Almoravid polity remained, in effect, a conquest state, dependent on new supplies of *ghanīma* (booty) to reward its supporters.

The Almoravid conquest of al-Andalus, 1086–1102

In June–July 1083 the Almoravids finally conquered Ceuta, the last outpost of the Zanāta, and put to death the ruler, al-Muʿizz b. Suqūt. The same summer, Alfonso VI of Leon-Castile (1072–1109), dissatisfied with the failure of al-Muʿtamid of Seville to pay the parias he required, launched a major expedition which ravaged the Seville countryside and reached Tarifa and the southernmost tip of al-Andalus. Christian power was irresistible. The point was confirmed when Alfonso VI entered Toledo in triumph on 25 May 1085 and went on to embark on the siege of Zaragoza the next winter.

13. R.A. Messier, 'The Almoravids, West Africa gold and the gold currency of the Mediterranean basin', *Journal of the Economic and Social History of the Orient* xviii (1974), 31–47.

There is some disagreement as to which of the Taifa kings first invited the Almoravids to cross into al-Andalus to defend them from the Christian menace.[14] It is probable that the Taifa ruler of Seville, al-Muʿtamid, had been in communication with Ibn Tāshfīn before 1086 and there are reports that he had lent naval support to the Almoravid conquest of Ceuta in 1083. According to the fullest account in the *Rawḍ al-Miʿṭār*, al-Muʿtamid summoned his neighbours, al-Mutawwakil of Badajoz and ʿAbd Allāh of Granada, and their *qāḍīs*, to a meeting. Here it was agreed that a mission led by the *qāḍī* of Cordoba, Ibn Adham, and al-Muʿtamid's *wazīr*, Ibn Zaydūn, should go to seek Ibn Tāshfīn's support. Al-Muʿtamid was by no means convinced: 'Better to pasture camels than be a swine-herd' was the terse summing up of his position as reported in the chronicles.

Tensions began to come to the surface even before Ibn Tāshfīn set foot on Iberian soil. He asked that Algeciras, where he was to land, should be evacuated by the ʿAbbadids to give him a secure foothold. They prevaricated but the Almoravid leader acted before they had time to resist. Five hundred advance troops were sent across and took possession of the town without resistance in July 1086. The main bulk of the Almoravid forces, said to have numbered 12,000, crossed soon after. They were greeted with enthusiasm by the local people who set up markets for them. Ibn Tāshfīn then moved on to Seville, where ʿAbd Allāh of Granada joined him, and they pressed on north to the Badajoz area, where they were joined by the local ruler al-Mutawwakil. Ibn Ṣumādiḥ of Almeria stayed at home pleading infirmity and the Taifa leaders of Valencia and Zaragoza were too far away and could hardly abandon their own threatened frontiers. Alfonso VI abandoned the siege of Zaragoza and marched down to meet this new threat. The two armies met at a place the Arabs called Zallāqa and the Christians Sagrajas to the north-east of Badajoz on Friday 23 October 1086. There are a number of confused accounts of the battle.[15] Neither of the two eye-witness accounts, a letter of Ibn Tāshfīn to the Zirid ruler of Tunis, which is very general, and the account in ʿAbd Allāh of Granada's *Memoirs*, which is very short, probably reflecting the small size of his own contribution, are much help. The fullest

14. Ibn Tāshfīn's invasions of al-Andalus are described in Lagardère, *Les Almoravides*, pp. 101–50, and Bosch Vila, *Los Almoravides*, pp. 132–64.

15. The sources and the history of the battle are fully analysed in A. Huici Miranda, *Las Grandes Batallas de la Reconquista durante las Invasiones Almoravides, Almohades y Benimerines* (Madrid, 1956), pp. 19–82.

account is the late-thirteenth-century geographical work, the *Rawḍ al-Miʿṭār* of al-Ḥimyarī, but this was composed 200 years after the event.[16] What is clear is that Alfonso was decisively defeated and retreated to Toledo in disorder, that al-Muʿtamid of Seville fought bravely and that the two Almoravid generals, Sīr b. Abī Bakr and Dāwud b. Ā'isha, played an important part.

Immediately after the battle, al-Muʿtamid suggested that the enemy be pursued and hunted down, but Ibn Tāshfīn wished to return to Seville and shortly after that to Morocco, though he is said to have left 3,000 troops to defend the east of al-Andalus. The most likely explanation for this is that he was concerned about the position in Morocco and was unwilling to leave his power base for too long and become entangled in the complex politics of the Taifa kingdoms. It was about this time, too, that his eldest son Sīr died. The next year his cousin Abū Bakr, whom he had supplanted, died far to the south in Ghana and Ibn Tāshfīn may have been concerned that his son Ibrāhīm would make another bid for the throne.

Whatever the reasons for his departure, the Andalusis soon began to regret his absence. Alfonso had been defeated but by no means broken; he continued to demand and receive parias and his men seized the fortress at Aledo, effectively blocking the route from Seville and Granada to the eastern provinces. From here the garrison raided Muslim territory at will. Valencia, theoretically ruled by the deposed al-Qādir of Toledo, was threatened by El Cid, and the problems of the Muslims were compounded by the increasingly bitter rivalry between al-Muʿtamid of Seville and Ibn Rashīq of Murcia. Now it was the turn of the notables (*wujūh*) of the eastern provinces to call on the Almoravids, a sign perhaps of the increasing popular support they were attracting in al-Andalus.

Ibn Tāshfīn arrived in Algeciras in May–June 1088 and was joined by al-Muʿtamid of Seville and ʿAbd Allāh b. Buluggīn of Granada, while Ibn Ṣumādiḥ of Almeria and Ibn Rashīq of Murcia sent support. The Muslim forces decided to capture the castle at Aledo.[17] From the beginning the expedition was dogged by rivalries between the Taifa kings. ʿAbd Allāh moaned continuously to Ibn Tāshfīn about the wickedness of his brother who had taken over Malaga which had been part of the Kingdom of Granada. At the siege of Aledo, Yūsuf asked the *fuqahā* (the authorities on

16. Ibn ʿAbd al-Munʿim al-Ḥimyarī, *Rawḍ al-Miʿṭar fi akhbār al-aqṭār*, ed. with French trans. E. Lévi-Provençal, *La Péninsule Ibérique au Moyen-Age* (Leiden, 1938), text pp. 83–95, trans. pp. 103–16.

17. For the siege see Huici Miranda, *Las Grandes Batallas*, pp. 85–99.

Muslim law) to adjudicate on the dispute between al-Muʿtamid of Seville and Ibn Rashīq. They found in favour of al-Muʿtamid and he ordered that Ibn Rashīq be arrested and dispossessed, but the incensed people of Murçia then refused to provide any supplies for the besiegers. To add to the difficulties of the Muslims, news came that Alfonso VI was marching to the aid of the beleaguered garrison. At the end of November, after four months of futile siege, Ibn Tāshfīn decided to return to North Africa.

The attempt on Aledo had been a fiasco and Ibn Tāshfīn seems to have decided that his attempts to cooperate with the Taifa kings were hopeless: he would return as undisputed leader of the Muslims or not at all. Alfonso VI regained the initiative. He sent his right-hand man, Alvar Fañez, to force ʿAbd Allāh of Granada to renew the parias, which he did on humiliating terms, and then turned his attention to al-Muʿtamid of Seville: it was as if the victory at Zallāqa had never been won. ʿAbd Allāh tried to excuse himself to his fellow Muslims, but by now he had many enemies at Ibn Tāshfīn's court and the Almoravid ruler was convinced that he was betraying the Muslim cause to the Christians.

In 1090 Ibn Tāshfīn arrived in Algeciras for the third time, determined to act on his own. In September he obliged ʿAbd Allāh to surrender Granada and took over Malaga from his brother Tamīm in October. Ibn Tāshfīn always seems to have been reluctant to spend much time in al-Andalus and he was back in Morocco by the end of the year. This time, however, he left his nephew Sīr b. Abī Bakr to continue his work. Ibn Tāshfīn's hostility and the declarations of the *fuqahā* of al-Andalus that the Taifa kings were impious and debauched and should be deposed finally drove al-Muʿtamid to the desperate expedient of seeking an alliance with Alfonso VI, so making all his enemies' accusations come true. Early 1091 saw the Almoravid forces taking Cordoba and the Guadalquivir valley and defeating a force led by Alvar Fañez which was coming to the aid of Seville. Al-Muʿtamid, faced by Almoravid force and the hostility of many of his own subjects, only put up a feeble resistance and in September 1091 Seville surrendered to Sīr b. Abī Bakr. Like ʿAbd Allāh of Granada, he was deported to North Africa and survived in 1095 as an exile in Aghmāt, close to Marrakesh. Later in 1091 other Almoravid armies took Aledo and Almeria. Al-Mutawwakil of Badajoz did not last much longer. Feeling insecure under Almoravid 'protection' he turned to Alfonso VI, offering to surrender Lisbon in return for military support. Sīr responded by taking over the whole of his kingdom in 1094.

Meanwhile, in Valencia, a different drama was being played out.[18] Here the coming of the Almoravids posed a serious challenge to the king, al-Qādir. Al-Qādir had lost Toledo to Alfonso VI and had been installed in Valencia by El Cid with a Castilian garrison to protect him. Even before the coming of the Almoravids, al-Qādir's rule was unpopular because of the taxes needed to pay the Christian troops. With the Almoravid armies now in Murcia, the prospect of liberation seemed at hand. In October 1092, when El Cid was away in Zaragoza, there was a *coup*. This was led by the *qāḍī*, Ibn Jaḥḥāf. A small force of Almoravid troops arrived and the Christians were driven out, while the miserable al-Qādir was dragged from his hiding place and executed. Then things began to go wrong for the insurgents. The Almoravids did not arrive in force and El Cid began to make preparations to regain the city. Furthermore, Ibn Jaḥḥāf began to set himself up as a monarch in the style of the Taifa kings, surrounding himself with a pomp and ceremony which Valencia could ill afford. Faced by El Cid approaching from the north and popular feeling in favour of the Almoravids within the city, Ibn Jaḥḥāf tried to play the same game as other Taifa rulers, agreeing to pay tribute to El Cid while negotiating with the Almoravids. When the Almoravid army, led by Ibn Tāshfīn's nephew Abū Bakr b. Ibrāhīm, finally arrived in September 1093, El Cid allied with Ibn Jaḥḥāf, while most Valencians seem to have supported an Almoravid take-over. They were disappointed. For reasons which are not entirely clear, the liberating army came within sight of the city walls but then retreated without striking a blow. Tortuous negotiations ensued, but eventually Ibn Jaḥḥāf decided he could not accept El Cid's conditions and once again the city was besieged by the Christians. Finally in May 1094 starvation forced the surrender of the city and El Cid's men entered in triumph.

Ibn Tāshfīn sent another army and in 1094 a considerable force led by another of his nephews, Muḥammad b. Ibrāhīm, reached the city only to be dispersed by El Cid in a daring night-time attack and forced to retreat to Jativa. After this, El Cid revenged himself savagely on what he took to be Ibn Jaḥḥāf's treachery by having him burned to death. A further Almoravid force under 'Alī b. al-Ḥājj was defeated at Bairen, south of the city, in 1097.

These humiliating defeats prompted another invasion by Ibn Tāshfīn in person in the summer of 1097. Muḥammad b. al-Ḥājj

18. The most recent discussion of these events can be found in P. Guichard, *Les Musulmans de Valence et la Reconquête* (2 vols, Damascus, 1990), i, pp. 65–79.

was sent against Toledo and defeated Alfonso VI at Consuegra, killing, amongst others, El Cid's son Diego. Meanwhile, Ibn Tāshfīn's son Muḥammad b. Ā'isha attacked Alvar Fañez in the old homelands of the Banū Dhī'l-Nūn between Zorita and Cuenca before turning his attention to ravaging the lands of Valencia. Against Alfonso VI and Alvar Fañez the Almoravid forces proved effective in the field, but it is noticeable that they did not take a single fortress of importance and their victories were ephemeral.

After El Cid's death on 10 July 1099, Valencia proved impossible to hold, despite the valiant efforts of his wife Jimena, and it was finally evacuated by the Christians in April–May 1102 and occupied by the forces of the veteran Almoravid commander Mazdalī. This completed the Almoravid occupation of al-Andalus with the exception of the Kingdom of Zaragoza in the north-east. To celebrate this triumph, Ibn Tāshfīn had his son 'Alī formally and publicly recognised as his heir. The King of Zaragoza was prudent enough to send his own son as ambassador on this occasion and a treaty was signed between the only two Muslim powers in the Iberian peninsula.

The establishment of the Almoravid regime in al-Andalus

The conquest of al-Andalus by the Lamtūna and their Berber allies was accomplished with surprisingly little violence. It was the subjection of a well-established and cultured society with a strong sense of its own history and identity by a group who were considered to be barbarians, yet the resistance was very slight.

Part of the explanation lies in the success of the Christians and the perilous position the Taifa kingdoms found themselves in. Al-Mu'tamid's bitter epigram about his choice between herding swine or herding camels reflects the sad reality of his position. To some extent this was the fault of the kings personally. Apart from al-Mu'tamid himself and his brave and effective son al-Rāḍī (executed by the Almoravid commander Garūr after the fall of Ronda in 1091), none of them seem to have been either able or determined. Even in his own memoirs, 'Abd Allāh of Granada presents himself as a feeble and incompetent failure, deserted by everyone he relied on, devoured by jealousy of his brother and quite incapable of standing up to outside pressures. None of the rest distinguished themselves and al-Qādir had the melancholy distinction of having lost not one but two major kingdoms (Toledo and Valencia) to the Christians.

But the problems went beyond personal failings. The issue of parias was central to the failure of the Taifas. Unlike the Almoravids, the Taifa kings were dependent for military support on professional soldiers who needed to be paid. The demand for parias meant, among other things, that no Taifa king could afford an effective military force. Al-Muʿtamid of Seville's men seem to have fought effectively at the battle of Zallāqa, but they were quite incapable of resisting the Christians without the support of the Almoravids. In his memoirs, ʿAbd Allāh b. Buluggīn mentions a number of military expeditions against rebels in his own kingdom and on his frontiers. On the rare occasions when he gives us numbers, they are very small: he speaks of 100 Zanāta Berbers in the garrison at Granada (though it is not clear that this was the total number) and says that his brother Tamīm had 300 at Malaga.[19] Numbers for Almoravid armies, by contrast, seem to have been much larger: disregarding the wilder estimates, it is clear that armies of 20,000 were known and that provincial forces could number around 5,000.[20]

Not only did the Taifa kings have very few troops, but their loyalty and proficiency were both doubtful and they were more concerned about the value of the *inzālāt*, the estates on which they subsisted, than about fighting. ʿAbd Allāh clearly regarded the possibility of resisting the armies of Alfonso VI or of Ibn Tāshfīn by force as completely out of the question. The other Taifa kings seem to have been in the same position and only in Seville, where al-Muʿtamid enjoyed widespread support, was there any military resistance to the North African take-over.

The reasons for the success of the Almoravids went beyond the military weaknesses of the Taifa kings. It is clear that, despite the fact that they were Berbers with a completely different lifestyle from the Andalusis, the Almoravids were widely welcomed by many sectors of society. This is in marked contrast with the unpopularity of the Berbers under the ʿAmirids and in the early days of the Taifa kings.

The invaders enjoyed widespread support among the *fuqahā* and the *qāḍīs*. The Almoravid movement had begun as a religious revival. The death of ʿAbd Allāh b. Yāsin had not been followed by

19. ʿAbd Allāh b. Buluggīn al-Ziri al-Ṣanhāji, *Tibyān*, trans. A.T. Tibi (Leiden, 1986), pp. 106, 140–1.

20. Lagardère, *Les Almoravides*, pp. 189–92.

the emergence of a new religious leader to take his place. Power had passed to the secular leaders of the Lamtūna, men like Abū Bakr and Ibn Tāshfīn who were pious but conscious of their ignorance of Islamic law. From the very beginning they showed a respect for the religious classes and relied on them for political as well as religious decisions. Ibn Tāshfīn summoned the *fuqahā* to Aledo to decide between the rival claims of al-Mu'tamid and Ibn Rashīq to Murcia and he accepted their judgement. He did not proceed with the deposition of the Taifa kings until they had been formally condemned under Islamic law. In return, the piety of the Almoravid leaders, their determination to pursue the *jihād* and their respect for the religious classes meant that the *fuqahā* supported their role. This can be seen clearly in the case of 'Abd Allāh b. Buluggīn of Granada. The *qāḍī* Aḥmad b. Khalaf al-Ghassānī, known as Ibn al-Qulay'ī,[21] a member of one of the most important religious families of Granada, had been one of the delegation of Andalusis who first went to Ibn Tāshfīn to ask for his intervention against Alfonso VI. He soon became an active opponent of 'Abd Allāh's, prejudicing Ibn Tāshfīn against him during the siege of Aledo. On his return to Granada, 'Abd Allāh wanted to have him executed but was dissuaded by his mother. Ibn al-Qulay'ī promptly defected to the Almoravids and 'Abd Allāh clearly thought that he was among those who were urging his deposition. He had no more luck with the next *qāḍī* of Granada, 'Īsā b. Sahl al-Asadī.[22] When Ibn Tāshfīn arrived at Ceuta, preparing for his third crossing into al-Andalus, 'Abd Allāh sent Ibn Sahl, amongst others, to him to put his case and say that he was prepared to cooperate loyally in the *jihād.* Ibn Sahl, however, used this opportunity to say how weak 'Abd Allāh's position in Granada was and (probably correctly) how most of the citizens were disaffected. Both Ibn al-Qulay'ī and Ibn Sahl came from ancient families which claimed Arab descent and 'Abd Allāh was for them an upstart Berber dynast with no claims on their loyalty.

There is considerable evidence that Ibn Sahl was correct in saying that most people supported a pro-Almoravid stance. Again, the best evidence comes from 'Abd Allāh b. Buluggīn's *Memoirs.* With engaging frankness, 'Abd Allāh makes it clear that his subjects preferred the prospect of Almoravid rule to his own. The siege of Aledo made this obvious: 'This was a campaign', he writes, 'in

21. 'Abd Allāh b. Buluggīn, *Tibyān,* trans., pp. 119–21 and n. 387.
22. Ibid., p. 247 and n. 407.

which God brought to light the princes' spiteful feelings towards one another. Their subjects [*raʿīya*] came in droves to lay their complaints against their rulers. These subjects made their *fuqahā* their intermediaries and relied on them. One of these was the *faqīh* Ibn al-Qulayʿī whose tent in that camp was like a magnet for all comers . . . The princes of al-Andalus at that time witnessed such insubordination on the part of their subjects, who refused to meet their tax obligations [*maghārim al-'iqṭāʿ*] at a time when their masters needed money to meet their expenses, that they became worried and suspicious.'[23] He goes on to complain that Ibn al-Qulayʿī was writing to his friends in Granada inciting them not to pay so that ʿAbd Allāh could not afford to buy food in the camp, and 'as a result, I was most outrageously ill-used'.

There was worse to come for, as ʿAbd Allah acknowledged, 'My subjects gave me some cause for concern because they were so anxious to see the end of the non-canonical taxes [*maghārim*] and because the attitude of the Almoravids, who were only concerned with the obligatory alms tax [*zakāt*] and the tithe [*ʿushr*] was well known'.[24] At that stage (before Ibn Tāshfīn's third and, for ʿAbd Allāh, fatal expedition) he still placed his trust in his fortresses to over-awe the people. He was soon undeceived as the Almoravids approached: 'Whenever a fortress resisted, the people would join the Almoravids in attacking it until it surrendered.'[25]

When the invaders approached Granada itself, ʿAbd Allāh knew that there was no hope of resistance and he gives us an analysis of why all classes would welcome the new regime, the Berber troops because they 'rejoiced at the arrival of their kinsmen', the merchants because they simply wanted to do business, the common people because they would only be required to pay alms tax and tithe. The Maghrebi courtiers (whom he describes as the mainstay of his regime) were the first to welcome his enemies. Slaves and Slavs, women and eunuchs, all were prepared to listen to the blandishments of the Almoravids.[26] In the end the unfortunate king was deserted by all except his aged mother.

The evidence is less full for other areas, but it suggests that the Kingdom of Granada was not unique. Even though al-Muʿtamid of Seville agreed to devote himself to the Holy War and removed the non-canonical taxes, all his 'fortresses were subject to subversion and in every part of his kingdom, his subjects rose against him'.[27]

23. Ibid., p. 119. 24. Ibid., p. 128. 25. Ibid., p. 150.
26. Ibid., pp. 152–3. 27. Ibid., p. 167.

It was internal subversion which led to the fall of Badajoz in 1094 and popular pressure and enthusiasm for the Almoravid cause which caused the downfall of al-Qādir in Valencia. Only in Seville and Zaragoza do the ruling dynasties seem to have had any popular support and it may be significant that both were ruled by old Andalusi Arab families.

The Taifa rulers were simply unable to survive off the proceeds of canonical taxation. They needed to pay professional armies and felt obliged to maintain courts to rival the reputation of Umayyad Cordoba, complete with luxurious palaces, poets, viziers and gardens. All these came very expensive and it was not just greed or wickedness which forced rulers to look to the *mukūs* or *maghārim*, the non-canonical taxes: after 1088 'Abd Allāh of Granada was forced to pay the parias out of the private fortune amassed by his predecessors and his complaints of poverty may have had some justification. These illegal taxes took many forms, and because they were 'illegal' and frequently improvised it is sometimes difficult to know what was involved. They included taxes on markets and trade, tolls for entering cities, purchase taxes, rents for stalls in the *suq*s and, most humiliatingly, a poll-tax on Muslims similar to that paid by Christians and Jews.[28] These revenues were especially valuable because they were easy to collect and they were paid in cash, not kind, and could rapidly be increased in time of emergency. The position in the countryside is much less clear. 'Abd Allāh's Berber soldiers seem to have been rewarded with estates (*inzālāt*, sing. *inzāl*) on whose produce they were expected to live. According to Ibn Ḥazm, a contemporary observer, they took between a third and a half of the proceeds, a far cry from the 10 per cent enjoined by Islamic law.[29]

It was in keeping with the rigorist view of Islam adopted by Ibn Yāsin that the Almoravids kept to the Quranic prescriptions, and it was one of the three points of their simple programme, the summons to righteousness, the redress of complaints and the abolition of the *maghārim*. The *fuqahā* approved because it was in accord with Islamic law and because many of them came from the commercial classes on whom the *maghārim* weighed most heavily; the common people approved because everyone likes the prospect of lower taxes.

28. For these taxes see the discussion in Lagardère, *Les Almoravides*, pp. 207–19, and the denunciation of such dues by Ibn Ḥazm discussed in P. Chalmeta, 'Concesiones territoriales en al-Andalus hasta la llegada de los almoravides', *Cuadernos de Historia. Anexos a la revista Hispania* vi (1975), 69–73.

29. *Inzālāt* are discussed by Tibi in 'Abd Allāh b. Buluggīn, *Tibyān*, n. 121 on p. 207.

The Almoravids were able to do this in the early stages because the state was expanding rapidly. ʿAbd Allāh's account shows that they were systematic and ruthless in the hunting down and confiscation of the treasuries of the Taifa kings, and some booty must also have been acquired from the Christians. Under Islamic law, the ruler was allowed to keep a fifth of all booty, in itself a strong incentive to persist in wars of conquest. They may also have benefited from the gold trade of the Sahara, enabling them to mint large quantities of fine gold coin to reward their troops and supporters. It is also probable that their expenditure was less than that of the Taifa kings. Ibn Tāshfīn himself seems to have maintained a fairly simple lifestyle and was content to give away windfalls, like the treasure confiscated from ʿAbd Allāh, to his followers. Ibn Tāshfīn recruited a small number of slave-soldiers and Andalusi horsemen who formed his *ḥashm*, but apart from these the vast majority of the Almoravid troops were Berber tribesmen. It is most unlikely that the Lamtūna and other Saharan nomads were paid cash salaries in the early stages of the movement. Later, modest salaries were paid: the anonymous *Ḥulūl al-Mawshīya*, commenting on the uncorrupted Saharan austerity of their troops, notes, 'No horseman was paid more than five dinars per month along with his expenses and the fodder for his horse', but adds that anyone who distinguished himself would be given a place (*mawḍiʿ*) whose revenues he could use.[30] Many of those who joined the Almoravid armies against the Christians were unpaid volunteers, choosing to make their contribution to the *jihād*. It was clearly felt that Almoravid troops lived simply. In addition to savings on military salaries, of course, the refusal of the Almoravids to pay parias must have helped to reduce expenditure. This fairly basic fiscal system could function adequately when Almoravid territory was expanding and there was still booty to be had. It seems likely, however, that it could not sustain the strains of defensive warfare and the later days of the Almoravid regime saw the introduction of some of the very fiscal abuses they had come to eradicate.

By the time Yūsuf b. Tāshfīn died, on the first day of the Muslim year 500 (2 September 1106), the Almoravids controlled Morocco and all of al-Andalus apart from the Kingdom of Zaragoza. Little military force had been required to do this and the Almoravids were swept to power on a wave of Muslim popular opinion. Apart from the reoccupation of Valencia in 1102, however, they had not

30. Anon, *Al-Ḥulūl al-Mawshīya*, ed. I.S. Allouche (Rabat, 1936), p. 67.

succeeded in winning back any of the lands lost to the Christians in the previous century and Toledo and the middle Tagus valley remained firmly under Castilian control.

The reign of ʿAlī b. Yūsuf b. Tāshfīn: the years of victory, 1106–17

There was no widespread disagreement about the succession, Ibn Tāshfīn having already secured the oath of allegiance to his son ʿAlī.[31] ʿAlī was now in his early twenties, having been born in Ceuta in 477/1084; his mother was a slave girl of Christian origin. He came from an urban background and there is no evidence that he ever lived the desert life or visited the Saharan homelands of his ancestors. His character is difficult to assess. He was certainly pious and generous, even easy-going, but he seems to have lacked his father's energy. As far as the Andalusis were concerned he was essentially an absentee monarch. In his reign of 37 years he visited al-Andalus only four times, in 1107 to organise the administration, for the *jihād* in the summers of 1109 and 1117, and to settle the disturbances in Cordoba in 1121. He did not visit al-Andalus at all in the last 21 years of his rule. Although he left some capable subordinates, real power remained in Marrakesh and after 1120 the Almoravid ruler became more and more preoccupied with Moroccan affairs as the Almohad threat grew.

ʿAlī's rule in al-Andalus can conveniently be divided into two halves. Between his accession in 1106 and the expedition to Coimbra in 1117, the Almoravid state remained stable and generally on the offensive. ʿAlī entrusted authority in al-Andalus to his brother Tamīm, who established himself in Granada which became the effective capital. Two veteran Almoravid commanders, close colleagues of his father's, held important commands in the west and east, Sīr b. Abī Bakr in Seville and Muḥammad b. al-Ḥājj in Valencia and, after its conquest in 1110, Zaragoza, and it was on these men that the conduct of the *jihād* largely rested.

The first main offensive was launched in the summer of 501/1108.[32] It was co-ordinated by Tamīm who summoned the troops of

31. For the best general account of ʿAlī's reign see Bosch Vila, *Los Almoravides*, pp. 173–251.

32. This campaign is thoroughly discussed in Huici Miranda, *Las Grandes Batallas*, pp. 103–34.

his brother, Muḥammad b. Ā'isha, from Murcia and Ibn Abī Rang, the governor of Cordoba. The objective was the Christian-held fortress of Ucles, the eastern plains of the old Taifa of Toledo, scene of campaigning in the last years of Ibn Tāshfīn. The small town of Ucles was soon taken but the ridge-top fortress held out, and news soon came that Alfonso VI was sending a relieving army under the command of the veteran Alvar Fañez. On 29 May the two armies met to the south-east of the castle. The Christians were decisively defeated and many of their leaders killed, including the young Sancho, only son and heir of Alfonso VI. The victory demonstrated the military effectiveness of the Almoravid field army, but its aftermath also illustrated its weaknesses. Tamīm immediately retired to Granada with his booty and had his secretary compose a grandiloquent letter of triumph to his brother in Marrakesh. Despite the victory, the army at Ucles was unable to reduce the castle and only succeeded in taking it by pretending to withdraw and surprising the garrison when they emerged. The fall of Ucles was followed by the abandonment by the Christians of Cuenca and Huete, effectively leaving the way open to Toledo.

The next summer, 'Alī sought to capitalise on this victory by attacking Toledo. He was certainly helped by the death of Alfonso VI at the end of June 1109 which left the Castilians preoccupied with the question of the succession. On 14 August his men stormed the fortifications of Talavera, on the Tagus to the east of Toledo. He then moved on to the city itself, the only Taifa capital to have fallen permanently to the Christians and a major insult to the prestige of Islam. The country to north and south was ravaged and the city invested for a month, but the garrison, led by Alvar Fañez, held out. The Almoravid army was unable to breach the defences of this superb natural fortress, and in the end retired. Once again their inability in siege warfare was glaringly apparent.

Zaragoza was the only Taifa kingdom to have survived Ibn Tāshfīn's take-over and there is some evidence that he intended it to remain as a bulwark against the Christians. Despite the competence of the ruler, al-Musta'īn, and his prompt submission to the Almoravids, it suffered from the same internal contradictions as the other Taifa states. The rulers were forced to pay parias to the Christian monarchs and this in turn left them vulnerable to the accusations of their subjects. A powerful pro-Almoravid party grew up in the city and al-Musta'īn felt obliged to lead an expedition against the Christians in 1110 to show his good faith. It was not a success and he was killed at Valtierra. His son 'Abd al-Malik, who took the title of 'Imād al-Dīn, was never really able to establish himself and was forced to flee the city. On 30 May Almoravid troops under Ibn al-Ḥājj encountered little resistance when they entered and put an end to the last of the Taifa states.

Offensive expeditions continued in west and east: Sīr b. Abī Bakr led an expedition in 1111 which secured the Tagus frontier in Portugal with the occupation of Lisbon and Santarem, and in 1112 Ibn al-Ḥājj used his new base in Zaragoza to raid north of the city of Huesca, recently taken by the Aragonese. It was the last time a Muslim army was ever to reach the foothills of the Pyrenees. In 1114 a large-scale expedition was undertaken against Catalonia by Ibn al-Ḥājj and Ibn Ā'isha of Valencia. The Almoravid armies ravaged the countryside and acquired considerable booty, but they were ambushed on their return and both commanders were killed. It was a serious loss of prestige and of two senior and effective generals.

The Almoravids were not defeated yet, however, and the next year the new governor of Zaragoza, 'Alī's cousin Abū Bakr b. Ibrāhīm b. Tīfilwīt, laid siege to Barcelona for twenty days before being forced to abandon it with the return of Count Ramon Berengar III from Majorca. In the same year the Balearic Islands were taken by an Almoravid fleet. They had been temporarily taken by the Catalans and Pisans on the death of the last of the local rulers, Mubāshir al-Dawla, originally a client of the Taifa ruler of Denia. Ironically, this final Almoravid conquest was also to prove to be their last refuge, when they were swept from the mainland of the Iberian peninsula by the Almohads. Finally, in 1117 'Alī himself led an expedition in the west which crossed the Tagus and took Coimbra. However, the city was abandoned after a few days and the expedition shows, not Almoravid power, but the fact that their offensive capacity was rapidly waning.

The structure of Almoravid government in al-Andalus

If the history of the Almoravids seems to be largely military, this very much reflects their role in al-Andalus. The chronicles on which we depend for our understanding of this period are largely concerned with military affairs and it is very difficult to discover much about the general impact of the Almoravids on Andalucian life and society. We do, however, have two sources which give a different point of view. One of these is the treatise by Ibn 'Abdūn.[33] The author, about whom nothing is known, was writing in Seville in Almoravid times, though unfortunately we cannot be more precise than that. His work is intended to be a manual on *ḥisba*, that is to say the ordering and regulation of the markets and other urban offices in the city. In this book he gives a considerable amount of information about the day-to-day running of a large Andalucian town in Almoravid times. The second, much more extensive, source is *Al-Mi'yar* of al-Wansharīsī.[34] Wansharīsī's work is a collection of the *fatwā*s or religious decisions made by respected *qāḍī*s on difficult cases. Most of these are concerned with fairly small-scale cases of personal property or commercial law, but like Ibn 'Abdūn's book, al-Wansharīsī's *Mi'yar* does provide interesting details of relations between rulers and ruled at this period.

It is impossible to tell how many Lamtūna and other Berber supporters of the Almoravids actually settled in al-Andalus. Estimates of their numbers at the battle of Zallāqa vary wildly, but may have lain between the 12,000 suggested by Ibn Kardabūs and the 20,000 of 'Abd al-Wāḥid al-Marrākushī. In 495/1101–2 Ibn Tāshfīn instructed his son to maintain (*tarakab*) 17,000 horsemen in al-Andalus: 4,000 in Seville, 1,000 in Cordoba, 1,000 in Granada, 4,000 in the Levante and the remainder (7,000) distributed along the frontiers. This accords well with the 4,000 troops Ibn Tāshfīn despatched to the Levante at the time of the siege of Aledo.[35] It is true these numbers refer to horsemen and there may have been large numbers of foot soldiers to accompany them, but if so, their presence has passed unremarked by the sources. These are not large numbers in themselves. Furthermore, there is no evidence of tribal immigration or of large-scale settlement. At the time of the anti-Almoravid movements in the 1140s, small numbers of identifiable Almoravids in provincial towns were hunted down and killed, implying a dispersed settlement and the preservation of a separate identity. The Almoravid presence was essentially military and essentially urban.

33. Ibn 'Abdūn, *Risāla fi qaḍā wa'l-ḥisba*, published in *Trois Traites de Hisba* (Cairo, 1955) but most conveniently accessible in the French translation by E. Lévi-Provençal, *Seville Musulmane* (Paris, 1947).

34. Al-Wansharīsī, *Al-Mi'yar al-mughrib wa'l-jāmi' al-mu'rib 'an fatāwā ahl Ifrīqīya wa'l-Andalus wa'l-Maghrib.* There is a twelve-volume lithograph edition made in Fes in 1314–15 A.H. I have used the discussion in Lagardère, *Le Vendredi de Zallāqa*, pp. 127–63.

35. See *Ḥulūl al-Mawshīya*, p. 57; Lagardère, *Le Vendredi de Zallāqa*, p. 44.

The ruling elite of Almoravid al-Andalus were drawn from a very restricted group. They held offices as governors of important towns, with Granada, Seville and al-Sharq being the most important. In al-Andalus, many of the most important positions were held by members of Ibn Tāshfīn's extended family, descendants of his great-grandfather, Turgūt b. Wartasin. Apart from the descendants of Ibn Tāshfīn himself, these formed a number of sub-dynasties, like the Banū Ḥājj and the Banū Mazdalī who supplied important military leaders for several generations.[36] It is perhaps a reflection of the importance of matrilineal kinship among the Berbers that some of the sub-dynasties took the name of their female ancestors, like the Banū Ā'isha (one of Ibn Tāshfīn's wives) and the Banū Fāṭima, descended from Sīr b. Abī Bakr's daughter.

Among the most famous of these kinsmen of Ibn Tāshfīn were Mazdalī b. Tilankan, Sīr b. Abī Bakr and Muḥammad b. al-Ḥājj. Mazdalī appears in 1073 taking Salé and Tlemcen in 1076. He seems to have been valued for his negotiating skills and it was he who persuaded Abū Bakr's son Ibrāhīm not to claim his father's rights in 1076. After the invasion of al-Andalus, he was made governor of Cordoba in 1091. In 1102 he was sent back to Tlemcen to resolve a frontier dispute by diplomacy and in 1106 it was again he who dissuaded Yaḥyā b. Abī Bakr, then governor of Fes, from challenging the rights of 'Alī b. Yūsuf to the throne. In 1111 he was appointed governor of Granada and spent the rest of his career in al-Andalus, leading expeditions against the Castilians until his death in battle in 1115. Several of his sons succeeded him in high office in al-Andalus: Muḥammad was governor of Cordoba in 1115 when he was killed in battle by the Castilians and Yaḥyā was the last Muslim governor of Zaragoza, where he died in 1118. Other sons supported the Almoravids against the Almohads in Morocco and Abū Bakr b. Mazdalī was governor of Tlemcen at the final débâcle of the Almoravid cause in 1142/3.

Sīr b. Abī Bakr, Ibn Tāshfīn's nephew and brother-in-law, appears as governor of Meknes in 1077/8 and was one of the leading Muslim generals at the battle of Zallāqa in 1086. In 1091 he took Seville and in 1094 Badajoz and he continued as governor, leading both defensive and offensive wars against the Christians in the western part of al-Andalus until his death from natural causes at Seville in 1113. His son Yaḥyā briefly succeeded him in Seville, but the family tradition was continued by Muḥammad, son of his

36. See the discussion in Lagardère, *Les Almoravides*, pp. 167–80.

daughter Fāṭima. Muḥammad b. Fāṭima was active in the retaking of Valencia in 1102 and was later governor there. In 1108 he was one of the generals at the Muslim victory of Ucles. Apart from a spell as governor of Fes in 1111–15 he remained in al-Andalus, dying in 1117/18 as governor of Seville.

Muḥammad b. al-Ḥājj took Cordoba for the Almoravids in 1091 and was afterwards governor of Granada. His brother ʿAlī was killed in 1103 fighting the Castilians near Talavera. In 1106, as governor of Cordoba, he refused to accept the accession of the young ʿAlī b. Yūsuf b. Tāshfīn, but he attracted no support and continued to serve the new sovereign until 1115 when, as governor of Zaragoza and Valencia, he was killed in battle with the Christians.

Similar career patterns can be found in other branches of the family. Almoravid government remained family government. Very few outsiders were assimilated into the elite. Not only were Andalusi Muslims completely excluded from military power, but even among the Berbers, power was concentrated in the hands of the Lamtūna chiefs, with a few from the other tribes of the deep desert, Massūfa and Guddāla. Other Ṣanhāja tribes like the Lamṭa and Gazzūla of the southern Atlas were largely excluded, as were other major tribal groups like the Zanāta and Maṣmūda who were allowed to provide soldiers but not generals.[37] This concentration of power persisted right to the end of the Almoravid state. As noted before, this made the leadership remarkably homogeneous but also very restricted. This became especially apparent as the generation of conquerors died off, Sīr b. Abī Bakr in 1113, Mazdalī and Muḥammad b. al-Ḥājj in 1115, leaving serious gaps in the leadership.

The Almoravid governors did not attract local support and they remained very separate from the bulk of the Andalusi population: the people of Cordoba, for example, did not support Ibn al-Ḥājj in 1106 when he stood out against the accession of ʿAlī b. Yūsuf. To see how the Andalusis regarded the Almoravids in their midst, it is instructive to turn to Ibn ʿAbdūn, who discusses the problems the presence of these outsiders could cause:

> No-one should wear the veil apart from the Ṣanhāja or Lamtūna or Lamṭī. The *ḥashm* [mercenary soldiers] or *ʿabīd* [slave soldiers] and others who do not need to be veiled do wear it among the people to terrorise them and commit all kinds of crimes because of the veil and the *sulṭān* [authorities] treat them leniently [? – text is corrupt here] but they are unruly. By this veiling, Almoravids who deserve

37. See the table in ibid., pp. 190–1.

> honour or respect or who have complaints which need to be seen to can be distinguished. If the *'abīd* and *ḥashm* are veiled it changes their appearance and one tends to treat them as people of a higher social status and treat them with honour and consideration which they do not deserve. No-one should go about armed in the city for that is an invitation to violence, especially with the Berbers who are a race who will kill or wound if they are annoyed.[38]

For Ibn 'Abdūn in the early twelfth century, the Almoravids are an alien minority in the Andalucian city, veiled and separate, to be treated with respect but bringing with them some dubious hangers-on. But precisely because they were an alien military presence, the local civilian elite enjoyed a wide measure of power and influence. Just as in the Near East the coming of the Turks between the tenth and twelfth centuries led to a flourishing of the urban patriciates of such cities as Damascus and Aleppo, so in al-Andalus the foreignness and inexperience of the Berbers meant that leaders of prominent local families could expand the scope of their activities.

In many respects, the government of an Andalucian city under the Almoravids was a partnership between the Almoravid military governor and the Andalucian *qāḍī*.[39] There were different ranks of *qāḍī*s for important and less important places, and specialist *qāḍī*s dealing with such topics as marriage, but the most important were the three *quḍāt al-jamā'at*. Just as al-Andalus was divided into three main military commands, west, centre and east under the Almoravids, so it was divided into three main judicial areas under the supervision of *qāḍī*s based at Seville, Cordoba and Murcia. *Qāḍī*s like Abū'l-Qāsim b. Ward of Granada (d. 1136), Abū'l-Walīd b. Rushd (grandfather of the philosopher Averroes) of Cordoba (d. 1126) and Abū Bakr b. al-'Arabī of Seville (d. 1148), all claiming Arab descent, were among the most powerful and influential men of their time. On occasion they played an important political role as intermediaries between the people and the Almoravids: when the people of Cordoba rose against the Almoravid governor in 1120, it was Ibn Rushd who negotiated a peaceful settlement; when the governor of Seville, 'Umar b. al-Ḥājj al-Lamtūnī, was killed by the forces of Alfonso VII outside the city walls, it was the *qāḍī* Muḥammad b. Asbagh who summoned help.

38. Ibn 'Abdūn, trans. Lévi-Provençal, pp. 61–3.

39. The role and succession of the *qāḍī*s is discussed in detail in Lagardère, *Le Vendredi de Zallāqa*, pp. 127–84. For the '*ulama*' in this period see also D. Urvoy, *Le Monde des ulemas andalous du Ve/XIe au VIIe/XIIIe siècles: étude sociologique* (Geneva, 1978).

In everyday administration, the *qāḍī* headed his own hierarchy. According to Ibn 'Abdūn, these included a lesser judge called the *ḥākim* and the *muḥtaṣib,* who supervised the markets and was the *qāḍī*'s right-hand man. All these officials should be Andalusis. It was the *qāḍī* who was in charge of the mosque and it was he, not the Almoravid governor (*ra'īs*), who led the prayers on Friday. He also controlled the *bayt māl al-muslimīn,* the treasury kept in the mosque for pious purposes. Ibn 'Abdūn was keen that his role should extend to other areas of government: the tax collectors (*kharrā*s) were to be lectured on their duties and obligations, and he describes the circumstances in which money can be given to the governor from the *bayt māl al-muslimīn* (only for projects which benefit the community, notably defence against the Christians).[40] He explains how the governor's *wazīr* should visit the *qāḍī* at least twice a day to be advised and how he should talk over ideas with the *qāḍī* before he presents them to his master. Ibn 'Abdūn, who is clearly making a political point here, shows us a *qāḍī* who exercises wide-ranging control over the everyday affairs of city and country and is closely involved in decision-making. He also shows how much administration was conducted by Andalusis.

The reign of 'Alī b. Yūsuf b. Tāshfīn: the years of decline, 1118–42

Almoravid rule in al-Andalus lasted barely a generation; there must have been many Andalusis, like the religious leader Abū Bakr b. al-'Arabī (1076–1148), who were born before it began and died after it was over. Like other nomad empires, it began to decline as soon as expansion had come to an end. From 1118 onwards, a new generation of Christian leaders from new and expanding kingdoms began to push their frontiers southwards at the expense of the faltering Almoravid government.

Despite the defeats at Zallāqa in 1086 and Ucles in 1108, Alfonso VI of Leon-Castile remained the most important leader in Christian Spain. However, after his death his kingdom was brought to the brink of collapse, not by Almoravid invasion but by his failure to leave a male heir to succeed him. After the death of his only son Sancho at Ucles, his daughter Urraca became his heir. Urraca had been married to Raymond of Burgundy, but he had died, leaving

40. Ibn 'Abdūn, trans. Lévi-Provençal, pp. 21–3.

her a widow with a young son called Alfonso, who later became Alfonso VII. Anxious to secure his daughter's protection in this male-dominated world, Alfonso VI married her to Alfonso I, ruler, since 1104, of the small upland kingdom of Aragon.

Urraca duly succeeded on her father's death in 1109, but the marriage was a failure and bitter hostility soon developed between Alfonso and his Aragonese supporters and the Castilians which led to desultory warfare. In 1126 Urraca died and her son Alfonso VII became King of Leon-Castile. Though he gradually restored the power of the monarchy, the weakness and divisions in the large kingdom allowed others to seize the political initiative.

Alfonso I of Aragon is known to history as 'the Battler', and he soon showed his determination to expand his small kingdom from its mountain fastnesses to the rich plains of the Ebro. In 1118 he seized Zaragoza and most of the central Ebro lands and by 1120 he had pushed on to take Calatayud and Daroca in the hills south of the river, so effectively doubling the size of his kingdom and taking possession of a major city. For the rest of his reign until his death in 1134, Alfonso devoted himself to maintaining his new conquests and taking advantage of Almoravid weakness. When he died, Aragon had established itself as one of the most important political units in the Iberian peninsula. The union of Aragon with the counties of Catalonia in 1137 meant the construction of a major Christian power bloc in the eastern half of the peninsula.

The weakness of Leon-Castile after 1109 allowed similar growth in the west. In 1096 another immigrant from Burgundy, Count Henry, had been given the hand of Teresa, Afonso VI's illegitimate daughter, in marriage and with it the county of Portugal. After Henry's death in 1112, Teresa continued to rule in her own right until in 1128 she was driven out by her son Afonso who became Count of Portugal. He was to rule, as Count and then King, until 1185 and effectively established Portugal as an independent political power. In the 1140s he assumed the title of King and this was gradually recognised by his Spanish neighbours and the papacy. Like his older contemporary, Alfonso of Aragon, Afonso of Portugal was determined to establish the viability of his kingdom by expanding it south at the expense of the Muslims. In this he was aided by Crusaders from northern Europe, on their way to the Holy Land, who helped him take Lisbon in 1147.

Al-Andalus was now faced not by one kingdom in the north but by three. Despite their rivalries, the rulers of the three kingdoms, Portugal, Leon-Castile and Aragon, were all determined to profit from Muslim weakness, if only to gain the resources to defend themselves successfully against their Christian neighbours. These were to be testing times for the Almoravid government.

According to the *Ḥulūl al-Mawshīya*, probably based on the insights of the Almoravid bureaucrat Ibn al-Ṣayrafī, Yūsuf b. Tāshfīn, on his deathbed in 1106, gave his son ʿAlī three pieces of advice: the first was not to aggravate the people of the Atlas Mountains and other Maṣmūda tribesmen, the second was to make a truce with the Banū Hūd (of Zaragoza) and keep them as a bulwark against the Christians, and the third was to favour and honour the people of Cordoba.[41] The unspoken implication is that ʿAlī did none of these and disaster ensued.

It was the second of these, the maintenance of the independence of Zaragoza, that caused the first major reverse.[42] Almoravid rule had only been established here in 1110 and it seems that the garrison, if it existed at all, was very small. Furthermore, the refusal of the Almoravids to pay pariaṣ meant that the King of Aragon, Alfonso the Battler (1104–34), no longer had any interest in preserving the city as in Muslim hands.[43] Early in 1118 ʿAbd Allāh b. Mazdalī, the governor, died and was not replaced and Alfonso saw his opportunity: the siege began on 22 May and continued through the summer and autumn. On 3 December the *qāḍī*, Thābit b. ʿAbd Allāh, wrote to Tamīm b. Yūsuf b. Tāshfīn in Valencia desperate for help, but only a small detachment was sent and on 18 December the city was obliged to surrender. ʿAlī b. Yūsuf, then in Cordoba, sent a major expedition to recover the lost lands made up of both Almoravids and Andalusi *muṭṭawiʿa* (volunteers), but they were decisively defeated at Cutanda in the summer of 1120, leaving many dead including ʿAbd Allāh b. al-Farrāʾ, the famous and learned *qāḍī* of Almeria. Calatayud fell soon after, in 1121, and Daroca in 1122. As Yūsuf's testament to his son had warned, the Almoravid takeover of Zaragoza led to direct attacks on Almoravid lands.

The loss of Zaragoza may have indirectly precipitated the next problem, the third of which Ibn Tāshfīn's testament had warned,

41. Quoted in *Ḥulūl al-Mawshīya*, p. 67.

42. For the conquest of Zaragoza see J.M. Lacarra, 'La conquista de Zaragoza por Alfonso I', *Al-Andalus* xii (1947), 65–96; and for a general account of the fall of Zaragoza and the other Muslim towns in the Ebro valley see D. Lomax, *The Reconquest of Spain* (London, 1978), pp. 80–6.

43. For recent accounts of the fall of Zaragoza see M.J. Viguera Molins, *Aragon Musulman* (Zaragoza, 1981), pp. 225–37, and C. Stalls, *Possessing the Land: Aragon's expansion into Islam's Ebro Frontier under Alfonso the Battler, 1104–1134* (Leiden, 1995), pp. 24–40.

namely the uprising of the people of Cordoba against the Almoravids in March 1121. Ibn al-Athīr gives us the fullest account:

> The Amīr al-Muslimīn ['Alī b. Yūsuf] had appointed as governor [of Cordoba] Abū Bakr Yaḥyā b. Rawād. On the Day of Sacrifice when the people had come out to enjoy themselves one of the *'abīd* [the slave soldiers Ibn 'Abdūn warned against] grabbed hold of a woman. She cried out to the Muslims for help and they came to her aid. A serious fight developed between the *'abīd* and the people of the town which lasted the whole day. There was open warfare until night came and the two sides separated. When the news reached the Amir Abū Bakr he gathered the *faqīh*s and the principal citizens [*a'yān*] who said, 'You should execute one of the *'abīd* who began the disturbance', but he refused and became angry. The next morning he prepared the arms and equipment to fight the people of the town so the *fuqahā*, the principal citizens and the young men of the town mounted and they fought him and forced him to flee. Then they laid siege to the palace and stormed it and he fled from them after a severe mauling. They then looted the palace and burned the houses of the Almoravids, pillaged their property and drove them from the town in disarray.
>
> When the news reached the Amīr al-Muslimīn, he was seriously concerned so he collected the troops of Ṣanhāja, Zanāta, the Berbers and others and formed them into a great army. He then crossed to al-Andalus in the year 515 [22 March 1121–11 March 1122] to attack them and laid siege to the city. The inhabitants fought him as people do when they are defending their lives, their families and their property. When the Amīr al-Muslimīn saw how fierce the resistance was, he sent envoys to them and they sought peace which he granted on condition that they compensated the Almoravids for the property they had stolen. Then the capital quietened down and the fighting stopped.[44]

The whole episode sheds interesting light on Almoravid rule. The Almoravids appear as a small number living in the palace compound. They could not defeat the people nor, apparently, were there sufficient Almoravid forces elsewhere in al-Andalus to do so; reinforcements had to be brought from Morocco. Clearly the uprising was the expression of widespread discontent and it may well have been linked to the fall of Zaragoza: the Almoravids were only acceptable as defenders of Islam and if they could not do that, they had no role. Also notable is the way in which all sections of

44. Ibn al-Athīr, *Al-Kāmil fī'l-Ta'rīkh*, ed. C.J. Tornberg (12 vols, Leiden, 1853–67), vol. x, p. 558.

the Cordovan population, including the *fuqahā*, joined in, though we know from other sources that the *qāḍī*, Abū'l-Walīd b. Rushd, played an important part in negotiating the settlement.

The loss of Zaragoza and the rebellion in Cordoba were damaging to Almoravid prestige but by no means fatal. It was the first of the dangers Ibn Tāshfīn had warned of, the Maṣmūda of the Atlas Mountains, which was to destroy the Almoravid empire.[45] This is not the place to discuss the origins of the Almohad movement[46] but to note its effects on the Almoravids. It was in 1120 that Muḥammad b. Tūmart returned to his native Morocco from the East and began preaching an interpretation of Islam at odds with the formalism of the Almoravids. Having failed to win support at Marrakesh he retired to the High Atlas, home to the Maṣmūda tribes from whom he himself originated. The Maṣmūda accepted his teaching and his leadership against the Ṣanhāja of the plains. For the next ten years Ibn Tūmart consolidated his hold over the mountains to the south and west of Marrakesh. This brought him into conflict with the Almoravid governor of Sūs, Abū Bakr b. Muḥammad al-Lamtūnī. In 1124 he established his base at Tīnmal, near enough Marrakesh to be a threat to the Almoravid capital but protected by steep mountains from attacks by the plainsmen.

'Alī b. Yūsuf sent numerous expeditions against them, but the Almoravid troops seem to have found it impossible to operate effectively in the high mountains and their armies were regularly ambushed and defeated. From 1125 they adopted a largely defensive strategy, building a series of fortresses, like the one at Tāsgīmūt whose impressive remains still exist, south of Marrakesh along the edge of the plains on which their capital stood. It was unfortunate for 'Alī b. Yūsuf that his capital lay so close to the mountains, but no attempt seems to have been made to move to a less exposed situation. By 1130 the Almohads felt strong enough to challenge the Almoravids on the plains and attacked Marrakesh itself. The campaign was not a success: 'Alī b. Yūsuf summoned troops from the Gharb of Morocco and Sijilmāssa, and the besieging army was defeated outside the walls of the city and forced to retire. Ibn Tūmart died a few months later at Tīnmal.

This setback damaged the Almohad movement less than might have been thought. 'Abd al-Mu'min had already been acknowledged as heir two years before and he took over command. The offensive

45. For the early history of the Almohad movement see below, pp. 196–200.
46. See below, pp. 196–200.

continued, though the Almohads were careful to keep to the shelter of the mountains for the time being. In 1132 the fortress of Tāsgīmūt fell to them and by 1140 they had completely taken over Sūs and soon after Sijilmāssa and Tāfīlālt.

'Ali b. Yūsuf called increasingly on the resources of al-Andalus to support his resistance to the Almohads. From 1125 the network of fortifications around Marrakesh was constructed by al-Falākī, said to have been a highway robber from al-Andalus reprieved by 'Alī b. Yūsuf and put to work. The victory of 1130 was brought about by one 'Abd Allāh b. Hamshak with around 100 horsemen from the frontier regions of al-Andalus. From 1132 'Alī became increasingly dependent on a Catalan mercenary leader, Reverter, a one-time viscount of Barcelona, who with his men formed the elite corps of the Almoravid army. In 1138 'Alī was forced to summon his son and eventual successor Tāshfīn from across the Straits. Tāshfīn had been a successful governor of al-Andalus since 1126 and had done much to stabilise the Almoravid position there; his departure was a serious blow.

After 1140 the Almoravid position in Morocco crumbled rapidly with the defection of many tribes, including the northern Ṣanhāja, to the new movement. Nonetheless, Tāshfīn and Reverter conducted a vigorous defence of the plains of central Morocco around Fes. The old Amīr al-Muslimīn, 'Alī b. Yūsuf, died in January 1143. He had not played any active role in the defence of his realm since the siege of Marrakesh in 1130 and he does not seem to have left the capital. His son Tāshfīn, who succeeded him, was much more effective, but the position was past saving.[47] The Almoravid cause was seriously weakened by divisions within their army: under the stress of defeat, old resentments between the Lamtūna and other tribes surfaced once more. A further blow was struck when Reverter was killed, probably in May or June 1144. A hard year of fighting ensued in the Tlemcen area as Tāshfīn sought allies among the Ṣanhāja of Algeria, but to no avail. Tāshfīn himself was killed in March 1145 without ever having been able to establish himself in Marrakesh. His shadowy successors could not prevent the Almohads, now finally strong enough to move into the plains, from taking Fes and the plains of western Morocco over the next two years. In March 1147 they finally stormed Marrakesh itself, putting an end to Almoravid rule with a systematic massacre. The fall of Tangier and Ceuta in May–June 1148 completed their conquest of Morocco.

47. Tāshfīn's reign is described in Bosch Vila, *Los Almoravides*, pp. 255–6.

The continuing preoccupation of ʻAli b. Yūsuf with the Almohad threat meant that the Almoravids of al-Andalus had more or less to fend for themselves. Until 1126 the overall commander was ʻAlī's brother Abū Ṭāhir Tamīm, but he was dismissed after the Almoravids suffered a major humiliation. In September 1125 Alfonso I of Aragon, possibly on the invitation of Mozarab Christians suffering under Almoravid rule, marched south with an army of 4,000 knights. He travelled down the east coast, bypassing the cities but passing through the countryside unopposed, until he reached Guadix in December. His main objective seems to have been Granada, but he found this too well fortified so he ravaged the Cordoba countryside. In March 1126 he defeated the army Tamīm finally sent against him at Arinzul near Lucena. Then he went to Motril on the south coast where he symbolically went fishing before returning to his homeland. A further humiliation for the Almoravid forces occurred in 1129 when Alfonso I raided deep into Valencia and defeated a large army, which included many black slaves, led by the governor of Seville, ʻAlī b. Majjuz, probably at Cullera or Alcala near Alcira.[48]

Alfonso's expedition to Granada had raised grave questions about the role of the Mozarabs in the eyes of many Muslims. We know that the status of the Jews declined under Almoravid rule. They no longer held the important offices they had under the Taifa kings and large sums were sometimes quite arbitrarily extracted from them. It is not clear that the status of the Mozarabs suffered to the same extent, since few of them had held high office. Whether they invited Alfonso I to al-Andalus is not clear, but many Muslims believed that they had. Furthermore, many Mozarabs joined his expedition and returned to the north when he did, rightly fearing reprisals. In the aftermath the *qāḍī*, Abū'l-Walīd b. Rushd, held that the Mozarabs had broken the pact they had with the Muslims by which they enjoyed freedom of worship and property. Numbers of them were deported to Morocco and the possessions of their churches and monasteries deemed forfeit to the state.[49] Like most such expulsions, this may have appeased the suspicions of the dominant group, but it must have seriously diminished the resource base of the Almoravid state, especially as the *jizya* on the protected peoples was one of the few taxes which had indisputable Quranic sanction.

48. These events are discussed in detail in Guichard, *Musulmans de Valence*, pp. 87–92. See also Stalls, *Possessing the Land*, pp. 51–2.
49. Lagardère, *Le Vendredi de Zallāqa*, pp. 135–7.

In the aftermath of the débâcles at Granada and Alcala, the Almoravid high command in al-Andalus was completely restructured. 'Alī b. Yūsuf despatched his dynamic and effective son Tāshfīn as governor of Granada and Almeria in 1129. In 1131 Cordoba was added to his command and he became the effective viceroy of al-Andalus until 1138, when he was recalled to Morocco to take over as heir apparent and lead the struggle against the Almohads.

This period also sees the emergence of a new force among the Almoravids of al-Andalus, the Banū Ghānīya. Yaḥyā b. 'Alī b. Ghāniya was a member of the ruling house on his mother's side, she being a relative of Yūsuf b. Tāshfīn, while his father was a chief of the Massūfa tribe. It may have been this tribal following which enabled him to put new life into the Almoravid forces. The family first appears in 1126/7 when Yaḥyā's brother Muḥammad was governor of the Balearic Islands, which were to remain under the rule of the Banū Ghānīya until the Almohad conquest of 1203. Yaḥyā was governor of Murcia before 1133 when he was transferred to Valencia to help combat the threat from Aragon. In 1134 he led the Muslim forces at the battle of Fraga and in 1136 he and the governor of Fraga, Sa'd b. Mardanīsh, reconquered Mequinenza, so re-establishing the Muslim position on the lower Ebro. Yaḥyā seems to have stayed in the Levante until 1143 or 1144 when he was transferred to Seville to face the growing danger of the rebellion of Ibn Qasī in the Algarve.

For a decade this new command more or less kept the Christians at bay and scored some notable successes. In 1130 Tāshfīn took the castle of Aceca south of Toledo and deported many of the garrison to Morocco. However, the heartlands of al-Andalus were still vulnerable, as was shown in 1133 when the militia of Toledo reached the gates of Seville and killed the governor, Abū Ḥafṣ 'Umar b. 'Alī b. al-Ḥājj. Only a rapid response by Tāshfīn prevented further damage being done. In 1134 Tāshfīn was able to counter-attack with a successful raid against Christian forces in the Caceres area. In 1136/7 he defeated the Castilians near Alcazar de San Juan and went on to sack the castle at Escalona, so bringing Muslim forces north of the Tagus once more.

In the Levante, too, the 1130s saw successes for Muslim arms. In 1130 the governor of Valencia defeated an Aragonese army operating nearby and killed Gaston de Béarn, a hero of the First Crusade who had also been prominent at the siege of Zaragoza. His head was paraded in the streets of Granada, which perhaps went some way to erasing memories of the humiliation of 1125/6. More significant was the victory at Fraga in 1134 and the death of Alfonso I. When Zaragoza fell to the Christians in 1118, the area around Lleida in the valley of the Segre had remained in Muslim hands and paid parias to Barcelona to ensure its survival. Alfonso was determined to destroy this anomalous outpost. In the summer of 1134 he laid siege to the small town of Fraga whose inhabitants put up a vigorous resistance and appealed for help. Unlike Tamīm in 1118, Tāshfīn replied promptly and sent an army under the command of Yaḥyā b. Ghānīya. Alfonso seems to have been over-confident and was worsted in battle, while a sally by the garrison of Fraga destroyed his camp. The king himself died of wounds soon after.

In the 1140s, however, the position of the Almoravids deteriorated rapidly. The real problems were in Morocco where the Almohad offensive consumed the resources of the empire. In al-Andalus the combination of military failure and increasing taxation led to widespread discontent. After the defeat of the Valencian army in 1129, the Amir ʿAlī b. Yūsuf ordered one of his secretaries, Abū Marwān b. Abī Hisal, to write to them to show them how angry he was at their poor performance. This he did with more zeal than was prudent: 'Sons of a disgraceful mother. You fled like wild asses. How long will critics expose your shame and a single horseman drive you back? There should be sheep being milked in the harnesses of your horses. We will punish you so that you do not cover your faces with veils and drive you back to your desert and purify the peninsula of your filth.' Powerful stuff, and the chronicler ʿAbd al-Wāḥid al-Marrākushī, who reports the incident, says that this letter was very well known and that many Andalusis, unhappy with Almoravid rule, learned it by heart.[50]

The *Chronicle* of Alfonso VII has the Andalusis express similar sentiments. During the raid on Seville in 1133, the Andalusis (whom the writer calls Agareni) wrote to Sayf al-Dawla, the Hudid pretender then fighting with the Castilians, saying, 'Speak with the king of the Christians and with him free us from the hands of the Moabites [Almoravids]. We will give the Leonese king parias [*tributa regalia*] larger than our fathers gave to his fathers and we will serve

50. ʿAbd al-Wāḥid al-Marrākushī, *Al-Muʿjib*, ed. M.S. al-'Uryan (Cairo, 1949), p. 176; discussed in Guichard, *Musulmans de Valence*, i, p. 92, and Viguera Molins, *Los Reinos de Taifas*, p. 182.

you and you and your sons will reign over us.'[51] Of course both the Marrākushī, who worked for the Almohads, and the anonymous Castilian chronicler are partisan and may have exaggerated, but events were to show that anti-Almoravid feeling was indeed widespread in al-Andalus. This feeling was soon to break out in the open revolts which finally destroyed Almoravid rule in al-Andalus.

51. Anon, *Chronica Adefonsi imperatoris*, cap. 41.

CHAPTER EIGHT

The Second Taifas

The weakness of the Almoravid regime in al-Andalus meant that communities were forced to look elsewhere for political and military leadership.[1] Of the Almoravid governors, only Yaḥyā b. Ghānīya in Seville made a determined effort to uphold the authority of the regime, though he was forced to rely on an alliance with Alfonso VII of Leon-Castile. In 1148 he lost Seville to the Almohads and retired to Granada where he died in 1149; Almoravid resistance in Granada continued until 1155. After 1155 the Banū Ghānīya were still able to hold on to the Balearic Islands and make trouble for the new masters of al-Andalus. In some places there was active rebellion against the Almoravids and they were driven out: from Badajoz, for example, there survives the epitaph of one 'Ubayd Allāh b. Muḥammad al-Māridi, 'the martyr, killed unjustly by the Veiled Ones on 25 March 1145',[2] presumably during the struggles which led to their abandonment of the city. In other places the Almoravids departed peacefully, leaving the local people to make their own arrangements. Between about 1144 and 1147 a new generation of Taifas emerged. They were only short-lived and precarious but their story does allow us to see beneath the surface of Andalusi politics to glimpse some of the structures beneath. The rulers of these new Taifas came from three distinct groups, the *qāḍīs*, almost always belonging to local patrician families of Arab descent, Andalusi military leaders, most of whom had served

1. The best general account of this period remains F. Codera y Zaidin, *Decadencia y Desaparicion de los Almoravides en Espana* (Zaragoza, 1899). See also the wide-ranging discussion in P. Guichard, *Les Musulmans de Valence et la Reconquête* (2 vols, Damascus, 1990–91), i, pp. 101–24.
2. E. Lévi-Provençal, *Inscriptions Arabes d'Espagne* (Leiden/Paris, 1931), no. 45, pp. 56–7.

with the Almoravids in junior capacities, and alternative religious leaders.

The existence of these new Taifas was overshadowed and threatened by Christian territorial advances.[3] Alfonso VII of Leon-Castile was quick to take advantage of the collapse of Almoravid rule. Already in May 1146 he was in Cordoba and had obliged Ibn Ghānīya, the Almoravid governor, to accept his overlordship. In January 1147 he took Calatrava and embarked on a land and sea campaign against Almeria. The Almeria campaign of 1147 was remarkable for the cooperation between Alfonso, Ramon Berengar IV of Aragon-Catalonia and Sancho Ramirez IV of Navarre, and for the role of Genoese naval power. Christian cooperation on this scale had not been seen before and it boded ill for the survival of al-Andalus. Alfonso and Sancho Ramirez travelled overland through Andalucia, taking Andujar and Baeza en route. At Almeria they met up with Ramon Berengar and the Genoese. The Almoravid fleet had withdrawn and on 17 October the city was obliged to surrender and was entrusted to the Genoese. Almeria was retaken for the Muslims by the Almohads ten years later, but its fall showed how united Christian armies combined with Italian naval power were more than the Andalusis could resist.

The Christians made more permanent gains elsewhere. In March 1147 Afonso Enriquez of Portugal took Santarem on the Tagus in a surprise attack and on 24 October captured Lisbon with the help of Crusaders from Cologne, Flanders and England. Meanwhile the final Muslim outposts in Catalonia were reduced, Tortosa in 1148, Lleida and Fraga in 1149. Apart from Calatrava and Almeria, none of these cities was retaken by the Almohads, and in both east and west al-Andalus had lost for ever, in these years of confusion and division, valuable and strategic territories.

The first major challenge to Almoravid rule within al-Andalus came from an alternative religious leader in the Algarve.[4] The Almoravid government, and their allies among the *fuqahā* of al-Andalus, had tended to preach a severe and perhaps rather unimaginative view of Islam in which correct performance of ritual was more important than inner spiritual development. Many in

3. For a clear summary of the Christian advances see B. Reilly, *The Contest of Christian and Muslim Spain, 1031–1157* (London, 1992), pp. 211–15.

4. For the Sufis political movements of this time see V. Lagardère, 'La Tariqa et la Révolte des Muridin en 539H/1144 en Andalus', in *Revue de l'Occident Musulman et de la Mediterranée* 35 (1983–4), 157–70, and J. Dreher, 'L'Imamat d'Ibn Qasī à Mertola', in *Mélanges de l'Institut Dominicain d'Etudes Orientales* (1988), 195–210.

al-Andalus wished to go further than this and looked for leadership to a group of Sufi teachers, based mostly in Almeria, who encouraged their followers to seek a more intense and personal communication with God. Among the most important of these were Ibn Barrajān and Ibn al-ʿArīf. They in turn derived much of their inspiration from the writings and teachings of the great imam al-Ghazzālī, especially his book *Iḥyā' ʿUlūm al-Dīn.* So concerned were the Almoravids by the effect of this work that shortly after his accession in 1106, the Amir ʿAlī b. Yūsuf b. Tāshfīn, along with the *qāḍī* of Cordoba, Ibn Ḥamdīn, and the *fuqahā* of the city arranged a public burning of all the copies they could find. Both Ibn Barrajān and Ibn al-ʿArīf were summoned to Marrakesh by the orders of ʿAlī b. Yūsuf in 1141 and cross-examined. While Ibn Barrajān was thrown into prison, where he soon died, Ibn al-ʿArīf was allowed to return to Almeria where he also perished, poisoned, it is said, by an aubergine fed to him by the *qāḍī.* These incidents were made much of by Almohad propagandists, suggesting that Sufis and Sufism had become a major focus of anti-Almoravid feeling in al-Andalus.

Almeria was not the only centre of Sufi activity. In the Algarve one Abū'l-Qāsim Aḥmad b. al-Ḥusayn al-Qasī, a Christian convert from Silves, had founded a small Sufi order which attracted a number of followers, the Murīdūn (the disciples) including Muḥammad b.ʿUmar b. al-Mundhir, an esteemed correspondent of Ibn al-ʿArīf's. Sufis preached asceticism and withdrawal from the affairs of the world and it seems as if Ibn Qasī's movement followed this pattern until after the arrest and death of the masters of Almeria in 1141. Ibn Qasī then abandoned this quietist attitude, proclaimed himself Imam and raised his followers in open rebellion.

He was immediately supported by Ibn al-Mundhir, who took Silves, and Sīdray b. Wazīr, governor of Beja. Together Ibn al-Mundhir and Ibn Wazīr took the castle of Monchique, where they killed the Almoravid garrison. Mertola was taken by surprise by only 70 men on 12 August 1144 and Ibn Qasī made it his capital. Soon after the governor of Niebla, the Andalusi Yūsuf b. Aḥmad al-Biṭrūjī, went over to the Mūridūn and the way to Seville seemed to be open. Here, however, they came up against the energetic Yaḥyā b. ʿAlī b. Ghānīya who drove them back and would probably have conquered Silves if he had not had to deal with the rebellion of Ibn Ḥamdīn in Cordoba. This military reverse was followed by a split between Ibn al-Mundhir and Ibn Qasī on one side and Sīdray b. Wazīr on the other which divided the movement and led Ibn Qasī to appeal for help from the Almohads. In September 1145 he went to Marrakesh in person where the Almohad Caliph received him, like other Andalusi notables, with favour, and in the summer of 1146 he was back in the Algarve with Almohad support. However, it seems that he was unwilling to accept Almohad leadership and negotiated to hand over Silves to the Christians. Not surprisingly, this move was extremely unpopular with the townspeople and in August/September 1151 he was murdered in his palace while his colleague, Ibn al-Mundhir, handed the town over to the Almohads.

Under Almoravid rule, the *qāḍīs* had in some ways become the civil governors of their cities and it was natural that the people should look to them for leadership. In Malaga, Jaen, Granada, Valencia and Cordoba, the *qāḍīs* took charge. The fullest account of how this happened comes from Cordoba.[5] Here, as in many cities, there were two rival families contending for the post, the Banū Rushd and the Banū Ḥamdīn, but the actual appointment of *qāḍī* remained in the gift of the Almoravid ruler. In 1137/8 Ḥamdīn b. Muḥammad b. Ḥamdīn, who claimed descent from the Arab tribe of Taghlib and that his ancestors had entered al-Andalus in the following of Balj b. Bishr al-Qushayrī in 741, was deposed in favour of Abū'l-Qāsim b. Rushd. However, this seems to have been a period of some disorder in the city and the upper classes (*khāssa*) felt that the new *qāḍī* was too weak. They appealed to Ibn Ḥamdīn and Ibn Rushd was obliged to resign. 'Alī b. Yūsuf, the Almoravid ruler, was reluctant to be dictated to in this way and left the city without an official *qāḍī* for a year until in 1141/2 he allowed the Cordovans to choose and they elected Ibn Ḥamdīn. At the beginning of 1145 the Cordovans expelled the Almoravid governor and rejected Almoravid rule. In February the people of Cordoba, *khāssa* and *'āmma* alike, assembled in the mosque and took the oath of allegiance to Ibn Ḥamdīn, not just as *qāḍī* but as *ra'īs*, or secular head, of the city, taking over all the administrative functions previously exercised by the Almoravid governor. He took the titles of *Amīr al-Muslimīn* and *Nāṣir al-Din* and settled in the palace of the caliphs, looking set to follow the example of the 'Abbadids of Seville a century before and establish himself as a Taifa ruler. However, his moment of glory was short-lived and he was soon dispossessed by Ibn Ghānīya.

Similar events took place in Valencia.[6] By March 1145 anti-

5. Ibn al-Khaṭīb, *A'mal al-a'lām fī man buyi'a qabla 'l-iḥtilām min mulūk al-Islām*, ed. E. Lévi-Provençal (Beirut, 1956), pp. 290–2; Codera y Zaidin, *Decadencia y Desaparicion*, pp. 56–63; Guichard, *Musulmans de Valence*, pp. 107–8.
6. Guichard, *Musulmans de Valence*, pp. 110–12.

Almoravid feeling in the city was growing, especially among the Andalusi *jund* who seem to have been the only military force there. The Almoravid governor, ʿAbd Allāh b. Muḥammad b. Ghānīya, and the *qāḍī*, Marwān b. ʿAbd al-ʿAzīz, tried to establish calm. The *qāḍī* spoke to the people in the mosque, urging them to accept the Almoravids because of their great contribution to the *jihād*, but the tide of sentiment was flowing too strongly against them and Ibn ʿAbd al-ʿAzīz was pressured by popular opinion, and especially by the Andalusi military leader Ibn ʿIyāḍ, into accepting the office of *raʾīs*. However, he soon ran into financial difficulties and was unable to pay the *jund*, who deposed him in November 1145 and replaced him with Ibn ʿIyāḍ.

We know less about the rule of the *qāḍīs* in the other cities, but it probably followed much the same course. Despite the wave of popular support which brought them to power, none of them were able to pay a reliable armed force or to maintain their authority for any length of time. There is an interesting contrast here with events in towns in northern Italy in the late eleventh and twelfth centuries. Here too the system of imperial government collapsed, but the people looked to the *boni homines*, the leading citizens of the town, and, rather than entrusting political power to an individual, gave it to a group, a sworn association, bound by oaths to uphold the interests of the city. In Italy the power vacuum led to the emergence of the first communes and a period of urban self-government; in al-Andalus power passed to an individual who was soon replaced by the representatives of a new military power.

The figure of Ibn ʿIyāḍ introduces us to the third of the groups which assumed power in these confused years, the Andalusi military leaders. As the role of the *jund* in Valencia shows, some of these were powerful enough to take over from the Almoravids when they were forced out. We know little of the origins of Sīdray b. Wazīr in Beja or Abū'l-Ghamr b. ʿAzzūn in Ronda, but they were clearly minor officials in the Almoravid military hierarchy who established themselves as independent dynasts. In a somewhat similar position was ʿAbd Allāh b. Maymūn, who was in charge of the Almoravid fleet. The people of Almeria asked him to become their *raʾīs* but he refused, saying that he would defend them against any enemy who came by sea but that they should entrust the rule of the city to another.[7] It is interesting to note that all of these readily submitted to the Almohads and all three families remained as leaders of

7. Ibid., p. 114.

the Andalusis in the Almohad regime until the thirteenth century, so providing an important element of continuity between Almoravid and Almohad government.

Two other military adventurers of Andalusi origin played a larger part in the history of the period of transition between the two Berber regimes, Sayf al-Dawla b. Hūd, known as al-Mustanṣir, and Ibn Mardanīsh. Sayf al-Dawla was the son of the last Hūdid ruler of Zaragoza, deposed by the Almoravids in 1110.[8] He had been established by the Castilians in the castle of Rueda de Jalon on the western fringes of his old kingdom. He now saw his opportunity and, with the support of Alfonso VII, decided to try his luck in al-Andalus. His first attempt was at Cordoba, where, in obscure circumstances, he was able to seize power briefly from Ibn Ḥamdīn in March 1145 but was unable to maintain himself in the face of popular hostility. He next went to the Levante, where he was invited by the Andalusi commander Ibn ʿIyāḍ to take over in Valencia and Murcia in January 1146. He proclaimed himself *Amīr al-Mu'minīn* or Caliph and took the regnal title of al-Mustanṣir, probably hoping to unite all the Andalusi factions under his leadership. However, his moment of glory did not last long and on 5 February he was defeated and killed by the Christians near Albacete.

More successful was his eventual successor in the Levante, Ibn Mardanīsh.[9] The name Mardanīsh may be an Arabisation of the Castilian Martinez, implying a Christian origin, but the Arabic sources firmly call him al-Judhāmī,[10] claiming that he, like the Hūdids, came from the Yemeni Arab tribe of Judhām. The first member of the family we hear of was Saʿd b. Mardanīsh, who was governor of Fraga and the frontier areas around and distinguished himself in the defence of the city against Alfonso I in 1134. The family seems to have moved south and joined the Andalusi *jund* in Valencia under Ibn ʿIyāḍ. In 1146 ʿAbd Allāh b. Mardanīsh was among those killed, along with Sayf al-Dawla b. Hūd, at Albacete.

In August 1147 Ibn ʿIyāḍ was killed in an obscure conflict, but before his death he had passed on his command of the Andalusi *jund* to Muḥammad b. Saʿd b. Mardanīsh, son of the defender of Fraga. Ibn Mardanīsh was to remain as ruler of the Levante until 1172. His dominions were surrounded by aggressive enemies. In

8. Codera y Zaidin, *Decadencia y Desaparicion*, pp. 71–88; Guichard, *Musulmans de Valence*, pp. 109, 112.

9. Codera y Zaidin, *Decadencia y Desaparicion*, pp. 111–53; Guichard, *Musulmans de Valence*, pp. 116–24.

10. Ibn al-Khaṭīb, *Aʿmāl*, p. 298.

the north, the last Muslim outposts in the Ebro valley were taken by 1149, while in the south the Castilians held Almeria until 1157. The western half of al-Andalus was being taken over by the Almohads who took Seville in 1147. For a decade, however, Ibn Mardanīsh was separated from them by the last Almoravids in Granada (until 1155) and by the Christians of Almeria (until 1157). Only after this were the Almohads able to direct the full force of their attack on Ibn Mardanīsh.

Faced by these threats, Ibn Mardanīsh put his trust in alliance with Castile. It suited the Castilians to have this Muslim ally against the growing power of the Almohads and they supplied him with troops and military assistance. This in turn laid him open to attacks by Almohad propagandists. We know almost nothing of the internal affairs of Ibn Mardanīsh's state. We know that his brother Yūsuf was governor of Valencia for the whole period and that until 1169 he also benefited from the support of his father-in-law, Ibn Hamushk, who had an independent lordship on the Almohad frontier at Segura, but more than that we cannot tell.

This state survived as long as its founder, though it was increasingly unable to defend itself against Almohad forces. When Ibn Mardanīsh died in 1172, his realm was taken over without strong opposition and his family, like those of Sīdray b. Wazīr, Ibn 'Azzūn and Ibn Maymūn before, were absorbed into the Almohad elite.

CHAPTER NINE

The Early Almohad Caliphate

The origins of the Almohad movement, c. 1100–30

The story of the Almohad caliphate begins, like the story of the Almoravids, with the journey of a young Berber from the south of Morocco to the Muslim east in search of learning.[1] Muḥammad b. Tūmart's early life is recorded in a number of accounts written by supporters of the Almohad movement, one of whom, al-Baydhaq,[2] was an eye-witness of many of the early events. These accounts were later incorporated by more sceptical editors like Ibn Idhārī and Ibn Khaldūn in their compilations. Despite this abundance of information, many of the details are obscured by the partiality of the writers. In other cases the events have undergone, on a smaller scale, the sort of elaboration given to the *Sīra* of the Prophet Muḥammad himself; the meeting of Ibn Tūmart with 'Abd al-Mu'min, an event of crucial importance in the history of the movement, is given in at

1. The best account of the Almohad empire is the magisterial work of A. Huici Miranda, *Historia Politica del Imperio Almohade* (2 vols, Tetouan, 1956–7). This fundamental work is now quite rare and the second volume especially difficult to find: it should certainly be reprinted. An interesting but much slighter account is R. Le Tourneau, *The Almohad Movement in North Africa in the Twelfth and Thirteenth Centuries* (Princeton, 1969). There is useful information in J.F.P. Hopkins, *Medieval Muslim Government in Barbary* (London, 1958), and a good recent survey in M.J. Viguera Molins, *Los Reinos de Taifas y Las Invasiones Magrebies* (Madrid, 1992), pp. 205–347. M. Fletcher's promised *Western Islam: the Almohad Renaissance* has not appeared at the time of writing, but readers can consult two of her articles, 'The anthropological context of Almohad history', *Hesperis-Tamuda* 26–7 (1988–9), 25–51, and 'Al-Andalus and North Africa in the Almohad ideology', in S.K. Jayyusi (ed.), *The Legacy of Muslim Spain* (Leiden, 1992), pp. 235–58.

2. Ed., with French trans., by E. Lévi-Provençal as *Documents inédits d'Histoire Almohade* (Paris, 1928).

least two versions, each full of circumstantial detail but incompatible with each other. As a result, while some of the details of what actually happened may be of questionable veracity, we do have a clear idea how his life was imagined and presented by the Almohad hierarchy in later years.

Ibn Tūmart was probably born between 1078 and 1082 in Ijilliz, a village in the Sūs, the great valley which separates the western range of the High Atlas from the Anti-Atlas to the south.[3] He came from the Harga tribe which was itself a branch of the Maṣmūda, as were the inhabitants of most of the villages of the Atlas. Even though they were geographically quite close, he came from a very different environment from the founders of the Almoravid movement. While the latter were children of the open deserts of the south, Ibn Tūmart was brought up in an agricultural environment, a land of narrow passes and villages perched on crags above the terraced fields where the people grew their vegetables and fruit trees: goats for milk and meat were their only livestock. The people were grouped into tribes for mutual support against outsiders, although in most respects the villages were effectively self-sufficient under their own chiefs.

We know nothing about his early life until in 1106/7 Ibn Tūmart went to al-Andalus, then, like Morocco, under Almoravid rule, to pursue his education. Soon, however, he was attracted to the richer learning to be found in the Muslim east and set out there. According to pious legend, he was taught in Baghdad by the Imam Muḥammad al-Ghazzālī (d. 1111), the greatest religious teacher of his age, who recognised the young man's promise. Al-Ghazzālī had recently published his famous *Iḥyā 'Ulūm al-Dīn* (*The Revival of the Religious Sciences*) and Ibn Tūmart was in his presence when news came that his great work had been publicly burned by the Almoravids. Hearing this, al-Ghazzālī was moved to prophesy that the young Ibn Tūmart would put an end to this obscurantist and impious dynasty. The message of the story is plain: Ibn Tūmart was the favoured pupil of the greatest Muslim intellectual of his age and his master had prophesied his future greatness. It was an important kind of legitimacy.

If he was entrusted with such a mission, he showed no urgency in fulfilling it. He left the east in about 1117 and returned through Tripoli and Mahdīya, arriving in Bougie in January 1119. Everywhere he went he preached a simple and puritanical Islam, condemning

3. For the early life and career of Ibn Tūmart see Huici Miranda, *Historia Politica*, i, pp. 23–65.

gaudy clothing, the mixing of people of the opposite sex on feast days, the selling of wine and all sorts of musical instruments, which he encouraged his followers to destroy. Not surprisingly, his activities made him unpopular in many quarters, but he did attract a small nucleus of followers. These included 'Abd Allāh b. Muḥsin al-Wansharisī, known as al-Bashīr, from the Oran area, 'Abd al-Mu'min b. 'Alī of the Kūmīya Berber tribe from near Tlemcen and al-Baydhaq, who was to write his master's biography.

The little party made its way from Bougie through Fes to the coast, finally reaching Marrakesh in 1120. He and his few followers were poverty-stricken (according to one report, 'Abd al-Mu'min was forced to swim the Bu Regreg River at Rabat because they could not afford the ferry fare for him) but not demoralised. When they reached Marrakesh, Ibn Tūmart went to the main mosque and, according to his biographers, immediately confronted the Almoravid Amir 'Alī b. Yūsuf b. Tāshfīn and the jurists who surrounded him and challenged them to a debate. We need not take all the details too seriously, for the topos of the forthright holy man defying the ruler is a common one in Islamic history and no doubt the details improved in the telling. It is clear that Ibn Tūmart tried to win over the Almoravid establishment and failed; what is less clear is the points on which they differed. Both believed in a puritanical Islam, though, if we believe the largely hostile sources, the Almoravids had departed from their original austerity. Ibn Tūmart sought the foundations of Muslim law in Qur'ān and Hadith alone, not in the writings of the jurists which may have alienated the *'ulamā*. He also insisted on the absolute unity of Allah. Of course, all Muslims believed in the unity and oneness of God, but he laid especial emphasis on this, denying that God had any attributes which could be distinguished from Him or that He had any anthropomorphic characteristics. It was from this that his followers were known as *Muwaḥḥidūn*, or those who affirm the unity of God, which becomes Hispanised as Almohade.

Ibn Tūmart also proclaimed his belief in a Mahdī and, soon, that he himself was the Mahdī. The Mahdī is said to be a spiritual leader, usually descended from 'Alī and Fāṭima and so from the Prophet Muḥammad himself, who will come to restore true Islam by virtue of his divine support. This belief is usually associated with a Shi'ite reverence for the House of 'Alī and, indeed, Ibn Tūmart acquired a highly tendentious 'Alid genealogy when he began to make his claims. Such a belief was, of course, irreconcilable with Almoravid views, but it is not clear that he espoused it until after his breach with the Almoravids in 1120 and his withdrawal to the mountains, and it may have been a result rather than a cause of this rebuff.

Apart from the claim that Ibn Tūmart was the Mahdī, there was little to distinguish Almohad teachings from those of their Almoravid enemies, and it must be remembered that Ibn Tūmart is said to have begun by trying to reform the Almoravids. The emphasis on certain comparatively minor issues like the alleged anthropomorphism of the Almoravids and their custom of veiling was probably due to the fact that these were the only noticeable differences and that they had to be stressed for propaganda purposes. The main body of Ibn Tūmart's criticism seems to have been directed at loose morals, just as ʿAbd Allāh b. Yāsin's had been, and he ridiculed the Almoravid men for wearing veils while their women did not (which is probably the basis for the Almohad accusation that the Almoravids were dominated by women, an assertion repeated by a number of modern historians).

ʿAlī b. Yūsuf was advised by his jurists to put the insolent preacher to death, but he was by nature a mild-mannered man and took the advice of others who urged that he should simply be expelled from the city. So after fourteen years of wandering, Ibn Tūmart left Marrakesh and returned to his native mountains.

In 1120 he made his way up the road which led to the pass at Tizi-n-Test and his native Sūs which lay beyond. On the way he received the support of Abū Ḥafṣ ʿUmar b. Yaḥyā al-Hintātī (or Intī), leader of Hintāta, probably the most important tribe in the area. Until his death in 1176, ʿUmar Intī was to be the most important member of the Almohad hierarchy after the caliphs and their families, and a notable warrior. His descendants, usually known as the Hafsids, were to rule in Tunis until 1574. By the end of the year he had established himself in a cave and begun his preaching. Always using the Berber vernacular, he called on his followers to support true religion and attack the Almoravids, who deserved to die for their anthropomorphism and their wearing of veils. Much of his prestige among the Berbers at this time seems to have rested on his reputation as a doer of wonders and miracles and a controller of supernatural powers, elements which later Almohad writers in al-Andalus tried to tone down or ignore.[4] He also laid more and more stress on the role of the Mahdī, whose virtues and accomplishments would transform the Muslim world. It must have

4. Discussed by Fletcher in 'Almohad ideology', in which she criticises Huici Miranda for underestimating the importance of this aspect of his early career.

been with satisfaction, if not surprise, therefore, that his followers, after a particularly eloquent Ramaḍān sermon in 515 (November–December 1121) proclaimed that he himself was the expected Mahdī. This newly acquired status meant that he could claim the power to interpret and decide the law and that resistance to him was also resistance to God and therefore apostasy, to be punished by death.

These heady days were followed by eight years of almost continuous warfare, when the Almohads defended themselves from Almoravid attacks from Sūs and Marrakesh. Gradually the Mahdī and his followers extended their power over the neighbouring Berber tribes. They did not always do it gently. Late in 1122 Ibn Tūmart moved his centre of operations to Tīnmal. Tīnmal lies in the centre of a small but fertile plain bordering the upper Wādī Nafīs. It is not far from the plains around Marrakesh but is protected from them by narrow gorges which could easily be defended against attack by a few men. Many of the original inhabitants of Tīnmal itself were driven out and slaughtered and the resistance of other 'hypocrites' was ended by purges and executions: the example of the Prophet's treatment of his enemies in Madīna cannot have been far from Ibn Tūmart's mind. The most extensive of these was the great *tamyīz* or purge conducted by al-Bashīr in the winter of 1129–30 when mass executions took place and a real reign of terror was introduced. Meanwhile the Almoravid ruler, 'Alī b. Yūsuf, was preoccupied by affairs in al-Andalus where Alfonso the Battler (King of Aragon, 1104–34) was threatening to extend his conquests, and he could spare neither leaders nor men for the campaign against the Almohads. While Ibn Tūmart fortified himself in Tīnmal, the Almoravids built a string of fortresses to contain him. The gradual build-up of Almohad power in the mountainous area around Tīnmal was followed by the disastrous attack on Marrakesh in 1130 which resulted in the death of many of the early adherents of the movement. This was followed shortly afterwards by the death of Muḥammad b. Tūmart himself in August 1130.[5]

'Abd al-Mu'min and the construction of the Almohad caliphate, 1130–63

The combination of military defeat and the death of the founder might easily have led to the collapse of the whole movement, but

5. See Huici Miranda, *Historia Politica*, i, pp. 78–89.

Ibn Tūmart had constructed and recruited a hierarchy with sufficient commitment and determination to keep the movement in being.[6] The details vary from one source to another and the system itself developed over time, but the main outlines are clear: there was an inner Council of Ten early followers of Ibn Tūmart, also known as the *Jumā'a*, to which was added a Council of Fifty, largely composed of tribal leaders from the Atlas area. As well as these there were the *Ahl al-Dār*, who were essentially the household of Ibn Tūmart, and the *Ṭalba* (sing. *Ṭālib*) and *Ḥuffāẓ* (sing. *Ḥāfiẓ*), who were originally missionaries sent out to spread Almohad doctrines.

Of the original Ten (according to the list provided by the *Kitāb al-Ansāb*, which seems to be the most reliable source), three at least, 'Abd al-Mu'min, al-Bashīr and 'Abd Allāh b. Ya'lā, known as Ibn Malwīya, had joined Ibn Tūmart during his stay in Bougie or soon after; most of the rest had local roots and included such tribal leaders as the Hafsid 'Umar al-Hintātī. Five of them, including al-Bashīr, perished in the disastrous attack on Marrakesh in 1130 and were not replaced, though their children often played an important part in Almohad politics. Ibn Malwīya was executed for opposing 'Abd al-Mu'min's assumption of power after 1132, and 'Umar Asnāj died of illness in 1142/3, leaving only 'Umar al-Hintātī and Ismā'īl al-Hazrajī alongside 'Abd al-Mu'min.

The sources which have come down to us suggest that the choice of 'Abd al-Mu'min as Caliph in succession to the Mahdī Ibn Tūmart was a natural one, but they may be concealing a real power struggle.[7] In his favour was the fact that he had joined the movement very early and had shown his competence as an organiser and soldier, but he remained an outsider among the Berber chiefs who formed its chief military support. There was opposition, from Ibn Tūmart's brothers and from Ibn al-Malwīya, one of the other surviving members of the Ten. It was a sign of both his leadership qualities and his ruthlessness that he was able not only to establish his personal power but to found a dynasty.

The first fifteen or so years of his leadership were occupied by

6. This hierarchy has been the subject of considerable discussion: see ibid., pp. 100–5; Hopkins, *Medieval Muslim Government*, pp. 85–111, who remarks: 'one is entitled to wonder whether the whole system existed at all except on paper or in the minds of its inventors' (p. 110). For the most recent assessment of the sources see M. Kisaichi, 'The Almohad social-political system or hierarchy in the reign of Ibn Tumart', *Memoirs of the Research Department of the Toyo Bunko* 48 (1990), 81–101.

7. His accession and the period to the fall of Marrakesh are described in Huici Miranda, *Historia Politica*, i, pp. 105–46.

the struggle against the Almoravids. Until 1141 the war was effectively a stalemate. The Almoravids could not crush the Almohads in the mountains while the latter could not challenge them on the plains and were intermittently distracted by disturbances among the tribes of the Sūs. In the spring of 1141 ʿAbd al-Muʾmin left Tīnmal on a seven-year campaign which was to end in the fall of Marrakesh. By the winter of 1142/3 the Almohad forces had worked their way along the mountains to ʿAbd al-Muʾmin's native land around Tlemcen. Here he was able to recruit members of his own tribe of Kūmīya and associated groups which, as well as providing reinforcements against the Almoravids, probably strengthened his position with his own followers. The death of the Catalan soldier of fortune Reverter and then of Tāshfīn b. ʿAlī at Oran in February 1145 allowed the Almohads to begin the final campaign against the cities of the plains, Fes, Salé and Marrakesh, which finally fell on 24 March 1147.

ʿAbd al-Muʾmin spent the rest of the year on the purification of Marrakesh and on suppressing yet another revolt in the Sūs, but he had time to send a small force to al-Andalus.[8] Even before the fall of Marrakesh, the minor rulers of al-Andalus, concerned at the growing power of the Christians and looking for a powerful ally against their Muslim rivals, had sent messengers to ʿAbd al-Muʾmin. They had good reason to be anxious. In 1147 Lisbon fell to Afonso Henriques (Count, then King, of Portugal, 1128–85) and an army of northern Crusaders, and Almeria was taken by Alfonso VII of Leon-Castile, while in the north-east Fraga, Lerida and Tortosa were all lost by 1149, putting an end to over four centuries of Muslim rule in the Ebro valley. The first to make contact with the Almohads seems to have been Ibn Qasī, the Sufi ruler of Silves, whose lands were being attacked by his neighbour Sīdray b. Wazīr, lord of Badajoz and Beja. He sent an ambassador as early as 1145 when ʿAbd al-Muʾmin was in Tlemcen, but negotiations broke down because Ibn Qasī's envoy refused to accept ʿAbd al-Muʾmin as the Mahdī. Soon after, the Almoravid naval commander (*ṣāḥib al-usṭūl*) ʿAlī b. ʿĪsā b. Maymūn defected and proclaimed himself independent in Cadiz. Ibn Qasī, now expelled from his lands, came in person and encouraged him to attack al-Andalus. In the spring of 1147 ʿAbd al-Muʾmin responded by sending a force commanded by a leading defector

8. The chronology of the first Almohad intervention in al-Andalus is confused, but I have followed Huici Miranda, *Historia Politica*, i, pp. 145, 156–8, which is based on Ibn Khaldūn, *Al-ʿIbār wa diwān al-mubtadāʾ waʾl-khabar* (8 vols, Beirut, 1981), vi, pp. 312–15.

from the Almoravids, Abū Isḥāq Barrāz b. Muḥammad al-Massūfī, which took Tarifa and Algeciras and accepted the submission of Abū'l-Ghamr b. 'Azzūn of Jerez. Bypassing Seville, still held by the Almoravids, they went on to the Algarve, where Yūsuf b. Aḥmad al-Bitrūjī of Niebla pledged obedience, and then to Mertola and Silves which were entrusted to Ibn Qasī. Finally they accepted the surrender of Sīdray b. Wazīr of Badajoz and Beja, so completing the subjection of the Algarve before the army settled for the winter in Mertola.

In January 1148 Barrāz, reinforced by his local supporters, took Seville by force, driving out the Almoravid garrison and killing in the process the son of the *qāḍī* Abū Bakr b. al-'Arabī. His father set out for Marrakesh to offer the city's submission to 'Abd al-Mu'min (another example of the role of the *qāḍī* as civic leader), but died en route. Ibn al-'Arabī and other members of the Andalusi elite seem to have seen no contradiction in serving first the Almoravids and then the Almohads. The local leaders who had made their submission were allowed to keep their lordships at this stage.

The progress of Almohad arms was interrupted by a massive revolt among the tribes of the Sūs and the western Atlas which soon attracted support from all over the Maghreb, Ceuta in the north and Sijilmāssa in the south being taken over by rebels. From al-Andalus, the Almoravid Ibn Ghānīya in Cordoba sent forces to aid the insurgents. It was not until May 1148 that the rebel leader al-Massatī was defeated and killed by the determination of the Caliph and his right-hand man, 'Umar al-Hintātī. 'Abd al-Mu'min then ordered an administrative reform to correct abuses and oppressive governors and, in a more sinister, almost Stalinist, manner, a widespread purge of suspect elements amongst the subordinate Berber tribes, which is said to have resulted in over 30,000 executions.[9]

These traumatic events had widespread repercussions in al-Andalus, where some of those who had accepted Almohad rule began to have second thoughts. The position was made worse, according to Ibn Khaldūn, by the two brothers of Ibn Tūmart the Mahdī, 'Abd al-'Azīz and 'Īsā, who had been sent into semi-exile in Seville, though it should be noted that there is a systematic attempt in the sources to blacken the reputation of Ibn Tūmart's brothers to justify 'Abd al-Mu'min's assumption of power. They are said to have plotted to assassinate Yūsuf al-Bitrūjī of Niebla. He and most of the other Andalusi leaders renounced their allegiance and Ibn

9. Huici Miranda, *Historia Politica*, i, p. 156.

Ghānīya came to take over Algeciras for the Almoravids: only Ibn 'Azzūn in Jerez and Ronda remained loyal.

This was the low point of Almohad fortunes, but the counter-attack soon began. Ibn 'Azzūn with Ibn Tūmart's brothers took Algeciras. Soon after, 'Abd al-Mu'min dispatched a large army of Almohads under Yūsuf b. Sulaymān (a member of the Fifty from Tīnmal) which undertook an extensive campaign as far as Silves and Badajoz. Faced by this new invasion and increasing Christian pressure on Cordoba, Ibn Ghānīya now sought to come to terms on condition that he was allowed to remain as local lord of Jaen. However, he was forced out of there by the troops of Alfonso VII (King of Castile and Leon, 1126–57) and retreated to Granada, now the last outpost of the Almoravids. Here he persuaded the governor, Maymūn b. Badr al-Lamtūnī, to accept terms, but he himself died, apparently of natural causes, at the end of 1148 or early 1149. His tomb was still known in Ibn Khaldūn's day.

The threat to Cordoba remained and the Almohads were obliged to call on their Andalusi allies to prevent Alfonso VII from taking the city. Ibn 'Azzūn and al-Bitrūjī were sent and later reinforced by Almohad troops led by Yaḥyā b. Yūmūr, one of the Fifty.[10] The city was saved for Islam and the inhabitants wrote to offer their submission to the Caliph in the summer of 1149, but the incident showed that the Almohads were heavily dependent on their local allies when it came to resisting the Christian advance. In 1150/1 a number of Andalusi leaders were summoned to Morocco to meet the Caliph at Salé. Among them were Sīdray b. Wazīr of Beja, al-Bitrūjī of Niebla, Ibn al-Ḥijjām, who appears as lord of Badajoz, and the ever faithful Ibn 'Azzūn of Jerez. They were received into the Caliph's favour and incorporated into the Almohad elite. They then returned to al-Andalus on condition that they gave up control over their own cities and attached themselves to the Almohad governor in Seville. On this basis the Almohad authorities began a partnership with the local Andalusi ruling class which was to serve both in good stead in the years to come. Sīdray b. Wazīr and the Ibn 'Azzūn brothers, Abū'l-Ghamr and Abū'l-'Alā, had particularly distinguished careers. Only the egregious Ibn Qasī, the only one of the Andalusi lords to claim religious as well as secular leadership, was excluded and there was continuing insecurity in the Algarve: from 1151 to 1167 Tavira was held by a pirate and brigand called 'Abd Allāh b. 'Ubayd Allāh who preyed on travellers by land and sea.

10. Ibid., p. 158.

These were modest beginnings to Almohad power in al-Andalus and for the next few years they were not developed. From 1151 to 1155 the Caliph was absorbed in African affairs, first with the building of his new fortress city at Rabat (the present Kasbah des Oudaïa, the walled nucleus of the old city) and then by a long campaign in the Maghreb. In 1152/3 he subdued much of modern Algeria including the main towns of Bougie and Constantine and defeated the Arab tribes in a battle at Setif near Constantine. In the aftermath of this battle, Arab tribes, notably the Banū Hilāl and the Banū Riyāḥ, were brought west to settle in the plains of Morocco and participate in the *jihād.* They were to be an important element in the Almohad armies, possibly because they provided useful cavalry, but they were hard to discipline and sometimes unreliable in battle. This transfer of Arab tribes marks the beginnings of the Arabisation of a countryside which seems to have been wholly Berber up to this point. In the thirteenth century, when Almohad power in Morocco was starting to disintegrate, these tribes were to prove a seriously disruptive presence. By September 1153 'Abd al-Mu'min was back in Marrakesh. During his absence it is said that Ibn Tūmart's brothers had been plotting against him. The brothers are consistently vilified in the chronicles for their moral failings, but whatever the truth of these allegations, they had good reason to fear that the polity their brother had founded was being taken over by a rival dynasty. They had some support among others who had been close to Ibn Tūmart, including members of his tribe of Harga. Many of these were executed and the brothers sent to Fes where they could be more easily watched.[11]

At the beginning of 1155, when this plot, if such it was, had been scotched, 'Abd al-Mu'min undertook a major political reorganisation which put his family firmly in control of the caliphate.[12] The first step was to secure the acknowledgement of his son Muḥammad as heir apparent in place, it seems, of the Hafsid 'Umar al-Hintātī, one of the original Ten companions of Ibn Tūmart and the most powerful man in the empire after the Caliph himself. Apparently he first gained the acceptance of the newly arrived Arabs and other groups outside the traditional Almohad elite and used their consent to put pressure on the latter. At an assembly in Salé, 'Umar

11. Ibid., ii, pp. 167–8.
12. Ibid., i, pp. 169–71. The relationships between tribe and dynasty are discussed in C. Hames, 'De la chefferie tribale à la dynastie étatique: généalogie et pouvoir à l'epoque Almohade-Hafside', in P. Bonte *et al.* (eds), *Al-Ansab: la quête des origines* (Paris, 1991).

and most of the old Almohads agreed to accept Muḥammad, but the action produced a final (and fatal) outburst of opposition from Ibn Tūmart's brothers, 'Abd al-'Azīz and 'Īsā, who escaped from Fes and attempted to mount a *coup d'état* in Marrakesh: they were thwarted by the citizens and killed in the ensuing mêlée.

'Abd al-Mu'min's next move, in 1155/6, was to secure control of all the most important provincial governorates for his own sons, of whom there were now fourteen. Up to this time, governors had been chosen from among the Almohad veterans, who would probably have objected to losing control of these offices, but the Caliph persuaded representatives from various provinces to request that his sons be appointed, and once again the old guard were obliged to accept. The fearful purges he had already conducted no doubt intimidated any who might have considered objecting. The pill was sweetened by appointing senior Almohads as chief advisers to each of the *sayyids*, as the young princes were called.[13] In North Africa, princes were appointed to Bougie, Tlemcen, Fes, Sūs and probably Tadla. In al-Andalus, *sayyid* Abū Ya'qūb Yūsuf was appointed to Seville with Abū Ja'far Aḥmad b. 'Aṭiya as *wazīr*, and *sayyid* Abū Sa'īd 'Uthmān to Algeciras and Malaga as well as the Straits with Ceuta and Tangier.

These changes gave the Almohad state a strongly hereditary character. With few exceptions, governors of important towns, Seville, Cordoba and Granada in al-Andalus, were to be members of the Caliph's family. However, the families of the Almohad elite also benefited from this. The sons of the Ten and the Fifty became a hereditary ruling class, with honoured positions at court and roles as commanders of armies or governors of smaller towns. The title of *ḥāfiẓ* was usually reserved for such people. In general, by this time *ḥāfiẓ* was a title given to civil or military commanders; the title *ṭālib*, on the other hand, was held by non-military figures among the religious classes. The closed nature of this ruling class may account for its cohesion, and civil wars within it were remarkably

13. Almohad naming practices are extremely confusing because the dynasty and their leading supporters tended to recycle a small number of Muslim given names, largely of biblical and Quranic origin (Ya'qūb/Jacob, Yūsuf/Joseph) or early Islamic ('Umar, 'Uthmān). To try to distinguish them they are often known by their *kunyas* (Abū so and so), but this does not always make recognition easier. A particular problem is distinguishing the family of the Berber Hintāta *shaykh* Abū Ḥafṣ 'Umar from the *sayyid* Abū Ḥafṣ 'Umar, brother and chief supporter of the Caliph Yūsuf I, both of whom founded important lineages. To try to limit the confusion, I shall use the title *sayyid* for all members of the Mu'minid house, which is the contemporary usage, and Hafsid for the descendants of Abū Ḥafṣ 'Umar al-Hintātī. Readers should also refer to the family tree on p. 314.

rare, but it also led to a certain fossilisation and dearth of leadership talent.

The elite were effectively in command of the Almohad armies. These are described as being composed of different elements. At the core were the Almohads, that is the members of the Maṣmūda tribes of the Atlas Mountains, who had been Ibn Tūmart's original followers. The fullest description of them is given by 'Abd al-Wāḥid al-Marrākushī, an Almohad bureaucrat writing at the beginning of the thirteenth century:

> The Almohad tribes who are called by this name, and form the army [*jund*], the collaborators and the helpers [*anṣār*] (the rest of the Berbers and the Maṣmūda are their subjects [*ra'īya*] and under their authority) are seven in number. The first of them is the tribe of Ibn Tūmart, the Harga, who are few in number compared with the other tribes. Then there is the tribe of 'Abd al-Mu'min, the Kūmiya, a large tribe with many branches. Neither in ancient or modern times were they known for leadership or great reputation: they were nothing but peasant farmers, shepherds and traders in the markets selling milk, firewood and other cheap goods . . . Today they are a people second to none in the Maghreb and have no rivals because 'Abd al-Mu'min originated from them, though some said he came from elsewhere as we mentioned above. Next there were the people of Tīnmal who came from different tribes but joined in taking the name of this place. Then there were the Hintāta, which was also a very large tribe, part of which enjoyed leadership and honour in ancient times, the Ganfīsa, a glorious and powerful tribe who spoke the purest and best Berber, and the Gadmīwa who were not entirely, but in part, subjects [*ra'īya*]. Finally there were those of the Ṣanhāja who had answered the call of the Almohads, and the Haskura.
>
> These are all the Almohad tribes entitled to the name: they take salaries ['*aṭā'*], form the armies and join in expeditions. All the other Maṣmūda tribes were subjects.[14]

The Almohads were divided into two groups, the salaried *jamā'a*, numbering about 10,000, who were permanently based in Marrakesh except when they went on major expeditions, and the *'umūm* of lower status who were based in provincial cities.

Next there were the Arabs, recruited first by 'Abd al-Mu'min during his campaigns in Tunisia and brought west. These Arabs seem to have fought, like the Almohads, in tribal units and under the command of their own chiefs. The third major element were

14. 'Abd al-Wāḥid al-Marrākushī, *Al-Mu'jib*, ed. M.S. al-'Uryan (Cairo, 1949), pp. 339–40; trans., A. Huici Miranda (Tetuan, 1955), pp. 279–80.

the Andalusis, who again fought under their own commanders. In 1186/7 a new group was added to the army when al-Manṣūr recruited a number of Ghuzz Turks who had left the service of the Ayyubids in Egypt. They became a privileged military elite, probably because of their skill in mounted archery. There was clearly some resentment among the Almohad at these new arrivals, especially as they were paid their salaries every month as opposed to three times a year like the Almohads. The Caliph attempted to excuse this by saying that they had no *'iqṭā'*s (fiefs) and so were totally dependent on their salaries, but al-Marrākushī notes sourly that their leaders were in fact given *'iqṭā'*s like the Almohads 'or even bigger' and says that one Sha'bān was given many villages in al-Andalus which brought in a revenue of some 9,000 *dīnārs*.[15]

It is not clear how these armies, which might number up to 100,000 for a major expedition, were paid. The Almohads did maintain *dīwāns* or *zimām*, lists of troops to be paid, and soldiers were inscribed (*marsūmīn*) in them, whether they were Almohads, Arabs or Andalusis. Payment (*'aṭā'*) seems to have been in cash and occasionally in gifts of clothing or arms. The revenues to pay these salaries were collected and distributed by a civilian bureaucracy, not by the soldiers themselves, so maintaining a degree of government control over the army. Sometimes they were given lands as fiefs, known as *'iqṭā'*, though it is not clear how widespread this was. The allocation of such fiefs does not mean that they lived on the lands from which they derived their revenues or that they collected the income directly themselves, which makes the *'iqṭā'* very different from the typical western European fief. We also hear of soldiers being assigned *sihām*, or shares of the revenue, which may have come from specified areas. It is not clear that salaries were regularly paid to all potential soldiers. It seems likely that Almohads employed in garrison duties were regularly paid, at least when resources permitted: when the Almohad garrison was settled in Granada after its recapture in 1162 they were given increases in their *barakāt* (lit. blessings) and *muwāsāt*, which seem to be alternative words for salaries.[16] For particular campaigns, on the other hand, large numbers of others were recruited and were paid as and when the Caliph had enough money.

It was characteristic of the Almohad caliphate that most of the court and the army moved with the Caliph. In his absence, only

15. Ibid., pp. 288–9; trans., pp. 240–1.

16. Ibn Ṣāḥib al-Ṣalāt, *Al-Mann bi'l-Imāma*, ed. A. al-Hadi al-Tazi (Beirut, 1964), p. 196; Spanish trans., A. Huici Miranda (Valencia, 1969), p. 47.

limited or defensive campaigns could be undertaken. ʿAbd al-Mu'min's preoccupation with the Bougie campaign and then with political reorganisation meant that little had been done to strengthen the Muslim position in al-Andalus. Alfonso VII was still threatening Granada and there had been a renewed anti-Almohad movement in Niebla, after which the Almohad governor, Yaḥyā b. Yūmūr, who had massacred many of the inhabitants, was disgraced and replaced.

The appointment of the two *sayyids* Yūsuf and ʿUthmān, both sons of the Caliph, to Seville and Malaga in 1156 signalled the beginning of a more active phase. Maymūn b. Badr al-Lamtūnī, the Almoravid governor of Granada, handed the city over to the Almohads and ʿUthmān took control. There were further successes in 1157. In the spring ʿUthmān began the siege of the Christian garrison of Almeria which had been seized by Alfonso VII ten years before. Despite attempts by Alfonso and the Muslim leader Ibn Mardanīsh of Murcia to relieve the city, the garrison was forced to surrender, probably in August. To add to the Muslims' good fortune, Alfonso VII himself died on 21 August, on the way north from Almeria. The two cities of Ubeda and Baeza, recently taken by the Christians, were abandoned. Much more important in the long run was the fact that Alfonso's death led to the division of Leon-Castile, united in 1072, into two separate kingdoms each ruled by its own sovereign. This division was to play a crucial part in the successes of the Almohads in al-Andalus as the two kingdoms were divided by bitter jealousies and rivalries. Leon, the smaller and weaker power, felt constantly threatened by Castile to the east and Portugal to the west; its kings, Fernando II (1157–88) and Alfonso IX (1188–1230), were often prepared to make alliances with the Muslims, or at least preserve a benevolent neutrality, if it would help preserve their independence. Furthermore, some Christian nobles, notably members of the Castro family, who were expelled from their lands during the Christian civil wars, were quite prepared to take service with the Almohads and contribute military power and, perhaps more important, intelligence and contacts to the Muslim war effort.[17]

The position was less secure in the west of al-Andalus. In the spring of 1158 the militia of Avila raided as far as Seville, defeating *sayyid* Yūsuf and killing several senior Almohads and Andalusi

17. For the history of the Castros in this period see J. Gonzalez, *El Reino de Castilla en la Epoca de Alfonso VIII* (3 vols, Madrid, 1960), i, pp. 321–36, though the author, who uses no Arabic sources, tends to play down the role of Pedro Fernandez de Castro (d. 1214) at the Almohad court.

lords Ibn 'Azzūn of Jerez and Ibn al-Ḥijjām of Badajoz. The young prince Yūsuf escaped with difficulty to the protection of the walls of Seville.[18]

Despite these reverses, 'Abd al-Mu'min continued to give priority to affairs in the eastern Maghreb. His next project was to take Tunisia, where the Normans from Sicily had established garrisons in most of the major coastal cities. With great pomp and ceremony he left Marrakesh in October 1158 and arrived outside Tunis in July 1159. The city soon surrendered and the Caliph went on to lay siege to the more strongly fortified city of al-Mahdīya. The Norman garrison held out here for almost six months until they finally capitulated in January 1160. Having achieved his main objectives, he returned slowly through the Maghreb, setting up a system of *kharāj* taxation, which seems to have been a sort of land tax, perhaps the first ever collected in these areas, and arranging for yet more Arabs to move west to Morocco.

It is not known if the Muslims of Seville were comforted by the grandiloquent letter from 'Abd al-Mu'min announcing his triumph at al-Mahdīya.[19] They certainly needed good news, for there was little else to cheer them up. As usual, the absence of the Caliph led to the paralysis of military activity. Not only were the Christians putting pressure on the frontier from Cordoba to the Algarve, but the eastern borders of Almohad control were being eroded by Ibn Mardanīsh of Murcia and Ibn Hamushk. On top of this, there was considerable popular antipathy to the Almohads even in Seville itself and morale was low.

It is at this juncture that the surviving section of the history of Ibn Ṣāḥib al-Ṣalāt opens, shedding a brilliant light on the hitherto obscure and confused history of Almohad al-Andalus. The narrative begins in 1159 with the attack of Ibn Mardanīsh on Cordoba: 'Raving, and unhinged by wine [anyone associating with Christians was liable to be accused of drunkenness], he believed that in the absence of the Commander of the Faithful 'Abd al-Mu'min he would conquer the Almohads in al-Andalus.'[20] At first, events suggested that he was right: the governor of Jaen, Muḥammad b. 'Alī al-Kūmī, from the Caliph's own tribe of Kūmīya, was persuaded to desert the Almohad cause.

Ibn Mardanīsh then moved on to Cordoba, which was defended by the *ḥāfiẓ* Abū Zayd 'Abd al-Raḥmān b. Tījīt, whose grandfather

18. Huici Miranda, *Historia Politica*, i, p. 184.
19. Ibn Ṣāḥib al-Ṣalāt, *Al-Mann bi'l-Imāma*, p. 119; trans., p. 16.
20. Ibid., p. 109; trans., pp. 11–12.

had been one of the original Council of Ten and was killed in 1130. It seemed as if the city would fall, but Abū Zayd concocted a scheme with the *qāḍī*, Akhīl b. Idrīs: they instructed one of the *qāḍī*'s servants to disguise himself as an oil seller from the Ajarafe near Seville and gave him a forged letter from the Andalusi noble Sīdray b. Wazīr for Ibn Mardanīsh which urged the latter to attack Seville instead, saying that he (Sīdray b. Wazīr) would guarantee entry to the city. The ruse worked and Ibn Mardanīsh abandoned the siege of Cordoba and set off for Seville, only to find the city firmly barred against him. The incident shows the military weakness of the Almohads at this time and the possibility that the Andalusi lords of the Seville area would join with Ibn Mardanīsh to expel them.

The same anxieties were being felt in Seville itself. Some Andalusis showed their loyalty to the new regime, like the *qāḍī*, Abū Bakr al-Ghāfiqī, and Abū'l-ʿAlā b. ʿAzzūn, who had succeeded his brother Abū'l-Ghamr and continued the family tradition of loyalty to the Almohads. With Ibn Mardanīsh outside the gates, however, the authorities were nervous and rounded up and executed anyone thought to be disloyal. In February–March 1160 a letter arrived detailing ʿAbd al-Muʾmin's conquests in Tunisia. They made the best of it: *sayyid* Abū Yaʿqūb Yūsuf ordered that the *ṭālib*s transcribe the letter and publicise it, beating the drums and reciting the victory poetry it contained, and banquets were given in the city so that the people could join in the celebrations. Almohad propaganda techniques were often more skilled than Almohad arms: at the same time, Abū Zayd made a careless sortie from Cordoba and was ambushed and killed by the troops of Ibn Hamushk.

On his return to Morocco in the summer of 1160, the Caliph prepared a major expedition to bolster the fragile Almohad presence in al-Andalus. Already in March he had written to his son, Abū Saʿīd ʿUthmān in Granada, ordering him, along with that Barrāz b. Muḥammad who had led the first Almohad forces to al-Andalus thirteen years before, and the famous architects Aḥmad b. Bāso of Seville and al-Ḥājj Yiʿīsh of Malaga, to come to Gibraltar and begin work on fortifications and palaces. Masons and craftsmen were brought from all the areas of al-Andalus under Almohad rule. He intended to use the Rock as a secure base from which to supervise affairs in al-Andalus while being able to return quickly to Morocco if the need should arise. The earliest surviving constructions on Gibraltar date from this period.[21]

21. Ibid., pp. 129–33; trans., pp. 21–3.

The Caliph finally crossed to Gibraltar in November 1160 where he prepared to receive his sons, *sayyid* Abū Ya'qūb Yūsuf of Seville and *sayyid* Abū Sa'īd 'Uthmān of Granada, together with the Almohads and leaders of Andalusi society. It was one of those formal, hierarchical court receptions which formed so large a part of Almohad political life. *Sayyid* Abū Ya'qūb Yūsuf's departure from Seville was marred by the news of a rebellion in nearby Carmona supported by Ibn Hamushk's men, and it was not until he had appointed men to deal with this that he was able to leave to meet his father. 'Abd al-Mu'min had been one of the Ten, so it was natural, according to Almohad protocol, that his son should be accompanied by sons of the Ten: accordingly he took with him sons of 'Umar Asnāj, the son of Ismā'īl b. Tījīt as well as the brother of 'Umar al-Hintātī. With them went many other Almohad cadres and leading Andalusis from Seville, the *qāḍī* Abū Bakr al-Ghāfiqī and the *ḥāfiẓ* Abū Bakr b. al-Jadd.

The court at Gibraltar was clearly a splendid affair: sermons were preached and poems recited, but it must have been something of a disappointment to supporters of the Almohad cause in al-Andalus. In January 1161 the Caliph returned to Marrakesh without penetrating any further into al-Andalus, and his sons returned to their governorates. On reaching Marrakesh, the Caliph sent reinforcements under the leadership of the veteran Almohad Yūsuf b. Sulaymān, who established himself in Cordoba, which was fortified and garrisoned.

Shortly afterwards, *sayyid* Abū Yūsuf Ya'qūb was summoned to Marrakesh to visit his father, who was said to be planning a major expedition to al-Andalus. He left in charge of Seville and the war against the rebels in Carmona the *ḥāfiẓ* Abū Muḥammad 'Abd Allāh, son of 'Umar Asnāj, one of the Ten. Abū Muḥammad led a force which included Abū'l-'Alā b. 'Azzūn and his followers, who are described as being enrolled in the government registers[22] and so were presumably being paid salaries and accepted as part of the Almohad regular army. It took a year to reduce the city and even then it only fell, on 30 December 1161, by treachery. Abū Muḥammad had the mosque washed out to cleanse it after the rebel occupation and the commander of Ibn Hamushk's forces, Ibn Abī Ja'far, was taken to Seville where he was crucified.

From his base at Jaen, Ibn Hamushk soon inflicted an even more humiliating reverse on the Almohads. In the spring of 1162

22. Ibid., p. 179; trans., p. 36. They are described as *marsūmūn fi zimām.*

his forces were let into the city of Granada, allegedly by a Jew who had been forcibly converted to Islam. The governor, *sayyid* Abū Saʿīd ʿUthmān, was with his father in Marrakesh and the Almohad garrison, taken by surprise, were forced to retreat to the old Alcazaba which stood on the north side of the River Darro, in what is now the Albaicin quarter, while Ibn Hamushk established himself on the Alhambra hill opposite. Ibn Hamushk immediately sent to Murcia to summon the assistance of Ibn Mardanīsh, who arrived with his own men and some 1,000 Christian horsemen and many more foot.

The garrison appealed to the Caliph for help. He immediately sent his son Abū Saʿīd ʿUthmān, who travelled by forced marches to the city. On the way he was joined by Abū Muḥammad ʿAbd Allāh, conqueror of Carmona, and the troops of Seville. Ibn Hamushk and his allies came out to meet them on the Vega. The Almohads, perhaps surprised by the presence of Ibn Mardanīsh and his Christian allies, were completely routed, many of them being brought down in the many irrigation channels which crossed the plain. Abū Muḥammad ʿAbd Allāh was killed and *sayyid* Abū Saʿīd ʿUthmān fled with difficulty to Malaga. It was the most serious reverse Almohad arms had suffered in al-Andalus.

The news of this fiasco reached the Caliph in Rabat. He immediately decided to send an army to restore the position and rescue the beleaguered Almohad garrison. An army of 20,000 comprised of Almohads, Arabs and salaried soldiers (*ajnād al-marsūmīn*) was recruited.[23] They were to be led by his son, Abū Yaʿqūb Yūsuf, and assisted by the veteran Almohad Yūsuf b. Sulaymān, to whom, as Huici observes,[24] the subsequent triumph should be credited. It was a fundamental part of the Caliph's dynastic policy to give his sons military commands, both to provide experience and to attach the army directly to the ruling family. The army went via Malaga where it was joined by *sayyid* Abū Saʿīd ʿUthmān, anxious no doubt to redeem his recent humiliation. When they arrived at Granada they found Ibn Hamushk and his men encamped in the fortress on the Alhambra hill and Ibn Mardanīsh, accompanied by 2,000 Christians and more than that number of his own men, on the Albaicin hill above the old Alcazaba on the other side of the Darro gorge. On the night of 12–13 July 1162, Muḥammad b. Sulaymān led a daring night march and fell upon Ibn Hamushk's men at dawn as they slept in their tents. The triumph was complete, Ibn Hamushk's

23. Ibid., p. 188; trans., p. 42.
24. Huici Miranda, *Historia Politica*, i, pp. 202–3.

men fled in panic down into the Darro gorge where many were killed, and he himself barely escaped to his base at Jaen. Ibn Mardanīsh also fled, leaving much of his army and equipment behind. The Almohad forces pursued their fleeing enemies to Jaen, where they ravaged the countryside.

The Almohads had now recovered this 'camel's hump of al-Andalus' (i.e. the most delicious part) and the Caliph was determined to keep it. The garrison that had held out in the Alcazaba was rewarded and compensated for lack of pay. A garrison of loyal Andalusis was established there along with the Almohads, and the hostile inhabitants were expelled. The Caliph also took care to supply the Alcazaba: 'He filled the store rooms of the Alcazaba with wheat, barley and salt and weapons like spears, shields [*daraq*], swords, bows, arrows and shields [*tarsiya*].'[25] All these were brought by sea from North Africa to Almuñecar on the coast and then transferred to Granada, suggesting that such supplies were unobtainable in al-Andalus which was effectively being subsidised by the African part of the empire. These supplies were kept in the Alcazaba until 1167/8 when they were distributed among the Almohads in lieu of pay: it was never easy to keep a fortress properly supplied.

In the aftermath of this triumph, the Caliph decided to transfer the capital of al-Andalus from Seville to Cordoba, because of both its central position and its ancient status as the capital of the Umayyads. The choice suggests a new confidence, at least on the part of the Caliph, and a new forward policy against both the Christians and Ibn Mardanīsh and his allies. Cordoba had suffered very badly during the civil wars of the period and Ibn Ṣāḥib al-Ṣalāt, who was an eye-witness, speaks of a ruined and deserted city whose inhabitants had fled. He claims that there were only 82 male inhabitants left, a detail supported by Ibn al-Abbār who describes them as being obliged to scratch a living by cultivating deserted lots within the city.[26]

The transfer of the administration to the new capital was entrusted to Barrāz b. Muḥammad al-Massūfī, the ex-Almoravid commander who had led the first Almohad army to al-Andalus. He remained an important figure in its administration until his death in 1163/4. He ordered the transfer of the *kuttāb* (secretaries) and *mushrifūn* (tax officers) from Seville accompanied by many of the leading citizens, though Ibn Ṣāḥib al-Ṣalāt succeeded in avoiding

25. Ibn Ṣāḥib al-Ṣalāt, *Al-Mann bi'l-Imāma*, p. 196; trans., p. 47.

26. Ibid., p. 199; trans., p. 49; Huici Miranda, *Historia Politica*, i, p. 204.

this draft by remaining in Seville to help with the accounts and the collection of *zakāt* (alms) there.[27]

On 26 September the victorious princes, *sayyid* Abū Ya'qūb Yūsuf and *sayyid* Abū Sa'īd 'Uthmān, with their military commander Yūsuf b. Sulaymān, arrived from Granada and were met by the inhabitants, old and new, at the Bāb al-Qanṭara (Gate of the Bridge). Reconstruction work began immediately, the architect Aḥmad b. Bāso was summoned and palaces, houses and fortifications built or restored. The *ṭālibs* of Cordoba had their names entered in the lists of those entitled to salaries. Muḥammad b. Sulaymān soon returned to Morocco with the Almohad and Arab troops. In December, *sayyid* Abū Ya'qūb Yūsuf was summoned by his father, who was making new arrangements for the succession, leaving his brother in Cordoba.

If the transfer of the capital had brought a new lease of life to Cordoba, it had brought poverty to Seville, now reduced to the status of a provincial city. Ibn Ṣāḥib al-Ṣālat laments the loss of status and, in doing so, gives an insight into the government of an Almohad provincial city. Yalūl b. Jaldās, a minor tribal leader, was in charge of the Almohads (*'ala shughl al-muwwaḥidīn*) in the city and Muḥammad b. Abī Sa'īd, known as Ibn al-Mu'alim, the financial administration (*'ala shughl al-makhzin*: it seems that this term, usually transliterated as *makhzen*, commonly used in Morocco for the financial administration of the government down to the twentieth century, was first used in Almohad times).[28] They would meet every morning to decide security matters before going about their separate business.

The Caliph died in May 1163 in Rabat, while collecting troops for the major expedition to al-Andalus he had long contemplated but never undertaken. Ibn Ṣāḥib al-Ṣalāt says that they numbered 100,000 horse and 100,000 foot and that their camp stretched as far as the spring at Gabula, some 19 kilometres from Rabat.[29] If the numbers are anything like correct, it was much the biggest army the Almohads had assembled. According to the Andalusi lord Sīdray b. Wazīr, who was present, the intention was to launch a four-pronged attack, against Portugal at Coimbra, Leon at Ciudad Rodrigo, and Castile at Toledo and Barcelona. The Caliph's death probably saved the Christians from a major invasion, though it is hard to see that

27. Ibn Ṣāḥib al-Ṣalāt, *Al-Mann bi'l-Imāma*, p. 203; trans., pp. 50–1.

28. See R. Dozy, *Supplément aux Dictionnaires Arabes* (2 vols, Leiden, 1967), i, p. 369.

29. Ibn Ṣāḥib al-Ṣalāt, *Al-Mann bi'l-Imāma*, pp. 214–15; trans., pp. 55–6.

such a large and diverse army would have been very effective and the problems of finding supplies would have been enormous.

The caliphate of Abū Yaʿqūb Yūsuf: the early years, 1163–72

As early as 1154 ʿAbd al-Muʾmin had secured the nomination of his son Muḥammad as heir. The sources accuse him of irreligious behaviour, like wine-drinking, but this may be no more than later attempts to blacken his reputation. Whatever the truth about this, Muḥammad was ousted from his position in a *coup d'état* managed by another of ʿAbd al-Muʾmin's sons, *sayyid* Abū Ḥafṣ ʿUmar. He seems to have been his father's chief adviser in the last years of his reign and was with him when he died. In circumstances which are not entirely clear, he managed to keep the death secret for long enough to ensure the succession of another brother, *sayyid* Abū Yaʿqūb Yūsuf, governor of Seville. This seems to have been the product of rivalry between different groups among ʿAbd al-Muʾmin's numerous sons: Abū Ḥafṣ ʿUmar and Abū Yaʿqūb Yūsuf shared the same mother, Zaynab, the daughter of Mūsā b. Sulaymān, a member of the Fifty, and they may have worked as a team. However, it was not only the displaced Muḥammad who was dissatisfied with this turn of events. The veteran Almohad ʿUmar al-Hintātī was absent at the time but seems to have acquiesced. Three other brothers, Abū Muḥammad ʿAbd Allāh of Bougie, Abūʾl-Ḥasan ʿAlī, who had taken his father's body to Tīnmal for burial, and Abū Saʿīd ʿUthmān of Cordoba seem to have objected. Abū Muḥammad soon met a mysterious death, but Abū Saʿīd, perhaps because of his position in the sensitive city of Cordoba, where he could easily have gone over to Ibn Mardanīsh and his allies, was treated with more respect: a deputation of senior Almohads visited him and accepted his excuses that his delay in recognising the new sovereign was due to illness and that rumours of his opposition were the work of slanderers. The deposed Muḥammad was allowed to live on in retirement in Marrakesh. This *coup* marked an important concentration of power within the ruling Muʾminid family: from this time it was only the descendants of Yūsuf and his full brother ʿUmar who were allowed to enjoy the senior positions in the Almohad state. The families of the rest of ʿAbd al-Muʾmin's sons were effectively deprived of these honours.

The new Caliph (who simply took the title of Amir until he was formally proclaimed as Amīr al-Mu'minīn, i.e. Caliph, in 1167/8. To avoid confusion, however, he will be referred to as Yūsuf I from now on) was an interesting personality. He was now 25 years old but was not without political experience, having been governor of Seville, off and on, since the age of eighteen, and he had participated in the successful reconquest of Granada from Ibn Hamushk. His father had been a great leader of armies, but Yūsuf did not inherit this quality. At crucial moments on campaign he showed himself hesitant and indecisive and this weakness was to prove fatal in the campaign against Santarem in 1184, which led to his death at the hands of the Christians. He also suffered from long periods of illness, perhaps depression, which interrupted the working of government. At the same time he was a genuine intellectual and bibliophile and had acquired an extensive knowledge of Arabic literature and religious writing during his stay in Seville. He was to gather round him a group of scholars, including Ibn Ṭufayl and Ibn Rushd (Averroes), and collected books like the Umayyad al-Ḥakam II (961–78) had before; a private collector in Seville recounts how this was done:

> The Commander of the Faithful came to hear [of my collections], so he sent Kāfūr the Eunuch with a selected group of slaves to my house when I was in the government offices [*dīwān*] and knew nothing about it. He ordered him not to frighten anyone in the house and not to take anything except books and then threatened him and those with him with the direst punishments if the people of the house lost so much as a pin. I was told about this while I was at the office and I thought that he intended to confiscate all my property, so, almost out of my mind, I rode to my house. There was the eunuch Kāfūr standing at the door and the books were being brought out to him. When he saw that I was obviously terrified, he said, 'Don't panic!' and added that the Caliph sent me his greetings and had mentioned me favourably and he carried on smiling until I relaxed. Then he said, 'Ask the members of your household if anyone has frightened them or if they are missing anything' and they replied, 'Nobody has frightened us and nothing is missing. Abū'l-Musk (Kāfūr) came and asked our permission three times and said that we were free to go. Then he himself went into the library store and ordered that the books be removed.' When I heard this all my anxiety disappeared.[30]

This collector was then given a profitable government position he had not previously expected. The anecdote is interesting: at one

30. 'Abd al-Wāḥid al-Marrākushī, *Al-Mu'jib*, pp. 238–9.

level it shows the Caliph as cultured and humane, at another it shows how the arbitrary exercise of power intimidated an ordinary citizen.

Book collecting was not, however, the new Caliph's overriding concern. His father just before he died had gathered a vast army at Rabat – a vast army to pursue the *jihād* in al-Andalus. ʿAbd al-Mu'min's death put a temporary end to these plans. After his accession, the Caliph had to go to the capital at Marrakesh to secure his position. It was not until early in 1165 that the Caliph, or rather his brother, *sayyid* Abū Ḥafṣ ʿUmar, who seems to have been in effective charge of the government at this time, was in a position to send reinforcements to al-Andalus. The first stage was to make sure of the loyalty of his half-brother, *sayyid* Abū Saʿīd ʿUthmān of Cordoba. Accordingly an expedition left Marrakesh in January 1165. It was led by *sayyid* Abū Ḥafṣ ʿUmar, accompanied by a number of senior Almohads, Andalusi leaders like Sīdray b. Wazīr and a group of 400 ex-Almoravid *shaykh*s of Massūfa and Lamtūna. The bulk of the force consisted of 4,000 Arab horsemen with two senior Almohads in charge of them. When he reached Gibraltar in February or March, Abū Saʿīd ʿUthmān came from Cordoba to pledge his loyalty to the Caliph along with other leading Andalusis, including a delegation from Seville, the *faqīh* Ibn al-Jadd, Abū Bakr al-Ghāfiqī the *qāḍī*, Ibn al-Muʿalim, head of the *makhzen*, and the chronicler Ibn Ṣāḥib al-Ṣalāt who, to his vast delight, was presented to the *sayyid* by his secretary, Abū'l-Ḥasan b. ʿAyyāsh, and favourably received.[31] It was the sort of political performance the Almohads did well: poems were recited and drums were banged, but after staying a fortnight Abū Ḥafṣ ʿUmar returned to Marrakesh, taking his brother, Abū Saʿīd ʿUthmān, with him. The Arab soldiers and their Almohad commanders were sent on to Cordoba to help defend it against Ibn Mardanīsh, and a detachment of 500 went to Badajoz which was, as ever, being threatened by the Christians.

No sooner had the two *sayyid*s, Abū Ḥafṣ ʿUmar and Abū Saʿīd ʿUthmān, returned to Marrakesh than they set out again for al-Andalus, and by September they were in Cordoba. They arrived determined to put an end to the menace posed by Ibn Mardanīsh and his supporters. Their first objective was the western outpost of his domains at Andujar, about 60 kilometres to the east of Cordoba, which was a constant threat to the city. Andujar fell easily and detachments were sent to pillage the surrounding countryside:

31. Ibn Ṣāḥib al-Ṣalāt, *Al-Mann bi'l-Imāma*, p. 253; trans., p. 71.

'they took the livestock from near and far and the hands of the Almohads were filled with booty and prisoners'. The windfall enabled the commanders to dish out provisions and money 'which redoubled their loyalty to them'.[32] The people of the area were certainly Muslims, yet the Almohads behaved as a conquering army. It seems as if they had brought neither supplies nor cash for payment of the troops and that the army was expected to survive off booty.

From Andujar they headed in the direction of Ibn Mardanīsh's capital at Murcia. They were met by Ibn Mardanīsh, who had summoned all the people of the Levante, his salaried soldiers and his Christian allies. The core of the Almohad force was composed of men from Tīnmal and the original Almohad tribes like Harga and Hintāta, but they were assisted by a number of Arabs from the Hilāl and Riyāḥ tribes and slaves. On 15 October a battle was fought at a site known to the Arabs as Faḥṣ al-Jullāb near Murcia and according to the Muslim accounts (we have no Christian ones) the forces of Ibn Mardanīsh were heavily defeated. Ibn Mardanīsh himself fled to the shelter of the walls of Murcia while the victorious Almohads dispersed to pillage the country without restraint. Letters describing the triumph were immediately dispatched to Seville and Marrakesh (the latter arrived on 31 October). With a typically Almohad display of grandiloquence and classical learning the victory was compared to Dhū Qār when the pre-Islamic Arabs had defeated the Persians.[33] As often, the reality was rather less decisive: Ibn Mardanīsh had been humiliated but the Almohads had not been able to mount a serious assault on the city of Murcia. They soon retired, Abū Saʿīd 'Uthmān remaining in Cordoba while Abū Ḥafṣ 'Umar with most of the troops returned to Marrakesh, where his brother the Caliph gave his army a triumphant reception. Each soldier was presented with a turban, a cloak and a length of linen. Each horseman received 20 gold *dīnār*s, while the chiefs of the Almohads and the Arabs had 100. Their names were all written down to ensure that the payment was distributed fairly.

New government appointments followed. In April 1166 Seville was entrusted not to a member of the ruling house (presumably because there were no suitable candidates) but to the son of one of Ibn Tūmart's closest associates, the *ḥāfiẓ* Abū 'Abd Allāh, son of Ismāʿīl b. Tījīt. He was dispatched with drums and banners through the streets of Marrakesh to the Fes Gate at the beginning of the

32. Ibid., p. 277; trans., p. 78. 33. Ibid., pp. 282–3; trans., pp. 79–80.

road which led to al-Andalus. With him were a number of senior Almohads, some Arab troops and a *wazīr*, the *ḥāfiẓ* Abū Zakariyā b. Yaḥyā b. Sinān, whose father had been one of the Fifty. By 4 May he was in Seville, where he took over from the Andalusi Abū'l-'Alā b. 'Azzūn, described as chief of the commanders and *shaykh*s of Seville. In September he was replaced by one of the Caliph's brothers, the *sayyid* Abū Ibrāhīm Ismā'īl, and early the next year he was ordered to take up the governorate of Granada. It is interesting to note that the orders for this transfer came from Marrakesh: Seville may have been the capital of Almohad al-Andalus, but in important matters, real power still lay with Marrakesh. Abū 'Abd Allāh remained a leading figure in al-Andalus until his death, aged only 36, in 1174. As well as his military achievements, which included the conquest of Baza, he had intellectual interests: he was learned in Qur'ān studies and legal affairs and built up a fine library of literature and history. The Almohad ruling class, perhaps imitating the Caliph, put a high value on learning.

Further government changes occurred the following year, in 1168. The main problem facing the Almohad administration in al-Andalus was not the Christian advance but the threat posed by Ibn Mardanīsh. Despite the defeat near Murcia, he was still capable of mounting a major offensive against Cordoba and other Almohad-controlled cities. In the spring of 1168 a party of his men raided as far as Ronda and took much of the town's livestock (it is noteworthy how much of the raiding of this period was concerned with rustling sheep and cattle). As they were returning to their base at Guadix they were attacked by a force led by Abū 'Abd Allāh, the governor of Granada, and defeated: the prisoners, including 53 Christians, were executed.

Almohad rule was also challenged in the west, notably by the guerrilla tactics of the Portuguese leader Giraldo Sempavor (the Fearless).[34] In 1165, at the same time as Almohad forces were pursuing and defeating Ibn Mardanīsh at Faḥṣ al-Jullāb, Giraldo, in a series of lightning attacks, took Trujillo, Evora and Caceres. The next spring he took Montanchez and Jurumeña to use as a base for attacking Badajoz. Ibn Ṣāḥib al-Ṣalāt describes him attacking on dark and stormy winter nights, running ladders up against the walls and surprising the sentries. Giraldo was basically a freelance and he is said to have sold Trujillo and Evora to the Portuguese Christians after he had taken them. By May 1169 Giraldo had entered the city

34. See D.W. Lomax, *The Reconquest of Spain* (London, 1978), pp. 113–14, for an outline of his career.

of Badajoz, and the King of Portugal, Afonso Henriques, had come to help him besiege the Almohad garrison still holding out in the Alcazaba.

It seemed as if Badajoz would soon fall, and the whole area with it. The Caliph in Marrakesh, now stirred into action, sent an army under the command of ʿUmar al-Hintātī, now the only surviving member of Ibn Tūmart's original Ten. Fortunately for the Muslims, they found an ally in the King of Leon, Fernando II, who had no desire to see Badajoz fall into Portuguese hands: if anyone were to take it from the Muslims it should be he. Accordingly, he made an alliance with the Almohads. The besieged garrison in Badajoz helped him to enter the city, and in the fighting Afonso Henriques was taken prisoner. He was allowed his liberty only on condition that he handed over all his recent gains. Fernando II retired and Badajoz once more returned to Muslim control, but Giraldo was still at large, threatening the city from his base at Jurumeña and ravaging the country around. In May 1170 the situation deteriorated yet further when Giraldo attacked and pillaged a convoy bringing supplies to the garrison and killed its commander.

Once again reinforcements had to be sent from Marrakesh, led this time by the Caliph's brother, Abū Ḥafṣ ʿUmar. As well as the Almohads, including his brother Abū Saʿīd ʿUthmān and a number of *ḥafizs*, sons of the Fifty, there were Andalusis resident in Marrakesh who were chosen for their knowledge of the country, among them Sīdray b. Wazīr and Abū'l-ʿAlā b. ʿAzzūn, the Almohads' leading Andalusi supporters. When they reached al-Andalus in September–October 1170, the *sayyid* Abū Saʿīd ʿUthmān was sent to Badajoz with the Andalusi leaders. The alliance with Fernando II was renewed at a meeting between him and Ibn Wazīr and Ibn ʿAzzūn on the fateful field of Zallāqa where the Almoravids had routed Alfonso VI 84 years previously. Ibn Wazīr, who was a friend and important source for the chronicler Ibn Ṣāḥib al-Ṣalāt, makes it clear that he was sent because he understood Spanish. In the course of the interview some Christians stole his turban; when he returned bareheaded, his commander, the *sayyid* Abū Saʿīd, gave him his own, an act of consideration for which the recipient was duly grateful.[35]

After the alliance was concluded, Giraldo was driven out of Jurumeña and Badajoz safeguarded, but the impression remains that it was an isolated garrison town in a ravaged and often hostile

35. For these campaigns see Ibn Ṣāḥib al-Ṣalāt, *Al-Mann bi'l-Imāma*, pp. 397–407, 424–6; trans., pp. 139–46, 154–7.

countryside, sustained only by tenuous links with Seville. Another convoy is recorded in 1171 and Ibn ʿAzzūn drove Giraldo's men out of the castle at Lobon, about 30 kilometres east of the city.[36] In 1173 a further convoy was sent, with 4,000 mounted troops guarding 3,000 mules carrying wheat, barley, flour, oil, salt, arms and all the provisions necessary for the people.

Badajoz remained something of a side-show. The main object of the 1170 expedition was to secure the submission or defeat of Ibn Mardanīsh. For all the talk of *jihād*, the subjection of the Muslims of al-Andalus remained the first priority. Despite his defeat at Faḥṣ al-Jullāb, Ibn Mardanīsh remained firmly in control of Murcia and Valencia. In the summer of 1169, however, he was seriously weakened by the defection of his father-in-law Ibn Hamushk who had been his ally since the arrival of the Almohads. The reason for the defection is said to have been resentment at Ibn Mardanīsh's humiliating divorce of Ibn Hamushk's daughter which left him fearing for his own life, but there may have been political differences as well. He came to Cordoba to pledge his submission. It was always part of Almohad strategy to welcome and honour Andalusis who accepted the Almohad doctrine and came over to them. Ibn Hamushk was received with honour in Marrakesh and given estates near Meknes. He soon became a prominent figure in Almohad armies operating in al-Andalus.

The Almohad leaders in al-Andalus, the *sayyid*s ʿUmar and ʿUthmān and the Hafsid ʿUmar al-Hintātī, spent the winter of 1170/1 in Seville, planning their next move. Guided by Ibn Hamushk, they set out from Cordoba via Lorca to Murcia. Ibn Mardanīsh's support seems to have been crumbling and in Lorca the people called in the Almohads to help rid them of Ibn Mardanīsh's half-Muslim, half-Christian garrison in the citadel. Almeria, Baza and Elche all pledged their allegiance. Ibn Mardanīsh himself, faced by these defections, seems to have become increasingly dependent on Christian support and his introduction of more Christians into the garrison at Valencia alienated many Muslims. The lord of Alcira went over to the Almohads and, during the summer of 1171, Ibn Mardanīsh tried unsuccessfully to take the city by siege. According to al-Baydhaq,[37] the defections went further and Ibn Mardanīsh's own brother, Abū'l-Ḥajjāj Yūsuf, governor of Valencia, submitted to the Almohads. For reasons which are not clear, the Almohad forces

36. Ibid., p. 497; trans., p. 187.
37. *Documents inédits d'Histoire Almohade,* ed. E. Lévi-Provençal (Paris, 1928), p. 215.

withdrew without taking Murcia, which remained in Ibn Mardanīsh's hands until his death the next year.[38]

The Huete campaign, 1172

In June 1171 the Caliph himself finally arrived in Seville. It was eight years since he had succeeded his father. During this time he had sent reinforcements to al-Andalus and his most trusted aides, including his brother *sayyid*, Abū Ḥafṣ 'Umar, and 'Umar al-Hintātī, but he himself had delayed, probably because he wished to make sure that there would be no disturbances in Marrakesh, where his brother Muḥammad, the original heir to 'Abd al-Mu'min, still lived. Furthermore, the Caliph was ill for most of 1169 and 1170 and was treated by eminent physicians, including the famous doctor and philosopher Ibn Ṭufayl.[39]

His expedition was carefully planned. To reinforce the Almohad forces, more Arabs were recruited in Tunisia, with poems being specially composed by Ibn Ṭufayl and the *wazīr* Ibn 'Ayyāsh to inspire them to the *jihād.* The leading figure among them was Jabāra b. Abī'l-'Aynayn of the Banū Riyāḥ who had fled to Egypt and the Hijaz to escape Almohad control but was now enticed to return. Money and horses were also collected: 4,000 horses and 500 loads of money from Tunisia and 1,000 horses and 50 loads of money from the Tlemcen area. In January 1171 receptions and parades were held in Marrakesh to encourage the loyalty of the Arabs to the Caliph, his family and the Almohad elite. A feast was given for 3,000 people in the Buhayra gardens outside the city walls and all the troops were reviewed. Ibn Ṣāḥib al-Ṣalāt, who was present with a delegation of Andalusis, records that there were violent quarrels between the rank and file of the Arabs and the Almohads.[40] The Arabs showed none of the customary awe and respect for the Caliph and he, for his part, turned a blind eye to their unruly behaviour. It did not bode well for the future campaign.

The troops, who were said to have numbered 10,000 Almohads and 10,000 Arabs,[41] were also paid. Abū 'Abd Allāh b. Muḥsin, who

38. The confused events of this year are discussed in P. Guichard, *Les Musulmans de Valence et la Reconquête* (2 vols, Damascus, 1990–1), i, pp. 125–6.

39. For the role of Ibn Ṭufayl and other important observations on the Almohad court see L. Conrad, 'An Andalusi physician at the court of the Muwahhids: some notes on the public career of Ibn Ṭufayl', *Al-Qantara* xvi (1995), 1–12.

40. Ibn Ṣāḥib al-Ṣalāt, *Al-Mann bi'l-Imāma*, pp. 463–5; trans., pp. 174–7.

41. Ibid., pp. 482–3; trans., p. 183.

was in charge of the *dīwān* in which the names of those to be paid were entered, described how he warned the Caliph that the numbers had greatly increased, but his master airily dismissed his anxieties, saying that he wanted to do his best for his soldiers. Ibn Ṣāḥib al-Ṣalāt, with a bureaucrat's eye for figures, notes the different rates of pay: among the Almohads, a fully equipped horseman was given 10 *dīnārs*, a partially equipped one 8, with 5 for a fully equipped foot soldier and 3 for the rest. The Arabs had a higher rate, 25 and 15 respectively for the horsemen and 6 for the foot soldiers: each Arab *shaykh* was given 50 and each *ra'īs* (paramount chief) 1,000. Three thousand horses were distributed among the Arabs as well as clothing materials and turbans. It seems as if these payments were not regular salaries but were made as and when resources were available. Ibn Ṣāḥib al-Ṣalāt says that all the troops were satisfied and that good relations prevailed,[42] but it is hard to believe that the Almohads were not resentful at the favours shown to the newly arrived Arabs.

On 13 March 1171 this large but unwieldy force left Marrakesh with great pomp, preceded by the Qur'āns of the Caliph 'Uthman and the Mahdī Ibn Tūmart, carried in great state. They reached Seville on 8 June and Cordoba eleven days later, where the Caliph remained to welcome his brother, *sayyid* Abū Ḥafṣ 'Umar, on his triumphant return from the campaign against Ibn Mardanīsh. By early September he was back in Seville, where he began a series of building projects and restorations.

The spring of 1172 brought good news to the Caliph. On 8 March 1172 Ibn Mardanīsh, now deserted by almost all his supporters including his brother Abū'l-Ḥajjāj, died of natural causes. His state was already on the verge of complete collapse and his death spelt the end of resistance. After a council, his family and followers decided to surrender to the Almohads. Despite the long years of hostility, the Almohads were happy to accept this submission and at the end of April, his son Hilāl came to Seville and was received with honour. As with the other lords of al-Andalus, Almohad policy was to incorporate the Banū Mardanīsh followers in the Almohad elite and use their talents and the support they enjoyed in the country. Hilāl b. Mardanīsh and his followers were lodged in the old palace of the Taifa king Muḥammad b. 'Abbād in Seville and showered with presents, while his soldiers, including one Sa'īd b. 'Īsā, described as lord of the frontier (*ṣāḥib al-thaghr*),

42. Ibid., pp. 465–6; trans., pp. 176–7.

formed a valuable part of the Almohad army.[43] The effect of this surrender was to increase the Andalusi element in the Almohad forces to balance the Almohads and Arabs. Meanwhile, Ibn Mardanīsh's old domains were governed by a leading Almohad. According to al-Baydhaq, elements of the Almohad army were also settled there, Arabs and Zanāta in Valencia, Haskura Berbers at Jativa and Murcia, people of Tīnmal at Lorca and Kūmīya Berbers at Almeria, but it is difficult to say how extensive such settlement was.[44]

Guichard has discussed the effect the Almohad take-over had in the Levante.[45] He concludes that the Almohad 'conquest' resulted in very few changes, except at the highest level. Even there, Yūsuf b. Mardanīsh remained governor of Valencia and it was only on his death in 1186 that he was replaced by an Almohad. The name of the Almohad caliph replaced that of the ʿAbbasid, still formally acknowledged by Ibn Mardanīsh, at the Friday prayers. It looks as if the *jund* and the religious dignitaries of the old regime continued in their functions, but there was more career mobility. Ibn al-Rumālya, for example, came originally from Granada, became *qāḍī* of Jativa in Ibn Mardanīsh's domains but returned to Granada as *qāḍī* between 1172 and his death in 1180. Service under Ibn Mardanīsh did not disqualify a man from serving the Almohads in high office: Ibn Hubaysh, prayer leader at the mosque in Murcia, went on to become *qāḍī* after the take-over. The most spectacular career was that of Ibn Ḥawt Allāh from Onda (about 50 kilometres north of Valencia) who became *qāḍī* successively of Cordoba, Murcia, Ceuta, Salé, Seville, Majorca and finally Granada, where he died in 1215. The incorporation of the Levante into the Almohad caliphate had surprisingly little effect on the structure of society or the personnel of government in the area.

The principal object of the Caliph's visit was a major expedition against the Christians. He had been advised by Ibn Mardanīsh's men that Huete was a suitable object for such an expedition as it was newly settled and inadequately defended. He eventually set out from Seville in June 1172. This expedition was the first determined attempt by an Almohad caliph in person to reverse the successes of the Reconquista. Ibn Ṣāḥib al-Ṣalāt, who was a participant, gives us a full and frank account of it,[46] and it is worth describing in some

43. Ibid., pp. 507–9; trans., pp. 193–4.
44. Al-Baydhaq, *Documents inédits*, ed. Lévi-Provençal, p. 215.
45. Guichard, *Musulmans de Valence*, i, pp. 127–9.
46. Ibn Ṣāḥib al-Ṣalāt, *Al-Mann bi'l-Imāma*, pp. 525–53; trans., pp. 204–24.

detail for it gives a clear idea of the strengths and weaknesses of the Almohad state at war. The army was large, perhaps more than 20,000,[47] and composed of Almohads, Arabs from Morocco and Andalusis. There were also a large number of non-combatants, like our author, for this was a peripatetic monarchy, like many in the contemporary Christian west, so there were bureaucrats and religious dignitaries.

After a pause at Cordoba, the army moved on to attack the castle at Vilches which Ibn Mardanīsh had handed over to the Christians after his quarrel with Ibn Hamushk, to whom it had previously belonged. It took only a day, 25 June, to reduce this Christian outpost, and the castle was handed back to Ibn Hamushk. By 30 June the army had reached Alcaraz where the Christian garrison asked for terms. The Muslims then moved into Christian territory, sticking close to their water supplies. On 6 July the Caliph camped on the River Jucar for his troops to rest while his experienced and competent brother, *sayyid* Abū Sa'īd 'Uthmān, who had served in al-Andalus since 1157, led an advance raiding party which included the Andalusi leaders Ibn 'Azzūn and Ibn Ḥamushk and their followers. There were some skirmishes in which the Arab contingents, of whose fighting abilities Ibn Ṣāḥib al-Ṣalāt had a very poor opinion, were worsted, but on 11 July the whole army assembled at Huete.

The chronicler gives us a detailed description of the army. There was no attempt to break up the tribal units and each tribe fought under its own chiefs. At the head was of course the Caliph himself, escorted by the sons of the Ten and the Fifty and other Almohad notables. Next came his right-hand man, his brother the *sayyid* Abū Ḥafṣ, and his other brothers: each brother had one of the old Almohad tribes with him, Abū Sa'īd 'Uthmān with Hintāta, Abū Zakarīyā Yaḥyā, governor of Bougie, with Kūmīya, Abū 'Alī al-Ḥusayn with Gomara, Abū Isḥāq Ibrāhīm with Gadmīwa and Abū Ibrāhīm Isma'il with Ganfīsa. There were also the religious dignitaries, including the *faqīh*s, Abū Bakr b. al-Jadd and Abū Muḥammad of Malaga, and the three *qāḍī*s, 'Īsā b. 'Imrān, Abū Muḥammad b. al-Ṣaffār and Abū'l-Walīd b. Rushd. The army advanced and the Caliph pitched the scarlet royal tent in a conspicuous position.

Huete was no Toledo: it has never been a big place, nor does it have strong natural fortifications. There was a citadel on a rounded hill and a small, inadequately fortified suburb at the foot of the hill

47. Lomax cites a figure of 100,000 but gives no reference (*Reconquest*, p. 114). Ibn Ṣāḥib al-Ṣalāt gives no overall figure, but mentions an expeditionary force of 12,000 being sent on ahead (*Al-Mann bi'l-Imāma*, p. 528; trans., p. 207).

by the small river. On 12 July a general assault was begun and most of the suburb was taken, forcing the defenders to flee to the citadel for refuge. At a crucial point, however, the momentum of attack was lost and reinforcements that could have carried the day were not sent. Abū'l-'Alā b. 'Azzūn, the Andalusi commander who played a leading role in that attack, later told Ibn Ṣāḥib al-Ṣalāt what had gone wrong:

> When I was fighting with the Christians in the tower, which was the heart of their resistance in the city of Huete, and victory and triumph over them were within our grasp, I saw none of the valiant soldiers or *shaykhs* or commanders who were supporting me. I rushed in person to the Caliph who was in session with his brother, the illustrious *sayyid* Abū Ḥafṣ and the *ṭālib*s of the court, discussing questions of religious dogma. I said to him, 'My lord the Caliph! send me reinforcements for I am on the point of victory!' I only wanted him to show himself on horseback so that the people and all the soldiers would see him and they would enter the city then and there. But he did not answer me and disregarded me for what he was doing. However the illustrious *sayyid* Abū Ḥafṣ replied to me and I realised that the intention of the *jihād* had been corrupted and that the expedition had failed. I returned despairing of victory and very preoccupied and thoughtful.[48]

After the failure of a direct assault, the Almohad army settled down for a siege, aiming to prevent the Christians from fetching water, and a quarter of the army was sent out to forage. The Caliph ordered that siege engines and towers should be constructed. Reinforcements arrived from Murcia led by the Almohad governor 'Umar al-Hintātī and Abū'l-Ḥajjāj b. Mardanīsh, who brought the men of the Levante.

Things soon began to go wrong. Even though it was July the weather turned against them. On the 14th there was a violent gale which destroyed many tents, and this was followed on the 16th by a thunderstorm. The next morning the Caliph ordered an assault but further heavy rain forced them to retire. When the weather cleared up in the afternoon the attack was renewed, but without significant results. The next morning the Caliph remained in his tent and he and his court seem to have been paralysed by depression or inertia. On the 19th the Christians made a successful sortie against the Haskūra Berbers, who fled; more disturbing, supplies began to run short. A third of each tribe was sent foraging but

48. Ibn Ṣāḥib al-Ṣalāt, *Al-Mann bi'l-Imāma*, p. 534; trans., p. 211.

without much success and prices rose. Two days later, on 21 July (a Friday), the preacher exhorted the army, first in Arabic and then in Berber, to remember their commitments to the *jihād* if they were true Almohads. But the problem lay with the commanders, not the rank and file.

News came from the Christian camp that the Christian forces under Alfonso VIII (King of Castile, 1158–1214) were preparing to raise the siege. At this the Caliph seems to have lost his nerve: on the Saturday night he ordered that the siege towers and engines be burned, and the chief of the mule-train was told to prepare his beasts to carry off the bells of the town church which had been taken in the first attack. The next day, 23 July, to the surprise and confusion of most of the army, the drums were beaten to announce departure. The siege had lasted less than a fortnight. As they were leaving in confusion and disorder, the Christians made a sally to burn and pillage the camp and slaughter the sick and weak.

The army headed east in the direction of Cuenca, the nearest Muslim town. Ibn Ṣāḥib al-Ṣalāt stresses that the march was orderly, but nothing could disguise the fact that, despite the large size of the army, the attack had been a fiasco. It is clear that the failure was partly one of leadership: at crucial moments neither the Caliph nor the Almohads who surrounded him seem to have been able to provide effective decision-making. But there were other problems too. No serious attempt was made to mount a formal siege. The engines and towers never seem to have been used (if they were ever finished) and were burned after only a few days. No thought seems to have been given to questions of supply before the problems became acute: once the country around Huete had been denuded, there were no reserves. The fact that the army had two different, mutually incomprehensible languages cannot have helped and their fighting in tribal groups would not have made for easy co-operation. As it was, almost all the effective fighting seems to have been done by Andalusi military leaders like Ibn ʿAzzūn and Abū'l-Ḥajjāj b. Mardanīsh, though this may simply reflect the viewpoint of Ibn Ṣāḥib al-Ṣalāt.

On 25 July the army reached the plains around Cuenca. While the main force made camp by the River Jucar, the Caliph, with his brothers and a number of other courtiers including Ibn Ṣāḥib al-Ṣalāt, rode off to inspect the city. The author gives a fascinating description of Cuenca just five years before the Christian reconquest. It was extremely well situated and the natural strength of the site was reinforced by strong walls; hidden stairs led down to the river to give access to the mills and for the collection of water in times of attack. The city was surrounded by trees and fields, especially orchards of walnuts. This impressive site could not, however, disguise the dangers which threatened it. Much of the surrounding countryside had been handed over to the Christians by Ibn Mardanīsh and the city had been blockaded for the last five months. The people were debilitated and very short of supplies. The Caliph set out to do what he could to remedy the position. The *ḥāfiẓ* 'Isā b. Makhlūf al-Gadmīwī conducted a census which found that there were just 700 inhabitants, including men, women and children. The Caliph ordered that they be given payments, 12 *dīnār*s to a horseman, 8 to a foot soldier and 4 to women and children. He also gave them arms and 70 cattle, which was all there were in the camp. Leading Almohads were encouraged to give alms in either cash or grain.

On 26 July a rumour spread that Alfonso VIII and his forces were approaching. The Caliph ordered that the army should move across the Jucar to put the river between them and the enemy. As had happened at Huete, moving the camp caused chaos and panic broke out as they forded the swift-flowing river. The next morning the Caliph held a council of war. The Almohads and Andalusis wanted to attack the Christian army, which was now on the other side of the river, but the Arabs, whom our author openly accuses of cowardice, refused, saying that they needed to fight in open country. On Friday 28 July a small force of Andalusis and Almohads, led by the indefatigable Ibn 'Azzūn, skirmished with the enemy while the main force prepared for battle the next day. But at dawn on the 29th, when Ibn 'Azzūn went out on patrol, he found that the enemy had struck camp and left during the night. The Almohads did not pursue them but ordered the army to march east. The 700 Muslims of Cuenca were abandoned to their fate: no garrison was left in the city and the supplies the citizens had been given would soon be exhausted. The Christians would be back as soon as the Almohad army had left.

The Caliph's intention was to go to Murcia to consolidate Almohad control over Ibn Mardanīsh's kingdom. The distances were not large but the Caliph had totally failed to take into account the provisioning of this large and unwieldy army on the desolate mountain roads in high summer: the journey turned into a sort of Almohad retreat from Moscow. On the first day of the march (30 July) the baggage train and the army became separated and by the 31st both men and mules were dying of hunger. There were further casualties on the steep hill leading down to the bridge over the River Cabriel. In an effort to restore morale, the Caliph ordered the chiefs to collect their tribesmen for review and payments were made, 5 *dīnār*s for a horseman and 2 for a foot soldier. This seems to have been the first time the troops had been paid since the expedition had set off two months previously and the immediate effect was to cause prices in the camp to rise sharply. Progress was slow and matters were not helped when the guides lost their way and the army was scattered in the defiles near Requeña, the Caliph and his brother Abū Ḥafṣ spending the night separately and without baggage.

On 6 August they reached the castle at Buñol on the edge of the plain of Valencia. The army had travelled about 150 kilometres in nine days of marching, an average speed of some 16 kilometres a day. For many the arrival at Buñol marked the end of the ordeal and Abū'l-Ḥajjāj b. Mardanīsh, who had presumably gone on ahead, sent a convoy of flour from Valencia. Most of the Andalusis and those whose names were not on the registers (who presumably had not been paid) now dispersed to Valencia or their own homes. Ibn Ṣāḥib al-Ṣalāt himself tried to buy something to eat at the castle of Buñol but could only find over-priced, unripe figs and went to Valencia: he had heard of the wonderful gardens which surrounded the city and he was not disappointed, but he notes cryptically that its weakness and fear of disturbances were already apparent. After three days he was back with the Caliph at Buñol and what was left of the army moved south to Jativa. By 17 August the Caliph was safely in Murcia where he was welcomed by Hilāl b. Mardanīsh. The Banū Mardanīsh were now high in his favour: Abū'l-Ḥajjāj Yūsuf was confirmed in charge of Valencia and its region and the local leaders were confirmed in the frontier fortresses. The historian compares the relationship of the Caliph to the Banū Mardanīsh at this time to that of the ʿAbbasid Caliph al-Ma'mūn (813–33) to his all-powerful vizier, al-Ḥasan b. Sahl. When the Caliph returned to Seville in October, the Banū Mardanīsh were further honoured: they were given the status of members of the Ten and Hilāl's brother Ghānim b. Muḥammad was given command of all the Andalusi troops. As the ultimate honour, the Caliph took Hilāl's sister as his wife.

Distinguished religious leaders came from Qayrawan and Tunis to congratulate the Caliph on his campaign, but in reality the achievement had been minimal. Huete had not been taken, Cuenca was doomed and the next spring the weakness of Almohad control was glaringly exposed when the Christian army of the city of Avila raided deep into Andalucia around Ecija and the countryside around Cordoba. They took 50,000 sheep, 12,000 cows and 150 men. A force of Almohads set off in pursuit, defeated the Christians on the plains of Calatrava and retrieved the stolen property. An expedition was then made to the Tagus valley around Talavera where a satisfyingly large number of beasts were taken, though no attempt was made to take the city. Needless to say, a victory reception was held in Seville and speeches were made in praise of the Caliph and the Almohads, but the Christian raid had shown how vulnerable even the heartlands of al-Andalus were.

Abū Yaʿqūb Yūsuf: the later years, 1173–84

After 1173 the pace of our narrative must change, for this marks the end of the surviving section of Ibn Ṣāḥib al-Ṣalāt's history. From this point we are largely dependent on the Almohad section of Ibn Idhārī's *Bayān al-Mughrib*, which is itself largely an epitome of the lost last section of Ibn Ṣāḥib al-Ṣalāt. Ibn Idhārī kept the bare bones of the narrative but edited out much of the detail which makes the original so interesting and entertaining.[49]

After his return from the Huete campaign, the Caliph remained in al-Andalus for another three years until March 1176, but he seems to have stayed in Seville and certainly led no more major offensive operations. It was rather a period of raid and counter-raid. It was also characterised by truces with Castile and Portugal when each of these monarchies was preoccupied with inter-Christian rivalries.

The fiasco at Huete had done nothing to safeguard the position of the Muslims of al-Andalus, and an impression of the prevailing insecurity can be gained from the melancholy history of Beja. This is fully reported by Ibn Idhārī from the lost section of Ibn Ṣāḥib al-Ṣalāt.[50] Ibn Ṣāḥib al-Ṣalāt had family connections among the leading citizens of the town and his account provides an interesting insight into provincial life away from the Caliph's court. Before the coming of the Almohads the town had been ruled by Sīdray b. Wazīr, the Andalusi noble, but he was replaced

49. The main narrative source for the remainder of Yūsuf I's reign is Ibn Idhārī al-Marrākushī, *Al-Bayān al-Mughrib fi akhbār al-Andalus wa'l-Maghrib*, Part III ed. Huici Miranda (Tetuan, 1963), pp. 99–140, and the period is discussed in Huici Miranda, *Historia Politica*, i, pp. 266–312.

50. Ibn Idhārī, *Al-Bayān*, iii, pp. 101–5.

by a series of Almohad *Ḥuffāẓ*, the best of whom, according to the chronicler, was the Berber 'Umar b. Tīmṣalīt al-Tīnmalī. Apparently there were considerable social tensions in the city between the leading citizens (*a'yān*) and the lower classes (*suffāl*), though the causes of these tensions are never explained. Early in 1172 an Almohad *ṭālib*, 'Umar b. Saḥnūn, was appointed governor. He is the villain of the account. He and the *qāḍī*, a rash and thoughtless man called 'Umar b. Zarqāj, began to persecute the leading citizens, extorting money from them by force and menaces while allowing disreputable elements to flourish.

In the late summer of the same year the Christians of Portugal launched a surprise night attack. The towers of the walls of the Alcazaba and the city were supposed to be guarded by sentries, but Ibn Saḥnūn had embezzled the meagre pay of one of these who had abandoned his post as a result. The Christians were able to take control of the tower and shouted to create a panic in the town. The population fled, among the first being Ibn Saḥnūn, who went into hiding to escape the wrath of the Caliph who had ordered his execution. Others were not so lucky and many of the citizens died in the mélêe, including Abū Ja'far b. Ismā'īl b. Ṣāḥib al-Ṣalāt, a relative of the chronicler. The Christians found that they could not hold the city so they simply burned it and left it in ruins, while the inhabitants scattered through the Almohad empire as far as Marrakesh, living on charity and hand-outs.

In 1174 there was a truce and the Portuguese agreed to hand Beja back. The Caliph, still in Seville, wrote to the inhabitants inviting them to return. They were received with honour in Seville and the *wazīr*, Ibn Jāmi', ushered them into a great court attended by Almohad notables, the leading Andalusi families including the Banū 'Azzūn, the Banū Mardanīsh and the Banū Hamushk, and leading ideologues (*ṭullāb*) like Abū Muḥammad al-Māliqī and Abū Bakr b. al-Jadd. The Caliph told them the good news and encouraged them to return, promising that he would soon send a party of Almohad soldiers with their wives and families who would settle with them.

It was not an auspicious homecoming: the place was devastated and the houses uninhabitable. They were only 200 men in the party and they decided to remove to the Alcazaba where they could defend themselves more easily, blocking up the gate which led from the fortress to the open country. In December, 'Umar b. Tīmṣalīt, now governor of Silves, arrived with 500 men to help with the rebuilding; the walls of the Alcazaba were repaired and work was started on the walls of the city, but after 'Umar left the next spring it seems that work stopped and the promised Almohad garrison never appeared. To make matters worse, the old social tensions seem to have re-emerged and the governor, the Andalusi noble Abū Bakr b. Wazīr, is accused of acting high-handedly towards the leading citizens. In the end 'Umar b. Tīmṣalīt was reappointed, to the satisfaction of the leading citizens (it is interesting that they preferred the Berber Ibn Tīmṣalīt to the Andalusi Ibn Wazīr). For a few months all was well: houses were reconstructed and the land around the city cultivated, and the people were able to send their tithes and the rents of the properties to Seville.

This happy state of affairs was short-lived. Early in 1178 Ibn Tīmṣalīt and 'Alī b. Wazīr launched a raid against the Christians but were surprised by a force from Santarem and captured: Ibn Tīmṣalīt was executed and Ibn Wazīr eventually ransomed for 4,000 *dīnār*s. The inhabitants of Beja did not wait for a Christian force to arrive but simply retreated to the comparative safety of Mertola: it was the ignominious end of four and a half centuries of Muslim rule in the city.

The Caliph and his court left Seville for Morocco in March 1176, taking with them most of the Almohads and their families as well as the Andalusi Banū Mardanīsh and Banū Hamushk. When he returned to Marrakesh, a plague broke out which claimed the lives of a number of leading Almohads including four of the Caliph's brothers and the veteran Hafsid 'Umar al-Hintātī, who died on his way from Cordoba to Marrakesh. His passing marked the end of an era: he was the last survivor of the original Ten who had followed Ibn Tūmart, and he and his family had played a vital role in securing the support of Hintāta and other Berber tribes for 'Abd al-Mu'min and his dynasty.

The Caliph's departure led to an immediate deterioration in the security position in al-Andalus. The Christian powers became more aggressive and the Caliph's brothers who had been left in charge, *sayyid* Abū'l-Ḥasan 'Alī in Cordoba and *sayyid* Abū 'Alī al-Ḥusayn in Seville, proved incapable of mounting an effective resistance. The Almohads seem to have found it difficult to organise defensive warfare or to provide garrisons for threatened outposts. Their response to Christian raids was usually a counter-raid as distraction or revenge. This could be effective in the short term but, as we saw in the case of Beja, failed to protect Muslim communities against renewed attack. The immediate challenge came at Cuenca where Alfonso VIII, in the first military campaign he led in person, began a siege in early 1177. The Almohad response was not to reinforce the defences of the city but to launch raids: the army of Cordoba moved in the direction of Calatrava and *sayyid* Abū 'Alī al-Ḥusayn led 4,000 horse and 4,000 foot from Seville against Talavera. Neither expedition achieved its objective and Cuenca finally fell in October.

It was the conflict with Leon rather than Almohad power that prevented Alfonso VIII from following up this success, but when the peace of Rioseco was signed in March 1181 he again had a free hand. The next year he began a major advance into al-Andalus, raiding the country around Cordoba, Granada and Ronda and reaching as far as Algeciras. He established a base at Setefilla, in the hills north of Lora del Rio, to house a garrison in the Guadalquivir valley, but this had to be given up in the face of Almohad pressure after the King had left. If the expedition did not produce permanent territorial gains for the Castilians, it did yield a satisfyingly large booty in cattle and sheep and 700 prisoners who were ransomed for 2,775 *dīnār*s.

Even more damaging were the raids by the Portuguese in the areas to the west and north of Seville. In 1178, as well as taking Beja, they burned Triana across the river from the capital itself. In 1182/3 a party set out from Lisbon and Santarem and ravaged the Ajarafe, the land of villages and olive orchards to the west of Seville. Some 1,000 horse and 1,000 foot took numerous captives and again almost reached the walls of Seville.

The Almohad response was feeble. *sayyid* Abū 'Alī al-Ḥusayn in Seville and his successor, the Caliph's young and inexperienced son *sayyid* Abū Isḥāq, failed to provide effective leadership and only a veteran Almohad, Yūsuf b. Wānnūdīn, one of the original Fifty, a man much admired by Ibn Ṣāḥib al-Ṣalāt, provided real leadership with raids on Talavera and Evora.

The struggle was also carried on at sea. In 1179 command of the fleet at Ceuta was entrusted to Ghānim b. Mardanīsh who led a raid on Lisbon in which two ships were captured. This in turn provoked a counter-raid on the island of Saltes at the mouth of the Rio Tinto in which Muslim prisoners were taken. The next year Ghānim led another raid on the Portuguese coast which ended in disaster: Ghānim and his brother 'Abd al-'Ulā and other Muslims were captured. Ghānim wrote a plaintive letter to the Caliph, then at Tlemcen, who instructed Ghānim's nephew, Hilāl b. Muḥammad, to go immediately to Marrakesh and raise the money for his ransom. In the summer of 1181 another naval campaign was led by

Ghānim's successor in Ceuta, 'Abd Allāh b. Jāmi', and Abū'l-'Abbās al-Ṣiqilī (the Sicilian) with the fleet of Seville. The two fleets, 40 ships in all, met at Cadiz. Sailing west they encountered the Lisbon fleet near Silves at exactly the place where Ibn Ghānim had been captured. Here they won a great victory, capturing 1,800 Christians and twenty ships with all their equipment for the loss of just one Muslim.[51]

Everywhere al-Andalus was under pressure: 'As long as the Caliph was absent', writes Ibn Idhārī, 'the Christians of Toledo and Santarem harassed the land of al-Andalus and raided near and far in the land of Islam. When the good news of the arrival of the Commander of the Faithful came, the people were carried away with enthusiasm for the *jihād* against the unbelieving enemies of Allah and were filled with courage to take revenge.'[52] The trouble was that the Caliph took his time and needed some persuading. After his return to Marrakesh in 1176 he had been distracted by the plague and in 1180 he decided that Tunisia had priority and began a long and expensive campaign there (he is said to have spent 1,000,000 *dīnār*s on paying the troops). Early in 1182 news came that he was back in the capital and a deputation from al-Andalus set out to impress on him the need for a major campaign; among them were his son Abū Isḥāq from Seville, his brother Abū 'Abd al-Raḥmān Ya'qūb from Murcia and the Almohad general Ibn Wānnūdīn.

Despite their pleas, the Caliph was still in no hurry, and during the rest of the year he busied himself with the extension of the city of Marrakesh to the south to accommodate his expanding court. It was not until September 1183 that he began to assemble an army for the expedition to al-Andalus, including ten siege engines (*manjanīq*). As part of his preparations he restructured the administration of al-Andalus, appointing his sons to the governorates of the four capitals (*qawā'id*): Abū Isḥāq to Seville, Abū Yaḥyā to Cordoba (at the request, we are told, of Abū'l-Walīd b. Rushd), Abū Zayd to Granada and Abū 'Abd Allāh to Murcia. This effectively marks the point when power passed to the new generation of the family of 'Abd al-Mu'min, effectively excluding his surviving brothers and their sons from the highest offices. He also appointed new *qāḍī*s to the main cities.[53]

He himself proceeded in his usual leisurely fashion and it was

51. Ibid., pp. 116–19, discusses this naval warfare. 52. Ibid., p. 116.
53. Ibid., p. 129.

not until June 1184 that the army crossed the Straits to Seville. Santarem was to be the object of the expedition. It was a sensible choice. It was more accessible than Christian bases like Talavera and Toledo and the Portuguese based in the city had been terrorising the Gharb as far as the walls of Seville. Here he was greeted with the usual formality by the dignitaries. He chose to dismiss Ibn Wānnūdīn, who, according to Ibn Ṣāḥib al-Ṣalāt, was ill at the time, thus depriving himself of the most experienced commander in the Almohad army. The army immediately set out via Badajoz to Santarem which they reached on 27 June.

The accounts of the events which followed are contradictory in different sources, but Huici Miranda has convincingly reconstructed them on the basis of the reports in Ibn Idhārī, which are in turn based on Ibn Ṣāḥib al-Ṣalāt and Abū'l-Ḥajjāj Yūsuf b. 'Umar, who were both eye-witnesses.[54] Santarem lies on a naturally fortified site on the right, northern, bank of the Tagus. The Caliph led his army across the river to attack. They were well supplied and morale was high. At first all went well and the *rabaḍ* or suburb outside the walls was taken. It seems that the Caliph then received intelligence that the King of Leon, Fernando II (1157–88), who had recently made peace with the Portuguese, was setting out to relieve the city. As at Huete in 1172, he suddenly lost his nerve: fearing that the army would be in a dangerously exposed position on the north bank of the river, on 2 July he ordered that the camp be moved across to the south bank. Despite his efforts, the decision resulted in confusion and the Caliph himself, in his conspicuous red command tent, was left almost alone on the north bank. At this moment the Christian garrison made a sortie and he was mortally wounded, dying a few days later as the defeated and demoralised army made its way back to Seville.

54. Huici Miranda, *Historia Politica*, iii, pp. 290–308.

CHAPTER TEN

The Later Almohad Caliphate

The caliphate of Abū Yūsuf Yaʿqūb al-Manṣūr, 1184–99

After Caliph Abū Yaʿqūb Yūsuf's death on 30 July 1184, the Almohad army made its way slowly back to Seville.[1] His death was kept a carefully guarded secret, the scarlet tent was pitched as usual and the servants went about their business in the normal manner. Meanwhile his cousin, the *sayyid* Abū Zayd ʿAbd al-Raḥmān b. ʿUmar b. ʿAbd al-Mu'min, gathered the dead Caliph's sons and the principal Almohad *shaykhs* and suggested the appointment of Abū Yūsuf Yaʿqūb, the dead man's son: this seems to have been accepted without open opposition. However, the new Caliph was careful not to make the news public until the army had returned to Seville and he had secured his grip on the reins of power. Even so, he thought it prudent to give out that his father had ordered that the people should renew their oaths of allegiance to him as heir apparent, and only after the leading figures in the state had all publicly pledged their loyalty did he reveal his father's death.

The new Caliph, who later took the title of al-Manṣūr, the Victorious, was probably 24 at the time of his accession. According to the Arabic sources he was stocky and dark-skinned with striking

1. The modern literature on the later Almohad caliphate is sparse. The best history remains A. Huici Miranda, *Historia Politica del Imperio Almohade* (2 vols, Tetuan, 1956–7). The reign of al-Manṣūr is covered in vol. i, pp. 313–90. There are shorter but still useful accounts in R. Le Tourneau, *The Almohad Movement in North Africa in the Twelfth and Thirteenth Centuries* (Princeton, 1969), pp. 71–114, and M.J. Viguera Molins, *Los Reinos de Taifas y Las Invasiones Magrebies* (Madrid, 1992), pp. 283–354. Also important, especially for the decline of Almohad government in al-Andalus, is P. Guichard, *Les Musulmans de Valence et la Reconquête* (2 vols, Damascus, 1990–1), i, pp. 125–65.

black eyes. He seems to have been a more determined and military figure than his father but with few of his intellectual interests. Perhaps partly as a result of this lack of literary patronage, we are very badly informed about his reign. There is no equivalent of Ibn Ṣāḥib al-Ṣalāt to give us inside information on court and government and we are largely dependent on the bare narrative of Ibn Idhārī, writing a century later, who seems to have used a court historian called Abū'l-Ḥajjāj Yūsuf b. 'Umar for at least some of his information. The narrative that results from this concentrates almost exclusively on the activities of the Caliph and especially on his military campaigns. We are almost completely in the dark about what went on in other areas of the Almohad caliphate, and even basic facts, like the names of the governors of Cordoba and Granada, are quite obscure.

The new Caliph's first move was to return to Marrakesh and establish his power there. Once again the affairs of al-Andalus and the *jihād* were put on the back burner while the Caliph devoted himself to the administration of the Maghreb. He left Seville on 2 September. On the way he met his cousin Abū Zakarīyā Yaḥyā b. 'Umar who had come from Tlemcen with 700 Arab horsemen for the *jihād*. Near Tarifa he entrusted his brothers Abū Isḥāq Ibrāhīm, Abū Yaḥyā and Abū Zayd Muḥammad with governorates in al-Andalus, but unfortunately we are not given any more details. The impression given is that the important posts remained firmly in the hands of the Mu'minid dynasty but that only two branches now had significant power, the sons of the Caliph Abū Ya'qūb Yūsuf and his closest ally, his brother 'Umar: all the other branches of this vast family seem to have been effectively excluded from the pickings of office.

The Caliph crossed the Straits and travelled via Rabat, where he first officially adopted the title of Commander of the Faithful, to Marrakesh, where he was installed by early October. Here he set about establishing his position. It seems that in his early life the new Caliph had acquired a reputation for loose living, and he now sought to counter this by a series of measures, including the enforcement of rules against alcoholic drinks. He also attempted to make it easier for petitioners to approach him with grievances and at first he declared his intention of holding an open court twice a week, but these seem to have degenerated into chaos and the practice was abandoned under pressure from Abū Zayd and other leading courtiers. He began the construction of a new palace quarter, al-Ṣāliḥa, to the south of the old Almoravid walls of Marrakesh: the mosque and walls he constructed still stand.

From the beginning of his reign, al-Manṣūr showed his enthusiasm for military expeditions and he would probably have resumed the *jihād* in al-Andalus but for the outbreak of major disturbances in the central and western Maghreb. This had begun in Majorca. The island had never been formally occupied by the Almohads but continued to be governed by the Banū Ghānīya, a branch of the Almoravids. Despite the long tradition of enmity between the two groups, Isḥāq b. Muḥammad b. Ghānīya had remained on good terms with the Almohads, sending gifts of booty which his men had taken in Mediterranean warfare. Isḥāq was succeeded by his son Muḥammad, who continued the same conciliatory line, but on the death of Abū Ya'qūb in 1184 he was deposed by his brothers who arrested the Almohad ambassadors and refused to accept Almohad authority. This would not have mattered very much if the revolt had been confined to the Balearic Islands, which were marginal to the Almohads' main concerns. However, the new ruler, 'Alī, made contact with partisans of the Hammadid dynasty in Bougie. The Hammadids had ruled Tlemcen before the rise of the Almohads and, like the Almoravids, they were Ṣanhāja Berbers. In the final years of Almoravid rule in Morocco they had been allies, and this old friendship was now revived. 'Alī sailed to Bougie with some 30 ships, 200 horse and 4,000 foot soldiers and took possession.

This marked the beginning of a prolonged, violent and destructive period of warfare between the Almohads and the Banū Ghānīya in North Africa which raged from Tlemcen in the west to Tunis in the east. The absence of 'Alī b. Ghānīya's troops left Majorca itself exposed and in 1185 an expeditionary force was sent to the island under the command of Abū'l-Ḥasan 'Alī b. Reverter, the son of the Almoravid general Reverter the Catalan who had, in circumstances of which we know nothing, joined the Almohad cause. He landed and made contact with the numerous Christian prisoners and together they took over the city. After some fighting he reached an agreement with the partisans of the Banū Ghānīya: the Christians were to go free and Ibn Reverter was paid a large sum in ransom money for members of the Banū Ghānīya he had captured. In return he agreed to leave the island, taking with him Muḥammad b. Isḥāq, the imprisoned brother who had remained loyal to the Almohads.[2] This *coup* did not bring Majorca under Almohad rule: by the early summer of 1186 'Abd Allāh b. Ghānīya had come back to the island and the Almohads were too preoccupied with the affairs of the Maghreb to respond.

2. Huici Miranda, *Historia Politica*, i, pp. 327–8.

The warfare in North Africa continued unabated and the Caliph himself was forced to intervene, leaving Marrakesh and arriving at Tunis in the spring of 1187. In June 1187 ʿAlī b. Ghānīya inflicted a massive defeat on an Almohad army led by the Caliph's cousin Abū Yūsuf Yaʿqūb at ʿUmra, near Gafsa in western Tunisia. In September the Caliph took his revenge when the Banū Ghānīya and their Arab and Berber allies were defeated at al-Ḥamma, and at the beginning of 1188 their stronghold at Gafsa was finally taken. Soon after, al-Manṣūr decided to return to Marrakesh.

He had begun to hear rumours that some of his relatives had been using his absence to conspire against him. One of these was his uncle Abū Isḥāq Ibrāhīm, who had been made governor of Tlemcen and had used his position to criticise the Caliph's plans. He was removed from office and was lynched by the crowd as he left the Caliph's presence. It seems that another uncle, Abū'l-Rabīʿ Sulaymān, governor of Tadla in central Morocco, had intended to join the conspiracy and he was arrested. In al-Andalus his own brother, Abū Ḥafṣ ʿUmar al-Rashīd, governor of Murcia, had entered into negotiations with Alfonso VIII when he heard of the Almohad defeat at ʿUmra. It may well be that he hoped to set up an independent state with Castilian support as Ibn Mardanīsh had done.[3] When the Caliph returned in triumph, al-Rashīd's followers deserted him and he went to Marrakesh, trusting in his brother's benevolence. None of the family of ʿAbd al-Mu'min had ever been executed before, but al-Manṣūr was taking no chances: Sulaymān and al-Rashīd were taken to Salé and killed. Al-Manṣūr is said to have felt great remorse on his deathbed for the execution of his relatives, and the incident is a first sign of those bitter divisions within the ruling family which were to be a major factor in the break-up of the caliphate.

The subjugation of the North African rebels had been a long hard campaign which had required all the resources of the Almohad state. It was not until 1190, six years after the defeat at Santarem and his own accession, that al-Manṣūr was able to turn his considerable military energies to the *jihād* in al-Andalus. These six years gave the Christians considerable opportunity for further expansion

3. See Ibn Idhārī al-Marrākushī, *Al-Bayān al-mughrib fi akhbār al-Andalus wa'l-Maghrib*, Part III (Almohads) ed. A. Huici Miranda (Tetuan, 1963), p. 172, trans. idem (2 vols, Tetuan, 1953), p. 146; Guichard, *Musulmans de Valence*, ii, p. 337, shows how al-Rashīd tried to take over the fiscal administration of Murcia for his own purposes, forcing the *ʿummāl* to hand over their cash and imprisoning the *mushrif* of Murcia for refusing to hand over his lists of taxpayers.

and it was only the quarrels between the Christian powers that prevented them from taking advantage of the Caliph's absence to launch a major offensive. In 1189, however, Sancho I of Portugal took advantage of help offered by volunteers from northern Europe to join the Third Crusade to take the important Muslim centre of Silves in the Algarve. The governor of Silves was, as was usual in the Almohad government of al-Andalus, a *ḥāfiẓ*, 'Īsā b. Abī Ḥafṣ b. 'Alī, who is said to have been inexperienced and to have failed to maintain the defences.[4] The attackers began by taking the castle of Alvor on the south coast where they put all 6,000 inhabitants to the sword. The siege of Silves was begun when Sancho arrived on 21 July and lasted some three months, during which time both the inhabitants and the attackers suffered badly from lack of supplies. It is indicative of the weakness of the Almohad military machine that neither the governor of Seville, the *sayyid* Abū Ḥafṣ Ya'qūb b. Abī Ḥafṣ, nor any other Almohad commander seems to have made an attempt to relieve the city. Finally, on 2 September the Muslims were compelled by hunger and thirst to ask for terms and were allowed to leave but lost all their possessions. Some of the Muslim inaction may be accounted for by the fact that Alfonso VIII made a simultaneous raid as far into Andalucia in the same summer. He is said to have raided the Cordoba area and then headed for Seville, where the Almohad resistance he encountered was divided and ill-planned.

It was in the nature of the Almohad state that only the Caliph could lead an expedition to counter the Christian offensive, and this he proceeded to do in the leisurely fashion which Huici Miranda notes as characteristic of the Almohads.[5] Not until January 1190 did he leave Marrakesh and, with a pause at Rabat for 40 days to gather his troops, he eventually crossed to Tarifa on 23 April, where he rested. He also received complaints from Andalusi delegations about the injustices committed by Almohad governors, but he sent them away with threats and accused them of undermining the Muslim cause. He ordered his cousin Ya'qūb b. Abī Ḥafṣ, governor of Seville, to gather an army from his own troops and those of Granada, volunteers (*muṭṭawi'a*) and Berbers of the Ṣanhāja and Haskūra tribes and to set out to Silves. By 6 June he was camped outside Silves and on 5 July the Almohad fleet arrived with siege engines and other military equipment. The preparations were to no avail,

4. Ibn Idhārī, *Al-Bayān*, Part III, p. 175; trans., p. 151.
5. Huici Miranda, *Historia Politica*, i, p. 341.

however, and the Muslim forces could not make any impression on the defences of the city.

Meanwhile the Caliph went to Cordoba where he stayed in the palace of the governor, his cousin Ya'qūb b. Abī Ḥafṣ. There was serious business to be done here and he concluded a peace with the Castilians: since he already had a truce with the Leonese, this meant that the Portuguese were isolated and would have to bear the full brunt of Muslim wrath. There was also an element of nostalgic tourism in his visit. He went to inspect the ruins of the long-deserted Umayyad palace at Madīnat al-Zahrā, destroyed by the Berbers in 1013. It was not the first time that the Caliph had shown an interest in historic monuments: when he was in Tunisia campaigning against the Banū Ghānīya, he had visited the venerable mosque of Qayrawān and, finding it somewhat dilapidated, had ordered repairs and new fabrics from Spain. The concern to identify with the glorious Muslim past, so clear from Almohad rhetoric, was here translated into concern for stones and mortar.

But the Caliph had not come to al-Andalus for sightseeing and he soon set off on campaign against the Portuguese after paying his troops a *baraka* (probably a one-off donative) and distributing banners in the mosque at Cordoba, just as the Umayyads had done before setting off on the *jihād*.[6] The army marched through the southern frontier areas of Portugal, burning crops and destroying vines, until they reached Torres Novas north of Santarem. Here the governor requested terms and he and his men were allowed to leave while the fortifications were razed, showing once again that the Almohads had no intention of holding their newly won gains. The army then moved north to the great fortress of Tomar, defended by the Templars, but a six-day military parade outside the walls showed clearly that a serious siege was beyond their capabilities. As had happened in the Huete campaign of 1172, the Almohad army began to suffer serious food shortages as the supplies they had brought from Cordoba ran out and they could find no more in the ravaged land. Hunger was followed by dysentery, the Caliph himself becoming ill, and the army returned to Seville on 26 July.

A grand parade was held to mark the return of the army and letters describing the triumph were sent out. But the reality was that, once again, Almohad arms had failed to make a real impression on the Christians, and the Caliph was determined to learn

6. For the Umayyad ceremonial, which the Almohads were clearly imitating, see E. Lévi-Provençal, *HEM*, iii, p. 90.

from his mistakes. He spent the winter in Seville and the next year began campaigning much earlier. He left Seville in April and began a siege of Alcacer do Sal, a small town on the coast south of Lisbon, known to the Arabs as Qaṣr Abī Dānis. It was not of major strategic importance and was probably chosen as an objective because access from the sea would mean that supplies could be brought by ship if necessary. This was a much more vigorous effort than the previous year's attack on Tomar. After the initial assault had failed, fourteen *manjanīq*s (trebuchets) were brought by sea and the defenders soon asked for terms. Unlike other conquests, a determined effort was made to establish a permanent Muslim presence in Alcacer do Sal. The Caliph appointed the Andalusi leader Muḥammad b. Sīdray b. Wazīr as commander and arranged that the inhabitants should be paid monthly allowances from the treasuries at Seville and Ceuta as an inducement to stay in this exposed position.[7] These brief details are interesting because they illustrate one of the main weaknesses of Almohad frontier policy. Towns established on the borders of Christian territory were not viable economically: they had to be sustained by subsidies from elsewhere. It was always difficult in a state with a fairly rudimentary fiscal administration like the Almohads' to provide regular subventions of this sort and they must have been stopped rapidly in times of civil war or other emergency nearer home. It is noteworthy too that these subsidies had to come from Seville and Ceuta, the Algarve itself presumably having neither the resources nor the administrative apparatus to sustain the outpost. By 27 June 1191 the Caliph was outside the walls of Silves and the city was soon taken by surprise attack when the defenders were off guard. By 25 July the survivors had left under safe conduct and the Almohad campaign had been brought to a triumphal conclusion.

Satisfied with his modest but much advertised success, the Caliph decided to return to Morocco. On 22 September he held a great reception at the Buḥayra in Seville to mark the beginning of Ramadan. He entrusted the governance of al-Andalus to his relatives (though unfortunately we are given no names) and crossed the Straits on 6 October. On his arrival at Marrakesh he fell seriously ill and, remembering no doubt his own uncertain claim to the throne, caused his son Muḥammad, the future al-Nāṣir, to be proclaimed heir. Delegations came from the most important *sayyid*s, his brother Abū Yaḥyā of Seville and Abū Zayd Muḥammad of

7. Ibn Idhārī, *Al-Bayān*, Part III, pp. 184–5; trans., pp. 169–70.

Ifrīqīya, to pledge their loyalty and Yūsuf b. al-Fakhkhār, the Jewish emissary of the King of Castile, came to renew the truces. On his recovery he devoted himself to building projects. At Rabat, the main assembly point for Almohad armes setting out for al-Andalus, he vastly extended the city from the small alcazaba constructed by ʿAbd al-Mu'min. An extensive new circuit of walls was built and a huge new mosque begun, though only the minaret was completed. At Seville he caused a new complex of fortress and palace to be constructed at Aznalfarache (Ḥiṣn al-Faraj: castle of relaxation) on the west bank of the Guadalquivir River. Tunisia remained disturbed: ʿAlī b. Ghānīya was succeeded by his brother Yaḥyā who continued to put himself at the head of the Arabs and other opponents of Almohad rule. The Caliph did not feel obliged to go east at this time, but the unrest meant, as ever, that he was obliged to send men and money to Tunisia and could not devote himself entirely to the defence of al-Andalus.

On 1 June 1195 the Caliph returned once more to al-Andalus. His first stop was Seville. On his approach he was met by the governor, Abū Yaḥyā, and a large number of the citizens, young and old. He himself lodged in the Buḥayra gardens but his court was billeted in houses in the town. Interestingly, this was arranged not by the governor but by the *shaykh* Abū Bakr b. Ẓuhr, who was assisted by other *shaykh*s of the town (*ashyākh al-balad*) in distributing the *bara'āt*, the notes which assigned lodgings. Who these *shaykh* s were is not clear but it does suggest some local participation in the administration of the city. The next day the Caliph rode to inspect his new buildings at Ḥiṣn al-Faraj and a sermon was preached in the great mosque his father had constructed in the city by the *khaṭīb* Abū ʿAlī b. al-Ḥajjāj. Then the army was paraded rank by rank and tribe by tribe in front of the Caliph, his family and the *kuttāb* and *wazīr*s, and they were paid their donatives (*murātibāt wa'l-barakāt*).[8]

On 22 June 1195 the Caliph left Seville. Passing through Cordoba and the defile of Despeñaperros, he reached the plain of Calatrava in early July. Meanwhile Alfonso VIII of Castile came south to challenge him, establishing himself near the newly built castle and settlement of Alarcos, the southernmost point in Castile.[9] The Castilian king, full of confidence in the size and strength

8. Ibid., pp. 192–3; trans., pp. 183–4.

9. The Alarcos campaign and its aftermath are studied in detail in A. Huici Miranda, *Las Grandes Batallas de la Reconquista durante las Invasiones Almoravides, Almohades y Benimerines* (Madrid, 1956), pp. 138–216, which includes a detailed critique of the sources.

of his army, refused to wait for reinforcements from Leon and determined to engage in battle immediately. Curiously, we have little reliable information about this major encounter, especially on the Muslim side. Many later Arabic accounts are a jumble of mostly legendary material and there is considerable confusion with the events surrounding the battle of Zallāqa (1086) about which we are much better informed. Ibn Idhārī gives us a short but sensible account, probably based on Yūsuf b. 'Umar's biography of al-Manṣūr, while Huici Miranda discovered an unexpectedly useful source in a commentary on a poem of al-Qarṭājanī by al-Sharīf al-Gharnāṭī (d. 1359) which adds some details favourable to the ancestors of the Hafsid dynasty of Tunisia, his patrons.

On 13 July the Muslim army assembled on the Campo de Calatrava. The *wazīr* Abū Yaḥyā, grandson of 'Abd al-Mu'min's ally Abū Ḥafṣ 'Umar al-Hintātī, gathered the leaders and they collectively asked that al-Manṣur pardon their sins. Next the Muslim troops were given an inspiring sermon by Abū 'Alī b. al-Ḥajjāj. Then, on the advice of the Andalusi leader Abū 'Abd Allāh b. Sanādīd, the Muslim army was divided into two groups. In the forefront was Abū Yaḥyā, with the Andalusis on the right wing and the Maghribis on the left, the volunteers, the Ghuzz (Turkmen) and archers in the vanguard and the Caliph's own tribe of Hintāta in the centre. Abū Khālid Maḥyū b. Abī Bakr, ancestor of the Merinid dynasty, was appointed by al-Manṣūr to command the Zanāta, and contingents are listed from the Arabs and other Berber tribes. The Muslims advanced slowly and battle was joined on 17 July on the open plains near the castle of Alarcos. The initial Castilian charge inflicted severe casualties on the advance guard and killed Abū Yaḥyā and many of the Hintāta but was eventually driven off with heavy losses. Ibn Sanādīd counter-attacked against the Castilians on the slopes around the castle and it was probably at this stage that al-Manṣūr joined the battle from the rear and routed the Christians. Some fled to the shelter of the castle, while Alfonso himself made for Toledo. Arab sources give very large numbers for the Christian casualties, 30,000 compared with 500 Muslim martyrs: even allowing for exaggeration, it was clearly a major defeat. The castle at Alarcos was compelled to surrender a few days later and the castles of Malagon, Benavente, Caracuel and Calatrava itself were taken without any serious resistance.

It is clear that there were many reasons for the Muslim victory. The over-confidence of Alfonso VIII, surprised by the effectiveness of the Muslim army after its poor showing at Huete in 1172 and

Santarem in 1184, and his rash refusal to wait for reinforcements contributed. On the Muslim side al-Manṣūr was clearly a more effective commander than his father, and the Muslim archers seem to have done great damage. Al-Manṣūr also enjoyed the support and advice of the dissident Castilian nobleman Pedro Fernandez de Castro and his followers. Much of the success, however, must be attributed to the fact that the Muslims were able to fight a pitched battle in open country soon after the expedition began: previous invasions had been frustrated by lack of supplies and disease. Probably because he realised this, al-Manṣūr did not pursue the fleeing enemy but retreated to Seville, which he reached in triumph on 7 August.

The Caliph spent the winter of 1195–96 gardening at his beloved Ḥiṣn al-Faraj, but the next spring, rejecting the pleas for peace brought by the ambassadors of Alfonso VIII, he launched a new campaign. On 15 April he left the city and headed north into Extremadura. He first laid siege to Montanchez. The garrison surrendered on condition that they be allowed to leave for the nearest Christian outpost. They were being escorted by Ibn Sanādīd, leader of the Andalusi vanguard in al-Manṣūr's army, when they were ambushed by a group of Arabs and slaughtered, much to the Caliph's fury. The next target was Trujillo, which was abandoned by its defenders, and then Plasencia, newly settled by Alfonso VIII, which was taken by assault; the bishop and many of the clergy were killed and others taken as prisoners to work on the new buildings at Rabat. The expedition then moved east between the Tagus and the Cordillera Central, ravaging the countryside around Talavera and the small outposts of Escalona and Maqueda. This culminated in a ten-day show of force outside Toledo when fields and vineyards were again ravaged. At the same time Castile was also attacked from the west by the Leonese King Alfonso IX aided by a Muslim contingent, and from the north-east by Sancho of Navarre. In mid-July al-Manṣūr turned south and by 6 August he was safely back in Seville, dispatching triumphant letters recounting his victories.

The next year he determined to repeat the success. This time he left Seville on 14 April and went to Cordoba, where he spent some time collecting supplies. He was also occupied in the trial and exile of the philosopher Averroes who had been accused by the Cordovans of heterodoxy: al-Manṣūr was probably trying to demonstrate his orthodoxy to the conservative religious leaders of al-Andalus and so encourage enthusiasm for the *jihād*. Then he moved north into Christian territory, ravaging the Tagus valley and trying to engage the Christians in battle. Alfonso VIII, with his new ally, the young Pedro II of Aragon, prudently retired behind the Guadarrama Mountains, not wishing to risk another encounter with the Almohad army in the open field. The Muslims went on to attack Madrid, which was ably defended by Diego Lopez de Haro, who had taken command of the castle of Alarcos after the disastrous battle of 1195, and then Guadalajara, where the defenders made a sortie while the Almohad forces were out foraging and pillaged their baggage train. Then the Caliph turned south, passing Huete, where his father had failed so miserably in 1172, and Cuenca, which had now been in Christian hands for twenty years, before returning to Seville on 19 August.

These two offensives mark the zenith of Almohad power in the peninsula, but at the same time they clearly show its limitations. Al-Manṣūr understood the need to move early in the year to take advantage of cooler weather and better supplies, and the need to move fast. He tried, unsuccessfully, to lure the Christian forces into battle. The weaknesses of the Almohad armies became glaringly apparent. The main problem was one of provisions. The Almohad state was too underdeveloped to organise a proper supply train and the army had to live off what it could plunder. This made it almost impossible to organise a prolonged siege which would have been necessary to reduce Talavera or Madrid, never mind Toledo. Al-Manṣūr seems to have realised this and taken no siege engines with him. The only hope for the Almohads was to repeat the success of Alarcos and engage the Christian army in the field, but Alfonso VIII had learned his lesson and was not to be drawn. For all the rhetoric, trumpets and drums, the Almohads never had the military stamina to have a serious chance of taking the Christian outposts in the Tagus valley, still less of attacking the areas to the north of the Cordillera Central.

The Caliph spent the winter in Seville, completing work on the mosque and the Giralda and enjoying the pleasures of his palace at Ḥiṣn al-Faraj. From the winter of 1196–97 we get a small insight into the civil administration of Seville in the reign. The Caliph was determined to root out corruption and set 50 clerks to work under the direction of Abū Muḥammad ʿAbd Allāh b. Yaḥyā and Abū ʿAbd Allāh al-Kātib examining the accounts of the various officials. They began with Dāwud b. Abī Dāwud who clearly had an important but unspecified office. He was fined 150,000 *dīnār*s for malpractices, but neither his family nor his servants were interrogated. Then Abū ʿAlī ʿUmar b. Ayyūb was fined 50,000 *dīnār*s and the two of them imprisoned. Unfortunately, we have no more information about either of them. To replace the disgraced officials, Abū Zayd ʿAbd al-Raḥmān b. Yujjān, nephew of the famous Abū Ḥafṣ ʿUmar al-Hintātī,[10] was appointed to control the fiscal affairs (*ashghāl*) of both al-Andalus and Morocco, including those of the Caliph, the government (*sulṭān*) and the *wizāra* as well as the affairs of the Almohads: for Ibn Yujjān, this was the beginning of a career which was to make him notorious in Almohad history. A great deal of money was collected. Abū'l-Qāsim b. Nuṣayr was appointed *mushrif* of Seville and the historian Yūsuf b. ʿUmar was removed from the service of the sons of the *sayyid* Abū Ḥafṣ to supervise the royal possessions (*al-mustakhlas*) in the Ajarafe and the city of Niebla and the redistribution of fiefs (*sihām*).

The Caliph had now spent almost three years away from Morocco and clearly felt it was time to return. He crossed the Straits on 30 March 1198. On his return to Marrakesh, his health began to fail and his last year was largely devoted to pious enterprises, including the building of a hospital and taking measures against the Jews.

While his military activities are well reported, it is difficult to say much about the internal administration of al-Andalus in al-Manṣūr's time. Some general points do emerge, however, from the political testament he is said to have left and which was widely remembered in Ibn Khaldūn's time.[11] It is said that he assembled all the leading figures in the Almohad regime in his new palace in al-Ṣāliḥa and addressed them, giving instructions as to how the state should be governed in the minority of his son and heir Muḥammad al-Nāṣir. Pride of place went to the *sayyid*s Abū'l-Ḥasan and Abū Zayd, sons of the *sayyid* Abū Ḥafṣ ʿUmar who had secured the accession of al-Manṣūr's father Abū Yaʿqūb. Abū Zayd himself had arranged al-Manṣūr's own accession and held the important post of governor of Ifrīqīya, while Abū'l-Ḥasan was the Caliph's deputy in Marrakesh and leader of the *sayyid*s, as well as being in charge of the building works at al-Ṣāliḥa. It is notable that they have precedence over the Caliph's own brothers. The other *sayyid*s were to be kept in the positions they held because attempts to remove them would result in internecine conflict.

10. Huici Miranda, *Historia Politica*, ii, p. 390.
11. Ibn Idhārī, *Al-Bayān*, Part III, pp. 206–9; trans., pp. 206–12.

Next on the list were the Hafsid *shaykh*s Abū Zakarīyā and Abū Muḥammad ʻAbd al-Wāḥid, descendants of Abū Ḥafṣ ʻUmar al-Hintātī, who were to be the young Caliph's advisers. After them came an Andalusi noble, Abū'l-Ghamr b. ʻAzzūn, whose father or grandfather had been one of the first to welcome Almohad forces in 1147 and whose family had played an important role as leader of Andalusi forces in the Almohad army. The next name is more surprising, Muḥammad b. Isḥāq, son of the Banū Ghānīya ruler of Majorca who had been deposed by his brothers for his loyalty to the Almohads.

He then went on to make his most celebrated remark, exhorting them to fear God and look after the orphans and the (female) orphan. On being asked who these were, he responded that they were the Muslims of al-Andalus and al-Andalus itself, instructing them to maintain the armies and fortify the frontiers. He went on to deal with different groups in the army. First of these were the Ghuzz Turks, instructing that they should be paid their salaries (*barakāt*). He explained that the Almohads had fiefs (*sihām*) to which they could return while the Ghuzz were entirely dependent on salaries. The Arabs were to be treated well and employed on military expeditions rather than being left in idleness to make trouble. The *ṭālib*s of the capital were instructed to look after the moral education of the young prince.

Two functionaries were then commended, the chief *qāḍī* Abū'l-Qāsim b. Bāqī and Abū Zayd ʻAbd al-Raḥmān b. Yujjān, in charge of the fiscal administration (*ashghāl*). Finally he came to the Almohad tribes, naming each one with their leaders.

Like most deathbed speeches, this has probably been elaborated by posterity, or even by some of the audience, but, in the absence of much other information, it gives us some insight into the structure of the Almohad regime at the end of al-Manṣūr's life.

The caliphate of al-Nāṣir, 1199–1213

Al-Manṣūr died in January 1199 and was succeeded by his son al-Nāṣir. We have a description of the young prince from someone who knew him personally:

> He had a clear complexion, a red beard, dark blue eyes, plump cheeks, average height; he often kept his eyes downcast and was very silent, mostly due to a speech defect from which he suffered; he was

> inscrutable, but at the same time mild, courageous, reluctant to shed blood, and not really disposed to undertake anything unless he had carefully studied it; he was accused of avarice.[12]

Although the new Caliph was only seventeen, he had been accepted as heir apparent by the Almohad establishment since he was nine, so his accession was attended by none of the uncertainty of those of his father and grandfather. Not surprisingly, the accent was on continuity in accordance with the arrangements in his father's testament. If the internal history of al-Andalus is dark in the reign of al-Manṣūr, it is completely blank for most of the period of his son's rule. His father had arranged a series of truces with the Christian leaders which neither side wished to breach, and there seem to have been no major internal disturbances. The first decade of the thirteenth century is probably the most obscure in the whole of the political history of al-Andalus from 711 to 1492 and even the identities of the most important figures are completely unknown to us.

The problems of North Africa consumed the energies and resources of the Almohad state. Ever since al-Manṣūr had left Tunisia ten years before, rebels, notably Yaḥyā b. Ghānīya, had been taking over more and more of the land. The new administration sent expeditions against him but they were defeated. There was even a rebellion much closer to home, in the Sūs, close to the very cradle of the Almohad movement. Faced by these problems, al-Nāṣir's tutors decided to strike at the stronghold of the Banū Ghānīya in the Balearic Islands.

ʿAbd Allāh b. Ghānīya, the ruler of Majorca since he had taken it from the Almohads in 1188, enjoyed good relations with the kingdom of Aragon and had made a trading and commercial treaty with Genoa. In the winter of 1199–1200 he attempted to expand his power and take Ibiza, but he was beaten back by the Almohads. The next winter, however, when the Almohad fleet was in Ceuta, he took Minorca. The next summer, 1202, Minorca was retaken by the Almohad fleet under *sayyid* Abū'l-ʿUlā the Elder. In 1203 a major assault was planned led by Abū'l-ʿUlā and the Hafsid Abū Saʿīd ʿUthmān b. Abī Ḥafṣ. The forces gathered at Denia, 1,200 horse, 700 archers and 15,000 foot. There were also a large number of ships, more than 130 of various sizes. The army was fully

12. See the account of ʿAbd al-Wāḥid al-Marrākushī, *Al-Muʿjib*, ed. M.S. al-'Uryan (Cairo, 1949), p. 307; trans. A. Huici Miranda (Tetuan, 1955), p. 255. I have quoted the translation in Le Tourneau, *The Almohad Movement*, p. 80, with minor emendations.

equipped with *manjaniqs* (siege engines) and supplies: it showed what the Almohads could do. The expedition sailed on 3 September 1203. Despite a vigorous resistance, 'Abd Allāh b. Ghānīya was killed and the capital surrendered, its inhabitants being given an amnesty. It was the Almohad empire's last major triumph.[13]

The conquest of Majorca simply intensified the struggle in North Africa, where Yaḥyā b. Ghānīya was now reinforced by refugees from the disaster in the Balearics. Once again the Caliph himself had to intervene. He gathered his troops in the traditional fashion at Rabat in February 1205 and set off to the west. In Tunisia he was engaged in a prolonged siege of 'Alī b. Ghānīya's stronghold at al-Mahdīya which finally fell on 11 January 1206. By the spring of 1207 Tunisia was subdued and an Almohad army under the Caliph's uncle Abū Isḥāq Ibrāhīm had made a show of force in Tripolitania. It was time for the Caliph to return to Marrakesh, but he (or his advisers) realised that rebellion would soon break out again after he had gone. He therefore decided on a major political initiative and appointed the Hafsid 'Abd al-Wāḥid as viceroy of Tunis, giving him full control of the collection of taxes and the raising of soldiers. In the short term it was a successful solution to the problem of ruling this turbulent area which had consumed so much Almohad treasure and blood, and the Caliph may even have been thinking that this solution would leave him with a free hand to concentrate on the affairs of al-Andalus. The Hafsids soon established their independent rule in Tunisia, though accepting the nominal authority of the Almohad caliph. This in itself may have meant little real diminution in the power of the Caliph, but it did mean that the Hafsid family, who had been the right-hand men of the caliphate from its earliest days, now had an alternative focus, and Hafsids would tend to make their careers and devote their talents to the new area of family interest in the east. Furthermore, it is likely that the Hafsids had played an important part in securing the loyalty of the mountain tribes, including of course the Hintāta from whom they sprang, to the Almohad state. Their departure helped to loosen these bonds.

In fact, the coming of the Hafsids in some ways simply displaced the centre of resistance to the central Maghreb. Yaḥyā b. Ghānīya turned his attention to Tlemcen, where the elderly governor, *sayyid* Abū'l-Ḥasan b. 'Umar, who had ruled the town for almost a quarter

13. Ibn Idhārī, *Al-Bayān*, Part III, pp. 215–16; trans., pp. 223–6. The chronology of the conquest is discussed in detail by Huici Miranda on p. 225 of the translation, n. 1. See also the account in Guichard, *Musulmans de Valence*, i, pp. 133–4.

of a century since 1185, proved incapable of resistance. He was replaced by one of the younger generation of the ruling family, Abū ʿImrān Mūsā b. Yūsuf b. ʿAbd al-Muʾmin, but he was defeated and killed by Yaḥyā and his Zanāta Berber allies, notably the Banū Marīn, later to be rulers of Morocco. In the end *sayyid* Abū Zakarīyā, governor of Fes, and the Hafsid Abū Zayd b. Yujjān were able to save Tlemcen for the Almohads, but the menace remained. By the end of 1209 real Almohad control seems to have ended at Tlemcen, only just to the east of the modern Morocco–Algeria frontier.

Meanwhile, in al-Andalus things seem to have been comparatively peaceful. Members of the ruling family continued to rotate between various governorates in the traditional Almohad fashion: in 1203 the Caliph wrote to Seville ordering that arms should be made and coats of mail bought. His uncle, *sayyid* Abū Isḥāq, was to be appointed governor of Seville and *sayyid* ʿAbd al-Wāḥid b. Abī Yaʿqūb governor of Silves and the Algarve, perhaps an upgrading of the office which had previously been held by a *ḥāfiẓ*.[14] Abū Yaḥyā b. Abī Sinān, probably a Berber *ḥāfiẓ*, was appointed governor of Badajoz and occupied himself with rebuilding its walls. It is worth noting in this context that the Almohad period saw a massive programme of fortification all over al-Andalus. Sometimes these were isolated castles, like the magnificent fortress of Alcala de Guadaira near Seville, but much more frequently the effort was put into city walls. Much of this work is undated, but it seems as if virtually every town of any importance had its walls either constructed or improved during the Almohad period. Apart from Seville itself, the finest surviving examples are to be found in Extremadura and the Algarve, at Badajoz, Caceres, Reina, Elvas and Silves.[15] These new works were usually constructed in rammed clay in the traditional Muslim fashion, but the Almohad period saw the introduction of large octagonal towers, the *torres albarranas* or towers projecting from the walls and connected to them by an arch or spur of the wall, and outer walls and barbicans.

In 1208/9 there was a new round of government appointments in al-Andalus and the Caliph appointed his brothers Abū Isḥāq to Seville, Abū Muḥammad to Murcia and Abū Yaḥyā to Valencia. With them went new civil servants, al-Ḥasan b. ʿAbd al-ʿAzīz over the chancery (*tawqīʿāt*) and Abū ʿAbd Allāh b. Manīʿ at the army office (*dīwān al-ʿaskar*). At the same time Abū ʿAbd Allāh al-Bājī was

14. Ibn Idhārī, *Al-Bayān*, Part III, p. 218; trans., pp. 227–8.
15. See L. Torres Balbas, *Ciudades Hispano-Musulmanas* 2nd edn (Madrid, 1985), pp. 475–501.

removed as *qāḍī* of Seville and was replaced by 'Abd al-Ḥaqq b. 'Abd al-Ḥaqq.[16] A further raft of appointments is recorded in 1210/11. New governors were appointed in Majorca and Murcia, where Abū 'Imrān b. Yāsin al-Hintātī replaced Abū'l-Ḥasan b. Wajjāj (both, it should be noted, Almohad *shaykhs*, not *sayyids*). The Caliph's brother Abū Isḥāq was removed from Seville at his own request and was replaced by his uncle Ibrāhīm who was transferred from Granada. The new governor of Granada, Abū 'Abd Allāh b. Abī Yaḥyā b. Abī Ḥafṣ, was transferred from Sijilmāssa in the south of Morocco. Changes were also made among the *qāḍīs*: Abū'l-Ḥasan al-Qaṣtallī was appointed to Murcia for the second time while the previous *qāḍī*, Abū Muḥammad b. Ḥawt Allāh, was transferred to Cordoba. Abū 'Alī al-Mālaqī was called from Cordoba to Marrakesh where he was made head of the *ṭālibs* of the court, as his father and brother had been before. Interestingly, one Abū'l-Jaysh b. Muḥārib took up the post of receiving, lodging, entertaining and interpreting for the ambassadors of the Christian kings. The record is dry and bald, but it does tell us something about the Almohad state at this period.[17] Offices circulated within a small and exclusive group, governors being chosen from the ruling family or the leading Almohads while *qāḍīs* mostly came from Andalusi families. There was a high degree of mobility among office holders, both governors and *qāḍīs* being transferred frequently from one city to another. The Andalusi military elite, like the Banū Wazīr and the Banū 'Azzūn, may have played a significant role in the army, but they were certainly excluded from the top positions in the administration. Since individuals seldom remained in one position for very long, it does not appear that they were able to build up local power bases: in appearance at least, the administration was very centralised, people being transferred by government order, and there is no record of a provincial governor resisting such a command. This policy must have meant that the Almohad ruling class remained very separate from the bulk of the people of al-Andalus and that they never built up the local contacts and networks which might have preserved their own rule and, ultimately, enabled the Muslims of the different cities of al-Andalus to work together and defend themselves and their society.

It was not until 1209 that the Christians began to take the offensive once more. The old king Alfonso VIII was anxious to avenge his defeat at Alarcos, while his ambitious son Fernando was keen to

16. Ibn Idhārī, *Al-Bayān*, Part III, pp. 230–1; trans., pp. 252–3.
17. Ibid., pp. 233–4; trans., pp. 257–8.

make a reputation in the Holy War. Pope Innocent III, ever keen to encourage the Crusade, whether in east or west, gave important support, above all by threatening the King of Leon, traditional ally of the Almohads, with ecclesiastical sanctions should he attack the Castilians. The Knights of Calatrava were desperate to win back the lands from which they had been so humiliatingly expelled in 1195. The king raided the areas around Jaen and Baeza while the Master of Calatrava gathered his men at the one remaining castle, Salvatierra on the southern fringes of the Campo de Calatrava, and raided south over the mountains to Andujar and Montoro, less than 50 kilometres from Cordoba itself. The Aragonese began to raid the Valencia area.

In 1210 al-Nāṣir was visited by a delegation from the Levante complaining about these attacks, and, with North Africa now comparatively stable, he decided to turn his attention to al-Andalus.[18] He wrote to the governors of Seville and Cordoba to assemble the armies, have the roads levelled and supplies prepared. He left Marrakesh on 6 February 1211 and went as usual to Rabat to gather his armies and on to the Straits. He found that supplies had not been made ready as ordered and the governors of Fes and Alcazarquivir were arrested and later executed for their negligence. By the beginning of June he was in Seville assembling troops from al-Andalus. The objective was the isolated fortress of Salvatierra, deep in Muslim territory, which the knights of Calatrava used as a base for raids. The siege began on 15 June. The castle was fiercely defended by its garrison of 400 knights, but the Almohad army was large and equipped with siege engines. Alfonso VIII, then at Talavera, did not wish to risk battle and the garrison were given permission to surrender after a siege of 51 days.[19] The triumph was duly publicised and the Caliph returned in triumph to Seville.

The next year, however, Alfonso, at the head of a large army which included the King of Aragon and contingents from all over Christian Spain and beyond the Pyrenees, was determined to take his revenge. He marched south through the plain of Calatrava towards the pass of Despeñaperros and Andalucia.

The castles of the Campo de Calatrava, which had been held by

18. For the campaigns of 1211 and 1212 see Huici Miranda, *Las Grandes Batallas*, pp. 231–327. For a more recent account see Guichard, *Musulmans de Valence*, i, pp. 134–6.

19. Ibn ʿAbd al-Munʿim al-Ḥimyarī, *Rawḍ al-Miʿṭār fi akhbār al-aqṭār*, French trans. by E. Lévi-Provençal, *La Péninsule Ibérique au Moyen-Age* (Leiden, 1938), pp. 108–9, trans., pp. 132–3, is the fullest description of the siege. The ruins of the castle can still be seen across the valley from the later headquarters of the Order at Calatrava la Nueva.

the Muslims since the battle of Alarcos in 1195, put up very little resistance apart from Old Calatrava itself, where the Andalusi *qā'id* (commander) Abū'l-Ḥajjāj b. Qādis conducted a vigorous defence with just 70 horsemen until, on 3 July, he was finally forced to surrender on terms. According to the often unreliable chronicler Ibn Abī Zar', he sent repeated messages to the Caliph describing the precarious state of his defences, but these were destroyed by the *wazīr* Ibn Jāmi' without the Caliph having ever seen them.[20] Al-Nāṣir, who left Seville in late June, seems to have decided to play a waiting game. He knew that the Christians were already short of supplies and he hoped that by the time they reached Andalucia, they would be starving and exhausted. Accordingly his army waited at the southern end of the great defile of Despeñaperros which leads from the Meseta down to the Guadalquivir valley. However, the Christian forces crossed the mountains by a side route and, on 16 July, inflicted a massive defeat on the Almohad army in a battle known to the Christians as Las Navas de Tolosa and to the Muslims as al-'Iqāb.

Both Muslim and Christian sources provide accounts of the battle, but neither provides any clear explanation of why the Almohad army performed so badly.[21] Certainly al-Nāṣir seems to have lacked his father's military determination and fled so rapidly that he had reached Jaen by nightfall. The Muslim troops seem to have been more lightly armed and lacking heavy cavalry to resist the Christian charges. There are also indications of divisions within the Muslim army. It may be that al-Nāṣir's execution of the two governors in 1212, a most unusual event in the Almohad state, had alienated many leading Almohads, especially as the Caliph also had a reputation for meanness and not paying allowances. According to 'Abd al-Wāḥid al-Marrākushī, writing only a few years after the events, the Almohad troops were paid every four months under al-Manṣūr, but al-Nāṣir had been much slower, especially in this campaign, and he had heard of groups of Almohads who had refused to fight at all and had fled at the first opportunity.[22] Ibn Idhārī says that the disaffection had been caused by al-Nāṣir's brutal punishment of officials who had failed to produce the supplies.[23] Other sources, like Ibn Abī Zar', writing a century later, as quoted

20. Ibn Abī Zar', *Rawḍ al-Qirṭās*, ed. C. Tornberg (Uppsala, 1843–46); Spanish trans. by A. Huici Miranda (2 vols, Valencia, 1964), pp. 462–3.
21. See the discussion in Huici Miranda, *Las Grandes Batallas*, on which mine is based.
22. 'Abd al-Wāḥid al-Marrākushī, *Al-Mu'jib*, p. 322; trans., p. 267.
23. Ibn Idhārī, *Al-Bayān*, Part III, p. 269; trans., p. 242.

by al-Maqqarī,[24] said that the main factor was tension between Andalusis and Almohads and that the defeat was precipitated by the failure of the Caliph and his *wazīr* to listen to the advice of experienced Andalusi leaders. Matters were brought to a head by the treatment of Ibn Qādis: when he reached the Caliph's camp, the *wazīr* Ibn Jāmiʿ prevented him from seeing his master and denounced him to the Caliph, who ordered his execution. This led to the disaffection of many of the Andalusi leaders and Ibn Qādis became a sort of hero for them and poems were circulated lamenting his death. The sources on the battle are too sparse for us to know the truth of these allegations, but we can be sure that al-Nāṣir and the Almohads were made scapegoats and widely held to blame for the catastrophe.

The Caliph fled ignominiously while the Christians moved on to storm Ubeda, taking a vast number of captives. Beyond that the immediate military consequences were not disastrous. Lack of supplies forced the Christian army to withdraw and the governors of Jaen, Granada and Cordoba were able to stabilise the position. The next year Christian expeditions took some minor fortresses, including Alcaraz, where the Muslim commander Ibn Faraj held out bravely. Muslim military organisation was not to be underestimated, as a group of 70 horse and 4,000 foot from Talavera found when they raided the Seville countryside in search of food and were annihilated by the local forces. If al-Nāṣir had been a different man, or even if he had lived longer, the disaster might have been retrieved. As it was, he retired to Marrakesh and seems to have made no effort to repair the damage done. It was there that he died, on 25 December 1213, aged only 32, assassinated, some said, by his own courtiers.

The collapse of Almohad rule in al-Andalus, 1213–28

The failure of the Christians to press home their advantage immediately after the defeat of the Muslims at Las Navas de Tolosa was partly a result of internal political changes. In 1213 Pedro II of Aragon-Catalonia, who had joined forces with the Castilians at Las Navas, was obliged to campaign north of the Pyrenees in support of the southern French nobles against the army of the Albigensian

24. Al-Maqqarī, *Nafḥ al-ṭīb min ghusn al-Andalus al-raṭīb*, trans. P. de Gayangos as *History of the Muhammedan Dynasties in Spain* (2 vols, London, 1840–41), ii, pp. 323–4.

Crusaders and was killed at the battle of Muret. He was succeeded by his five-year-old son Jaime, later famous as 'the Conqueror', who took some time to establish his authority.

The next year the veteran King of Castile, Alfonso VIII, vanquished at Alarcos in 1195 and victor at Las Navas in 1212, died. His son Enrique I was only eleven and Castile was preoccupied by the struggle over the regency. In Portugal the young King Afonso II (1211–23) was prevented by health problems and internal divisions from attacking al-Andalus. Enrique of Castile died in 1217 after only three years as king, but his formidable elder sister, Berenguela, now separated from her husband, Alfonso IX of Leon, caused her young son Fernando III to be proclaimed King. By 1225 Fernando was old and established enough to begin campaigning against the Muslims. In 1230 he succeeded his estranged father Alfonso IX as King of Leon, so reuniting the kingdoms of Leon and Castile. This union was an event of major importance in the history of the Reconquista. The two kingdoms had been divided since the death of Alfonso VII in 1157, and throughout the 73 years of separation the kings of Leon had regarded the Castilians as the chief threat and the Almohads as potential allies. But for this division, it is unlikely that the caliphs would have been able to resist Christian advances as effectively as they had. The union of Leon and Castile, and the coming of age of Jaime of Aragon-Catalonia, meant that the political problems of the Christian kingdoms were at an end and both Castile and Aragon were led by young and ambitious monarchs. This was fateful news for the divided and leaderless Muslims of al-Andalus.

Before his death, al-Nāṣir is said to have nominated his son Yūsuf as his heir. Whether this was in fact the case is not clear, but it certainly suited the controlling figures at the court in Marrakesh, the *wazīr* Ibn Jāmiʿ and the *ṣāḥib al-ashghāl* ʿAbd al-ʿAzīz b. Abī Zayd, to secure the accession of the boy, who seems to have been a timid youth of about ten years old. The oath of allegiance was taken to him on the day that his father was buried.

Among the brief and rather colourless notices of the period, we have a description of this oath-taking by an eye-witness, the chronicler ʿAbd al-Wāḥid al-Marrākushī, whose lively but often unreliable account of the period was written shortly afterwards from memory while he was in exile in Egypt:

> The oath of allegiance was taken to this Abū Yaʿqūb on the day his father was buried. I am not certain if his father had designated him as heir or not but I do know that he had turned against him in his

last days when he heard stories about his evil conduct. Those of the royal family who took the oath were Abū Mūsā ʿĪsā b. ʿAbd al-Muʾmin, his grandfather's uncle who had been attacked by the Majorcans [the followers of Ibn Ghānīya] in Bougie, who was the last surviving son of ʿAbd al-Muʾmin and I have still not heard that he has died. Then there was Abū Zakarīyā Yaḥyā b. Abī Ḥafṣ b. ʿUmar b. ʿAbd al-Muʾmin. These two were standing by his head to summon the people. Among the Almohads there were Abū Muḥammad ʿAbd al-ʿAzīz b. ʿUmar b. Zayd al-Hintātī whose father had been the first *wazīr* of Abū Yūsuf, as has already been mentioned, and Abū ʿAlī ʿUmar b. Mūsā b. ʿAbd al-Wāḥid al-Sharqī and Abū Marwān Muḥammad b. ʿAbd al-Malik b. Yūsuf b. Sulaymān of the people of Tīnmal.

The inner circle [*khāṣṣa*] took the oath on the Thursday, the Almohad *shaykh*s and the rest of the royal family on the Friday, and the general populace on the Saturday. I attended on that day and Abū ʿAbd Allāh b. ʿAyyāsh the secretary stood up and said to the people:

'Swear allegiance to the Commander of the Faithful, son of the Commanders of the Faithful as the companions of the Prophet of God swore to him, promising him submission and obedience in matters pleasing and hateful, easy and difficult, and to give counsel to him, his officers and the community of the Muslims. This is what you owe him. He is obliged not to detain your military contingents (after the campaign), not to keep for himself what should be for the public benefit, to pay your salaries [*ʿaṭā'*] on time and not to seclude himself away from you. May God help you to fulfil this and help him in the affairs of yours which have been entrusted to him.' He repeated these words to each group until the swearing of allegiance had been finished.[25]

This vignette illustrates again that the ruling group formed a very close circle: no-one could become part of the inner elite unless their grandfather or great-grandfather had served with ʿAbd al-Muʾmin. There was no chance that the increasingly powerful Banū Marīn, Berber chiefs for example, could be incorporated in the ruling group. The Arabs and Ghuzz who had formed an important part of the military in the previous century do not seem to have a role here either. Among this conservative ruling class the main concern seems to have been the distribution of lucrative governorates amongst its members, and they seem to have failed to realise the threats posed to the whole empire in a changing world. The nature of the oath is interesting too. The people are encouraged to obey the Caliph as the Companions obeyed the Prophet Muḥammad. It

25. ʿAbd al-Wāḥid al-Marrākushī, *Al-Muʿjib,* pp. 325–7; trans., pp. 270–1.

is true that this reinforces the idea that the Caliph was the rightful successor of the Prophet, which had been a feature of Almohad propaganda since early days, but it is striking that there is no mention of the Mahdī and no specifically religious obligations. In a simple way, this was a contractual monarchy and the new Caliph's promises to remedy certain grievances about military recruitment, taxation and the holding of audiences is a faint echo of developments in the contemporary Christian world.

The new Caliph, who took the formal title of al-Mustanṣir,[26] was too young to take effective control of policy and the oligarchy effectively divided up the spoils of empire. He himself never seems to have left the capital: as Ibn Idhārī notes, 'his father gave him as tutors some Almohad *shaykhs* who dominated him during his reign. He undertook no expeditions or campaigns of note but his days were peaceful apart from some revolts. He entrusted the government of the Maghreb and al-Andalus to his paternal uncles and his relatives'.[27] Among the most important of these were his father's brothers ʿAbd Allāh, Abū'l-ʿUlā, Abū Mūsā and Abū'l-Ḥasan, who became governors of Murcia, Cordoba, Malaga and Granada respectively and may have formed an important pressure group.

Despite the Christian victory of 1212, al-Andalus remained largely peaceful. The Caliph's advisers took care to renew truces with the Castilians, and the Christians were in any case preoccupied with internal affairs and famine. Only on the Portuguese front were there any serious problems and these were largely precipitated by external intervention. In the summer of 1217 a fleet of German Crusaders on their way to the Holy Land stopped off at Lisbon and agreed to join an attack on Alcacer do Sal, whose capture by al-Manṣūr in 1192 had been the most important permanent conquest of his reign. The assault began on 30 July. Muḥammad b. Sīdray, who had been appointed as governor at the time of the Muslim reconquest, had been succeeded by his son ʿAbd Allāh who took charge of the defence. He sought help from the governors of Badajoz, Cordoba, Seville and Jaen who sent troops and a small fleet. The Muslim relief force was easily defeated and on 18 October the defenders were obliged to ask for terms. These were harsh: they were allowed to leave in safety but could not take any of their possessions. Ibn Wazīr himself agreed to convert to Christianity but, after a few days, he escaped to Muslim territory. The German Crusaders moved on

26. For al-Mustanṣir's reign see Huici Miranda, *Historia Politica*, ii, pp. 437–52.
27. Ibn Idhārī, *Al-Bayān*, Part III, p. 243; trans., p. 275.

and no further attacks were made at this stage, but the Muslims must still have felt threatened for between 1219 and 1221 the governor of Seville, Abū'l-ʿUlā the elder, constructed a wall and ditch around the city, some of which still survives by the Puerta Macarena on the north side of the old city, and the great polygonal tower, known as the Torre del Oro, on the banks of the Guadalquivir. And Muslim strongholds were still capable of fierce resistance: both Caceres in the west and Requeña in the east defended themselves successfully against determined Christian attacks.

As ever, the fate of al-Andalus was decided in Morocco. Here too the years of Yūsuf II's reign were largely peaceful, but it was more a peace of exhaustion than strength. As in Castile, these were years of famine and starvation and the depopulated Moroccan countryside was increasingly ravaged by Berber and Arab tribes, notably the Banū Marīn who moved up from the Sijilmāssa area to the plains between Taza and Fes. Gradually, the country slipped out of Almohad control.

On 4 January 1224 the young Caliph died: some said that he was gored to death by a pet cow, as he kept cows and horses which he had imported from Andalucia. He left no children, which in the hereditary monarchy that had been established by ʿAbd al-Mu'min led to immediate problems. The *wazīr* ʿUthman b. Jāmiʿ immediately gathered the Almohad *shaykh*s and had them elect a senior member of the family, Yūsuf's great-uncle, ʿAbd al-Wāḥid b. Yūsuf. Despite the fact that he was now in his sixties, the choice was not unreasonable, and ʿAbd al-Wāḥid al-Marrākushī, who knew him personally, speaks of his excellent qualities. He was also experienced, having been appointed governor of Malaga in 1202, then given command of the Haskūra Berber tribe in 1206. He then did a spell as governor of Sijilmāssa and, from 1221, of Seville, but was back in Marrakesh in 1224.

Whatever his qualities, his hurried appointment aroused considerable opposition. His determination to rule effectively angered many of the Almohad *shaykh*s who wished for a more compliant sovereign. It also represented an important shift in the balance of power within the ruling family, and the brothers of al-Nāṣir, with their important group of governorates in al-Andalus, were not prepared to see another branch of the family take over. This might not have come to open conflict but for fierce rivalries in the administration. The family of Ibn Jāmiʿ had served as *wazīr*s almost continuously since Ibrāhīm b. Jāmiʿ, a coppersmith by trade whose family originated in Toledo, had offered his services to ʿAbd al-Mu'min.[28] Despite a period of exile in Merida in the reign of Yūsuf I, the family had re-established itself and its current head, 'Uthmān b. 'Abd Allāh b. Ibrāhīm b. Jāmi', was head of the administration and effectively kingmaker. He had, however, an increasingly influential rival, Abū Zayd 'Abd al-Raḥmān b. Mūsā b. Yujjān, widely respected for his skills in financial administration. Furthermore, as the nephew of 'Umar al-Hintātī, Ibn Yujjān had powerful connections among the Almohad tribal leaders. Al-Manṣūr had had a high opinion of his abilities and probity and he had continued in high office throughout the reign of al-Nāṣir. With the accession of the boy-caliph Yūsuf II, Ibn Jāmi' saw his chance to dispose of his hated rival who was imprisoned and then exiled to Chinchilla near Albacete: the Almohads often used remote outposts on the Christian frontier as a place of political exile.

On the accession of the aged 'Abd al-Wāḥid b. Yūsuf in 1224, Ibn Yujjān was released and made his way to Murcia. Here he joined up with the governor, 'Abd Allāh. Both knew they had no political future under a government dominated by Ibn Jāmi' and 'Abd al-Wāḥid and they began to work to overthrow it. Two months after the accession of 'Abd al-Wāḥid, 'Abd Allāh was proclaimed Caliph in Murcia with the title of al-'Ādil.[29] At first all went well: with the support of his brothers he was able to take over most of al-Andalus and drive Abd al-Wāḥid's governor out of Seville. Furthermore, Ibn Yujjān's allies among the Almohad chiefs in Marrakesh rallied to his cause: Abū Zakarīyā, the *shaykh* of Hintāta and Yūsuf b. 'Alī of Tīnmal forced Ibn Jāmi' into exile in the Atlas where he was soon done to death. Shortly afterwards, in September 1224, the aged Caliph was deposed and murdered in Marrakesh.

The deposition and death of 'Abd al-Wāḥid b. Yūsuf, known to the Arab sources as *al-makhlū'* (the deposed one), marked a major turning point in Almohad history. Since the time of the first Caliph 'Abd al-Mu'min, the Almohad empire had been a hereditary dynastic state. The ruling family was extremely numerous but, despite some indications of dissent, in the reign of al-Manṣūr for example, it had remained united. There was no rule of primogeniture to decide which of a Caliph's sons should succeed him, and yet, astonishingly, there had been no open and violent succession disputes. The caliphate had remained securely in the hands of the descendants of Yūsuf I while the descendants of his brother and chief

28. For the history of the family see Huici Miranda, *Historia Politica*, ii, p. 448 n. 1.

29. For his reign see ibid., pp. 452–63.

supporter, Abū Ḥafṣ ʿUmar, had been content to play an important role in government without ever claiming supreme power. This cohesion was a major factor in securing the success and stability of the regime. Once it had been broken, it was never recovered: even if other circumstances had been favourable, it would have been difficult to heal the wounds, but against a background of gathering crisis, of famine and plague, of Christian advances in al-Andalus and Merinid attacks in Morocco, it was impossible.

For a moment it must have seemed that al-ʿĀdil would reunite the Almohads, but this was not to be: if he had a claim to the throne, others did as well. The only powerful people in al-Andalus who refused to accept him as caliph were the governor of Valencia, Abū Zayd and his brothers, ʿAbd Allāh and Abū Dabbūs.[30] These were the descendants of the *sayyid* Abū Ḥafṣ ʿUmar and they seem to have felt that the time had come for them to make a bid for power in their own name, with the result that there followed a violent and destructive conflict between the two branches of the ruling family. ʿAbd Allāh, who had been deprived of his position as governor of Jaen by al-ʿĀdil, moved north to Baeza, close to the frontier with the Christians, which he took over, intending to make it his power base. As a result of this he was known to the Arab historians as al-Bayyāsī (the Baezan). Once precariously established, he made another move which was to have disastrous consequences for al-Andalus: he sought an alliance with Fernando III of Castile and agreed to become his vassal. In September 1224 Fernando came to Baeza to accept his homage in person; as Lomax graphically puts it, 'This alliance was to be the lever with which Fernando split the Almohad empire.'[31]

Meanwhile, al-ʿĀdil sent two expeditions in the winter of 1224–25 to try to dislodge him. Despite the fact that he could only muster 100 Muslim horsemen in addition to his Christian mercenaries, al-Bayyāsī was able to defeat both attacks, inflicting a reputation for cowardice and incompetence on al-ʿĀdil's family. This reputation was reinforced when the Portuguese raided the lands around Seville in the early summer of 1225. We have an almost contemporary description of what followed which sheds some light on the failure of the Almohad regime:

> The Portuguese had come to raid this region and had pillaged and taken what they found. Al-ʿĀdil, the ruler of the Maghreb, was in

30. See Guichard, *Musulmans de Valence*, i, pp. 136–8, for a good account of this period.
31. D.W. Lomax, *The Reconquest of Spain* (London, 1978), p. 137.

Seville at the time with his *wazīr*, Abū Zayd b. Yujjān, and the high officials and Almohad *shaykh*s. They had neither the money nor the means to resist the enemy: the power of the empire was then in decline and the lustre of the dynasty tarnished. If a disaster afflicted one of its subjects, if his flocks were raided, he could not hope for any help or get any assistance. The news of the Portuguese attack reached Seville a few days before the encounter we are going to describe. A large number of the common people gathered in the great mosque and when the Friday prayer was over, they got up and shouted at the authorities demanding that they make a sortie against the enemy. The next day, Saturday, a herald went through the town to tell the people that a sortie had been arranged. The people prepared and equipped themselves. Some left the city that very day. When Sunday came there was a levée en masse, and all the Sevillians, great and small, went out of the city on all sorts of mounts, some with arms, some without as if they were going on picnics to their gardens and meadows. A group of them went in the direction of Tejada, accompanied by less than a hundred horsemen. The Christians were there in considerable numbers, protected with coats of mail and well-armed while the majority of the Muslims were unarmed and powerless: they were only the people of the *suq*s and tradesmen. The commander of the group of regular soldiers from Seville was Abū Muḥammad ʿAbd Allāh b. Abī Bakr b. Yazīd who understood warfare much better than this rabble and crowd who knew nothing. They shouted to him that they were going to meet the enemy but he forbade them and tried to warn them. They paid no attention and only wanted to come face to face with the Christians and they abused and insulted him so he became disgusted with them and left along with the horsemen who were with him. He had, furthermore, discovered that they were up against an enemy greatly superior in number against whom he could do nothing. Seeing the regular troops retiring, the Christians began to move towards the people of Seville. The latter, seeing them approach, began to flee and the killing started. Some were slain and large numbers were taken prisoner, while an equal number escaped. Afterwards people differed about the numbers of Sevillians who were killed or taken prisoner on that day, some exaggerating in one way, others in the other. The first gave a figure of 20,000 while others gave a lower estimate. Allah knows best. Al-ʿĀdil then left Seville to return to the capital Marrakesh in November–December of this year [1225].[32]

The account tells us a good deal about the malaise of al-Andalus. There was no lack of popular enthusiasm for the struggle against the Christians but the Almohad and Andalusi military caste seem to have been unable to provide leadership. Perhaps the most telling

32. Al-Ḥimyarī, *Rawḍ al-Miʿṭār*, pp. 128–9; trans., pp. 156–7.

bit is the sharp differentiation between the military and civilian populations. The civilians have no military equipment and no idea of the dangers they are facing. The Almohad elite seems to have made no effort to use this popular enthusiasm to raise a local militia or any sort of defence forces for the city. This gulf between the military and civilian is in striking contrast to the situation in the Christian towns of the frontier regions, where virtually the entire adult male population was trained in the use of arms and could man the walls or raid deep into Muslim territory.

Meanwhile al-Bayyāsī sought to expand his power in the shadow of his new overlord. In June 1225 Fernando arrived with a large army and began a destructive military expedition in Andalucia, taking Priego and Loja and ravaging the Vega of Granada. After the expedition was over, al-Bayyāsī was established in Cordoba and the surrounding areas with Christian support. In exchange for this help, al-Bayyāsī agreed to cede three fortresses to Fernando, Baños de la Encina, where the old castle built by the Umayyads still stands, Salvatierra, where the knights of Calatrava had held out until 1211, and the small and isolated outpost of Capilla to the north-west. The first two surrendered on his orders but the people of Capilla put up a vigorous resistance. From 7 June until it fell on 15 August Fernando conducted a major siege of the castle. The defenders hoped in vain for relief from Seville while the Christians were sustained by large quantities of supplies sent by al-Bayyāsī. His action aroused violent hostility among many Muslims, and soon after the people of Cordoba rose against him and he was killed as he tried to escape, his head being sent as a trophy to al-ʿĀdil in Marrakesh. Al-ʿĀdil in turn had little time to enjoy his triumph. He soon fell out with Ibn Yujjān and many of his Berber allies and was assassinated in Marrakesh on 4 October 1227.

In Seville his effective and ruthless brother Abū'l-ʿUlā now caused himself to be proclaimed Caliph with the title of al-Ma'mūn. He immediately made a truce with Fernando for the winter of 1227–28 in exchange for a payment of 300,000 maravedis. He used the breathing space to try to secure his acceptance in Marrakesh, but increasing and violent divisions amongst the Almohad tribes made this impossible.

In the circumstances, it is not surprising that many Andalusis thought they would be better off without the Almohads:[33] as the

33. The best account of this post-Almohad period in al-Andalus is Guichard, *Musulmans de Valence*, i, pp. 139–65. For a detailed chronology of this complex period see E. Molina Lopez, 'Por una cronologia historica sobre el Sarq al-Andalus (S. XIII)', in *Sharq al-Andalus* 3 (1986), 39–55.

Christians advanced, al-ʿĀdil and al-Maʾmūn were seen to devote their energies to establishing themselves in Marrakesh, while al-Bayyāsī was popularly regarded as a traitor. Nor were the Andalusis lacking in fighting spirit. The successful defences of Caceres and Requeña, the heroic resistance of Capilla showed this. There were demonstrations of popular enthusiasm for warfare against the Christians: it was popular clamour that led to the disastrous sortie of the people of Seville against the Portuguese, and the Murcians launched a similarly unsuccessful attack at Aspe in the same year. The determination of the people of Cordoba and Baeza not to have Christian troops in their cities was a major factor in al-Bayyāsī's downfall. It was not so much enthusiasm for the *jihād* as a stubborn determination to protect their homes and their faith and they badly needed effective leadership.

It was against this background that Muḥammad b. Yūsuf b. Hūd al-Judhāmī appeared on the scene. He was, or was said to have been, a descendant of the Hudids who had been the last Taifa rulers of Zaragoza, dispossessed by the Almoravids in 1110. He was a regular soldier in the *jund* of Murcia who raised a rebellion in the Ricote area to the north-west of the city, probably in May 1228. His programme was openly anti-Almohad and he slaughtered them and their allies at every opportunity. His simple programme seems to have commanded considerable popular support and he soon defeated the governor of Murcia, the *sayyid* Abū'l-ʿAbbās b. Abī Mūsā b. ʿAbd al-Muʾmin, and the *sayyid* Abū Zayd, governor of Valencia. In Cordoba the people rose against the Almohad governor appointed by al-Maʾmūn, the *sayyid* Abū'l-Rabīʿ, killed him and drove out the Almohads. The military defeat of the Almohads was followed by a rejection of their ideology: Ibn Hūd sent messengers to the distant court of the ʿAbbasid caliphs in Baghdad, pledging allegiance to them as caliphs, while he himself took the title of Amir al-Muslimin which had been used by the Almoravids. This pledge of allegiance brought the part of al-Andalus he ruled back into the Sunni world, but its main purpose was the public repudiation of the Almohads and all their works.

Ibn Hūd's success was confirmed by the decision of al-Maʾmūn, the Almohad caliph in Seville, to move to Marrakesh, always the real seat of Almohad power, to dispossess a rival caliph.[34] In October 1228, accompanied by most of the surviving Almohads and a force of some 500 Christian knights, he crossed the Straits. His departure marks the effective end of Almohad rule in al-Andalus. It

34. For al-Maʾmūn's reign see Huici Miranda, *Historia Politica*, ii, pp. 471–80.

also deprived al-Andalus of a large part of its professional defenders. The Almohad army never seems to have recovered from the casualties inflicted on it at Las Navas de Tolosa. After 1212 there is no record of Almohad troops facing the Christians again and the Arabs and Ghuzz, who had formed an important part of the army before, completely disappear from the scene. Some sources speak of much of Morocco being depopulated by the defeat,[35] and the surviving members of the Almohad tribes confined themselves to Marrakesh and the mountains to the south where they had originated, refusing to answer desperate appeals for help from al-Andalus.

Once in Marrakesh, al-Ma'mūn defeated his rival and seems to have been determined to destroy the traditional bases of Almohad authority. He formally repudiated the doctrines of Ibn Tūmart and announced his adherence to Sunni Islam. At the same time he allied himself with the increasingly important Khult tribe (who seem to have been newcomers to the political scene) and embarked on a systematic massacre of the leaders of the Hintāta and the people of Tīnmal, the mainstays of the Almohad regime since its inception. Why he should have acted with such ferocity is not clear, but his actions led to a definitive break with the Hafsids of Tunisia and destroyed the credibility of the Almohads in their own heartland.

The twilight of al-Andalus, 1228–48

The twenty years between the departure of the Almohads and the fall of Seville to the Christians (1228–48) are among the most confusing and complex in the entire political history of al-Andalus, and the problems are compounded by the fact that we only have a few narrative sources, Ibn Idhārī, Ibn Khaldūn, Ibn al-Khaṭīb and al-Maqqarī, all of which were written well after the events they describe. Certain general themes are clear, however. The first is the rise to power of figures with Andalusi backgrounds. Of course Andalusi chiefs like the Banū Wazīr and the Banū 'Azzūn had played an important role under the Almohads, but now a new and different group became rulers in their own right. Some, like the Banū Hūd and the Banū Mardanīsh, sprang from families which had been prominent in Andalusi history in previous centuries; others, like the Banū'l-Aḥmar, were effectively new. In some cities, notably Seville, leadership was provided by the heads of families who had

35. Al-Makkari (trans.), *Mohammedan Dynasties*, ii, p. 323.

long been distinguished in the civil administration, like the Banū Abī'l-Bāqī and the Banū'l-Jadd.

The second characteristic feature of this period is the role of popular opinion in choosing rulers. Ibn Hūd succeeded because he attracted popular support, Muḥammad b. Yūsuf al-Aḥmar became ruler of Arjona after he was chosen by an assembly in the mosque, and Seville was effectively ruled by an oligarchic council. There was also a general quest for legitimacy now that the Almohad caliphate could no longer provide this. Ibn Hūd turned to the 'Abbasid caliphs, who sent messengers to give him investiture and high-sounding titles but no practical support. Other rulers, like Zayyān b. Mardanīsh and the oligarchs of Seville, pledged allegiance to the Hafsid rulers of Tunisia who might at least provide some military backing. As with early periods of Taifa rule, this lack of a constitutional framework certainly contributed to the political instability. The overwhelming need, however, was to find rulers who could either resist the Christians or cooperate with them effectively. It is easy to dismiss the Andalusis of this period as being fickle and feckless, forever appointing and rejecting rulers. But the truth is that these people were desperate and time was running out: this was not a situation where men could put up with an inadequate leader in the hope that things might get better. Many of the rebellions and *coups* of the time should be understood, not as jealous striving for power at the expense of the Muslims, but the actions of would-be leaders frustrated by the failures of their present masters.

The events took place against a background of economic and social disruption. Our sources tell us little enough about these matters: the narrative chroniclers mention details only in passing and there are none of the documentary sources which illuminate the broader history of Christian Europe in the twelfth and thirteenth centuries. However, we can be sure that the uncertainty and sporadic violence of the period must have had a deleterious effect on the rural economy. The Christian raids were often stock rustling as much as religious warfare and this may be a sign that much of the cultivated land of Andalucia was now given over to pasture. Some cities like Valencia, Murcia, Granada, Malaga and Seville were clearly still thriving and probably benefited from the increasing commercial activities of Genoese and other Italian merchants in the area. But other inland towns – the examples of Cuenca (lost to the Christians in 1177), Badajoz and Beja have already been cited – seem to have been depopulated, impoverished and even dangerous. We know that members of many leading families emigrated to the comparative security of the Maghreb, and many humbler people probably made unrecorded moves in the same direction. The depopulation and impoverishment of southern Spain and Portugal, often cited as a consequence of the Reconquista, may in some areas have been a cause of it.

For al-Andalus, the final fate of the Almohads was now irrelevant; the real question was whether Ibn Hūd would be able to unite the country and defend it against the Christians. In November 1229 the people of Seville held a public debate in which it was agreed that they would accept his authority and acknowledge the 'Abbasid caliphate.

Ibn Hūd, who took the quasi-caliphal title of al-Mutawwakil, was now accepted in the whole of al-Andalus except Valencia, but his success did not last long. His first task was to deal with the Christian threat. In March 1230 he went north to confront the King of Leon, who was laying siege to Merida, and the knights of Santiago, who had taken over Montanchez. Despite his own courage and the superior numbers of his troops, he was decisively defeated at Alange. The defeat was a disaster for al-Andalus. Not only were Badajoz and the rest of Extremadura soon lost, but the credibility of Ibn Hūd as a leader was fatally damaged and many Andalusis who had previously supported him began to look elsewhere. Attempts have been made to portray Ibn Hūd's regime as essentially 'populist' and demagogic and to argue that he fell because the 'aristocracy' like Ibn al-Aḥmar and Ibn Mardanīsh opposed him.[36] In fact there is no real evidence for this at all. It is not clear how, if at all, Ibn al-Aḥmar, for example, was more aristocratic than Ibn Hūd, and there is no reason to suggest that this was a social conflict. The fact is that Ibn Hūd benefited from widespread discontent at all levels of society and this support began to drift away when the defeat at Badajoz showed that he could not deliver military success. One by one the major Muslim cities, each looking to their own salvation, were overwhelmed by the enemy.

Majorca was one of the first victims of this great Christian advance and the only conquest for which we have an extended Arabic account by an eye-witness: Aḥmad b. 'Abd Allāh al-Makhzūmī wrote a history of Majorca where he lived for many years. After the Christian conquest he went into exile in North Africa and died in Tunis in 1251. Unhappily, his history is largely lost, but his account of the conquest of Majorca was incorporated in al-Maqqarī's

36. The issue is discussed in Guichard, *Musulmans de Valence*, i, pp. 149–50.

History.[37] His account is highly critical of the last Almohad governor, Muḥammad b. ʿAlī, whom he blames for provoking the Christians by capturing their ships and alienating the leading Muslims by his cruelty and arbitrary executions: even as the sails of the Catalan fleet were sighted, he was preparing to execute 50 of the leading citizens: 'Muḥammad then pardoned the fifty citizens who had been sentenced to death, and having apprised them of the arrival of the enemy, bade them go home and prepare for the defence of the city. Accordingly they all went home and were received by their families as if they had just risen from the tomb.' It is scarcely surprising in these circumstances that the defence was unsuccessful. The city was conquered on 31 December 1230 and guerrilla resistance in the rest of the island subdued during the next year.

The Muslims of Minorca were luckier, at least at first. In 1231 the Minorcans agreed to pay tribute and acknowledge the overlordship of the King of Aragon, in exchange for being allowed a large measure of self-government. Under the rule of the wise and learned Saʿīd b. al-Ḥakam al-Qurashī, the island even became something of a centre of Muslim culture. All this was brought to an end, however, when the Aragonese invaded the island in 1282 and sold virtually the entire Muslim population as slaves, repeopling it with Catalans. Ibiza was taken in 1235 by an expedition financed and led by Guillem de Montgri, sacristan of Girona cathedral.[38]

In Valencia the collapse of Almohad government in Seville left the local governor, the *sayyid* Abū Zayd, isolated as the last Almohad leader in al-Andalus. In 1226 he had made a treaty with James I of Aragon, granting him a tribute which amounted to a fifth of the revenues of the province. As elsewhere, this inability to resist the Christians made him widely unpopular and in late 1228 or early 1229, shortly after the rising of Ibn Hūd in Murcia, he was deposed by rebellion. He and the remaining Almohads were forced to flee to Segorbe on the Aragonese frontier. Here he lived until his death (1264–68) as a vassal of the Aragonese. He ended by converting to Christianity and his lordship was inherited by his daughter and her Christian husband (though his sons remained Muslim).[39] The

37. Al-Makkari (trans.), *Mohammedan Dynasties,* ii, pp. 329–32.

38. The fate of the Balearic Islands immediately after the Reconquista has recently been investigated by D. Abulafia, *A Mediterranean Emporium* (Cambridge, 1994), esp. pp. 65–72 on Minorca.

39. R.I. Burns, 'Daughter of Abu Zayd, last Almohad ruler of Valencia', *Viator* 24 (1993), and M. de Epalza, 'La Caiguda de Valencia i altres Caigudes d'Al-Andalus, segons l'Obra en Prosa d'Ibn al-Abbar', in *Ibn Al-Abbar: Politic i Escriptor Arab Valencia,* ed. M. de Epalza (Valencia, 1990).

leader of the anti-Almohad *coup* was Zayyān b. Mardanīsh (Zayyān b. Mudāfi' b. Yūsuf b. Sa'd b. Mardanīsh), a direct descendant of that Ibn Mardanīsh who had resisted the Almohads for so long. The family had been incorporated into the Almohad elite, and though we do not hear much about them after the Almohad take-over of the Levante in 1172, they clearly maintained their influence in the Valencia area. Zayyān took over Valencia and his cousin Muḥammad b. Subay' b. Yūsuf ruled in Denia. We know a certain amount about Zayyān's rule in the area because Ibn al-Abbār, author of biographical dictionaries and poems, was for a time his *wazīr*, and though he does not give a connected account of the period, he does offer a few details beyond the bare outlines provided by more general annalists.[40] Like Ibn Hūd, Zayyān acknowledged the 'Abbasid caliphate. He was able to maintain his independence of Ibn Hūd but not to resist the Christians effectively. His rule was dominated by a losing battle with the Aragonese and the gradual erosion of his domains, events about which the Muslim sources say little but which are covered in more detail by the autobiography of Jaime I of Aragon[41] and later Christian sources. The Aragonese advance was inexorable: in July 1233 Zayyān was unable to give any support to the defenders of Burriana, who were forced to surrender after a hard-fought siege of two months. In 1236 the Aragonese occupied Puig, only about 20 kilometres north of the capital itself. Ibn Zayyān made a final desperate attempt to dislodge them. He gathered all the troops he could, said by Christian sources to have numbered 600 horse and 11,000 foot, and sent them against the Christian garrison of about 100 knights and 2,000–3,000 foot. Some of the Muslim foot, notably crossbow men from frontier areas like Jerica, Segorbe and Onda, are said to have fought well, but it was literally an uphill struggle on difficult terrain and the mass of the Muslim infantry soon broke and fled. The battle, known to the Muslims as the battle of Anīsha, was really the *coup de grâce* for Valencia. In the aftermath of the disaster, Ibn al-Abbār was sent to Tunis to try to get support from the Hafsid ruler, but though a small fleet was sent, they were unable to land and the Valencians were obliged to face the Christians on their own. The final siege began on 23 April and on 22 September the defenders were obliged to ask for terms. Ibn al-Abbār, who was an eye-witness, described the scene:

40. See Guichard, *Musulmans de Valence*, i, pp. 146–9.
41. This is available in an English translation: *Chronicle of James I of Aragon*, trans. J. Forster (2 vols, London, 1883).

> Abū Jumayl Zayyān b. Mudāfi b. Sa'd al-Judhāmī came out of the city of which he was then Amir and the head of his household and the leaders of the civil and military administration [*wujūh al-ṭulba wa'l-jund*]. The tyrant [Jaime I], dressed in his most splendid clothes and surrounded by his nobles, advanced from the camp at al-Ruṣāfa where he had been since the beginning of the siege. They met at Walaja [immediately south-east of the city] and an agreement was made whereby the tyrant took the city without fighting and that, for twenty days, the inhabitants were able to move out with their possessions. I was present at all these events.[42]

Zayyān himself was able to retreat to Cullera and Denia to the south, but the Christian advance continued. After the assassination of Ibn Hūd in Almeria in January 1238, apparently for personal reasons, the people of Murcia chose as ruler a leading member of the city patriciate, 'Aziz b. Khaṭṭāb, but he is said to have been short of money and failed to resist the Christians. In April 1239 the Murcians turned to Zayyān b. Mardanīsh, whose military reputation had survived the collapse at Valencia, but he too proved unsatisfactory and at the beginning of 1241 he was driven out and spent the rest of his life in Alicante and then, from 1247, in exile in Tunis. The Murcians then turned to the son of Ibn Hūd, but their fate was already sealed. The Castilians, alarmed lest the Nasrid Ibn al-Aḥmar of Granada should try to take over Murcia, advanced, and by 5 July 1243 they had occupied the citadel, though Murcia survived as a vassal kingdom until it was finally taken over by the Castilians in 1266.[43]

Elsewhere the pattern was repeated: cities were vigorously defended by their inhabitants but there was a serious lack of trained and equipped military personnel, little co-operation between cities and no realistic prospects of outside help. Cordoba fell on 29 June 1236, despite the efforts of Ibn Hūd to come to its rescue. By 1249–50 all the cities of the Algarve had fallen to the Portuguese, and in south-west Spain only Niebla survived until 1262 as a vassal kingdom.

In Seville the response of the people to the collapse of the Hudid effort was to turn to Abū Marwān Aḥmad al-Bājī, who came from an important family in the city. He was proclaimed ruler and took the imposing title of al-Mu'taḍid in November 1231. However, he

42. Ibn al-Abbār, *Hullat al-Siyāra,* quoted by Guichard, *Musulmans de Valence,* i, p. 149.

43. For the history of Murcia as a Christian protectorate see L.P. Harvey, *Islamic Spain, 1250–1500* (Chicago, 1990), pp. 44–8.

was killed two years later by the Nasrid Ibn al-Aḥmar, who sent his right-hand man Ibn Ashqilūla to take the city in his name. Again there was a popular revolution and less than a month later Ibn Ashqilūla was driven out and Seville returned to the obedience of Ibn Hūd. The leading figure in the city was now Abū ʿAmr b. al-Jadd, who came from another long-established family of *qāḍī*s and *ʿulamā*, and it was he who persuaded the citizens to return their allegiance to the Almohads after the death of Ibn Hūd in 1238. From then until his death in 1246 Ibn al-Jadd was effective ruler of the city, the last in a line of patrician rulers of Seville which had included Ibn al-Ḥajjāj in the tenth century and Ibn ʿAbbād in the eleventh. He adopted a policy of strict subservience to the demands of Fernando III which, for a time, kept the city safe but made him very unpopular, especially with the *mughāwira* or frontier soldiers whose pay he cut. In 1246 it was the leader of these troops, one Sakkāf, who murdered him. For the last two years of Muslim rule, Seville was run by a council which included Sakkāf, Yaḥya b. Khaldūn, relative of the historian Ibn Khaldūn and representative of a family which had been prominent in the city since the end of the ninth century, and other members of the local patriciate.[44] But it was too late to save Islamic Seville: many leading citizens had already emigrated to North Africa, and with the Castilians in Cordoba, the Guadalquivir valley was effectively lost. Fernando III used the death of Ibn al-Jadd as a pretext for invasion. Fernando, aided by Ibn al-Aḥmar, could not take the city by force but had to resort to starving it out. Eloquent pleas in letter and poetry were sent to North African rulers and the Hafsids did send a fleet which the Christians drove off, but no help was forthcoming from Morocco where the last Almohads and the Merinids were preoccupied by their own struggles. Finally, on or about 23 November 1248,[45] after a siege of a year and a half, the inhabitants asked for terms. They were given a month to leave with all the possessions they could take and on 22 December Fernando entered the city as conqueror.

44. For Seville in this period see R. Valencia, 'Los Dirigentes de la Sevilla Arabe en torno a 1248', in E. Cabrera (ed.), *Andalucia entre Oriente y Occidente* (Actas de V Coloquio Internacional de Historia Medieval de Andalucia, Cordoba, 1988).

45. The different dates are discussed by Valencia in 'Los Dirigentes', p. 33.

CHAPTER ELEVEN

The Nasrids of Granada

Ibn al-Aḥmar and the foundation of the Nasrid kingdom, 1232–73

The foundations of the Kingdom of Granada were laid in the turbulent years of the second quarter of the thirteenth century.[1] The triumphant progress of the Christian reconquest of the 1230s and 1240s reached its culmination with the taking of Seville in 1248. It must have seemed to many on both sides of the religious divide that the catastrophe would engulf the whole of al-Andalus, but in fact this did not happen and the Kingdom of Granada was to survive for another two and a half centuries.

The history of the Kingdom of Granada is frustratingly difficult to discuss in any depth. We can be reasonably sure about the comings and goings of the rulers and the progress of warfare against the Christians but little else. This makes for a linear narrative rather than political analysis. We know little about events outside the capital and we have virtually no information about the provincial governors. This in turn makes it very difficult to understand the civil wars, especially those in the fifteenth century, which played such an important part in the decline of the kingdom. We know that there were important families like the Banū Sarrāj and Banū Kumāsha,

1. The fundamental study of the Nasrid kingdom is R. Arié, *L'Espagne musulmane au temps des Nasrides 1232–1492* (Paris, 1973; new edn Paris, 1990), which deals with all aspects of the life of the kingdom. This should now be supplemented by L.P. Harvey, *Islamic Spain, 1250–1500* (Chicago, 1990), which treats Mudejars (Muslims living under Christian rule) as well as the Kingdom of Granada and makes extensive use of Christian chronicles in addition to the sometimes meagre Arabic sources. Also important for the thirteenth and fourteenth centuries is M.A. Manzano Rodriguez, *La Intervencion de los Benimerines en la Peninsula Iberica* (Madrid, 1992).

but we cannot tell the basis of their power: was it control over the government in Granada or did they have local power bases where they could raise money and military support to pursue their ambitions at the centre? Were there differences of policy towards Castile, a peace party and a war party? Did commercial interests play a part in deciding policy? The answer to these central questions is quite obscure and much of the political history can seem like no more than a series of damaging and pointless palace intrigues.

In 1231 Ibn Hūd had been defeated by the Leonese at Alanje and this defeat, with the subsequent loss of Badajoz and the rest of Extremadura, had fatally undermined his credibility as leader and protector of the Muslims of al-Andalus. All over the country, people began to turn to local strong men who might be able to save them. So it was that the Muslims of the small town of Arjona, in the Guadalquivir valley some 80 kilometres east of Cordoba, gathered at prayers on the final Friday of Ramadan 629 (18 April 1232) and agreed to accept the authority of Muḥammad b. Yūsuf b. Naṣr, known as Ibn al-Aḥmar. Though later attempts were made to find a distinguished ancestry for Ibn al-Aḥmar, it is clear that his origins were fairly modest but that he had acquired a reputation because of his austere piety and his success and energy as a warrior on the Christian frontier, now dangerously close to Arjona. He must have had companions, a war-band, probably formed from Andalusi soldiers who had fought in the Almohad armies and volunteer fighters for the faith, including his relations called the Banū Ashqilūla, with whom he worked in partnership for most of his rule. He was also joined by leading Muslim families who had been driven from their cities by the Christians, families like the Banū'l-Mawl of Cordoba and the Banū Sanādīd of Jaen, who had served the Almohads: they and, presumably, their retainers and followers now joined the army of the Nasrid.[2]

A century later Ibn Khaldūn put the rise of Ibn al-Aḥmar in perspective:

> The Nasrids belonged to one of the Arab families that had supported the Umayyad dynasty, a few survivors of which remained. When the Andalusis were no longer ruled by the Umayyads and the Almoravids and Almohads became their rulers, they detested this domination. Their oppression weighed heavily on them and their hearts were full of hate and indignation against the new rulers.
>
> Near the end of Almohad rule, the Almohad lords handed over

2. Arié, *L'Espagne musulmane*, p. 238.

> many of their strongholds to the Christian ruler in order to gain his support for their attempts to capture the capital city of Marrakesh. This caused the remnants of the Andalusis who represented the ancient group feeling to unite. They were descendants of Arab families who had to some degree kept away from urban civilisation and cities [which Ibn Khaldūn saw as very debilitating] and were firmly rooted in the military life. They included Ibn Hūd, Ibn al-Aḥmar and Ibn Mardanīsh and others like them.[3] Ibn Hūd seized power, and proclaimed the authority of the 'Abbasid Caliphate in the East, and caused the people to revolt against the Almohads. Allegiance to them was denounced and they were driven out. Ibn Hūd thus became independent ruler of al-Andalus. Then Ibn al-Aḥmar rose to power in opposition to Ibn Hūd. He proclaimed the authority of Ibn Abī Ḥafṣ, the ruler of Tunisia, and seized power with a group of relatives who were called 'the chiefs' [*al-ru'asā'*]. He needed no more people than these because there were so few people in al-Andalus possessing a government [*sulṭān*] and subjects [*ra'īya*]. Ibn al-Aḥmar then sought support against the Christians from Zanāta princes who came to him from across the sea. These Zanāta princes became his associates in the defence of the frontier regions and the manning of the garrisons.
>
> Now the Zanāta (Merinid) ruler of the Maghreb had hopes of winning power in al-Andalus but these Zanāta princes who were Ibn al-Aḥmar's associates defended him. His power eventually was firmly established. The people became used to his rule and could do nothing against him. He bequeathed his power to his descendants, who have held it down to the present.[4]

The appearance of this strong man, now known as *al-shaykh*, which in this context probably just means 'the boss', attracted support from other areas, including Jaen. Not everyone was prepared to accept his harsh government, however, even in the crisis situation in which the Muslims of al-Andalus found themselves. In Cordoba the patrician Banū'l-Mawl, the leading family in the city, were hostile to Ibn Hūd and sought to engage Ibn al-Aḥmar as their military protector, but a few months under his control convinced them that Ibn Hūd had a lighter touch. In Seville, too, the Banū'l-Bājī first welcomed and then rejected his authority. He was more successful in smaller centres: Guadix and Baza came over to him in 1232, Granada in May 1237, Almeria in 1238 and Malaga in 1238 or 1239. In none of these cases did Ibn al-Aḥmar have to conquer

3. For the Ibn Hūd and Ibn Mardanīsh referred to, see pp. 265–71 above.
4. Ibn Khaldūn, *Al-'Ibār wa diwān al-mubtadā' wa'l-khabar*, ed. S. Zakkar (8 vols, Beirut, 1981), i, pp. 207–8; trans. F. Rosenthal, *Muqaddima* (3 vols, London, 1958), i, pp. 334–6. I have slightly adapted Rosenthal's translation.

the cities concerned and the people seem to have been only too relieved to accept an effective leader. The foundations of the Kingdom of Granada were laid by consent, not force.

Ibn al-Aḥmar continued to strengthen his position with a cynical disregard for the interests of the Muslim community which must have appalled many: he was an ally of the Castilians when they took Cordoba in January 1236. This did not initially protect his domains: in 1244 Arjona itself was taken and in the summer of 1245 the Castilians mounted a siege of Jaen. The inhabitants sustained a seven-month siege with grim determination, but Muḥammad's attempts to send in supplies proved unsuccessful. Then in March 1246 he decided on a major volte-face. He met Fernando III and agreed to surrender the city and become the vassal of the Castilian king in return for a twenty-year truce. The inhabitants realised that they had no choice but to surrender and the preacher concluded his final address in the great mosque with the words: 'This is the last [Muslim] sermon which will ever be preached in Jaen.' He was right: the Muslim inhabitants of all the cities conquered by the Castilians so quickly at this time were driven out, and there was to be no return:

> Farewell, farewell Jaen, I shed my tears like a scattering of pearls.
> I hate to leave you, but that is the judgment of Time

a local poet lamented.[5]

Two years later Muḥammad demonstrated his loyalties again when he sent a contingent of his men to help the Christians in the final siege of Seville. Ibn al-Aḥmar used his relationship with Fernando III to establish his position in Granada and the south. The Christian sources say that he became the King's vassal, but too much importance should not be attached to this. At various times Ibn al-Aḥmar pledged his loyalty to Ibn Hūd, the 'Abbasid caliphs of Baghdad and the Hafsids of Tunis. All these moves were temporary and tactical. More striking was his policy of accepting the Castilian alliance, buying peace for himself with the catastrophe of other, expendable, Muslims.

The Jaen agreement of 1246 and the fall of Seville in 1248 decided the political and geographical basis of the new kingdom.[6]

5. Both quoted in Ibn 'Abd al-Mun'im al-Ḥimyarī, *Rawḍ al-Mi'ṭār fi akhbār al-aqṭār*, pp. 71–2; French trans. by E. Lévi-Provençal, *La Péninsule Ibérique au Moyen-Age* (Leiden, 1938), pp. 88–90.

6. For his reign see Arié, *L'Espagne musulmane,* pp. 61–8, and Harvey, *Islamic Spain,* pp. 20–40.

Between 1246 and 1264 Ibn al-Aḥmar was largely at peace with his over-mighty Castilian overlords and these years must have provided a vital breathing space in which the new state could become established. Ibn al-Aḥmar established himself in the fortress of the Alhambra, which his dynasty was to make so famous. The city was flooded with refugees from captured towns and the settlement engulfed the old Alcazaba and extended up the hill now known as the Albaicin, from the refugees from Baeza who settled there. The presence of large numbers of refugees was one of the reasons why the kingdom was able to survive so long. It was very densely populated in comparison with the surrounding plains of Christian Andalucia which were very sparsely inhabited, especially after the further expulsions of Muslims which followed the revolts of 1264–66.

The meagre evidence suggests that the Kingdom of Granada was both densely populated and comparatively prosperous, although, as Lévi-Provençal observed, we know much less about the economic state of the Kingdom of Granada than we do of the caliphate of Cordoba half a millennium earlier.[7] In contrast to Christian Spain, where the production of wool from merino sheep was coming to dominate the agricultural economy, Granada seems to have had a mixed agricultural economy. Silk and dried fruits were exported in significant quantities to Italy and northern Europe. Most of the external trade was in the hands of Genoese merchants who established trading colonies in Malaga, Almeria and Granada. In contrast to earlier periods, commerce with the Muslim east seems to have almost completely dried up, though grain may have been imported from the Maghreb. The city of Granada itself expanded and new quarters like the Albaicin to the north and the Antequeruela (inhabited by people from Antequera which fell to the Castilians in 1410) to the south were developed, partly to house refugees who arrived from Christian-held territories. The population has been estimated at 50,000, perhaps half of that of Cordoba in the tenth century, although the estimates are very speculative. But it is the Alhambra palace itself which survives to give us the fullest impression of the wealth of this last remaining Muslim enclave.

The frontiers of the kingdom established at this time were to remain almost unaltered until the 1480s, except in the extreme west where Tarifa and Algeciras were lost. The kingdom included

7. For the economy see Arié, *L'Espagne musulmane*, pp. 344–63; O.R. Constable, *Trade and Traders in Muslim Spain* (Cambridge, 1994), pp. 209–39.

the modern provinces of Almeria, Granada, Malaga and some of the most eastern areas of Cadiz. In addition to the capital itself it contained some important cities, notably Malaga, Almeria, Ronda and Guadix, and rich agricultural areas, especially in the Vegas of Granada and Malaga. The control of ports like Malaga and Almeria meant that Italian merchants could come without going through Castilian territory and that there were direct communications with the Muslim states of North Africa. Much of the kingdom enjoyed good natural frontiers, steep mountains and ravines in the north-west and upland semi-desert in the north-east. In two areas, however, it was particularly vulnerable: the first was the area to the north of the Straits of Gibraltar where Tarifa, Algeciras and Gibraltar itself offered a tempting strategic prize to the Castilians. The second was more central. With the loss of Jaen to the Christians, Granada itself was uncomfortably close to the frontier, which in many cases was less than 50 kilometres away. This meant that there was a constant struggle for control of the castles, especially on the main invasion route from the north-west. The Muslims were determined to hold Loja, Iznajar, Montefrio, Illora and Moclin to guard the approaches to the capital from attacks from the Christian bases at Alcala la Real, Alcaudete, Priego and Cabra. Much of the warfare between the two sides was concerned with the possession of these small but vital strongholds.

This first period of stability was brought to an end with the revolt of the Mudejars (1264–66).[8] The Mudejars were those Muslims who had chosen to live and remain under Christian rule. There had been such Muslims in Castile and Aragon for two centuries by this time who seem to have enjoyed a degree of tolerance and religious freedom and showed no signs of joining a Muslim rebellion. It was different for those who had been subjected by the thirteenth-century Reconquista. In a few areas like Niebla and Murcia they enjoyed virtual self-government under Muslim lords, but in others Christian rule was more direct and harsh.

It is not clear whether the initiative for the rebellion came from Ibn al-Aḥmar or from the Mudejars. Ibn al-Aḥmar must have been aware that the King of Castile, Alfonso X (1252–84), was increasingly preoccupied by other concerns. He had also established good relations with the Hafsids of Tunisia, who might be expected to help, and, more important, with the Merinids in Morocco, who had now replaced the last Almohads and were eager to establish

8. On which see Harvey, *Islamic Spain*, pp. 51–4.

their legitimacy by contributing to the *jihād*. A Berber contingent crossed the Straits to Tarifa, where Ibn al-Aḥmar welcomed them. Muḥammad had observed the fate of the other Muslim rulers of al-Andalus and he must have felt that now was the time to break the Christian stranglehold.

At first things went well: the lord of Murcia, son of Ibn al-Aḥmar's old rival, Ibn Hūd, accepted the authority of Granada, and in the lower Guadalquivir valley, at Jerez, Utrera and Lebrija, the Muslims, encouraged by the arrival of the Merinid forces, attempted to drive out the Christian garrisons. The Christians soon struck back: Jaime I (King of Aragon, 1213–76) retook Murcia and Alfonso X invaded the Vega of Granada in the summer of 1265. By the end of the year it was all over and Ibn al-Aḥmar had to make his peace as best he could. The failure was a disaster for the Mudejars: mass expulsions and ethnic cleansing took place in the lands under Castilian rule, with the result that there were virtually no Muslims left in Christian Andalucia.

One of the reasons for Ibn al-Aḥmar's failure was that he was faced with a challenge in his own lands from none other than the Banū Ashqilūla who had been his partners in the early days.[9] The root of the problem seems to have been Ibn al-Aḥmar's determination to secure the succession for his sons Muḥammad and Yūsuf, which the Banū Ashqilūla knew would ultimately exclude them from power. They rebelled in their stronghold at Malaga in 1266 and invited the aid of Alfonso X. There followed a period of confused warfare and diplomacy which was made more complicated by the revolt of a group of Castilian barons under Nuño Gonzalez de Lara against Alfonso X in 1272. Ibn al-Aḥmar was delighted to welcome the rebel barons to his court.

The problems had still not been solved when Muḥammad died after a fall from his horse on 22 January 1273. Fortunately his son, also called Muḥammad and known as *al-faqīh* (the religious lawyer), was already experienced in both war and diplomacy. Aged 38, he took over immediately.

Because of the nature of the sources, we are much better informed about military and diplomatic events than about domestic developments. Despite, or perhaps because of, the wealth of detail, these military and diplomatic manoeuvres can be bewildering and pointless to the historian, just as, presumably, they were bewildering to many people at the time. However, each of the parties did

9. The struggle is discussed in ibid., pp. 31–7.

have long-term interests which they attempted to pursue with some consistency.

Nasrids, Merinids and Castilians, 1273–1333

Muḥammad II's reign (1273–1302)[10] saw the emergence of the Nasrid diplomatic system, a balancing of forces which, when successful, secured the power of the kings of Granada and the safety of their realm. There were three main protagonists in the system, the rulers of Granada, the kings of Castile and the Merinid sultans of Fes. Each of these players had their own objectives. The kings of Granada sought above all to survive with their frontiers intact, but in their more optimistic moments they also wanted to regain some of the territories lost to the Christians. Their ambitions seem to have been realistic in this respect: their targets were small towns on the frontier, like Alcaudete and Martos which the Christians used as bases for attack, rather than Cordoba or Seville. The Nasrids were also determined not to be swallowed up into some Moroccan empire as the Taifa kingdoms of the eleventh century had been. They were anxious to keep the Merinids at arm's length, happy to accept them as allies when it suited but wary of their intentions and determined not to allow them any foothold in their kingdom, and this involved trying to control the Straits at Algeciras, Gibraltar and Ceuta. Nasrid diplomacy was aimed at preserving a balance of power and, above all, at preventing an alliance of Castilians and Merinids.

The objectives of the Castilians were more complex than might at first appear. They seem to have had very little desire to take over Granada and complete the Reconquista. They did want to prevent Muslim raids on their territory and to force the Nasrids to pay tribute, which was an important source of income to the Castilian crown which was frequently in financial difficulties. Essentially, the kingdom was more valuable to the kings of Castile alive than dead: if it had been conquered, its lands would have had to be distributed among the Castilian nobility. In addition, the Castilians were already finding it difficult to attract enough settlers to occupy the newly conquered lands of Christian Andalucia. There is little indication of any systematic attempt at conquest and the principal gain the Christians did make, Tarifa in 1292, was taken from the Merinids,

10. For his reign see Arié, *L'Espagne musulmane*, pp. 68–84; Harvey, *Islamic Spain*, pp. 151–64.

not the Nasrids, the object being to prevent North Africans from crossing the Straits of Gibraltar. Muḥammad II of Granada supported the siege and took the opportunity to drive Merinid troops out of Estepona, which they had recently occupied.

The Merinids were a Berber dynasty based on the support of the Zanāta group of tribes, as the Almoravids had been on the Ṣanhāja and the Almohads on the Maṣmūda, but they differed from their predecessors in having no religious or ideological basis to their rule: the Merinid empire had been established by tribal chiefs, not religious reformers. Nonetheless they saw themselves as successors to the Almohads and tried, at least at times, to act as protectors of the Muslims of al-Andalus. Like many Muslim dynasts before them, they saw leadership of the *jihād* as a way of establishing their right to rule with the *'ulamā* and the wider Muslim public. Forays into Christian Andalucia also gave the opportunity for their Berber followers to acquire booty, mostly in the form of sheep and cattle. Merinid armies were largely composed of lightly armed horsemen and they moved quickly, at least compared with the ponderous progress of the Almohads, but they never developed any real expertise in siege warfare: they could, and did, ride up to the walls of Seville but they could never have mounted an effective assault.

In addition to these major players, each of the parties was also faced by internal opposition. The Kingdom of Granada was the most cohesive of the polities but was weakened from time to time by internal disturbances, like the revolt of the Banū Ashqilūla in the late thirteenth century and succession disputes in the fourteenth and fifteenth, all of which were exploited by its enemies. Castile was plagued with internal strife from the later days of Alfonso X as well as by the intermittent hostility of Aragon, Portugal and Navarre. For long periods the frontier lords of Christian Andalucia faced the Muslims without any leadership or support from their kings. The Merinid sultanate was divided by succession crises, tribal revolts and the establishment of a separate, rival, Berber state under the 'Abd al-Wādids of Tlemcen.

From the first appearance of Merinid forces on Andalusi soil at the time of the Mudejar revolt in 1264 until their final defeat at the battle of the Rio Salado in 1340, these different interests constantly arranged and rearranged themselves like the patterns in a kaleidoscope, changing according to their perceived needs and relative strengths. Despite intermittent reference to the *jihād*, neither Muslims nor Christians seem to have felt any inhibitions about making alliances with the infidel.

Muḥammad II's reign saw important changes in the composition of the army.[11] In addition to the Andalusi *jund*, Muḥammad recruited Zanāta Berbers who became an important element, perhaps the most important element in the army of the Kingdom of Granada. These Berbers, known as *ghāzī*s, or warriors for the faith, were mostly political exiles from the Merinid sultanate. The earliest of them had appeared in 1264 in the reign of Muḥammad I after a failed rebellion in Morocco, and a second wave came at the beginning of Muḥammad II's reign after a number of leading Merinid families in the Gomara mountains, notably the Banū 'Abd Allāh and the Banū Idrīs, had rebelled in protest at the Sultan Abū Yūsuf's decision to appoint his own son as heir apparent. Like the Zirids at the beginning of the eleventh century, these Berber groups came with their own chiefs and seem to have maintained their kinship bonds. They were settled in Granada where they gave their names to the Zenete quarter just below the old Alcazaba and the Gomares (after the Gomara mountains of northern Morocco where many of them were recruited) below the Alhambra itself. As so often, these military outsiders made heavy financial and political demands, consuming a large part of the tax revenue and living in elegant palaces. That they were not always welcomed by the locals is suggested by the report that when a group of rebels in Ronda surrendered to Muḥammad II in 1295, one of the conditions they made was that the *ghāzī*s from Africa would not be settled in the town.[12]

These Zanāta proved the most effective soldiers in the Nasrid armies. We have little idea of overall numbers, though a Christian document of 1303 speaks of 7,000 being dismissed by Muḥammad III,[13] which suggests that there may have been as many as 10,000 at times, though the 600 whom Muḥammad V sent to help his suzerain Pedro the Cruel of Castile (1350–69) was probably a more typical force.[14] They brought with them their own distinctive fighting techniques. It seems that up to the mid-thirteenth century, Andalusi and Christian horsemen had fought with similar equipment, coats of mail and lances, though Christian knights were probably more heavily armed and armoured. In the fourteenth and fifteenth centuries, Christians increasingly used plate armour, which was never adopted by the Muslims, while the Andalusis began to fight in the

11. For a full discussion of the Nasrid army see Arié, *L'Espagne musulmane*, pp. 229–76.
12. Manzano Rodriguez, *La Intervencion de los Benimerines*, p. 332.
13. Ibid., p. 330.
14. Arié, *L'Espagne musulmane*, p. 252 n. 6.

Berber fashion. With light armour, small lances and sabres, riding their ponies with short stirrups, they were dangerous and highly mobile opponents who gave their name to the Spanish language (*jinete* meaning horseman from Zanāta) and played a major part in defeating the Castilian forces. They were also recruited by Christian rulers: in 1301, for example, Muḥammad II agreed to send a corps of Zanāta to Jaime II of Aragon in exchange for galleys. Right up to the last days of the Kingdom of Granada, these Berbers formed the backbone of the army and in one sense the survival of the kingdom can be ascribed to the use of the revenues of Granada to pay the Zanāta to fight the Christians.[15]

The Zanāta soldiers were recruited and led by exiled members of the Merinid ruling family who held the powerful office of *shaykh al-ghuzāt* or chief of the *ghāzī*s. There were three main sub-dynasties of these Merinid leaders, the Banū ʿAbd al-Ḥaqq, the Banū Raḥḥū and the Banū Abīʾl-ʿUlā, who were switched round according to political circumstance. The leaders of the *ghāzī*s were often good military leaders but politically demanding: ʿUthmān b. Abīʾl-ʿUlā held office through the reigns of Ismāʿīl I (1314–25) and Muḥammad IV (1325–33), and in 1319 he won a brilliant victory over the Castilians at the battle of the Vega, but when Muḥammad IV tried to establish close relations with the then Merinid ruler, ʿUthmān's sworn enemy, the military leader had no compunction in murdering his sovereign. It was not surprising therefore that Muḥammad V finally suppressed the office in 1374. Thereafter, Berber troops continued to play an important role in the Nasrid armies, but they were commanded by members of the Nasrid families or Andalusi generals.

Not all warfare was cavalry warfare. The crossbow was the classic infantry weapon, both for attack and defence. Muḥammad II, like his Almohad predecessors, embarked on a large programme of fortification, and this was continued by his fourteenth-century successors, notably Muḥammad V (1362–91). City walls were strengthened and, in the case of Granada, extended to take in the newly settled Albaicin. The Alhambra itself was surrounded by massive walls and towers and Muḥammad V united Alhambra and city in a single defensive system. Unlike the Almohads, who had concentrated their efforts on city fortifications, the Nasrids also built isolated castles, with square, vaulted donjons and outer enceintes: there are good

15. For the Zanāta see ibid., pp. 238–57, and Manzano Rodriguez, *La Intervencion de los Benimerines*, pp. 321–71.

surviving examples at Zahara and Teba, in the west of the kingdom, and at Moclin guarding the northern approaches of Granada. There were also smaller watch towers and places of refuge where peasants could take refuge from Christian attacks: Muḥammad III (1302–9) built five in the Vega of Granada, and at the time of the Christian conquest in 1489 there were said to have been almost 1,000 small towers in the huerta of Baza. The siege and defence of castles characterised frontier warfare around Granada right up to the final Christian conquest.[16]

The early years of Muḥammad II's reign were occupied by his attempt to destroy the power of the rebel Banū Ashqilūla. The problem was that the rebels had powerful friends. Muḥammad met Alfonso X in Seville in 1273, but even though he agreed to pay 300,000 maravedis per year, the Castilian king still kept in touch with them. Worse still, when the Merinid sultan Abū Yūsuf came to Tarifa in 1275, he received the Banū Ashqilūla as well as the Nasrids and made no distinction between them. In 1278 the Banū Ashqilūla felt obliged to hand over their base at Malaga to Abū Yūsuf, who appointed his uncle to rule the town: as Ibn Khaldūn noted, it was all uncomfortably reminiscent of the early days of the Almoravid presence in al-Andalus. The Merinids, not the Castilians, had now become the main threat to Granada and Muḥammad incited the Muslim ruler of Tlemcen to attack them and was able to prise Malaga from their hands in February 1279. In 1281 there was a triple alliance of Castilians, Merinids and Banū Ashqilūla against Granada and Malaga, but Muḥammad's Berber troops proved their worth and the attackers were driven off. The deaths of Alfonso X in 1284 and Abū Yūsuf the Merinid in 1286 meant that Muḥammad's main enemies were preoccupied by internal affairs, and in 1288 the Banū Ashqilūla were finally forced to abandon their last base at Guadix and emigrate to Morocco.

The Merinids retained Tarifa, to the discomfort of the Nasrids and the new King of Castile, Sancho IV (1284–95), and Muḥammad put together an alliance with the ruler of Tlemcen to attack the Merinid outpost. The Nasrids attacked Merinid possessions while the city itself fell to Sancho in October 1292. Muḥammad found, however, that he had tried to be too clever: when he went to see Sancho in Cordoba in December of the same year to receive the keys of the city according to their agreement, he was met with a stony refusal and there was nothing he could do about it. Tarifa,

16. For military architecture see Arié, *L'Espagne musulmane*, pp. 320–8.

in its strategic position on the Straits, was lost to the Muslims for ever. However, in the aftermath of this débâcle the Merinid sultan Abū Ya'qūb handed over all his remaining possessions in al-Andalus, including Algeciras.

In 1295 Sancho IV died and the accession of his young son Fernando IV (1295–1312) to the throne of Castile allowed Muḥammad to take the offensive, often in alliance with James II of Aragon. Between 1295 and his death in 1302 he was able to retake the frontier forts of Alcaudete and Quesada and raid the Guadalquivir valley, but, despite intrigues and negotiations, he was unable to secure the return of Tarifa to Muslim hands.

Muḥammad II was succeeded by his son, Muḥammad III (1302–9).[17] He seems to have been a strange character, with a reputation for bizarre cruelty, and it was alleged that he had in fact poisoned his father. However, he played much the same diplomatic and military game as his father and grandfather had before him. For the first year he continued his father's policy of raiding Castile and maintaining an alliance with Aragon and the Merinids. In 1303, however, Fernando IV established effective control in Castile and forced a complete turnabout in policy. Muḥammad was obliged to make peace and to pay the tribute his father had paid to Sancho IV. This change immediately alienated the Merinids because it meant the abandonment of the *jihād* and of Aragon, even though Muḥammad maintained a position of strict neutrality between the two major Christian powers and dismissed 6,000 of his Berber troops.

Now that the Castilian frontier was peaceful, Muḥammad turned his attention to seizing control of the Straits from the Merinids. He ordered the governor of Malaga, his cousin the Abū Sa'īd Faraj, to raise a rebellion in Ceuta and he made contact with the dissident Merinid 'Uthmān b. Abī'l-'Ulā, whose family were to hold the office of *shaykh al-ghuzāt* in Granada for much of the fourteenth century.[18] 'Uthmān raised a rebellion in the Gumara mountains in 1307 and Ceuta came under Nasrid rule. Muḥammad, aided by dissident Berbers, was able to prevent the Merinids retaking it, but more serious problems loomed. His triumph in Ceuta seems to have encouraged his enemies to unite against him, for the Christian powers put aside their differences. On 19 December at Alacala de Henares, Fernando IV of Castile and Jaime II of Aragon agreed to mount a

17. For his reign see ibid., pp. 84–9; Harvey, *Islamic Spain*, pp. 165–70.

18. On this family see M.A. Manzano Rodriguez, 'Los Banū Abī'l-'Ulā', in M. Marin *et al.* (eds), *Estudios Onomastico-Biograficos de Al-Andalus* (5 vols, Madrid, 1988–92), v, pp. 199–227.

joint expedition to invade Granada and divide up the kingdom, the Aragonese taking Almeria, the Castilians the rest. The Merinids were drawn into the alliance by the prospect of recovering Ceuta.

This dangerous situation was turned into a crisis by internal disagreements in Granada itself. Muḥammad had been obliged to suppress a revolt by Abū'l-Ḥajjāj b. Naṣr, a relative of his who was governor of Guadix in 1303. In March 1309 the *wazīr* Ibn al-Ḥakīm al-Rundī was assassinated by his rival, 'Atiq b. al-Mawl, and his body abused by an angry mob. Muḥammad himself was forced to abdicate in favour of his brother Naṣr. It is not clear what the reasons for this *coup d'état* were, but it may be that many in Granada were concerned that his foreign policies were leading the kingdom to destruction. It is also likely that his dismissal of many Berber troops and ill-treatment of others had stirred up hatred in many quarters.

His brother Naṣr (1309–14) took immediate steps to break out of the isolation.[19] He needed to move fast, for in the summer of 1309 Fernando IV took Gibraltar with the aid of Aragonese galleys operating in the Straits and in August a large Aragonese expedition arrived to lay siege to Almeria. As soon as he came to the throne, Naṣr sent a message to the Merinid court to ask for peace. The process was aided in July when a rebellion in Ceuta turned the city over to the Merinids and 'Uthmān b. Abī'l-'Ulā was encouraged to come to Granada with his followers, so removing the major bones of contention between the two Muslim powers. Merinid forces landed in al-Andalus to defend Algeciras and the new Sultan, Abū'l-Rabī', wrote to Jaime II of Aragon urging him to make peace with Granada and encouraging Majorcan merchants to come to Morocco. Algeciras resisted Castilian attacks as the people of Almeria resisted the Aragonese throughout the autumn of 1309. By early 1310 the danger was over, the Aragonese had retreated, and though the Castilians took a few castles, their attacks came to an end with the death of Fernando IV in 1312.

Despite this diplomatic success, Naṣr had aroused opposition within the ruling elite. In 1312 a rebellion was raised by his cousin Ismā'īl supported by 'Uthmān b. Abī'l-'Ulā, now in Granada as leader of the *ghāzīs*. Naṣr made the mistake of seeking aid from the Castilians, which made him even more unpopular. As the rebels approached Granada, there was an uprising in the city supported by the *wazīr* Ibn al-Mawl and the leading *shaykhs*. The people of the Albaicin opened the gates to Ismā'īl's forces and on 8 February

19. Arié, *L'Espagne musulmane*, pp. 89–93; Harvey, *Islamic Spain*, pp. 171–80.

1314 Naṣr was obliged to leave the city and retire to the modest position of provincial governor in Guadix.

Ismāʿīl I (1314–25) proved a vigorous and effective ruler.[20] His main problem was the rogue activities of his deposed cousin. Naṣr had no scruples about forming an alliance with the Castilians for the invasion of Granada and his position in Guadix allowed for easy communication with the Christians. It was fortunate for Granada that the King of Castile, Alfonso XI (1312–50), was a minor and that his two regents, the princes Pedro and Juan, were not particularly effective, but the threat was certainly real and the Merinids showed no wish to intervene on behalf of their co-religionists. After some siege warfare on the frontiers, the Castilians launched a major assault in the summer of 1319, laying siege to Granada itself. On 26 June, however, the Castilian army was decisively defeated in the Vega, both the co-regents being killed. It was probably the most decisive victory the Nasrids ever won over the Castilians, and reports of it, suitably exaggerated, were widely circulated in the Muslim world.

The battle of the Vega saved the kingdom and put an end to Naṣr's hopes of restoring his position. In 1324–25 Ismāʿīl was even able to take the offensive and recover Baza and Martos. He might have achieved much more had he not been assassinated by his cousin Muḥammad b. Ismāʿīl, lord of Algeciras, on 6 July 1325, apparently as a result of a personal grudge.

His son and successor Muḥammad IV (1325–33) was still young and his youth allowed factional strife to develop.[21] At the heart of this were the Banū Abīʾl-ʿUlā, led by the redoubtable ʿUthmān. They were the backbone of the Granadan forces and responsible for the successes of Granadan arms against the Castilians. However, they were not always popular with the Andalusis, especially because of their financial demands, and they were opposed to close relations between Granada and their enemies/kinsmen the Merinids. At this period they came close to acting as a praetorian guard and dominating the kingdom entirely. In 1327–28 they secured the assassination of the *wazīr* Ibn al-Maḥrūq and took charge of the young prince.

As usual, internal discord coincided with external threat. In 1325 Alfonso XI of Castile attained his majority and set about establishing his reputation as a Crusader. His attempts to secure effective

20. Arié, *L'Espagne musulmane*, pp. 93–8; Harvey, *Islamic Spain*, pp. 180–7.
21. Arié, *L'Espagne musulmane*, pp. 98–101; Harvey, *Islamic Spain*, pp. 187–9.

support from France and Aragon failed, but the Castilian army was still formidable and volunteers from northern Europe joined the expedition. Once again frontier forts, including Teba,[22] were captured, though the Merinids succeeded in taking Gibraltar for Islam. The Granadan army performed well but the Zanāta military, led by the Banū Abī'l-'Ulā, became dissatisfied with the young King, who was assassinated on 25 August 1333, apparently because of his close relations with the Merinid sultan Abū'l-Ḥasan.

The golden years of the Nasrid kingdom: Yūsuf I and Muḥammad V, 1333–91

The accession of his brother Yūsuf I (1333–54)[23] marks the beginning of the golden years of the Nasrid kingdom, years when the kingdom was prosperous and not seriously threatened by outside attack, years when the great historian and literateur Ibn al-Khaṭīb (d. 1374) flourished, and years in which the beautiful palaces of the Alhambra were constructed.

The new king's first actions were to revenge his brother by driving the Banū'l-'Ulā from his kingdom. They took refuge in Tunis and were replaced as leader of the *ghāzīs* by the Merinid Yaḥyā b. 'Umar b. Raḥḥū. Needless to say, his main preoccupation was defending his realm against the crusading King of Castile. Alfonso XI was determined to retake Gibraltar and so prevent North African armies from crossing the Straits. The conflict came to a head in 1340. The first stage was a naval battle in which the ships of the Merinids, with help from the Hafsids of Tunisia, defeated the Castilian fleet, supported by the Catalans: Muslim naval power was still a force to be reckoned with. The land battle turned out very differently. On 30 October 1340 a Christian force led by Alfonso XI and his father-in-law Afonso IV of Portugal (1325–57) decisively defeated the Merinid and Nasrid army on the Rio Salado.[24] The Merinid Abū'l-Ḥasan fled back to Morocco and Yūsuf I to Granada.

The Christian victory was of great importance, in both the short and the long term. In the short term it avenged the defeat in the

22. It was while participating in the attack on Teba that Sir James Douglas, who was carrying the heart of Robert Bruce, King of Scots, to the Holy Land, was killed in battle.

23. Arié, *L'Espagne musulmane*, pp. 101–9; Harvey, *Islamic Spain*, pp. 190–205.

24. The campaign is described in A. Huici Miranda, *Las Grandes Batallas de la Reconquista durante las Invasiones Almoravides, Almohades y Benimerines* (Madrid, 1956), pp. 329–87.

Vega in 1319. It also allowed the Castilians to take Priego and Alcala la Real in 1342, both vital points on the road which led to Granada from the north-west. After a hard-fought siege in which the Muslim defenders, mostly Merinid troops, used cannon for the first time in the Iberian peninsula,[25] Algeciras was taken by Alfonso XI in 1344. This was an international Crusade which attracted attention from all over Europe: Alfonso had the support of Henry of Lancaster, the Earl of Salisbury, the King of Navarre and Gaston, Count of Foix, though these foreign grandees do not seem to have had the stamina for a long siege.

In the longer term, the Battle of the Rio Salado meant the end of Merinid activity in al-Andalus and, as it turned out, the end of any large-scale North African participation in the military affairs of the Iberian peninsula. Since 1086 when Yūsuf b. Tāshfīn and his Almoravid followers had first landed, Berbers from Morocco had played a vital role in sustaining al-Andalus against the Christians while, at the same time, undermining its home-grown elites. Now all that was at an end. This was partly because the Merinid regime disintegrated in the second half of the fourteenth century and was not replaced by a strong successor, but partly too because the loss of access to the Straits at Tarifa or Algeciras meant that it was impossible to move large forces into al-Andalus. Smaller groups could and did make the longer sea voyage to Malaga or Almeria, but mass invasions were a thing of the past. The Nasrids had, in fact, to work out their own salvation.

In fact, the aftermath was less catastrophic than it might have been. In 1350 Alfonso XI perished while besieging Gibraltar, a royal victim of the Black Death, and his young son Pedro I (known as the Cruel or the Justiciar, 1350–69) had problems enough of his own and was keen to be on good terms with the Muslims.

Yūsuf's successful reign was brought to an abrupt end in 1354 when he was assassinated in the great mosque in Granada, apparently by a madman. Muḥammad V (1354–59 and 1362–91) was only sixteen when he came to the throne[26] and the government was run by the *ḥājib* Riḍwān who had served his father, Yaḥyā b. ʿUmar b. Raḥḥū, chief of the *ghāzī*s, and the young Ibn al-Khaṭīb who acted as *wazīr*. This group adopted a policy of peace with Castile, agreeing to pay tribute and send military support: in the naval warfare between Castile and Aragon in the summer of 1359, for example,

25. Harvey, *Islamic Spain*, p. 200.
26. For his reigns and the intervening usurpations see Arié, *L'Espagne musulmane*, pp. 106–21; Harvey, *Islamic Spain*, pp. 206–19.

Muḥammad not only put Nasrid ports at the disposal of the Castilian fleet but contributed three galleys himself. A more peaceful and lasting testimony to the good relations can be seen in the Alcazar of Seville, where the Castilian royal palace was largely built in the Granadan style during this period. Pedro was widely criticised in Castile for his liking for Muslim things and his reign represents a high point in this cultural interchange.

Muḥammad's first reign was brought to an end by a palace intrigue between members of the ruling family. The *coup* of August 1359 was led by his half-brother Ismāʿīl, apparently incited by his mother Maryam and an ambitious cousin, the *ra'īs* Abū ʿAbd Allāh Muḥammad. The unfortunate Riḍwān was killed but Muḥammad himself was able to escape to Guadix, where he was supported by the chief of the local *ghāzī*s, ʿAlī b. Badr al-Dīn b. Mūsā b. Raḥḥū, and then to the Merinid court in Fes.

Ismāʿīl II (1359–60) had little chance to enjoy his power before he was murdered on 24 June 1360 by his ambitious co-conspirator Abū ʿAbd Allāh, who now became Sultan as Muḥammad VI (1360–62). But Muḥammad V had not been entirely abandoned by his Castilian overlord and in February 1362 he was able to return: he had financial support from Castile and the backing of the *shaykh al-ghuzāt* ʿUthmān b. Yaḥyā b. Raḥḥū and of ʿAlī b. Kumāsha. ʿAlī was a member of a family, probably from Vera on the Murcian frontier of the kingdom, which was to play a major role in Granadan politics right up to 1492. Meeting Pedro and his army at Casares, they marched on Granada and Muḥammad VI fled. Ill-advised by Idrīs b. ʿAbī'l-ʿUlā, the deposed Muḥammad VI threw himself on the mercy of Pedro the Cruel. There was none: Pedro fully understood the value of his alliance with Muḥammad V and the supplicant was executed.

On his return to power, Muḥammad V continued the peaceful policies of his first reign, and the kingdom seems to have been remarkably free of internal dissension. In about 1370 he made a major change to the administration when he suppressed the office of *shaykh al-ghuzāt* and brought the Berber troops under the direct command of the Nasrid family. While this may have reduced the problems caused when Berber leaders like ʿUthmān b. Abī'l-ʿUlā became too powerful, it may have encouraged the growth of faction and rivalry within the Nasrid house and among other members of the elite which is so typical of the Nasrid state in the fifteenth century. Individual princes attracted the loyalty of groups of soldiers and leading families like the Banū Sarrāj and the Banū Kumāsha acquired power bases in the army which they used to push the claims of different members of the dynasty to the throne.

Muḥammad's reign also saw the high point of Nasrid culture. In the literary field, the dominating figure was the writer and politician Lisān al-Dīn Ibn al-Khaṭīb (1313–75). Born in Loja, he was educated in Granada where his father was working for Ismā'īl I. After his father was killed in the disastrous defeat of the Muslims on the Rio Salado in 1340, the young Ibn al-Khaṭīb continued in the royal service, becoming *kātib al-inshā'* (chancellor) and *wazīr* to Yūsuf I in 1349 after his predecessor 'Alī b. Jayyāb had died of the Black Death. He continued in office under Muḥammad V and followed him into exile when he was temporarily deposed in 1359. While in exile, he made useful contacts at the Merinid court and in some ways seems to have felt more at ease there than in Granada. In 1362, when Muḥammad was restored, he became *wazīr* again but clearly felt that his position was insecure, largely because of the rivalry of the poet Ibn Zamrak. In 1371 he defected to the Merinids but even here he was attacked by rivals and finally murdered in 1375. Despite the ups and downs of his administrative career, he found the time to write on many different subjects and his three history books are one of the major sources for the Nasrid kingdom.

Ibn al-Khaṭīb's successor as *wazīr* was Ibn Zamrak (d. 1392), son of a metal-worker from the Albaicin quarter of Granada, who produced some of the most notable poetry of the kingdom. It was his verse, carved in stucco, that decorated and explained the Court of the Lions, perhaps the most exquisite part of the Alhambra palace, which was constructed during Muḥammad's reign.[27]

This cultural activity was made possible by the success of Muḥammad V's foreign policy, and none played the Nasrid political game with more skill than he. He was aided by circumstances: the civil wars which culminated in the murder of Pedro the Cruel by his half-brother Henry of Trastamara in 1369 meant that the Castilians were in no position to threaten Granada. The first two Trastamara kings of Castile, Henry II (1369–79) and John I (1379–90), were too weak and insecure to launch major campaigns. Nor was the independence of Granada seriously threatened by the Merinids: after the death of 'Abd al-'Azīz in 1372 the sultanate was undermined by succession disputes which meant that Merinid contenders looked to Granada for support and favours.

27. See O. Grabar, *The Alhambra* (London, 1978), pp. 144–7.

Muḥammad knew that the Castilians were the main threat to Granada and he resolutely pursued a policy of peace with them. From 1362 on Pedro I was threatened by his rival Henry of Trastamara. Muḥammad supported Pedro, partly no doubt because of Pedro's close relations with Granada but partly too because Pedro held Christian Andalucia which bordered on his kingdom. He sent 600 horsemen, commanded by Faraj b. Riḍwān, to help him. This aroused the hostility of the Aragonese, allies of Henry, and Granadan ships were attacked: Muḥammad proclaimed a *jihād* and was sent money, supplies and men by Mūsā II, lord of Tlemcen. In 1366 Henry of Trastamara took Seville while Pedro fled north. Muḥammad was ever the pragmatist and the interests of Granada took precedence over any other loyalties, so when Henry began to attack the frontiers of Granada, Muḥammad made peace with him and his Aragonese allies in 1366–67. When Pedro reappeared in 1367 Muḥammad once again changed allegiance and, acting as Pedro's ally, sacked Jaen, Ubeda and Baeza, which were held by supporters of Henry, and even reached the walls of Cordoba.

The assassination of Pedro at Montiel on 22 March 1369 and the confusion which followed allowed Muḥammad to consolidate his position on the frontier to the north of Granada and retake Algeciras. From 1370 until Muḥammad's death in 1391 there was a long period of almost complete peace, the halcyon days perhaps of the Kingdom of Granada.

Internal divisions and external threats, 1391–1464

The death of Muḥammad V saw an outbreak of palace intrigue of which we know the barest details: the historical writings of Ibn al-Khaṭīb only go as far as the 1360s and those of Ibn Khaldūn to 1393; we are without any good Arabic source for the bulk of the fifteenth century and are heavily dependent on fragments gleaned from Christian chronicles. Muḥammad V was succeeded by his eldest son, Yūsuf II (1391–92).[28] He was at first dominated by his father's freedman Khālid, who murdered the new king's three brothers before being murdered himself as the new monarch

28. For the period 1391–1410 see Arié, *L'Espagne musulmane*, pp. 121–9; Harvey, *Islamic Spain*, pp. 220–42.

asserted his personal rule. Yūsuf was aided by his *wazīr*, the poet Ibn Zamrak. Yūsuf died of natural causes in October 1392. Helped by members of the court, his younger son Muḥammad (Muḥammad VII, 1392–1408) seized power and put his elder brother under arrest at Salobreña on the south coast. Ibn Zamrak was removed and a new *wazīr*, Muḥammad b. ʿĀṣim, appointed.

Fortunately for the Granadans, the Kingdom of Castile was equally disturbed during the minority of Henry III (1390–1406) and internal conflict did not put the frontier in danger. Rogue elements in Castile did sometimes cause problems. In April 1394 the Master of the Order of Alcantara, Martin Yañez de la Barbuda, decided to prove his Crusader credentials and led 400 of his knights and a motley group of followers against Granada. No sooner had they reached the Vega of Granada than the Nasrid army fell on them and wiped them out. Muḥammad VII protested to the Castilian king about this breach of the truce then in force and the embarrassed monarch publicly disassociated himself from the Master's actions. At one level this showed the effectiveness of Granadan arms and the unwillingness of the Castilian crown to open hostilities, but there was another, more worrying, aspect: the incident showed that the Crusading spirit was still very much alive among some of the Castilian nobility and that attacks on Granada were considered a significant way of making a reputation.

However, it was not until 1405 that large-scale hostilities began again. The initiative seems to have been taken by the Granadans, who launched an offensive on the frontiers of Murcia. Henry III protested. From the slender evidence, it looks as if there was a peace party in Granada headed by the brothers ʿAlī, ʿAbd Allāh and Saʿd al-Amīn who negotiated with the Castilian court through the Master of Santiago. Muḥammad VII, however, seems to have been little inclined to peace and led an offensive in October 1406 in which a Castilian force led by the governor of Jaen, Pedro Manrique, was defeated by the Granadans.

Castilian revenge was postponed by the death of King Henry III and the accession of the young John II (1406–54). However, the young king's uncle Fernando assumed the regency and assembled the Cortes in Toledo and asked for troops and resources for a major campaign. Throughout 1407 the kingdom was attacked from different directions. On the Murcian frontier, Vera and Zurgena were sacked, and in the west Zahara was taken by Fernando, using cannon to great effect for the first time. Fernando then broke off and retired to Seville for the winter, but the Granadans counter-attacked at Alcaudete, to the north of the capital. In the spring of 1408 a truce was negotiated by ʿAbd Allāh al-Amīn.

The warlike Muḥammad VII died on 13 May 1408 and was succeeded by his brother Yūsuf (Yūsuf III, 1408–17) who was brought from his confinement at Salobreña, but the change of monarch seems to have brought no major changes of policy. Desultory warfare continued until in 1410 the regent of Castile, Fernando, decided on a major campaign. The object of attack was to be the small town of Antequera on the exposed northern flank of the mountains to the west of Granada. It does not seem to have been a place of great importance but its castle with its massive square keep was certainly well fortified. At the end of April the city was surrounded. This was a serious siege with artillery and other engines. On 6 May a relief army led by the King of Granada's brothers, ʿAlī and Aḥmad, was driven off but the citizens defended themselves vigorously with cannon and it was not until 25 September that the city was finally forced to surrender: the people (said by a Christian eye-witness to have numbered 895 men, 770 women and 863 children, total 2,528, hardly a very large city[29]) were allowed to leave for nearby Archidona with their goods and the mosque was turned into a church. Much was made of this conquest in Castile (the only accounts we have of it are Castilian) and Fernando was known thereafter as 'El de Antequera', but in fact the gain was small enough and one small town had occupied the strength of the Castilian army for a whole campaigning season. No attempt was made to capitalise on the victory, and Fernando was soon after chosen as the new King of Aragon which meant that he had more pressing concerns than pursuing a crusade against the Kingdom of Granada. A truce was signed in which the Granadans were, as usual, obliged to release prisoners but escaped the obligation of paying tribute; in fact it seems as if no tribute had been paid since the 1370s.[30]

The years 1410–28 were a period of external peace and internal turmoil for the Kingdom of Granada.[31] The reasons for the internal dissension are hard to discover, especially as we are almost entirely dependent on Castilian chronicles for this period which, while they give full details of battles, only report the bare outlines of the internal politics of the kingdom. These were dramatic enough in

29. *Chronicle of John II*, quoted in Harvey, *Islamic Spain*, p. 241.
30. Harvey, *Islamic Spain*, p. 239.
31. Covered in Arié, *L'Espagne musulmane*, pp. 129–33, and Harvey, *Islamic Spain*, pp. 235–50.

themselves, with frequent depositions and murders. The politics of Granada in the fifteenth century were dominated by the violent feuds of a small number of families who sought to have their candidates imposed as rulers. Relations with Castile, increasingly the only foreign policy issue that mattered, were dominated by questions of truce and tribute: rulers who failed to secure truces or, alternatively, paid too much for them were liable to become the objects of popular wrath and to lose their thrones. The main feud seems to have been between the family of the Banū Sarrāj and their enemies. The Banū Sarrāj (the Abencerrajes of Castilian legend) were newcomers to the Granadan political scene. The name Sarrāj, which means a saddler, is common enough, and attempts to link them with earlier bearers of the name may be far-fetched.[32] They seem to have been a family of Andalusi origin who appear as military commanders in Guadix and Illora. The ruthless aggrandisement of one family naturally provoked the resentment and envy of others. It is hard to see any issues of principle or policy in these conflicts and they seem to have been simple factional rivalries, struggling for control of the Alhambra and the trappings of power. It would be difficult to exaggerate the damage this did to the Granadan kingdom, for the pretenders always called in Castilian help in pursuing their ambitions, and Castilian help always carried a heavy price.

The Banū Sarrāj had their opportunity when Yūsuf III died in 1417, leaving the eight-year-old Muḥammad VIII as his successor under the tutelage of ʿAlī al-Amīn. The Banū Sarrāj, who were determined to end the power of the al-Amīn family, lighted on an ambitious cousin of the dead Sultan, Muḥammad, known as al-Aysar (the left-handed). In 1419 they launched a *coup*, Muḥammad VIII was deposed and Muḥammad IX installed as ruler. He was to enjoy no less than four separate reigns before his death in 1453/4 and he virtually presided over the destruction of the kingdom.

Muḥammad VIII was still alive, confined in the castle of Salobreña on the south coast which became the Nasrid state prison, and he still had friends in the capital. In 1427 there was a popular uprising in the city, probably because Muḥammad IX had made an expensive truce with the Castilians. The political initiative was taken by one Riḍwān Bannigash (Spanish Venegas). Riḍwān was said to have been a captive of Christian origin, brought up and educated, like an Ottoman Janissary, in the Nasrid court. He now drove the Banū

32. The origins of the Banū Sarrāj are fully discussed in Arié, *L'Espagne musulmane*, p. 130 n. 5 and p. 131 n. 1.

Sarrāj from Granada and Muḥammad IX took refuge in Tunisia, while Sa'd al-Amīn negotiated with John II of Castile on behalf of the new government. However, Yūsuf b. Sarrāj with 300 men contacted the Castilians at Lorca and then went on to Tunis. Muḥammad IX and Yūsuf b. Ṣarrāj then returned to al-Andalus with 500 troops sent by the Hafsid ruler of Tunisia and Muḥammad succeeded in recovering his throne. Finally, in 1431 Muḥammad IX killed his cousin and rival Muḥammad VIII in his gaol at Salobreña.

Meanwhile the Castilians prepared a large-scale expedition because Muḥammad IX had refused to acknowledge the Castilian kings as his overlords. As usual the Castilians were aided by dissidents in Granada. After the death of Muḥammad VIII, Riḍwān had chosen as his candidate one Yūsuf (Yūsuf IV, 1431–32). Yūsuf was not actually a Nasrid in the male line: his maternal grandfather had been that Muḥammad VI who had briefly interrupted the reign of Muḥammad V, but his father was Ibn al-Mawl, a descendant of the family that had left Cordoba when it fell to the Christians in 1236 and emigrated to Granada. The Castilian expedition was full of chivalric encounters and sound and fury but achieved very little beyond ravaging the land around Granada. John II and Alvaro de Luna established themselves in the Vega. A victory of sorts was achieved: known as the battle of Higueruela (the little fig-tree), it was little more than a cavalry skirmish, and when the Castilians pursued the Muslims to the walls of Granada, they were driven off by crossbowmen. This battle was widely reported and grew in importance with the retelling. In the late sixteenth century it formed the subject of a large and detailed painting in the Escorial Palace which is an important source for the arms and armour of the period.[33]

After this military parade the Castilian army retired, having achieved little more than the wasting of the Vega and the enhancement of their own self-esteem. In the aftermath of the battle the supporters of Yūsuf b. al-Mawl, with Castilian support, gradually took over more and more cities until on 1 January 1432 he was accepted as ruler in Granada itself. In exchange for Castilian support he made a humiliating treaty which included the provisions that he should pay a tribute of 20,000 *dīnār*s a year, release all Christian prisoners, do military service and attend the Cortes in person if it was held south of Toledo, or send his son if it was held to the north. This treaty made him deeply unpopular in the country and Muḥammad IX now attracted more and more support. In the

33. For the battle see ibid., pp. 133–5, and for the painting, ibid., p. 234.

spring of 1432 there was a *coup d'état* in Granada and Yūsuf was besieged in the Alhambra. Attempts by Castilian troops to rescue him failed and in April Muḥammad IX was established in the city and Yūsuf put to death. Castilian force was not enough to sustain a subservient and unpopular ruler.

Muḥammad IX was now restored for his longest period as ruler (1432–45), aided by Ibn ʿAbd al-Barr as *wazīr,* Ibn Kumāsha and Saʿd al-Amīn, all members of the elite of the kingdom. Riḍwān, meanwhile, had taken refuge in Castile, but this was a long way from being a time of peace. John II and Alvaro de Luna were embroiled in internal conflicts and arranged truces between 1439 and 1446 which allowed Granada some respite. As so often, this allowed internal conflicts to break out there. Muḥammad IX seems to have made many enemies and in 1445 he was deposed by Muḥammad X, the Lame, governor of Almeria. Muḥammad X was Muḥammad IX's nephew and had been his main military supporter at the time of the battle of Higueruela in 1431. The Banū Sarrāj opposed the new king and fled to Montefrio on the Castilian frontier. Here they established their own candidate, who took the title of Yūsuf V. He had been educated at the Castilian court and was a protégé of Alvaro de Luna, which of course made him deeply suspect in Granada. In 1446 Muḥammad X was back in power and in 1447 Muḥammad IX re-established himself for his fourth and last reign (1447–53/4).[34]

Frontier warfare began again after 1446 but its character had changed. The King of Castile was preoccupied with internal affairs and the conflicts were now at a more local level between the Granadans and the Castilian nobility of Andalucia and Murcia, men like Pedro Fajardo, alcalde of Lorca, known as El Bravo in the Castilian romances. In this warfare of raids and counter-raids, the Granadans often took the offensive: in 1452, for example, the chief of the Gomara mercenaries, with the governors of Guadix, Baza, Almeria and Vera, led an expedition of 600 horse and 1,500 foot deep into Murcian territory. This expedition ended in disaster when the raiding party was defeated in pitched battle on its way home and the Commanders of Granada, Baza and Almeria killed, at least according to the Castilian chronicler on whom we depend.[35] Frontier fortresses changed hands frequently, but the Granadans were more than able to hold their own.

34. See ibid., pp. 135–46, and Harvey, *Islamic Spain,* pp. 243–60.
35. Harvey, *Islamic Spain,* p. 258.

Muḥammad IX died in 1453 or 1454. A forceful and violent ruler, he was probably the most effective of the fifteenth-century kings of Granada, pursuing a policy of opposition and resistance to Castilian demands and pressures. He had appointed as his heir the son of his cousin Muḥammad VIII, perhaps in a gesture to heal the rifts in the ruling house, and he now became king as Muḥammad XI, known to the Christian sources as El Chiquito. The Banū Sarrāj, however, had other ideas and found a candidate called Abū Naṣr Saʿd, who had spent a long time at the Castilian court. They caused him to be proclaimed at Archidona with Castilian support. The kingdom was divided between them, Muḥammad XI El Chiquito having Granada, Malaga, Guadix and Gibraltar while Saʿd had Archidona and Ronda. It is possible that we are seeing here the Banū Sarrāj favouring candidates like Yūsuf IV and Saʿd who had lived at the Castilian court and might be expected to follow pro-Castilian policies, while their opponents favoured a more antagonistic line. This may, however, be reading too much long-term political importance into feuds which were based on little more than greed and opportunism.

Matters were made worse for Granada by the accession of a new king in Castile, Henry IV (1454–74). In the early years of his reign, before he was overwhelmed with internal political problems, Henry sought to establish himself as a Crusader against Granada. It does not seem as if he was trying to conquer the city. He did not besiege major strongholds in a systematic way, but rather ravaged the country as a form of economic warfare. These raids seriously undermined the prosperity of the kingdom, especially as they penetrated to areas like the Vega of Malaga which had been practically immune from previous incursions. In 1455 he raided the Vega of Granada and the Malaga area but was deterred from attacking the city by the garrison of 1,500 Granadan horsemen commanded by Ibn ʿAbd al-Barr and Ibn Kumāsha.

These incursions allowed Saʿd to take the Alhambra from Muḥammad XI, who fled, but Saʿd's abject submission to Castilian demands led to a revolt in the city. Muḥammad XI was invited to return but fell into an ambush laid by Saʿd's son Abū'l-Ḥasan ʿAlī. He had his throat cut open in one of the chambers giving onto the Court of the Lions in the Alhambra and his children were suffocated. In 1456 Henry led a major raiding party to the Vega of Malaga and thence along the coast to Fuengirola, where he captured the Umayyad castle where the people had tried to defend themselves, and so on to Tarifa.

Abū Naṣr Sa'd, now sole monarch, was not inactive, and Granadan raiding parties reached Jaen. It was he who ordered the massacre of the Banū Sarrāj at a banquet in the Alhambra, an incident long remembered in history and legend. The massacre was by no means complete, and the surviving members of the family and their supporters now established themselves in Malaga which they used as a base for re-establishing their position. Sa'd was helped by the fact that in 1457 Henry IV had to go north to face domestic opposition and the war against Granada was left to frontier lords, many of whom were in active rebellion against their sovereign; even so, Gibraltar finally fell into Christian hands in 1461, partly because of the disturbances caused by the fall of the Banū Sarrāj.

The decline and fall of the Kingdom of Granada, 1464–92

In 1464 Sa'd was deposed by his own son, Abū'l-Ḥasan 'Alī, aided by the Banū Sarrāj, and sent to the fortress at Salobreña. 'Alī (1464–82), known to the Christians as Muley Hacen, had spent many years at the Castilian court.[36] The Arabic chronicle *Nubdhat al-'aṣr*,[37] which opens at this point and gives us a Muslim viewpoint on Granadan affairs once again, speaks of his firm and just rule and the prosperity which resulted, at least at the beginning of his reign. Later Christian sources describe the King's alleged infatuation with an ex-Christian slave, Thurāyā, and the jealousies this aroused at court: moral decay at the centre led to political defeat. But the only near-contemporary Muslim source mentions nothing of this and the military record suggests that both Abū'l-Ḥasan and his kingdom held their own against the Castilians until his death.

Frontier warfare and skirmishing with rival Christian powers continued. A series of events in 1471 illustrates how complex relations were. In May Miguel Lucas, Constable of Jaen, and Alonso de Aguilar attempted to take Montejicar by surprise, but the Granadans were warned by the Count of Cabra who sent his son with 500 knights and 2,000 foot to help the Muslims, and the attempt failed. In response, 3,000 Muslim horsemen assembled and pillaged the

36. For his reign see Arié, *L'Espagne musulmane*, pp. 147–56, and Harvey, *Islamic Spain*, pp. 265–74.

37. *Nubdhat al-'aṣr fi akhbār Banī Naṣr*, ed. A. Bustani with Spanish trans. C. Quiros (Larache, 1940).

area around Porcuna, taking 400 captives. At the same time, the Marquis of Cadiz seized Cardela in the west and his rival appealed for help to Abū'l-Ḥasan who retook the place from the Marquis. The events of 1471, by no means untypical, show how rivalries and jealousies on the Christian side often outweighed any considerations of Holy War against the Muslims and how, in these fairly small-scale encounters, the troops of Granada were able to put up a good fight against Christian armies. The accession of Isabella to the Castilian throne in 1474 made little difference at first: preoccupied with securing her own position in Castile, she entrusted the Marquis of Cabra with the task of securing truces with Granada. Raids continued: in 1477 the Sultan penetrated deep into Murcian territory, sacked the town of Cieza which belonged to the Order of Santiago and returned with 700 prisoners. The continued vitality of the Kingdom of Granada can be seen in the reconquest of the fortress of Zahara. On 27 December 1481 a force of 300 horse and 4,000 foot from the Ronda area, led by one Ibrāhīm al-Ḥakīm, stormed the castle and took more than 100 prisoners back.

The taking of Zahara was the last time the Muslims were able to take and garrison a fortress. In 1479 Fernando of Aragon succeeded his father as King (Fernando V, 1479–1516), and he and his wife Isabella of Castile decided on a systematic war of conquest against the Kingdom of Granada. This warfare was very different from the raiding and counter-raiding of earlier years. The Andalucian aristocracy were ordered by the Catholic kings (Fernando and Isabella) and siege equipment was always taken.

The first sign of this new aggressiveness was the spectacular conquest of Alhama de Granada in 1482. The small town of Alhama was thought to be impregnable and had never been subject to Christian attack before. It lay in the heart of the kingdom, on the road from Granada to Malaga. When it was taken by storm after a surprise attack led by Rodrigo Ponce de Leon at the end of February, it must have sent shock waves throughout the kingdom, especially when three efforts to dislodge the invaders in the summer of 1482 failed. However, the Christians did not have it all their own way: in July 1482 a Castilian force besieging Loja was driven off with serious losses by the Granadan captain ʿAli al-ʿAṭṭār, and in the spring of 1483 a Castilian force heading for Malaga was ambushed and badly mauled in mountain country by a Muslim force led by the Sultan's brother, Muḥammad b. Saʿd.

As so often in the fifteenth century, the Kingdom of Granada showed it could defend itself against outside attack but not against internal dissension. In July 1482 the tough old king Abū'l-Ḥasan was driven out of Granada by a *coup* led by his son Abū 'Abd Allāh Muḥammad (the Boabdil of the Christian sources) and the Banū Sarrāj and other Granadan nobles. The cause of their dissatisfaction seems to have been the harsh taxation Abū'l-Ḥasan had to raise to fund the war against the Christians, especially after the devastation of the Vega of Granada. The King and his brother Muḥammad b. Sa'd were obliged to flee to Malaga. There were now two monarchs, the old king with his warlike brother Muḥammad and Abū'l-Qāsim Bannigash in Malaga, and Boabdil with his *wazīr* Ibn Kumāsha and the Banū Sarrāj in Granada. Worse was to follow. Boabdil, in an attempt to acquire a military reputation to establish his position, attempted to take Lucena from the Castilians in 1483 and allowed himself to be captured. He was only released after making the most humiliating concessions to his captors, including leaving his son and the sons of most of his principal supporters as hostages. His capitulation to the Castilian terms seems to have destroyed his credibility in Granada and there survives a *fatwa* in which all the leading jurists of the city, including the chief *qāḍī* Ibn al-Azraq, denounced him as a rebel against God.[38] Faced with this hostility, he retired to establish himself in Guadix. His father, despite increasing illness and the onset of blindness, continued to lead the Granadan forces, pillaging the area around Teba with a force of 1,200 horse and 4,000 foot.

From 1484 onwards the Castilian campaigns continued without cease. The story of the Christian victory has been told many times.[39] It is clear that the Castilian armies were larger than the Muslims' and were deployed with persistence and determination. They also made full and effective use of artillery, which meant that the fortresses that had protected Granada for so long could now be taken: the fall of Ronda in 1486, for example, was the direct result of a heavy bombardment by cannon. Crops and fruit trees were destroyed in a systematic way to prevent the defenders from amassing supplies and their government from collecting money. The Christians were also aided by the absence of any effective support from the rest of the Muslim world. The sovereigns of North Africa were too feeble to intervene and had in any case been effectively neutralised by the diplomacy of the Catholic kings. In a desperate attempt

38. See F. de la Granja, 'Condena de Boabdil por los alfaquies de Granada', in *Al-Andalus* 36 (1971), 145–76.

39. From the Muslim point of view in Arié, *L'Espagne musulmane*, pp. 147–78, and Harvey, *Islamic Spain*, pp. 283–323.

to raise support, the Andalusi Ibn al-Azraq visited the court of the great Mamluke ruler Qā'iṭ Bey in Cairo in 1487, but while sympathetic, he confined himself to sending two friars from the Church of the Holy Sepulchre in Jerusalem, then under Mamluke rule, with a letter appealing to the Catholic kings to spare Granada. The emissaries were received with honour and Fernando replied to the effect that the civil and religious rights of the Muslims would be respected when they surrendered. There were no more letters.

Astonishingly, given the imminence of the Christian threat, Granada continued to be wracked by internal feuds which resulted in bloody fighting in the streets of the capital on at least three occasions in the 1480s. At the beginning of 1485 Abū'l-Ḥasan, increasingly enfeebled by illness, had resigned his power in favour of his brother Muḥammad b. Sa'd. Muḥammad, who was given the nickname of al-Zaghal (the brave), became the mainstay of the Muslim resistance. In March 1486 Boabdil, who had taken refuge in Christian territory, reappeared on the scene. He seems to have attracted support in the Albaicin quarter of Granada, said to have been inhabited by shepherds and peasants anxious to remain at peace with the Castilians (according to the *Nubdhat al-'aṣr*[40]). Between March and May there was a fierce struggle between Boabdil and his followers in the Albaicin and the partisans of Muḥammad b. Sa'd in the Alhambra, after which Boabdil was forced to acknowledge his uncle as sovereign.

In the spring of 1486 Boabdil was leading the last resistance of Loja against the Catholic kings. The city fell on 30 May, leaving the Vega of Granada undefended against Christian attack. The inhabitants were allowed to emigrate but Boabdil remained, for a second time, prisoner in Castilian hands. He was soon released and promised a principality including Guadix and Baza in exchange for his oath of allegiance. They knew their man well, for on his release he resumed the civil war against his uncle. By October 1486 he was re-established in the Albaicin, aided by arms and supplies from Christian territory. Once again the capital was plunged into bloodshed and on 29 April 1487 he finally triumphed and took the Alhambra, executing the warriors who had opposed him. Once in control, he again approached the Catholic kings with an offer to surrender the city itself in exchange for a principality in the east of the kingdom; his *wazīr*, Abū'l-Qāsim al-Mulīh, was to be given Andarax.

At the same time, al-Zaghal was trying vainly to support the

40. Text, p. 17; trans., pp. 19–20.

Muslims of Velez Malaga, under close siege from the Christians. On 3 May the town surrendered and al-Zaghal retired to Almeria. The Castilians moved on to Malaga. The citizens, led by Aḥmad al-Thaghrī (the Frontiersman) and supported by a North African garrison, resisted fiercely, but constant bombardment and lack of supplies forced them to surrender on 18 August. Boabdil seems to have co-operated actively with the Castilian forces, destroying a small relief force which his uncle, al-Zaghal, had managed to gather. It was the most difficult siege of the war and a mortal blow for the Muslim kingdom. Because of their fierce resistance, there were no easy terms for the inhabitants, who were all taken prisoner: this no doubt encouraged many other small towns to submit without a struggle. Now only Granada itself and the east of the kingdom remained in Muslim hands. Here al-Zaghal continued a fierce resistance throughout 1488, harassing the Christians as far as Alcala la Real and the Vega of Granada. The Catholic kings realised they had to break his power before attacking Granada and in the summer of 1489 they laid siege to Baza. Al-Zaghal sent all the reinforcements he could to the city under the leadership of Yaḥyā al-Najjār, but in the end it was not enough. On 28 November, after a siege of more than five months, the city surrendered. Both Christian and Muslim sources suggest that many of the leading citizens in Baza, and probably other towns as well, were negotiating to make peace with the Christians, in some cases even offering to convert if they could retain their possessions. The commander, Yaḥyā, is said to have become a Christian and to have been left in control of his estates, on condition that the news of his conversion did not become public until after the fall of Guadix.

The fall of Baza meant the end of serious military resistance. Al-Zaghal had been unable to save it and seems to have lost heart, surrendering Almeria on 22 December and Guadix on the 30th in exchange for a small principality in the Alpujarras around Andarax and Lanjaron. He soon realised that all was lost and, selling his rights to the Castilians for 30,000 castellanos of gold, set sail for Oran.

Granada was now on its own. Boabdil now found that the Catholic kings were not prepared to honour their previous generous promises. The citizens resisted with an energy born of despair, Boabdil himself leading raids on Christian territory. Throughout 1490 and 1491 the noose tightened on the city: famine became more and more acute as supplies were systematically cut off. On 25 November 1491 Ibn al-Mulīh signed the documents of surrender in the Christian camp at Santa Fe.[41] There was still some anxiety that popular resistance would continue, so on 1 January 1492 Ibn al-Mulīh and the army commander Ibn Kumāsha led Gutierre de Cardenas and others to the old Nasrid throne room in the Comares tower of the Alhambra, where Boabdil handed over the keys of the city. Then the Castilian flag was raised on the Torre de Vela, the great donjon of the fortress of the Alhambra. The political history of al-Andalus was over.

41. The capitulations are translated and discussed in Harvey, *Islamic Spain*, pp. 314–21.

Farewell to al-Andalus

Spain and Portugal are not now Muslim countries and the name of al-Andalus survives only as a memory of past greatness. In the final analysis this is not because the Muslims who once inhabited the larger part of these two countries converted to Christianity of their own free will, but because they were defeated militarily and, ultimately, presented with the choice of conversion or expulsion. Why then did Muslim political society fail?

Some of the answers to this question are unknowable given the information at our disposal. There may have been demographic factors: the Christian population may have grown faster than the Muslim for some reason, and simple Malthusian pressures forced them to conquer new lands. Yet there is no evidence for this, and in many areas the Christian settlers of reconquered lands were few and not sufficiently numerous to occupy the countryside. However, it does seem clear that at some periods from 1100 onwards, al-Andalus was haemorrhaging people, especially from exposed frontier areas like Cuenca and Beja. There was emigration even from more central areas and we see that old-established families like the Banū Khaldūn had largely abandoned Seville in the half-century before the Christian conquest of 1248. The Almohad empire facilitated this as ambitious Andalusis could find employment in Marrakesh or Hafsid Tunis. In the thirteenth century, Andalusi scholars are found in considerable numbers in the Middle East.

Strategic factors played an important part. It is probable that after the loss of Toledo in 1085, al-Andalus was never viable as an independent state but was forced to look to North Africa for help. Only after 1250 when Muslim rule was confined to the Kingdom of Granada did the Muslims again have sustainable borders.

North African military support brought temporary relief from Christian advances, but there were problems attached. The major concern of both Almoravids and Almohads was to maintain their empire in Morocco: al-Andalus was important as the setting for the *jihād* which could confer legitimacy on their rule, but it was not central and they could and did withdraw their troops to try to save their positions at home. It was problems in Africa, not Christian attacks in al-Andalus, that brought both regimes down. The Almoravids and Almohads were always regarded as outsiders in al-Andalus, tolerated but not loved or integrated. When their military power failed and their fiscal demands increased, the Andalusis saw no need to accept them any more.

Muslim disunity was a major cause of weakness. Immediately after the death of al-Muẓaffar in 1008, different factions began to search for Christian allies and the pattern continued. The Taifa kings of Zaragoza and Toledo sought, and paid heavily for, Christian allies, Ibn Mardanīsh in the twelfth century depended on Christian support to sustain his independence in the face of Almohad advance, and Ibn al-Aḥmar in the 1240s owed much of his rise to power to his position as a vassal and ally of the Castilian king. Muslim political disunity inevitably resulted in Christian military advance.

But this can only be part of the answer. Christian Spain too was torn by feuds: brothers fought over succession, the kings of Castile and Aragon struggled for supremacy in the border regions and the kings of Leon in the second half of the twelfth century were happy to accept the Almohads as allies against their cousins in Castile and Portugal. Yet Christian disunity did not have the same catastrophic consequences and Christians did not allow Muslim princes to fight their battles. The Taifa kings of Zaragoza and Toledo in the eleventh century did invite Christian troops into their enemies' lands. Alfonso VI may have taken refuge in Muslim Toledo but he never employed the armies of Toledo to ravage the lands of his brother Sancho. The struggle between the kings of Castile and Leon after 1157 was as fierce as any conflict with the Muslims, but neither side invited Almohad armies into their lands.

This may have been because Muslim armies were inferior in tactics and equipment. This is difficult to judge and we must not lose sight of the fact that the Muslims won major victories, at Zallāqa in 1086 and Alarcos in 1195 amongst others. But the eagerness with which Muslims sought Christian military support from the beginning of the eleventh century suggests that Christian knights were regarded as superior warriors. The Christians began to advance when the mailed knight became the dominant military figure. Throughout the Mediterranean world in the late eleventh and twelfth centuries, knights from north-west Europe proved their superiority over lighter armed Muslim, Lombard or Byzantine troops. In the Crusader east, this superiority was soon countered by the mounted archery of the Turks and the organisational ability of the Mamlukes. In al-Andalus they do not seem to have met their match among the lightly armed Berber horsemen.

Siege warfare was another area of Muslim military weakness. After 1000, if the Christians captured a town or city, they held it. There are a few exceptions, like Valencia in 1102 and Almeria in 1157, but both of these were isolated outposts. Despite victories on the field of battle, the Muslims were never able to mount an effective siege of Toledo. When Lisbon fell in 1147 or Cuenca in 1177, they were never subsequently threatened by Muslim armies. When the Almohads attempted the siege of even a small town like Huete, the result was a fiasco. This was not because Muslims in general were unable to mount sieges: the Mamlukes of Egypt were superbly effective in this branch of warfare. What we can say with confidence is that the Muslims of al-Andalus seem to have been unable to take well-fortified and defended cities.

As early as the tenth century, the eastern geographer Ibn Ḥawqal had noted the unwillingness of native Andalusis to become soldiers. The military reforms of ʻAbd al-Raḥmān al-Nāṣir and al-Manṣūr institutionalised the exclusion of most Andalusis from the army. The Taifa kings failed to recruit effective armies locally and the coming of the Almoravids meant that the defence of the country was entrusted to Berbers. This exclusion was never complete and there were always examples of Andalusi soldiers, like the Tujībīs under al-Manṣūr and the Banū ʻAzzūn and Banū Wazīr under the Almohads, who did play an important, if secondary, military role, but they were exceptional.

This meant that there was a large non-military, civilian population in al-Andalus, untrained in warfare and unequipped. They relied on the professional soldiers to defend them and when, with the collapse of the caliphate, the Almoravids or the Almohads, these professional soldiers were no longer available, the local people could not mount a successful resistance. Along with this concentration of military power in a caste of professional solders went the concentration of political power in the hands of the rulers. Under the Umayyads, the lords of the Marches had considerable autonomy and the power to lead defensive and offensive campaigns on their own initiative. Under the Almoravids and Almohads, such local initiatives ceased to be possible. This is especially true under the centralised Almohad caliphate when the prolonged absences of the caliphs effectively paralysed both offensive and defensive war efforts.

Christian Spain and Portugal during this period have been

described as a 'society organised for war'.[1] The Christians seem to have been able to mobilise a much higher proportion of their populations for warfare, in royal armies, in the armies of the military orders and in the armies of the towns. The gulf between the military castes and the rest of the population did not exist. Furthermore, there were many different centres of command. Not only were there three or four frontier monarchies but there were military orders, nobles' followings and town armies with their own command structure, capable of independent action. Muslim society had no equivalent of an adventurer like Giraldo Sempavor or military forces like the aggressive and effective militia of Avila in the second half of the twelfth century. If royal power was enfeebled by minority or civil war, as in Castile after 1157, there were others who could and did assume a leadership role.

Both Christians and Muslims developed an ideology of Holy War, or *jihād*. How far this motivated the participants in the long struggle for control of the Iberian peninsula is difficult to say. Both sides believed they had God and right on their side. The Christians also benefited intermittently from the arrival of Crusaders from north of the Pyrenees, notably the Flemish and English who helped in the siege of Lisbon in 1147, but there are other examples through to the fourteenth century. There is, however, little evidence of mass enthusiasm or participation from within Christian Spain of the sort that accompanied the First Crusade.

The Muslims benefited more continuously from the spirit of *jihād* preached by Almoravids, Almohads and, to a lesser extent, Merinids. Guichard has convincingly argued, however, that *jihād* was not a major concern for the Muslims of al-Andalus.[2] The pursuit of the *jihād* was left to the state. From Umayyad times, the rulers of al-Andalus had used the leadership of Holy War to assert their legitimacy as rulers of the Muslims of al-Andalus. However, there is little evidence of mass popular or voluntary participation.

In the end, it is probably impossible to tell how far these various factors, demography, military technology and military and political structures, led to the demise of al-Andalus. But it remains a central and intriguing question why the self-confident and dominant Muslim political society of the year 1000 should have divided, shrunk and, eventually, half a millennium later, disappeared from Iberian soil completely.

1. E. Lourie, 'A society organised for war: medieval Spain', *Past & Present* 33–5 (1966), 55–76.

2. On which see the important discussion in P. Guichard, *Les Musulmans de Valence et la Reconquête* (2 vols, Damascus, 1990–91), i, pp. 117–18.

Appendix 1: Governors of al-Andalus and Taifa Kings

Governors of al-Andalus with dates of appointment

711	Mūsā b. Nuṣayr
714	ʿAbd al-ʿAzīz b. Mūsā
716	Ayyūb b. Ḥabīb al-Lakhmī
716	al-Ḥurr b. ʿAbd al-Raḥmān al-Thaqafī
718	al-Samḥ b. Mālik al-Khawlānī
721	ʿAbd al-Raḥmān b. ʿAbd Allāh al-Ghāfiqī
721	ʿAnbasa b. Suḥaym al-Kalbī
726	ʿUdhra b. ʿAbd Allāh al-Fihrī
727	Yaḥyā b. Salama al-Kalbī
728	Ḥudhayfa b. al-Aḥwaṣ al-Ashjaʿī
728	ʿUthmān b. Abī Nisʿa al-Khathʿamī
729	al-Haytham b. ʿUbayd al-Kinānī
730	Muḥammad b. ʿAbd Allāh al-Ashjaʿī
730	ʿAbd al-Raḥmān b. ʿAbd Allāh al-Ghāfiqī
732	ʿAbd al-Malik b. Qaṭan al-Fihrī
734	ʿUqba b. al-Ḥajjāj al-Salūlī
740	ʿAbd al-Malik b. Qaṭan al-Fihrī
741	Balj b. Bishr al-Qushayrī
743	Abū'l-Khaṭṭār al-Ḥusām b. Ḍirār al-Kalbī
745	Thawāba b. Salāma al-Judhāmī
747–56	Yūsuf b. ʿAbd al-Raḥmān al-Fihrī

Rulers of the major Taifa kingdoms with dates of accession

SEVILLE

1023	Muḥammad b. Ismāʿīl b. ʿAbbād
1042	ʿAbbād b. Muḥammad al-Muʿtaḍid

1069	Muḥammad b. ʿAbbād al-Muʿtamid
1091	City conquered by the Almoravids

GRANADA

1013	Zāwī b. Zīrī al-Ṣanhājī
1019/20	Ḥabbūs b. Māksan b. Zīrī
1038	Bādīs b. Ḥabbūs
1073	ʿAbd Allāh b. Buluggīn b. Bādīs
1090	City conquered by the Almoravids

CORDOBA

1031	Jahwar b. Muḥammad b. Jahwar
1043	Muḥammad b. Jahwar al-Rashīd
1063	ʿAbd al-Malik b. Muḥammad al-Manṣūr
1069	City annexed by Seville

TOLEDO

1012/13	Yaʿīsh b. Muḥammad b. Yaʿīsh al-Qādī
1018	Ismāʿīl b. Dhīʾl-Nūn
1043/4	Yaḥyā b. Ismāʿīl al-Maʾmūn
1075	Yaḥyā b. Hishām b. Yaḥyā al-Qādir
1085	City conquered by Alfonso VI of Castile

BADAJOZ

1012/13	Sābūr al-Siqlabī
1022	ʿAbd Allāh b. Muḥammad Ibn al-Afṭas al-Manṣūr
1045	Muḥammad b. ʿAbd Allāh al-Muẓaffar
1068	ʿUmar b. Muḥammad al-Mutawwakil
1094	City conquered by the Almoravids

ZARAGOZA

1010	al-Mundhir b. Yaḥyā al-Tujībī
1021/2	Yaḥyā b. al-Mundhir

1036	al-Mundhir b. Yaḥyā b. al-Mundhir
1038/9	ʻAbd Allāh b. al-Ḥakam al-Tujībī
1038–39	Sulaymān b. Hūd al-Judhāmī, al-Mustaʻīn
1049/50	Aḥmad b. Sulaymān al-Muqtadir
1081–82	Yūsuf b. Aḥmad al-Mu'tamin
1085	Aḥmad b. Yūsuf al-Mustaʻīn II
1110	City conquered by the Almoravids

*Appendix 2: Family Trees of the Ruling Dynasties of al-Andalus**

Umayyad rulers of al-Andalus

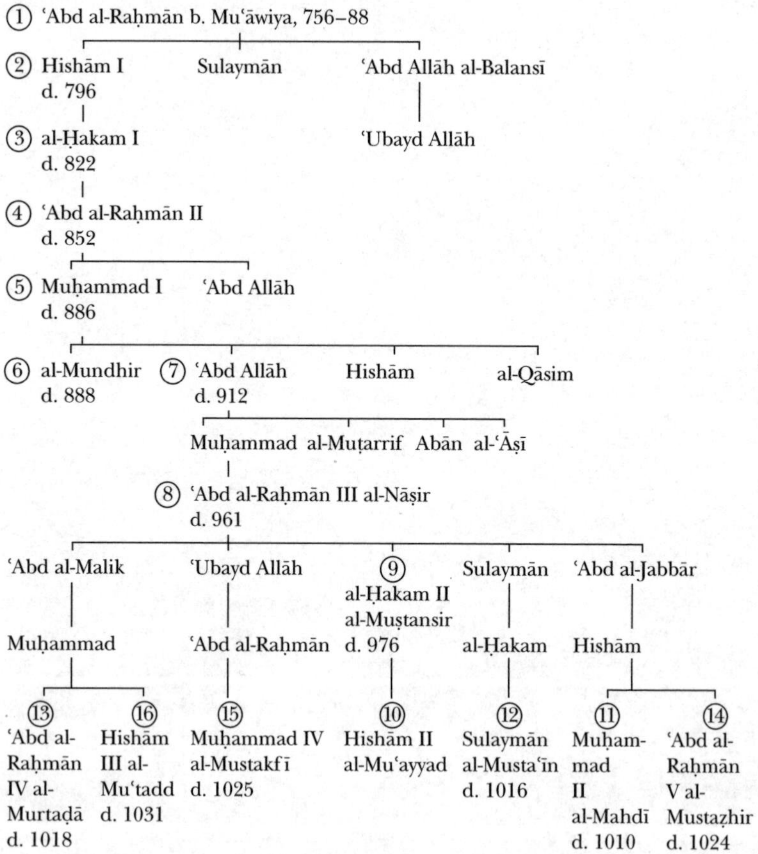

* In all cases, the numbers in circles give the order in which they ruled.

The Almoravid ruling dynasty

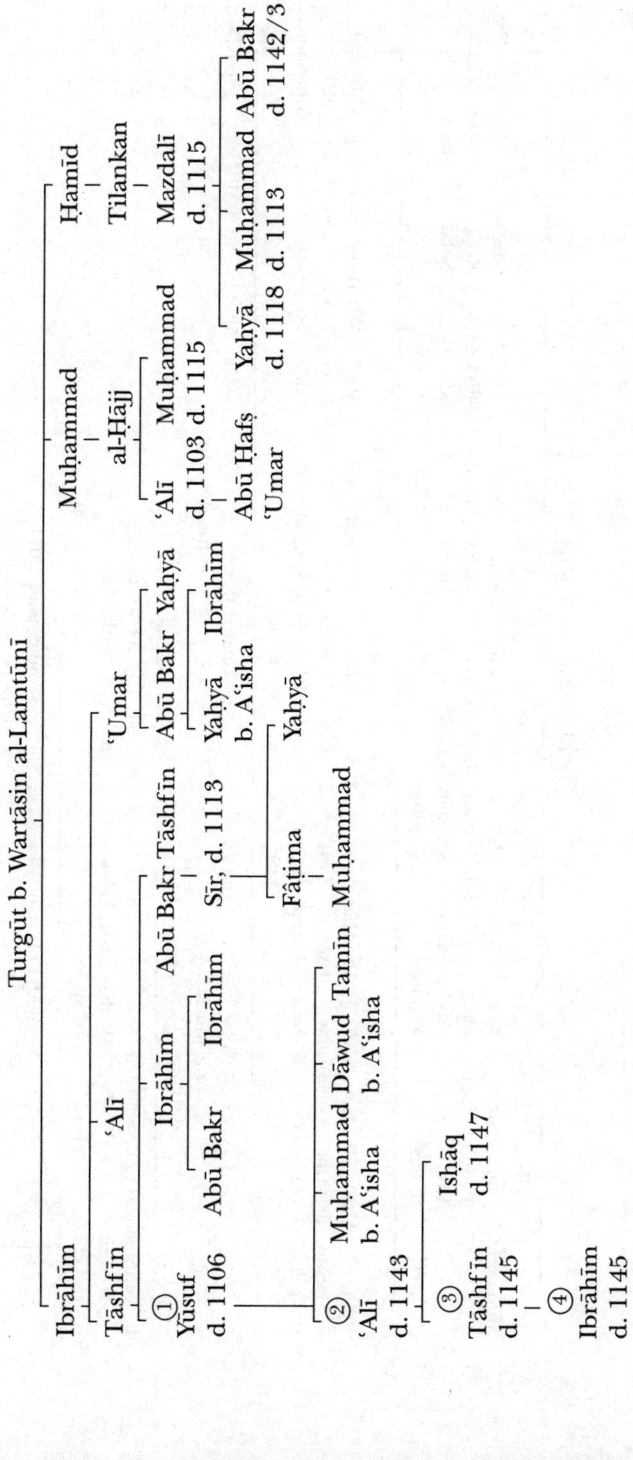

The Almohad ruling dynasty (sayyids)

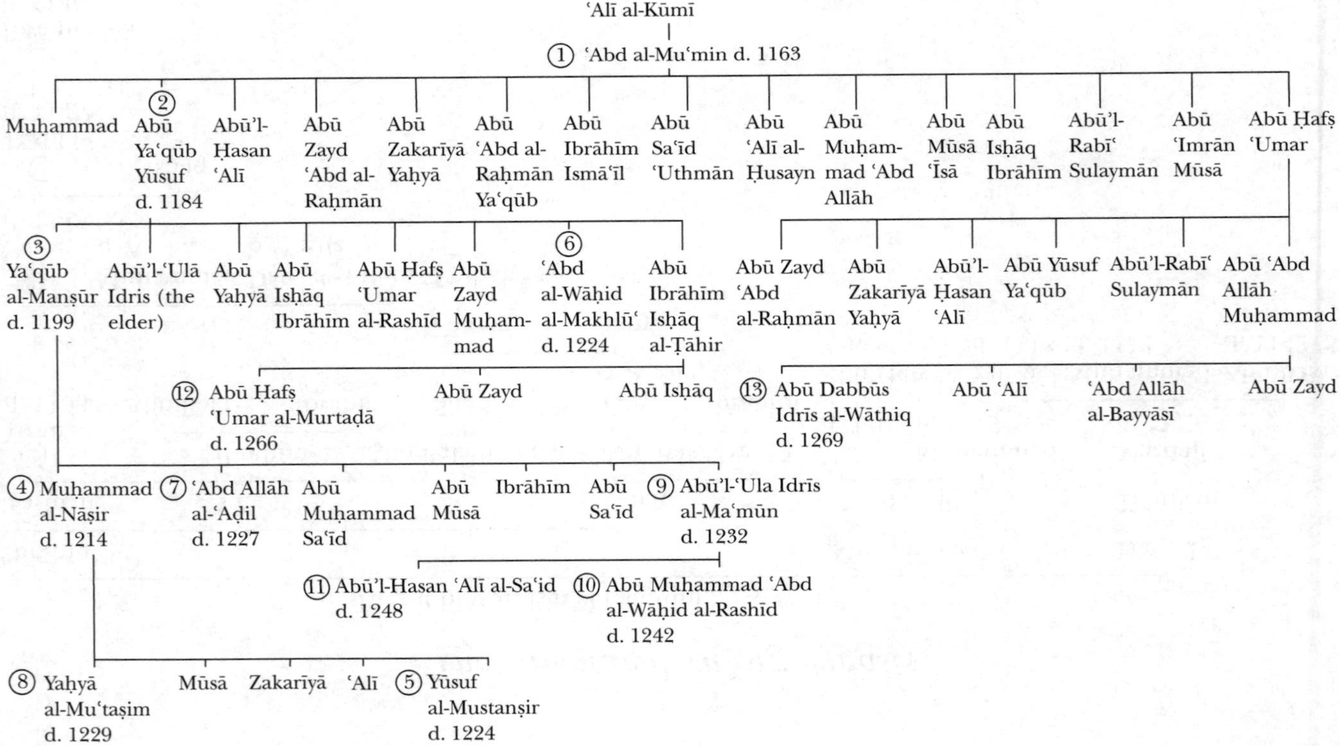

The Nasrids of Granada (Banū'l-Aḥmar)

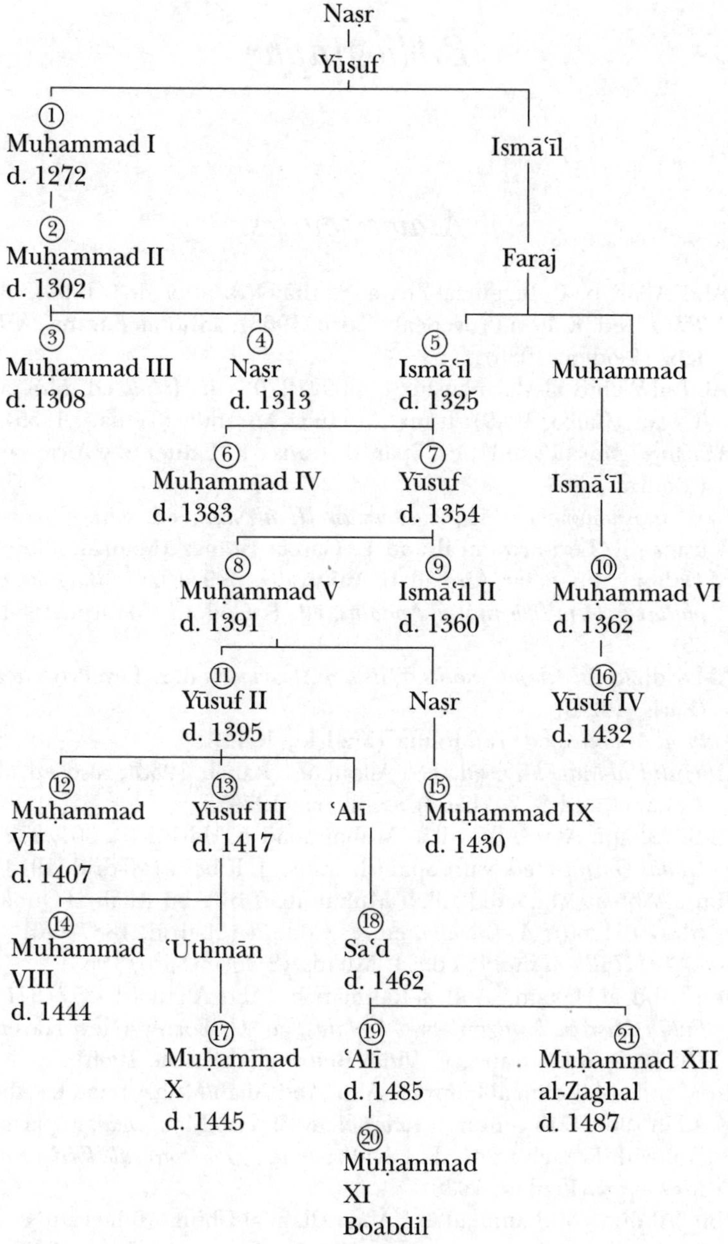

Bibliography

Arabic sources

'Abd Allāh b. Buluggīn al-Ziri al-Ṣanhāji (d. after 483/1090), *Al-Tibyān*, ed. E. Lévi-Provençal (Cairo, 1963); annotated trans., A.T. Tibi (Leiden, 1986).

'Abd al-Wāḥid al-Marrākushī (c. 669/1270), *Al-Mu'jib*, ed. M.S. al-'Uryan (Cairo, 1949); trans. A. Huici Miranda (Tetuan, 1955).

Akhbār al-Majmū'a, ed. and Spanish trans., E. Lafuente y Alcantara (Madrid, 1867).

Cronica Anonima de 'Abd al-Raḥmān III al-Nāṣir, ed. with Spanish trans., E. Lévi-Provençal and E. Garcia Gomez (Madrid, 1950).

Al-Dabbī, Abū Ja'far Aḥmad b. Yaḥyā (d. 599/1024), *Bughyat al-multamis fī ta'rīkh rijāl al-Andalus*, ed. F. Codera (Madrid, 1884–85).

Al-Baydhaq, *Documents inédits d'Histoire Almohade*, ed. E. Lévi-Provençal (Paris, 1928).

Fatḥ al-Andalus, ed. L. Molina (Madrid, 1994).

Al-Ḥulūl al-Mawshīya, ed. I.S. Allouche (Rabat, 1936); also ed. A. Zamama and S. Zakkar (Casablanca, 1979).

Al-Khushānī, Abū 'Abd Allāh Muḥammad b. Ḥārith (d. 361/972), *Quḍāt Qurṭuba*, ed. with Spanish trans., J. Ribera (Madrid, 1914).

Ibn al-Abbār, Abū 'Abd Allāh Muḥammad b. 'Abd Allāb al-Quḍā'ī (d. 658/1260), *Al-Takmila*, ed. F. Codera (Madrid, 1887–90).

——, *Al-Ḥulla al-siyarā'*, ed. H. Mu'nis (2 vols, Cairo, 1963).

Ibn 'Abd al-Ḥakam, 'Abd al-Raḥmān b. 'Abd Allāh (d. 257/871), *Futūḥ Miṣr wa'l-Maghrib wa'l-Andalus*, ed. C. Torrey (New Haven, 1922); Spanish trans., E. Vidal Beltran (Valencia, 1966).

Ibn 'Abd al-Mun'im al-Ḥimyarī, Abū 'Abd Allāh Muḥammad b. 'Abd Allāh (9th/15th century), *Rawḍ al-Mi'ṭār fi akhbār al-aqṭār*, in partial edn with French trans., E. Lévi-Provençal, *La Péninsule Ibérique au Moyen-Age* (Leiden, 1938).

Ibn 'Abdūn, Muḥammad b. 'Abd Allāh al-Ishbīlī (6th/12th century), *Seville Musulmane*, trans. E. Lévi-Provençal (Paris, 1947).

Ibn Abī Zar', Abū'l-Ḥasan 'Alī b. 'Abd Allāh al-Fāsī (8th/14th century), *Rawḍ al-Qirṭās*, ed. C. Tornberg (Uppsala, 1843–46); Spanish trans., A. Huici Miranda (2 vols, Valencia, 1964).

Ibn al-Athīr, Abū'l-Ḥasan Muḥammad b. 'Alī (d. 630/1233), *Al-Kāmil fī'l-Ta'rīkh*, ed. C.J. Tornberg (12 vols, Leiden, 1853–67); partial French trans., E. Fagnan, *Annales du Maghreb et de l'Espagne* (Algiers, 1901).

Ibn Bashkuwāl, Abū'l-Qāsim Khalaf b. 'Abd al-Malik (d. 578/1183), *Al-Ṣila fī ta'rīkh a'immat al-Andalus*, ed. F. Codera (Madrid, 1882); also ed. I. al-Husayni (Cairo, 1955).

Ibn Bassām, Abū'l-Ḥasan 'Alī al-Shantarīnī (d. 542/1147), *Al-Dhakhīra fī maḥāsin ahl al-Jazīra*, ed. I. 'Abbas (Beirut, 1978).

Ibn al-Faraḍi, Abū'l-Walīd 'Abd Allāh b. Muḥammad (d. 403/1013), *Ta'rīkh 'ulamā' al-Andalus*, ed. F. Codera (Madrid, 1890); also ed. I. al-Husayni (Cairo, 1954).

Ibn Ḥabīb, 'Abd al-Malik (d. 238/852), *Kitāb al-Ta'rīkh*, ed. J. Aguadé (Madrid, 1991).

Ibn Ḥawqal, Abū'l-Qāsim Muḥammad b. Ḥawqal (c. 380/990), *Ṣūrat al-arḍ*, ed. J.H. Kramers (Leiden, 1939).

Ibn Ḥayyān, Abū Marwān Ḥayyān b. Khalaf al-Qurṭubī (d. 469/1076), *Al-Muqtabis min anbā ahl al-Andalus (Al-Muqtabis II)*, ed. M.A. Makki (Cairo, 1971).

——, *Al-Muqtabis fi ta'rīkh rijāl al-Andalus (Al-Muqtabis III)*, ed. M. Antuña (Paris, 1937).

——, *Al-Muqtabis V*, ed. P. Chalmeta, F. Corriente and M. Sobh (Madrid, 1979); Spanish trans., M. Viguera and F. Corriente (Zaragoza, 1981).

——, *Al-Muqtabis fi akhbār balad al-Andalus (al-Ḥakam II) (Al-Muqtabis VII)*, ed. A.A. al-Hajji (Beirut, 1965); Spanish trans., E. Garcia Gomez, *Anales Palatinos del Califa de Cordoba al-Hakam II* (Madrid, 1967).

Ibn Ḥazm, Abū Muḥammad 'Alī b. Sa'īd al-Qurṭubī (d. 456/1064), *Jamharat ansāb al-'Arab*, ed. A. Harun (Cairo, 1962).

——, *Rasā'il Ibn Ḥazm*, ed. I. 'Abbas (Cairo, 1955).

——, *The Ring of the Dove*, trans. A.J. Arberry (London, 1953).

Ibn Idhārī al-Marrākushī, Abū'l-'Abbās Aḥmad b. Muḥammad (c. 712/1312), *Al-Bayān al-mughrib fi akhbār al-Andalus wa'l-Maghrib*, vols. I–II ed. E. Lévi-Provençal and G.S. Colin (Leiden, 1948); vol. III ed. E. Lévi-Provençal (Paris, 1930); vol. IV ed. I. Abbas (Beirut, 1967); Part III (Almohads) ed. A. Huici Miranda (Tetuan, 1963), trans. idem (2 vols, Tetuan, 1953).

Ibn al-Kardabūs, Abū Marwān 'Abd al-Malik al-Tawzari (6th/12th century), *Al-Iktifā' fī akhbār al-khulafā'*, ed. A.M. al-'Abbadi (Madrid, 1965–66); Spanish trans., F. Maillo (Madrid, 1986).

Ibn Khaldūn, Abū Zayd ʿAbd al-Raḥmān al-Ḥaḍramī (d. 808/1406), *Al-ʿIbār wa diwān al-mubtadā' wa'l-khabar*, ed. S. Zakkar (8 vols, Beirut, 1981); annotated trans. of the *Muqaddima* (Introduction), F. Rosenthal (3 vols, London, 1958).

Ibn al-Khaṭīb, Abū ʿAbd Allāh Lisān al-Dīn Muḥammad b. ʿAbd Allāh (d. 776/1374), *Aʿmāl al-aʿlām fī man buyiʿa qabla 'l-iḥtilām min mulūk al-lslām*, ed. E. Lévi-Provençal (Beirut, 1956).

——, *Al-Iḥāṭa fi akhbār Gharnāṭa*, ed. M. 'Inan (4 vols, Cairo, 1973–77).

——, *Al-Lamḥa al-badriya fi ta'rīkh al-dawla al-naṣriya* (Beirut, 1978).

Ibn al-Qaṭṭān, Abū Muḥammad Ḥasan b. ʿAlī al-Marrākushī (7th/13th century), *Nuẓm al-jumān li-tartīb mā salafa min akhbār al-zamān*, ed. M.A. Makki (Tetuan, 1964, and Beirut, 1990).

Ibn al-Qūṭīya, Abū Bakr Muḥammad b. ʿUmar (d. 367/977), *Ta'rīkh iftitāḥ al-Andalus*, ed. and trans. J.M. Nichols (unpublished PhD thesis, Chapel Hill, 1975; available on University Microfilms International); also ed. with Spanish trans., J. Ribera (Madrid, 1868).

Ibn Ṣāḥib al-Ṣalāt, Abū Marwān ʿAbd al-Malik b. Muḥammad al-Bājī (c. 594/1198), *Al-Mann bi'l-Imāma*, ed. A. al-Hadi al-Tazi (Beirut, 1964); Spanish trans., A. Huici Miranda (Valencia, 1969).

Ibn Saʿīd, Abū'l-Ḥasan ʿAlī b. Mūsā b. Saʿīd al-Maghribī (d. 685/1286), *Al-Mughrib fī ḥulā al-Maghrib*, ed. S. Dayf (2 vols, Cairo, 1953–55).

Al-Idrīsī, Abū ʿAbd Allāh Muḥammad b. Muḥammad al-Ḥammūdī (c. 560/1164), *Nuzhat al-mushtāq* (Naples, 1982).

Al-Maqqarī, Shihāb al-dīn Abū'l-ʿAbbās Aḥmad b. Muḥammad al-Tilimsānī (d. 1041/1631), *Nafḥ al-ṭīb min ghuṣn al-Andalus al-raṭīb*, ed. I. 'Abbas (Beirut, 1968); trans., P. de Gayangos, *History of the Mohammaden Dynasties in Spain* (2 vols, London, 1840–41).

Nubdhat al-ʿaṣr fi akhbār Banī Naṣr, ed. A. Bustani with Spanish trans. C. Quiros (Larache, 1940).

Al-ʿUdhrī, Aḥmad b. ʿUmar al-Dalā'i (d. 478/1085), *Nuṣūṣ ʿan al-Andalus min kitab Tarṣīʿ al-akhbār wa tawzīʿ al-āthār*, ed. A. al-Ahwani (Madrid, 1956).

Al-Wansharīsī, Abū'l-ʿAbbās Aḥmad b. Yaḥyā al-Tilimsānī (d. 914/1508), *Al-Mi'yar al-mughrib wa'l-jāmiʿ al-muʿrib ʿan fatāwā ahl Ifrīqiya wa'l-Andalus wa'l-Maghrib* (Fez, 1896–97), ed. M. Hajji (Beirut, 1981–83).

Latin sources cited in text

Cronica Mozarabe de 754, ed. with Spanish trans., E. Lopez Pereira (Zaragoza, 1980).

Chronicle of Alfonso III in *Cronicas Asturianas*, ed. J. Gil Fernandez *et al.* (Oviedo, 1985).

Conquerors and Chroniclers of Early Medieval Spain, trans. K.B. Wolf (Liverpool, 1990), includes translations of the *Chronicles* of 754 and Alfonso III.

Chronica Adefonsi imperatoris, ed. A. Maya Sanchez, in *Chronica Hispana saeculi XII. Pars I*, pp. 109–248 (Corpus Christianorum, Continuatio Medievalis lxxi, Turnhout, 1990).

An introductory selection of secondary works

ABULAFIA, D., *A Mediterranean Emporium* (Cambridge, 1994).

ACIEN ALMANSA, M., *Entre el feudalismo y el Islam: 'Umar Ibn Ḥafṣun en los historiadores, en las fuentes y en la historia* (Granada, 1994).

AGUILAR SEBASTIAN, V., 'Aportacion de los Arabes nomadas a la organizacion militar del ejercito Almohade', *Al-Qantara* xiv (1993), 303–415.

ARIÉ, R., *L'Espagne musulmane au temps des Nasrides (1232–1492)* (Paris, 1973; 2nd edn, Paris, 1990).

——, *Espana Musulmana (siglos viii–xv)* (Madrid, 1984).

——, *Etudes sur la civilisation de l'Espagne musulmane* (Leiden, 1990).

——, *El reino nasri de Granada (1232–1492)* (Madrid, 1992).

AVILA, M.L., 'La proclamacion (bay'a) de Hišam II, ano 976 d.C.', *Al-Qantara* i (1980), 79–114.

——, *La sociedad hispanomusulmana al final del califato* (Madrid, 1985).

BALANA I ABADIA, P., *Els Musulmans a Catalunya (713–1153)* (Barcelona, 1993).

BARCELO, M., 'El hiato en las acuñaciones de oro en al-Andalus, 127–317/774(5)–929', *Moneda y Credito* 132 (1975), 33–71.

——, 'Un estudio sobre la estructura fiscal y procedimientos contables del emirato omeya de Cordoba (130–300/755–912) y del califato (300–366/912–976)', *Acta Medievalia* v–vi (1984–85), 45–72.

BAZZANA, A., CRESSIER, P. and GUICHARD, P., *Les Châteaux ruraux d'al-Andalus* (Madrid, 1988).

BONTE, P. ET AL (EDS), *Al-Ansab: la quête des origines* (Paris, 1991).

BOSCH VILA, J., *Albarracin Musulman* (Teruel, 1959).

——, *La Sevilla Islamica* (Seville, 1984).

——, *Los Almoravides,* ed. E. Molina Lopez (Granada, 1990).

BOVILL, E.W., *The Golden Trade of the Moors* 2nd edn (Oxford, 1970).

BULLIET, R., *Conversion to Islam in the Medieval Period: An Essay in Quantitive History* (Cambridge, Mass., 1979).

BURNS, R.I., *The Crusader Kingdom of Valencia* (2 vols, Cambridge, Mass., 1967).

——, *Moors and Crusaders in Mediterranean Spain* (London, 1978).

——, 'Daughter of Abu Zayd, last Almohad ruler of Valencia', *Viator* 24 (1993), 143–87.

CAÑADA JUSTE, A., 'Los Banū Qasī (714–924)', *Principe de Viana* clviii–clix (1980), 5–90.

CHALMETA, P., 'Concesiones territoriales en al-Andalus hasta la llegada de los almoravides', *Cuadernos de Historia. Anexos a la revista Hispania* vi (1975), 1–90.

——, 'Simancas y Alhandega', *Hispania* xxxvi (1976), 359–444.

——, *Invasion e Islamizacion: la sumision de Hispania y la formacion de al-Andalus* (Madrid, 1994).

CHEJNE, A., *Muslim Spain: its history and culture* (Minneapolis, 1974).

CODERA Y ZAIDIN, F., *Decadencia y Desaparicion de los Almoravides en Espana* (Zaragoza, 1899).

COLLINS, R., *Early Medieval Spain: Unity in Diversity, 400–1000* (London, 1983).

——, *The Arab Conquest of Spain* (Oxford, 1989).

CONRAD, L., 'An Andalusi physician at the court of the Muwahhids: some notes on the public career of Ibn Ṭufayl', *Al-Qantara* xvi (1995), 3–13.

CONSTABLE, O.R., *Trade and Traders in Muslim Spain* (Cambridge, 1994).

COOPE, J.A., *The Martyrs of Cordoba* (Nebraska, 1995).

CRONE, P., *Slaves on Horses. The Evolution of Islamic Polity* (Cambridge, 1980).

Cuadernos de Madinat al-Zahra (3 vols, Cordoba, 1987, 1988–90, 1991).

DEVERDUN, G., *Marrakesh des origines à 1912* (2 vols, Rabat, 1959).

DOZY, R., *Supplément aux Dictionnaires Arabes* (2 vols, Leiden, 1967).

DREHER, J., 'L'Imamat d'Ibn Qasī à Mertola', *Mélanges de l'Institut Dominicain d'Etudes Orientales* (1988), 195–210.

DUNLOP, D.M., 'The Dhunnunids of Toledo', *Journal of the Royal Asiatic Society* (1942–43), 77–96.

DE EPALZA, M. and RUBIERA, M.J., *Xativa Musulmana* (Xativa, 1987).

—— (ED.), *Ibn al-Abbar, Politic i Escriptor Arab Valencia* (Valencia, 1990).

FIERRO BELLO, M.I., 'Bazī', mawla de 'Abd al-Rahman I y sus descendientes', *Al-Qantara* viii (1987), 99–118.

——, *La heterodoxia en al-Andalus durante el periodo Omeya* (Madrid, 1988).

FLETCHER, M., 'The anthropological context of Almohad history', *Hesperis-Tamuda* 26–7 (1988–89), 25–51.

FLETCHER, R., *Moorish Spain* (London, 1992).

GLICK, T., *Islamic and Christian Spain in the Early Middle Ages* (Princeton, 1979).

GONZALES, J., *El Reino de Castilla en la Epoca de Alfonso VIII* (3 vols, Madrid, 1960).

GRABAR, O., *The Alhambra* (London, 1978).

DE LA GRANJA, F., 'Condena de Boabdil por los alfaquies de Granada', *Al-Andalus* 36 (1971), 145–76.

GUICHARD, P., *Structures sociales 'orientales' et 'occidentales' dans l'Espagne musulmane* (Paris, 1977).

——, *Les Musulmans de Valence et la Reconquête* (2 vols, Damascus, 1990–91).

AL-HAJJI, A., *Andalucian Diplomatic Relations with Western Europe during the Umayyad Period* (Beirut, 1970).

HANDLER, A., *The Zirids of Granada* (Coral Gables, Florida, 1974).

HARVEY, L.P., *Islamic Spain, 1250–1500* (Chicago, 1990).

HAWTING, G., *The First Dynasty of Islam* (London, 1986).

HEM: E. Lévi-Provençal, *Histoire de l'Espagne Musulmane* (3 vols, Leiden/Paris, 1950–53).

HERNANDEZ GIMENEZ, F., *Madinat al-Zahra* (Granada, 1985).

HOPKINS, J.F.P., *Medieval Muslim Government in Barbary* (London, 1958).

HUICI MIRANDA, A., *Historia Politica del Imperio Almohade* (2 vols, Tetuan, 1956–57).

——, *Las Grandes Batallas de la Reconquista durante las Invasiones Almoravides, Almohades y Benimerines* (Madrid, 1956).

——, 'La participacion de los grandes jeques en el gobierno del Imperio Almohade', *Tamuda* 6 (1958), 239–75.

——, *Historia Musulmana de Valencia* (Valencia, 1969).

IDRIS, H.R., 'Les Aftasides de Badajoz', *Al-Andalus* xxx (1965), 277–90.

——, 'Les Birzalides de Carmona', *Al-Andalus* xxx (1965), 49–62.

JAYYUSI, S.K. (ED.), *The Legacy of Muslim Spain* (Leiden, 1992).

KENNEDY, H., *The Early Abbasid Caliphate: A Political History* (London, 1981).

——, *The Prophet and the Age of the Caliphates* (London, 1986).

——, 'Byzantine–Arab diplomacy in the Near East', in *Byzantine Diplomacy,* ed. J. SHEPARD and S. FRANKLIN (Aldershot, 1992), pp. 133–43.

KISAICHI, M., 'The Almohad social-political system or hierarchy in the reign of Ibn Tumart', *Memoirs of the Research Department of the Toyo Bunko* 48 (1990), 81–101.

LACARRA, J.M., 'La conquista de Zaragoza por Alfonso I', *Al-Andalus* xii (1947), 65–96.

LAGARDÈRE, V., 'La Tariqa et la révolte des Muridin en 539H/1144 en Andalus', *Revue de l'Occident Musulman et de la Mediterranée* 35 (1983–84), 157–70.

——, *Le Vendredi de Zallaqa: 23 Octobre 1086* (Paris, 1989).

——, *Les Almoravides* (Paris, 1989).

——, *Campagnes et paysans d'Al-Andalus* (Paris, 1993).

——, 'Structures étatiques et communautés rurales: les impositions legales et illegales en al-Andalus et au Maghreb (XIe–XVe)', *Studia Islamica* 80 (1994), 57–95.

LATHAM, J.D., *From Muslim Spain to Barbary: Studies in the History and Culture of the Muslim West* (London, 1986).

LE TOURNEAU, R., *The Almohad Movement in North Africa in the 12th and 13th Centuries* (Princeton, 1969).

LÉVI-PROVENÇAL, E., *Inscriptions Arabes d'Espagne* (Leiden/Paris, 1931).

——, *Histoire de l'Espagne Musulmane* (3 vols, Leiden/Paris, 1950–53) (abbreviated to *HEM* in notes to this book).

——, 'Le titre souverain des Almoravides et sa légitimation par le califat Abasside', *Arabica* iii (1955), 265–80.

LEVTZION, N. and HOPKINS, J.F.P., *Corpus of Early Arabic Sources for West African History* (Cambridge, 1981).

LOMAX, D.W., *The Reconquest of Spain* (London, 1978).

MAKKI, M., 'The political history of al-Andalus', in Jayyusi, *Legacy of Muslim Spain* (see above), pp. 3–87.

MANZANO MORENO, E., 'La rebelion del ano 754 en la Marca Superior y su tratamiento en las cronicas arabes', *Studia Historica* iv, 2 (1985), 185–205.

——, *La Frontera de Al-Andalus en epoca de los Omeyas* (Madrid, 1991).

——, 'Oriental "topoi" in Andalucian historical sources', *Arabica* 39 (1992), 42–58.

——, 'Arabes, berberes e indigeuas: al-Andalus en su primer periodo de formacion', paper presented at the Congress on *Incastellamento*, French School in Rome, 1994. In press.

——, 'El asentamiento y la organizacion de los ŷund-s sirios en al-Andalus', *Al-Qantara* xiv (1993), 327–59.

MANZANO RODRIGUEZ, M.A., *La Intervencion de los Benimerines en la Peninsula Iberica* (Madrid, 1992).

MARIN, M., *Individuo y Sociedad en al-Andalus* (Madrid, 1992).

MARIN, M. ET AL (EDS), *Estudios Onomastico-Biograficos de Al-Andalus* (5 vols, Madrid, 1988–92).

MARTINEZ-GROS, G., *L'idéologie omeyyade: la construction de la legitimite du Califat de Cordoue (Xe–XIe siècles)* (Madrid, 1992).

MELVILLE, C. and UBAYDLI, A., *Christians and Moors in Spain. vol iii Arabic Sources* (Warminster, 1992).

MEOUAK, M., 'Hierarchie des fonctions militaires et corps d'armée en al-Andalus umayyade', *Al-Qantara* xiv (1993), 361–92.

——, 'Notes sur le vizirat et les vizirs en al-Andalus a l'époque umayyade', *Studia Islamica* lxxviii (1993), 181–90.

MESSIER, R.A., 'The Almoravids, West Africa gold and the gold currency of the Mediterranean basin', *Journal of the Economic and Social History of the Orient* xviii (1974), 31–47.

MOLINA LOPEZ, E., 'Por una cronologia historica sobre el Sarq al-Andalus (S.XIII)', *Sharq al-Andalus* 3 (1986), 39–55.

MONES, H., 'Consideraciones sobre la epoca de los Reyes de Taifas', *Al-Andalus* xxxi (1966), 302–28.

MONROE, J.T., *The Shu'ubiyya in al-Andalus* (Berkeley-Los Angeles, 1969).

MORAES FARIAS, P.F., 'The Almoravids: some questions concerning the character of the movement during the period of closest contact with the Western Sudan', *Bulletin de l'Institut fondamental d'Afrique noire* 29 (1967), 794–878.

MUNZEL, B., *Feinde, Nachbarn, Bundnisparter* (Munster, 1994).

NOTH, A. and CONRAD, L.I., *The Early Arabic Historical Tradition* (Princeton, 1994).

PAVON, B., *Ciudades Hispanomusulmanas* (Madrid, 1992).

REILLY, B., *The Contest of Christian and Muslim Spain, 1031–1157* (London, 1992).

——, *The Medieval Spains* (Cambridge, 1993).

RUBIERA MATA, M.J., *La Taifa de Denia* (Alicante, 1985).

SANCHEZ-ALBORNOZ, C., *El 'Ajbar Maymu'a'. Cuestiones historiograficas que suscita* (Buenos Aires, 1944).

——, *Despoblacion y repoblacion del valle del Duero* (Buenos Aires, 1966).

SCALES, P.C., *The Fall of the Caliphate of Cordoba* (Leiden, 1994).

SENAC, P., *Musulmans et Sarrasins dans la sud de la Gaule du viii*[e] *au xi*[e] *siècle* (Paris, 1980).

SHNEIDMAN, J.L., *The Rise of the Aragonese-Catalan Empire* (2 vols, New York, 1970).

STALLS, C., *Possessing the Land: Aragon's expansion into Islam's Ebro Frontier under Alfonso the Battler, 1104–1134* (Leiden, 1995).

TAHA, A.D., *The Muslim Conquest and Settlement of North Africa and Spain* (London and New York, 1989).

TORRES BALBAS, L., *Ciudades Hispano-Musulmanas* (2nd edn, Madrid, 1985).

TURK, A., 'El reino de Zaragoza en el siglo xi de Cristo', *Revista del Instituto de Estudios Islamicos en Madrid* 17 (1972–73), 7–122, 18 (1974–75), 7–74.

URVOY, D., *Le Monde des Ulemas andalous du V*[e]*/XI*[e] *au VII*[e]*/XIII*[e] *siècles* (Geneva, 1978).

VALENCIA, R., 'Los Dirigentes de la Sevilla Arabe en torno a 1248', in E. Cabrera (ED.), *Andalucia entre Oriente y Occidente* (Actas de V Coloquio Internacional de Historia Medieval de Andalucia, Cordoba, 1988), 31–6.

VALLEJO TRIANO, A., *El Salon de Abd al-Rahman III* (Cordoba, 1995).

VALLVÉ BERMEJO, J., 'La Cora de Jaen', *Al-Andalus* 34 (1969), 55–82.

——, 'La Cora de Tudmir', *Al-Andalus* 37 (1972), 145–89.

——, *La Division territorial de la Espana Musulmana* (Madrid, 1986).

——, *El Califato de Cordoba* (Madrid, 1992).

VERLINDEN, G., *L'esclavage dans l'Europe Medievale* (Bruges, 1955).

VIGUERA MOLINS, M.J., *Aragon Musulman* (Zaragoza, 1981).

——, *Los Reinos de Taifas y las Invasiones Magrebies* (Madrid, 1992).

—— (ed.), *Los Reinos de Taifas: al-Andalus en el Siglo XI.* vol viii-i of *Historia de Espana Menendez Pidal* (Madrid, 1994).

WASSERSTEIN, D., *The Rise and Fall of the Party Kings* (Princeton, 1985).

——, *The Caliphate in the West* (Oxford, 1993).

WATT, W.M., *A History of Islamic Spain* (Edinburgh, 1965).

WOLF, K.B., *Christian Martyrs in Muslim Spain* (Cambridge, 1988).

Maps

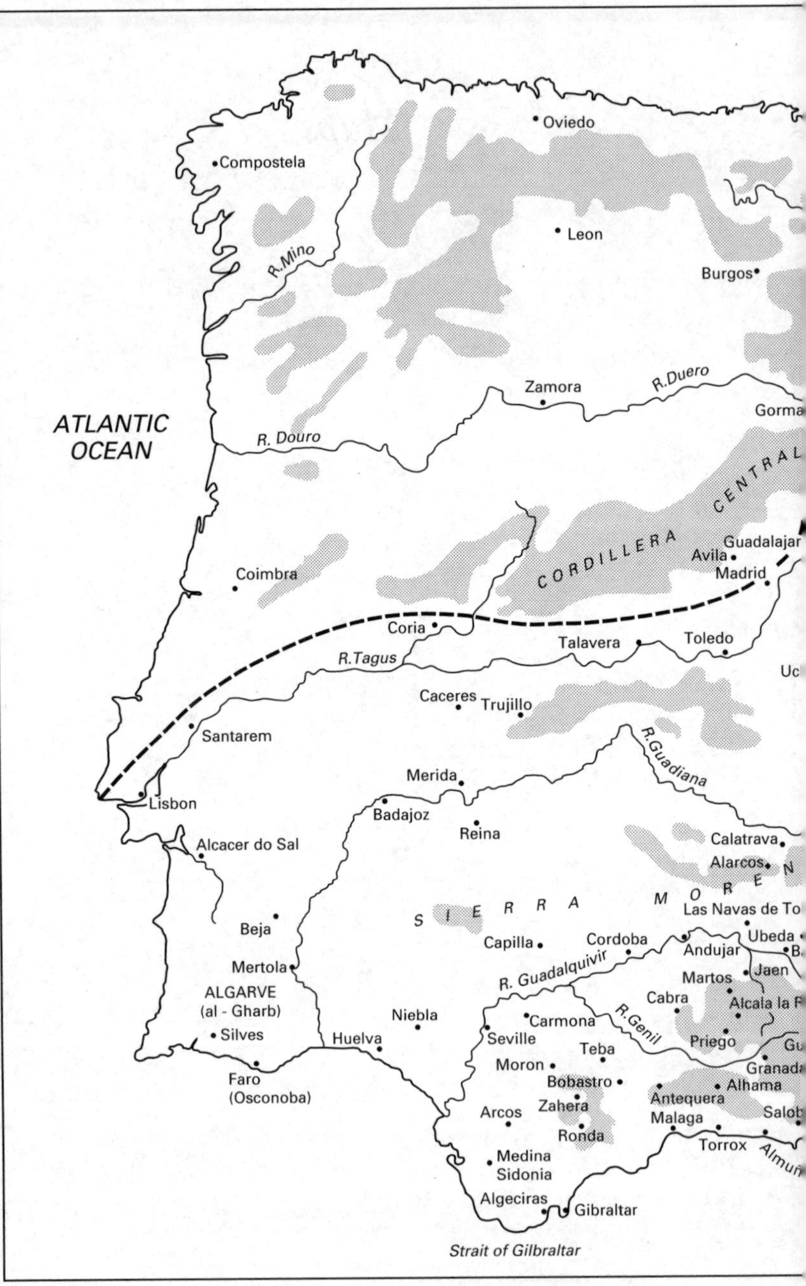

Al-Andalus (Spain and Portugal)

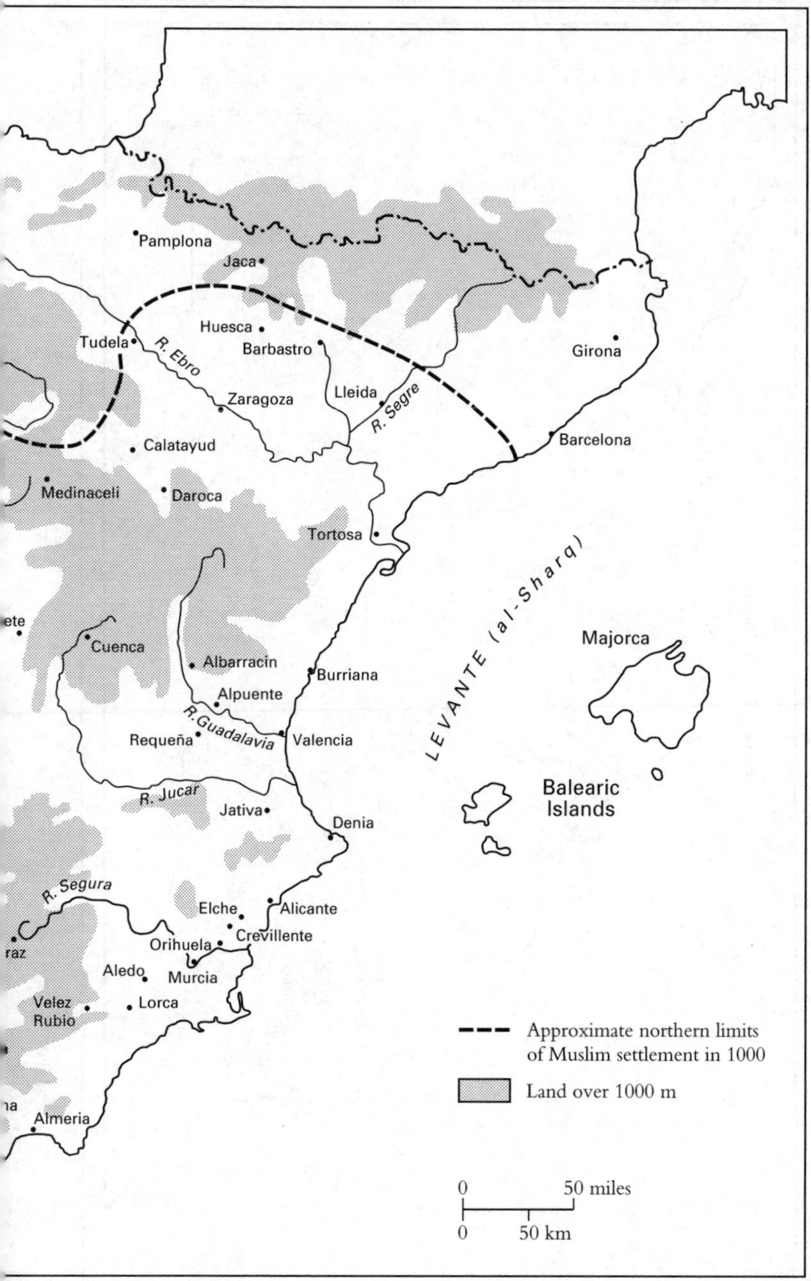
Pamplona
Jaca
Huesca
Barbastro
Tudela
R. Ebro
Girona
Lleida
R. Segre
Zaragoza
Barcelona
Calatayud
Medinaceli
Daroca
Tortosa
LEVANTE (al-Sharq)
ete
Cuenca
Majorca
Albarracin
Burriana
Alpuente
R. Guadalavia
Requeña
Valencia
R. Jucar
Jativa
Balearic Islands
Denia
R. Segura
Elche
Alicante
Crevillente
Orihuela
raz
Aledo
Murcia
Velez Rubio
Lorca
Approximate northern limits of Muslim settlement in 1000
Land over 1000 m
na
Almeria
0 50 miles
0 50 km

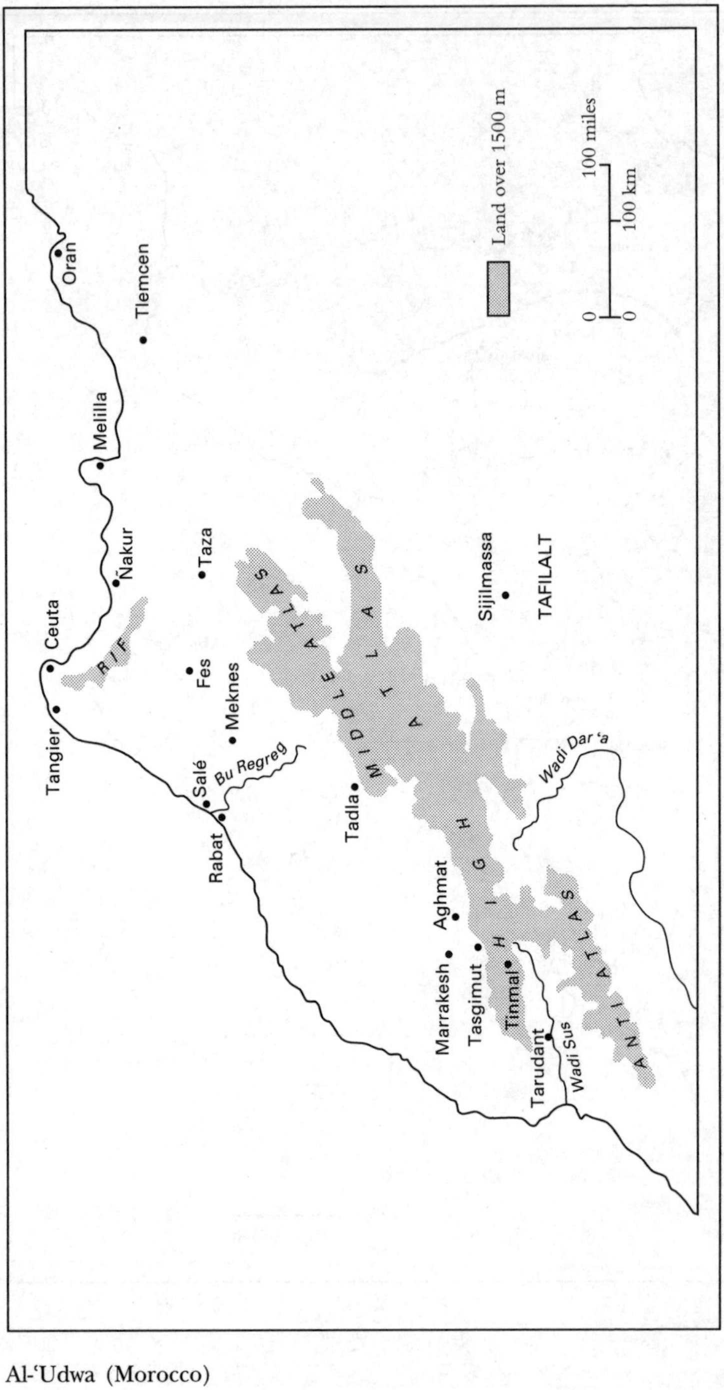

Al-ʻUdwa (Morocco)

Index

Abān, son of the Amīr ʻAbd Allāh, 78, 82
ʻAbbādids of Seville, 135–6, 138, 144–5, 162–4, 272
ʻAbbās b. Aḥmad b. Abī ʻAbda, 78
al-ʻAbbās b. Firnās, 46
ʻAbbasids, 31, 34–5, 36, 40, 44, 45, 49, 68, 84, 101, 111, 130, 131, 225, 265, 267
ʻAbd Allāh b. ʻAbd al-ʻAzīz al-Ḥajar, 115–16
ʻAbd Allāh b. ʻAbd al-Raḥmān I, 38–9, 41–2
ʻAbd Allāh b. ʻAbd al-Raḥmān II, 63–4
ʻAbd Allāh al-Bayyāsī, *sayyid*, 262, 264–5
ʻAbd Allāh b. Buluggīn, 111–12, 118–19, 134, 141, 147–9, 162, 166–9
ʻAbd Allāh b. al-Ḥakam al-Tujībī, 136
ʻAbd Allāh b. Hamshak, 184
ʻAbd Allāh b. Jāmiʻ, 235
ʻAbd Allāh b. Khālid, 31
ʻAbd Allāh b. Kulayb b. Thaʻlaba, 53, 56
ʻAbd Allāh b. Mardanīsh, 194
ʻAbd Allāh b. Maryam, 135
ʻAbd Allāh b. Maymūn, 193, 195
ʻAbd Allāh b. Mazdalī, 181
ʻAbd Allāh b. Muḥammad al-Amīr, 16, 65, 68, 73–82, 86
ʻAbd Allāh b. Muḥammad b. Abī ʻĀmir, 115
ʻAbd Allāh b. Muḥammad, lord of Badajoz, 92
ʻAbd Allāh b. Muḥammad b. Ghāniya, 193, 239, 250–1
ʻAbd Allāh b. Muḥammad b. Sīdray b. Wazīr, 259
ʻAbd Allāh b. Sinān, 45
ʻAbd Allāh b. ʻUmar b. Asnāj, 212, 213
ʻAbd Allāh b. Umayya al-Kātib, 68
ʻAbd Allāh b. Yaʻlā, Ibn al-Malwīya, 201
ʻAbd Allah b. Yāsin, 156–8, 167, 170, 199
ʻAbd al-ʻAzīz, Merinid sultan, 291
ʻAbd al-ʻAzīz b. Abī Zayd, 257
ʻAbd al-ʻAzīz al-ʻĀmirī, ruler of Valencia, 140, 142
ʻAbd al-ʻAzīz b. Mūsa b. Nuṣayr, 12, 17, 19
ʻAbd al-ʻAzīz b. Tūmart, 203–4, 205–6
ʻAbd al-Ḥaqq b. ʻAbd al-Ḥaqq, *qāḍī*, Seville, 253
ʻAbd al-Karīm b. al-Mughīth, 32, 40, 43, 45, 50, 55, 64
ʻAbd al-Malik b. al-Mughīth, 40, 55, 56
ʻAbd al-Malik b. al-Mustaʻīn, 174
ʻAbd al-Malik al-Muẓaffar, 115, 121, 122–4
ʻAbd al-Malik b. Qaṭan al-Fihrī, 25, 27
ʻAbd al-Malik b. Razīn, 139
ʻAbd al-Malik b. ʻUmar b. Marwān, 32, 35, 36
ʻAbd al-Mu'min b. ʻAlī, Almohad caliph, 183, 196, 201–16, 218
ʻAbd al-Raḥmān I, 28, 30–8, 40, 45, 49, 64
ʻAbd al-Raḥmān II, 16, 21, 44–62, 63, 75, 81, 97, 100, 102, 106, 117
ʻAbd al-Raḥmān III al-Nāṣir, 79, 81, 82–99
ʻAbd al-Raḥmān b. ʻAbd Allāh al-Ghāfiqī, 19, 20, 22, 65
ʻAbd al-Raḥmān al-Fihrī, 31
ʻAbd al-Raḥmān b. Hishām, 133
ʻAbd al-Raḥmān b. al-Muṭarrif al-Tujībī, 115, 116, 136
ʻAbd al-Raḥmān b. Saʻīd, ruler of Beja, 83, 91

'Abd al-Raḥmān Sanchuelo, 120, 124–5, 130
'Abd al-Rahmān b. Rustam, 45
'Abd al-Raḥmān b. Yaḥyā al-Tujībī, 102, 116
'Abd al-Ra'ūf, Banū, 85
'Abd al-Razzāq b. 'Isā, 77
'Abd al-Wādids of Tlemcen, 281
'Abd al-Wāḥid b. Abī Ya'qūb, *sayyid*, 252
'Abd al-Wāḥid al-Makhlū', Almohad caliph, 260–1
'Abd al-Wāḥid al-Marrākushī, 175, 188, 189, 255, 257–8
'Abd al-Wāḥid b. 'Umar, Hafsid, 251
'Abdūs, Banū, 69
Abencerrajes: see Sarrāj, Banū
Abī 'Abda, Banū, 65, 76, 85, 113, 137
Abū'l-'Abbās al-Siqillī, 235
Abū 'Abd Allāh b. Abī Zamanīn, *qāḍī* of Granada, 142
Abū 'Abd Allāh al-Bājī, *qāḍī*, 252–3
Abū 'Abd Allāh Ismā'īl b. Tījīt, 219, 220
Abū 'Abd Allāh al-Kātib, 247
Abū 'Abd Allāh b. Manī'
Abū 'Abd Allāh b. Muḥsin, 223
Abū 'Abd Allāh b. Sanādīd, 245, 246
Abū 'Abd Allāh b. Abī Yaḥyā, 253
Abū 'Abd al-Raḥmān Ya'qūb b. 'Abd al-Mu'min, *sayyid*, 235
Abū 'Alī al-Ḥusayn, *sayyid*, 226, 233, 234
Abū 'Alī al-Ḥajjāj, 244, 245
Abū 'Alī al-Sarrāj, 71
Abū 'Amr Yaḥyā b. Muḥammad b. al-Jadd, *qāḍī* of Seville
Abū Bakr 'Alī b. Wazīr, 233
Abū Bakr b. al-'Arabī, *qāḍī* of Seville, 178, 179, 203
Abū Bakr al-Ghāfiqī, *qāḍī* of Seville, 211, 212, 218
Abū Bakr b. Ibrāhīm, 165, 174
Abū Bakr b. al-Jadd, 212, 218, 228
Abū Bakr b. Mazdalī, 176
Abū Bakr b. Muḥammad al-Lamtūni, 183
Abū Bakr al-Turṭūshī, 117–8
Abū Bakr b. 'Umar b. Turgūt, 156–9, 133
Abū Bakr b. Ẓuhr, 244
Abū Dabbūs al-Wāthiq, Almohad caliph, 262
Abū Ḥafṣ Intī: see 'Umar b. Yaḥyā al-Hintātī
Abū Ḥafṣ 'Umar b. 'Abd al-Mu'min, *sayyid*, 216, 218, 219, 221–4, 226, 230
Abū Ḥafṣ 'Umar al-Rashīd b. Yūsuf I, *sayyid*, 240
Abū Ḥafṣ Ya'qūb b. Abī Ḥafṣ 'Umar, *sayyid*, 241, 242
Abū'l-Hajjāj b. Qādis, 254, 256
Abū'l-Ḥasan, Merinid sultan, 288
Abū'l-Ḥasan 'Alī (Muley Hacen), Nasrid ruler, 299–301
Abū'l-Ḥasan 'Alī b. Abī Ḥafṣ 'Umar, *sayyid*, 248
Abū'l-Ḥasan 'Alī b. 'Abd al-Mu'min, *sayyid*, 216, 233
Abū'l-Ḥasan b. Ayyāsh, 218, 223
Abū'l-Ḥasan b. al-Wajjāj, 253
Abū Ibrāhīm Ismā'īl, *sayyid*, 220, 226
Abū 'Imrān b. Yāsin al-Hintātī, 253
Abū Isḥāq Ibrāhīm b. 'Abd al-Mu'min *sayyid*, 240
Abū Isḥāq b. al-Manṣūr, *sayyid*, 252, 253
Abū Isḥāq Ibrāhīm b. Yūsuf I, *sayyid*, 234, 235, 238, 251, 252
Abū Muḥammad 'Abd Allāh b. Yaḥyā, 247
Abū Muḥammad 'Abd Allāh b. 'Abd al-Mu'min, *sayyid*, 216
Abū Muḥammad 'Abd al-Wāḥid, Hafsid, 249
Abū Muḥammad Sa'd b. al-Manṣūr, *sayyid*, 252
Abū Mūsā 'Īsā b. 'Abd al-Mu'min, *sayyid*, 258
Abū Mūsā b. al-Manṣūr, *sayyid*, 259
Abū'l-Qāsim Bannigash, 301
Abū'l-Qāsim b. Bāqī, *qāḍī*, 249
Abū'l-Qāsim b. al-Mulīh, *wazīr*, 302, 303–4
Abū'l-Qāsim b. Nuṣayr, 248
Abū'l-Qāsim b. Rushd, 192
Abū'l-Qāsim b. Ward, *qāḍī* of Granada, 178
Abū'l-Rabī', Merinid sultan, 286

Abū'l-Rabī' Sulaymān b. 'Abd al-Mu'min, *sayyid*, 240
Abū Sa'īd Faraj al-Naṣrī, 285
Abū Sa'īd 'Uthmān, Hafsid, 250
Abū Sa'īd 'Uthmān, *sayyid*, 206, 209, 221–3, 215–6, 218–9, 221–2, 226
Abū'l-Shammākh Muḥammad b. Ibrāhīm al-Judhāmī, 47, 50
Abū'l-'Ūla' the Elder, *sayyid*, 250, 259, 260
Abū'l-Walīd b. Rushd, *qāḍī* of Cordoba, 178, 183, 185, 226
Abū Yaḥyā b. al-Manṣūr, *sayyid*, 252
Abū Yaḥyā b. Yūsuf I, *sayyid*, 235, 238, 243, 244
Abū Ya'qūb, Merinid sultan, 285
Abū Ya'qūb Yūsuf I, Almohad caliph, 206, 209, 210–3, 215, 216–37
Abū Yūsuf, Merinid Ssultan, 282–4
Abū Yūsuf Ya'qūb, Almohad caliph: see al-Manṣūr
Abū'l-Walīd Muḥammad b. Rushd (Averroes), 235, 246
Abū Zakarīya, Hafsid, 249
Abū Zakarīya Yaḥyā b. 'Abd al-Mu'min, *sayyid*, 226
Abū Zakarīya Yaḥyā b. Sinān, 220
Abū Zakarīya Yaḥyā b. 'Umar, *sayyid*, 238, 252, 258
Abū Zayd 'Abd al-Raḥmān b. Tījīt, 210–1
Abū Zayd 'Abd al-Raḥmān b. 'Umar, *sayyid*, 237, 248
Abū Zayd Muḥammad b. Yūsuf I, *sayyid*, 235, 238, 247
Abū Zayd b. Muḥammad of Valencia, *sayyid*, 265, 269–70
Aceca, 186
Al-'Ādil, 'Abd Allāh b. al-Manṣūr, Almohad caliph, 259, 261–5
Afonso I of Portugal, 180, 190, 202, 221
Afonso II of Portugal, 257
Afonso IV of Portugal, 288
Aftasids of Badajoz, 138–9, 144–7, 150
Aghmāt, 141, 164
Aḥmad b. 'Abd Allāh al-Makhzūmī, 269–9
Aḥmad b. Abī 'Abda, 78, 85, 89
Aḥmad b. 'Aṭiya, Abū Ja'far, 206
Aḥmad al-Bāqī, *qāḍī*, 90
Aḥmad b. al-Barā' al-Umawī, 80
Aḥmad b. Bāso, 211, 215
Aḥmad b. Isḥāq al-Qurashī, 87, 93
Aḥmad b. Maslama b. al-Ḥajjāj, 88
Aḥmad b. Muḥammad al-Bājī, al-Mu'taḍid, *ruler* of Seville, 271–2
Aḥmad b. Muḥamad b. Ḥudayr, 88
Aḥmad b. Mūsā al-Rāzī, 7, 50
Aḥmad b. Ya'lā, 94
Akhbār al-Majmū'a, 7, 19, 49
Akhīl b. Idrīs, *qāḍī* Cordoba, 211
Akhila, 10
al-'Alā' b. al-Mughīth al-Yaḥṣubī, 34–5
Alamundo, 10
Alanje, battle of, 268, 274
Alarcos, battle of, 244–6
Alava, 55, 65
Albacete, 194
Albaicin, Granada, 213, 277, 283, 286, 302
Albarracin, 94, 103, 139–40, 145
Albuniel, 79
Alcala de Guadaira, 252
Alcala la Real, 278, 289, 303
Alcaraz, 226, 256
Alcacer do Sal, 243, 259
Alcazar de San Juan, 186
Alcaudete, 278, 280, 285, 294
Aledo, 153, 158, 163–4, 167, 175
Alfonso I, 28, 60
Alfonso II, 60
Alfonso III, 61, 70, 71, 77
Alfonso VI, 139, 147, 151–2, 161–6, 167, 173, 179–80
Alfonso VII, 178, 180, 189, 190, 194, 202, 209
Alfonso VIII, 228–9, 233–4, 244–6, 247, 253–5, 257
Alfonso IX, 209, 246, 257
Alfonso X, 278, 279, 284
Alfonso XI, 287, 288, 289
Alfonso I of Aragan, 180, 181, 185, 187
Algeciras, 3, 12, 66, 128, 143, 144, 150, 162, 203, 206, 234, 277, 280, 285, 286, 289
Alhama de Granada, 300
Alhambra, Granada, 99, 213, 277, 283, 291, 303–4

Alhandega, battle of, 84, 86, 87, 93–4, 98, 102, 128
'Alī al-'Aṭṭār, 300
'Alī b. Badr al-Dīn b. Mūsā b. Raḥḥū, 290
'Alī b. al-Ḥājj, 165
'Alī al-Ḥammūdī, 128–9
'Alī b. 'Īsā b. Maymūn, 202
'Alī b. Isḥāq b. Ghānīya, 239–40
'Alī b. Jayyāb, 291
'Alī b. Kumāsha, 290, 297, 298
'Alī b. Majjuz, 185
'Alī b. Reverter, 239
'Alī b. Yūsuf b. Tāshfīn, 172–4, 176, 177, 179–87, 191, 198, 200
Alicun de Ortega, 799
Aljaferia Palace, 132
Almeria, 76, 97, 129, 140, 141, 145, 186, 190, 191, 193, 195, 209, 222, 225, 275, 278, 286, 303
Alpuente, 131, 145
Alpujarras, 303
Alquezar, 150
Alvar Fañez, 153, 164, 166, 173
Alvaro de Luna, 296, 297
Al-Amīn, Banū, 293, 294, 295, 296
'Amrūs, Banū, 15, 39, 56, 72
'Amrūs b. Yūsuf, 39, 54, 57, 58
'Anbasa b. Suḥaym al-Kalbī, 18, 19, 22
Andarax valley, 76, 302
Andujar, 190, 218–9, 254
Anīsha, battle of, 270
Antequera, 277, 294
Angelino, Banū, 75
'Aqabat al-Baqar, 127
Aragon, 150, 180
Archidona, 26, 294, 298
Arcos, 136, 146
Ardobast, Count, 10, 17, 26, 33
Arjona, 267, 274, 275
Aṣbagh b. Wansūs al-Miknāsī, 42, 56
Ashqilūla, Banū, 274, 279, 281, 284
al-'Āṣī b. 'Abd Allāh al-Amīr, 78, 82, 87
al-'Āṣi b. al-Ḥakam al-Tujībī, 102
Aspe, 265
Astorga, 29, 54
Asturias, 3, 40, 54, 60
'Aṭīq b. al-Mawl, 286
Atlas mountains, 155, 157, 161, 181, 183, 197, 203, 207
Autun, 22
Averroes,: see Abū'l-Walīd b. Rushd
Avila, 209, 230
Awdaghast, 155
Awlīl, 155
Aznalfarache (Ḥiṣn al-Faraj), 244, 246, 247

Badajoz, 65, 70, 80, 91–2, 150, 170, 189, 202–4, 221, 252, 267–8, 274
Badajoz, Taifa kings of, 131, 138–9, 144
Badr, *mawla* 'Abd al-Raḥmān I, 31–2, 34
Badr b. Aḥmad, 86, 88
Baeza, 78, 190, 209, 253, 263, 265, 292
Bairen, 165
Bakrī family, 132, 137, 154–5
baladīyūn, 25, 33, 50
Balearic Islands, 53, 140, 174, 186, 189, 239, 250–1
Balj b. Bishr al-Qushayrī, 18, 24–5, 52
Baños de la Encina, 264
Barbastro, 150, 151
Barcelona, 37, 54, 61, 65, 119, 127, 174, 185, 215
Barghawāṭa Berbers, 158
Barrāz b. Muḥammad al-Massūfī, 203, 214
Al-Bashīr, 'Abd Allāh b. Muḥsin, 198, 200, 201
Basques, 3, 14, 37, 61, 89, 109, 120
Al-Baydhaq, Abū Bakr b. 'Alī, 196, 222, 225
Baza, 220, 222, 275, 284, 287, 302, 303
Beja, 34, 35, 53–4, 71, 83, 91, 191, 193, 202–4, 231–3, 267
Belillos, castle, 148
Benavente, 245
Berenguela, queen, 257
Birzāl, Banū, 104–5, 113, 131, 142–3
Bobastro, 73, 77, 83, 88–9
Bougie, 206, 209, 210, 239
Buluggīn b. Zīrī al-Ṣanhājī, 103, 105, 121
Buñol, 230
Burriana, 270
Buyids, 111, 131
Byzantines, 2, 3, 10, 16, 60, 97–8, 104, 106

Cabra, 66, 278
Caceres, 186, 220, 252, 265
Cadiz, 235
Calatayud, 57, 72, 80, 92, 102, 103, 136, 180, 181
Calatrava 16, 57, 66, 69, 126, 190, 234, 244–5, 253–5
Cantuarias, 153
Capilla, 264, 265
Caracuel de Calatrava, 245
Carcassonne, 40, 56
Carmona, 12, 34, 66, 76, 88, 131, 136, 142, 144, 212
Carolingians, 22, 38, 54, 58, 61–2, 75
Castro family, 209
Ceuta, 10, 24, 96, 104, 128, 160, 161, 162, 184, 203, 206, 234, 243, 280, 285, 286
Charlemagne, 37, 42, 61
Chronicle of 754, 9, 13, 24
Chronicle of Alfonso III, 13, 58, 70
Chronicle of Alfonso VII, 187
Chronicle of Moissac, 38
El Cid, 46, 152, 163, 165–6
Ciudad Rodrigo, 215
Clunia, 89
Coimbra, 29, 150, 174, 215
coinage, 21, 45, 90–1
Comes, son of Antonian, 68
Consuegra, 166
conversion to Islam, 67–8
Cordoba, Muslim conquest, 11, 14
  becomes capital, 16
  urban development, 107
  siege of, 124–9
  mosque of, 38, 40, 46, 63, 105–6, 119, 123, 133
  Taifa rulers of, 137, 144–5
  Almoravids and Almohads in, 181–3, 214–5
  Christian conquest of 271, 276
Coria, 29, 36, 76, 150, 152
Covadonga, 21, 60
Cuenca, 173, 228–9, 233–4, 267
Cullera, 271

Dammarīs of Moron, 143
Dar'a, Wādī, 155, 157
Daroca, 72, 80, 92, 136, 180
Dāwud b. Ā'isha, 163, 174
Dāwud b. Abī Dāwud, 247
Daysam b. Isḥāq, 75, 79
Denia, 131, 133, 140, 145, 174, 250, 271
Dhu'l-Nunids, 69, 80, 85, 92–4, 103, 116, 139, 144–6, 151–3
Diego Lopez de Haro, 247
dīwān, xii, 5, 16, 31, 45, 50, 87, 125, 161, 208, 224
Duero River, 28, 61, 89, 93, 95, 100
Durrī al-Ṣiqlabī, 86, 93

Ebro Valley, 12, 16, 17, 37, 38, 39, 55, 57, 89, 92–3, 186, 194: *see also* Upper March
Ecija, 231
Egica, King, 1, 10, 66, 88
Elche, 222
Elvas, 252
Elvira, 11, 16, 26, 32, 53, 66, 133, 142
Enrique I of Castile, 257
Escalona, 186, 246
San Esteban de Gormaz, 85, 89
Estepona, 281
Eulogius, martyr, 48
Evora, 220, 234
Extremadura, 18, 56, 246, 274

Faḥṣ al-Ballūṭ, 66
Fā'iq al-Ṣiqlabī, 112–3
Al-Falakī, 184
faqīh, fuqahā, xii, 40, 163–4, 167–8, 169, 170, 183, 190, 226, 279
Faraj b. Khayr al-Ṭūṭāliqī, 53–4
Faraj b. Riḍwān, 292
Faro, 71, 84: *see also* Ocsonoba
fatā, fityān, xii, 51, 63, 86, 117
Fatimids, 36, 90, 96–7, 103, 104, 121
Fatḥ b. Mūsā b. Dhī'l-Nūn, 80
Fernando I, king, 146–7, 150, 151
Fernando II of Leon, 209, 221, 236
Fernando III, 254, 257, 262, 264, 272, 276
Fernando IV, 284, 285, 286
Fernando de Antequera, 294
Fes, 44, 64, 95, 96, 121, 160, 161, 177, 202, 206
Fiñana, 88
Fortun Garces, king of Navarre, 82

Fortun b. Muḥammad al-Shabrīṭī, 94
Fraga, 186, 187, 190, 194
France, 18, 19, 21, 28, 97
Fuengirola, castle, 96, 294
Futays, Banū, 85, 113, 123
Fraxinetum, 97

Gadmīwa, Berber tribe, 207, 226
Galicia, 12, 28, 55, 0, 65, 147
Ganfīsa, Berber tribe, 207, 226
Garcia, king of Galicia, 147, 151
Garci Fernandez, Count of Castile, 101, 115, 116
Garcia Ramirez, Count of Viguera, 126, 128
Garcia Sanchez, King of Navarre, 145
Garūr, Almoravid leader, 166
Gaston de Béarn, 186
Gazzūla, Berber tribe, 155
Genoese, 277
Ghālib b. ʿAbd al-Raḥmān al-Ṣiqlabī, 86, 94–5, 100–2, 104, 110, 117
Ghānīya, Banū, 186, 189, 239, 250–1
ghāzī, xii, 282, 283, 286, 289–90
Ghazzāli, Imām, 191, 197
ghulām, ghilmān, xii, 39, 86, 113
Ghuzz Turks, 208, 245, 249, 258, 266
Gibraltar, 10, 211–2, 218, 278, 280, 286, 299
Giraldo Sempavor, 220–2
Girona, 29, 37, 38, 56, 61
Gomara Berbers, 226, 282, 297
Gormaz, 100, 101
Granada, Taifa kings of 133, 141–5
  Nasrid rule in, 273–304
  Christian conquest of 302–4
  see also Albaicin, Alhambra
Guadalajara, 29, 69, 72, 145, 247
Guadix, 177, 275, 278, 284, 286, 290, 298, 301, 302, 303
Guazalete River, 69
Guadalquivir Valley, 16, 17, 18, 47, 52, 57, 98, 107, 133, 164, 272, 279, 285
Guddāla, Berber tribe, 155, 156, 157, 159, 177
Guillem de Montfri, 269

Ḥabūs b. Māksan al-Zīrī, 112, 142
Ḥafṣ b. Ḥafṣūn, 83
Hafsids of Tunisia, 251, 266, 267, 270, 272, 275, 276, 278, 288
ḥājib, xii, 44–5, 64, 111, 125, 131, 136
Banū'l-Hājj, 176
Al-Ḥājj Yaʿīsh, architect, 211
Al-Ḥajjāj, Banū, 75–6, 88, 134, 272
Al-Ḥakam I, Amīr, 41–4, 49–50, 51, 52, 54, 55, 57, 58, 66, 117
Al-Ḥakam II al-Mustanṣir, Caliph, 99–106, 109–110, 117, 119, 135
Ḥamīd al-Zajjālī, 68
Al-Ḥamma, battle of, 240
Ḥammūdi family, 128–9, 130, 135, 143, 145
Harga, Berber tribe, 197, 205, 219
Ḥārith b. Bazīʿ, 69
al-Ḥasan b. Gannūn al-Idrīsī, 100, 104
Hāshim b. ʿAbd al-ʿAzīz, 65, 68, 70–1
Haskūra, Berber tribe, 207, 225, 227
Henry II of Trastamara, 291–2
Henry III, 293
Henry IV, 298
Higueruela, battle of, 296, 297
Hilāl, Arab tribe, 205, 219
Hilāl al-Madyūnī, 36
Hilāl b. Mardanīsh, 224, 230, 234
Hintāta, Berber tribe, 207, 219, 233, 251, 266
Hishām I al-Amīr, 37, 38–41, 54, 55, 64
Hishām II al-Mu'ayyad, Caliph, 109–10, 120, 124, 125, 127, 129, 130–1, 136
Hishām b. Muḥammad al-Muṣḥafī, 101
Hishām b. ʿUrwa al-Fihrī, 34
Holy War: see *jihād*
Hostegesis, bishop, 51
Ḥudayr, Banū, 85, 123
Hudids of Zaragoza, 131, 136–7, 145–7, 187, 194, 219, 265–8, 275, 276
Huelva, 137, 144
Huesca, 15, 29, 42, 55, 57, 72, 92, 136
Huete, 80, 92, 103, 173, 225–8
Ḥulūl al-Mawshīya, 171, 181
Hurayz b. Hābil, 78
al-Ḥurr b. ʿAbd al-Raḥmān al-Thaqafī, 21
al-Ḥusām b. Ḍirār al-Kalbī, Abū'l-Khaṭṭār, 25–6

al-Ḥusayn b. Yaḥyā b. Sa'd b. Ubāda, 37

Ibiza, 250, 269
Ibn al-Abbār, historian, 214, 271–2
Ibn 'Abd al-Barr, Nasrid *wazīr*, 297, 298
Ibn 'Abd Rabbīhi, 76
Ibn 'Abdūn, 175, 177–8, 179, 182
Ibn Abī Rang, 173
Ibn Abī Zar', 157, 255
Ibn Adham, *qāḍī* of Cordoba, 162
Ibn 'Ammār, 148
Ibn al-Andalusi, (Ja 'far b. 'Alī b. Ḥamdūn), 103, 104, 105, 114–5
Ibn al-'Arīf, Sufi, 191
Ibn al-Athīr, historian, 182
Ibn Ayyāsh, Abū'l-Ḥasan, 218, 223
Ibn al-Azraq, *qāḍī* Granada, 301, 302
Ibn 'Azzūn, Abu'l-Ghamr, 193, 195, 203, 204, 210, 211
Ibn 'Azzūn, Abu'l-'Alā', 204, 211, 220, 221–2, 226–8
Ibn 'Azzūn, Abū'l-Ghamr II, 249
Ibn Barrajān, Sufi, 191
Ibn Dhakwān, *qāḍī* of Cordoba, 127, 135
Ibn al-Faraḍī, historian, 127
Ibn Hafṣūn, 'Umar, 68, 69, 72–4, 77–8, 84, 88–9, 96
Ibn al-Ḥakīm al-Rundī, 286
Ibn Ḥamdīn, *qāḍī* of Cordoba, 191–2
Ibn Hamushk, 195, 210, 211, 212–4, 221–2, 226
Ibn Ḥawqal, 86, 87
Ibn Ḥawt Allāh, *qāḍī*, 225, 253
Ibn Ḥayyan, Abū Marwān, historian, 7, 9, 53, 59, 63, 64, 65, 66, 73, 76, 78, 98, 99–100, 101, 102, 110, 132, 137, 151
Ibn Ḥazm, 132, 133
Ibn al-Ḥijjām, 204, 210
Ibn Ḥubaysh, *qāḍī*, Murcia, 225
Ibn Hudhayl, 78
Ibn Idhārī, historian, 7, 22, 63, 65, 73, 99, 115, 123, 143, 157, 196, 235, 245, 255, 259, 266
Ibn Iyād, 193, 194
Ibn Jaḥḥāf, *qāḍī* Valencia, 165
Ibn Jahwar, Abū'l-Ḥasan, 129
Ibn Jāmi', family of, 260–1
Ibn Kardabūs, 175
Ibn Khaldūn, historian, 196, 203, 204, 266, 272, 274–5, 284, 292
Ibn al-Khaṭīb, historian, 9, 266, 288, 289, 290, 292
Ibn al-Maḥrūq, Nasrid *wazīr*, 287
Ibn Mardanīsh, Muḥammad b. Sa'd, 194–5, 209, 210–11, 213–14, 219, 220, 221–2, 224, 226, 229
Ibn Marwān al-Jillīqī, 'Abd al-Raḥmān, 56, 65, 68, 70–1, 75, 80, 91–2
Ibn al-Mufrij, 63
Ibn Mundhir *al-faqīh*, 91
Ibn al-Mundhir, Sufi, 191, 192
Ibn Qasī, Aḥmad b. al-Ḥusayn, 191–2, 202–3, 204
Ibn al-Qiṭṭ, 71
Ibn al-Qulay'ī, *qāḍī* Granada, 168, 169
Ibn al-Qūṭīya, 7, 17, 43, 63, 64, 65, 66, 68, 69, 73, 80
Ibn Rashīq, ruler of Murcia, 163, 164, 168
Ibn al-Royolo, 145
Ibn al-Rumālya, *qāḍī*, 225
Ibn Ṣāḥib al-Ṣalat, historian, 210, 214, 215, 218, 221, 223–4, 225–31, 232, 234, 236
Ibn al-Ṣayrafī, historian, 181
Ibn Ṣumādiḥ, 140, 162, 163
Ibn Ṭufayl, 217, 223
Ibn Yujjān, Abū Zayd 'Abd al-Raḥmān, 248, 249, 252, 261, 263, 264
Ibn Zamrak, Nasrid *wazīr*, 290, 293
Ibrāhīm b. Abī Bakr, 163, 176
Ibrāhīm b. al-Ḥajjāj, 75–6, 77, 88
Ibrāhīm al-Ḥakīm, 300
Idrisids, 95, 104, 128–9
Ifrīqīya, 10, 16, 19, 31: *see also* Tunisia
Ijilliz, 197
Illora, 278
Iñigo Arista, King of Pamplona, 61
Al-'Iqāb, battle: *see* Las Navas de Tolosa
'Īsā b. Aḥmad al-Rāzi, historian, 7, 100, 102, 104
'Īsā b. 'Imrān, *qāḍī*, 226
'Īsā b. Sahl al-Asadī, *qāḍī* Granada, 168
'Īsā b. Sa'īd al-Yaḥṣubī, 123, 125
'Īsā b. Shuhayd, 40, 45, 50, 64, 66

'Īsā b. Tūmart, 203, 205–6
Isḥāq b. al-Mundhir, 43
Ismā'īl I, Nasrid ruler, 283, 287–91
Ismā'īl II, Nasrid ruler, 290
Ismā'īl b. 'Abbād, 135, 138
Ismā'īl b. 'Abd al-Raḥmān b. Dhī'l-Nūn, 139, 141, 152
Iznajar, 278
'Izz al-Dawla, lord of Moron, 131

Jabāra b. Abī'l-'Aynayn, 225
Jābir b. Labīd, 49
Jaen, 26, 46, 66, 129, 142, 192, 204, 210, 212, 253, 274, 275–6, 278, 292, 299
Ja'far b. 'Uthmān al-Muṣḥafī, 101–2, 104, 112–14
Jahwarid rulers of Cordoba, 137, 144
Jaime I, the Conqueror, 257, 279
Jaime II, 285–6
Jativa, 80, 165, 225
Jaw'dhar al-Ṣiqlabī, 112–13
Jawhar, Fatimid general, 97, 103
Jayfar b. Mukassir, 56
Jerez, 203, 204, 279
Jerica, 270
Jews, 11, 13–14, 49, 145, 161, 213
jihād, xii, 22, 44, 46, 53, 66–7, 71, 77, 64–5, 89–90, 112, 119–20, 123, 151, 157, 169, 171, 172, 205, 218, 223, 226, 235, 238–9, 246, 265, 281, 285, 305–6
jizya, xii, 6, 17, 51, 59, 68, 170, 185
John I, 291
John II, 293, 296, 297
John of Gorze, 97
Joseph b. Samuel b. Naghrila, 145
Judhām, Arab tribe, 17, 27
Julian, Count, 8, 10
jund, xii, 23, 26, 31, 33, 35–6, 49–50, 52, 66, 68, 87, 94, 102, 103, 117–19, 193, 225, 282
Junquera, battle of, 89
Jurumeña, 221

Kāfūr the Eunuch, 217
Kāhina, 5
Kalb, Arab tribe, 25
Khalaf b. Bakr, ruler of Ocsonoba, 84
Khaldūn, Banū, 75–6, 134
Al-Khandaq: *see* Alhandega
Kharijites, 23, 36, 41, 95, 96–7, 105
Khawlān, Arab tribe, 17
Khayrān al-Ṣiqlabī, ruler of Almeria, 129, 140
Khizrūnis of Arcos, 143
Khult, Berber tribe, 266
Kumāsha, Banū, 273, 290, 301, 303
Kūmiya, Berber tribe, 198, 202, 207, 210, 225, 226

Lakhm, Arab tribe, 17, 27, 135
Lamego, 150
Lamṭa, Berber tribe, 155, 177
Lamtūna, Berber tribe, 155–61, 166, 175, 177, 184, 218
Lanjaron, 303
Lebrija, 279
Leon, 29, 54, 55, 61, 89, 106, 138, 147, 150, 151
Lerida: *see* Lleida
Linares, 70
Lisbon, 47, 138, 164, 174, 180, 190, 234, 235
Lleida 55, 123, 136, 147, 187, 190
Lobon, 222
Loja, 264, 278, 290, 300, 302
Lorca, 75, 79, 89, 222
Louis the Pious, 54
Lower March, 52, 56–7, 70–1
Lubb b. Mūsā b. Qasī, 69
Lubb b. Ṭarbīsha, 89, 92
Lucena, 185, 301

Ma'āfir, Arab tribe, 17, 124
Madīnat al-Zāhira, 114, 125
Madīnat al-Zahra, 98–9, 100, 102, 104, 105, 114, 132, 242
Madrid, 29
maghārim, xii, 43, 79, 158, 169, 170
Al-Mahdī, Caliph: see Muhammad II
Maḥyū b. Abi Bakr, 245
Majorca, 101, 145, 174, 239, 250–1, 252, 268–9
makhzen, 215
Malaga, 11, 13, 26, 66, 143, 145, 163, 164, 167, 192, 209, 275, 278, 284, 298
Malagon, 245
Mālik b. Anas, 40–1

Al-Ma'mūn, Almohad caliph, 259, 264–6
Ma'n b. 'Abd al-'Azīz al-Tujībī, 114–15
Al-Manṣūr, Almohad Caliph, 208, 237–49, 261
Al-Manṣūr: *see* Muḥammad b. Abī 'Āmir
Al-Maqqarī, historian, 256, 266, 268
Maqueda, 246
Marrakesh, foundation of, 159
Almohad building in, 238, 249
Martos, 280, 287
Martyrs of Cordoba, 48
Marwān b. 'Abd al-'Azīz, *qāḍī* Valencia, 193
Maṣmūda Berbers, 155, 157, 181, 183, 197, 207
Masrūr al-Khādim, 43
Massūfa, Berber tribe, 155, 177, 186, 218
Mas'ūd b. Tajīt, ruler of Merida, 91
Matrūḥ b. Sulaymān b. Yaqẓān, 39
mawlā, mawālī, xii, 6, 26, 31–2, 34, 49, 50, 56, 57, 59, 64, 65, 67, 78, 85, 94, 137
Maymūn b. Badr al-Lamtūnī, 204, 209
Mazdalī b. Tilankan, 160, 166, 176, 177
Medellin, 36
Medina Sidonia, 11, 16, 51, 66, 88
Medinaceli, 9, 69, 89, 100, 114, 117, 126
Melilla, 96
Meknes, 160, 176, 222
Mequiñenza, 186
Merida, 12, 14, 25, 37, 38, 52, 56, 57, 70, 91–2, 268
Merinids, 245, 262, 278–9, 280, 291
Mertola, 144, 191, 203, 233
Middle March, 52, 57, 100, 114
Minorca, 250, 269
Moclin, 278
Monchique, castle, 191
Montanchez, 264, 268
Montefrio, 278, 297, 299
Montejicar, 79
Montiel, 185
Montoro, 254
Moron, 51, 66, 131, 143, 144
Mozarabs, 48, 73
Mubārak al-Ṣiqlabī, ruler of Valencia, 140
Mubāshir al-Dawla, 174
Muḍar, Arab tribe, 4, 47: *see also* Qays
Mudejars, 278–9, 281
al-Mughīra b. 'Abd al-Raḥmān III, 112–13
al-Mughīra b. al-Ḥakam I, 44
Mughīth al-Rūmī, 11, 14, 32
Muḥammad I al-Amīr, 55, 63–71
Muḥammad II al-Mahdī, Caliph, 125–8
Muḥammad I, Nasrid ruler, 267, 268, 271, 272, 273–80, 282
Muḥammad II, Nasrid ruler, 279, 280–5
Muḥammad III, Nasrid ruler, 282, 284, 285–6
Muḥammad IV, Nasrid ruler, 283, 287–8
Muḥammad V, Nasrid ruler, 282, 283, 289–92
Muḥammad IV, Nasrid ruler, 290
Muḥammad VII, Nasrid ruler, 293–4
Muḥammad VIII, Nasrid ruler, 295, 298
Muḥammad IX, Nasrid ruler, 295, 296–8
Muḥammad X, Nasrid ruler, 297
Muḥammad XI el Chiquito, Nasrid ruler, 298
Muḥammad XII, Boabdil, Nasrid ruler, 301–4
Muḥammad b. 'Abbād, ruler of Seville, 131
Muḥammad b. 'Abd Allāh al-Amīr, 74
Muḥammad b. 'Abd al-Mu'min, 215
Muḥammad b. 'Abd al-Raḥmān al-Tujībī, 80–1, 85
Muḥammad b. Abī 'Āmir al-Manṣūr, 105, 109–122, 124–5, 130, 131, 136, 140, 141
Muḥammad b. Abī Sa'īd, Ibn al-Mu'alim, 215, 218
Muḥammad b. Ā'isha, Almoravid, 166, 173
Muḥammad b. 'Alī b. Ghānīya, 186
Muḥammad b. 'Alī al-Kūmī, 210
Muḥammad b. Aṣbagh, *qāḍī* of Seville
Muḥammad b. 'Āṣim, Nasrid *wazīr.* 293
Muḥammad b. Fāṭima b. Sīr, Almoravid, 177

Muḥammad b. Ghālib, 76
Muḥammad b. al-Ḥājj, Almoravid, 172, 174, 176, 177
Muḥammad b. Ḥāshim al-Tujībī, 92–3
Muḥammad b. Ibrāhīm, Almoravid, 165
Muḥammad b. Isḥāq b. Ghāniya, 239, 249
Muḥammad b. Ismā'īl al-Naṣrī, 287
Muḥammad b. Ismā'īl b. Qasī, 70
Muḥammad b. Ibrāhīm b. al-Ḥajjāj, 83, 88
Muḥammad b. Kawthar, 68
Muḥammad b. Khazar al-Zanātī, 96
Muḥammad b. Lubb b. Qasī, 81
Muḥammad b. Mazdalī, Almoravid, 176
Muḥammad b. Mūsā al-Wazīr, 65
Muḥammad al-Muẓaffar, ruler of Badajoz, 138–9, 147
Muḥammad b. al-Qāsim, 42
Muḥammad b. al-Qāsim b. Ṭumlus, 104
Muḥammad al-Rashīd, ruler of Cordoba, 137
Muḥammad b. Rustam, 45, 47, 50
Muḥammad b. Sa'd al-Zaghal, 300–3
Muḥammad b. Sīdray b. Wazīr, 243, 259
Muḥammad b. Tūmart al-Mahdī, 183, 196–200, 201, 205
Muḥammad b. Yūsuf al-Fihrī, 34
Muḥammad b. Yūsuf b. Hūd, 265–72
Al-Mu'izz b. Suqūt of Ceuta, 161
Mujāhid al-Ṣiqlabī, 122, 140
Al-Mundhir al-Amīr, 64, 65, 73, 81
Al-Mundhir b. 'Abd al-Raḥmān II, 55
Al-Mundhir b. Yaḥyā al-Tujībī, 136
Muqātil, ruler of Tortosa, 140
al-Muqtadir, ruler of Zaragoza, 131
Murcia, 15, 17, 75, 79, 89, 158, 164, 165, 168, 194, 213, 219, 222–3, 227, 235, 251, 252, 267, 271
Al-Murtaḍā, Caliph, 136, 142
Mūsā b. Abī'l-'Āfiya al-Miknāsī, 96
Mūsā b. Sulaymān, Almohad, 216
Al-Musta'īn, ruler of Zaragoza, 173–4
Al-Mu'taḍid, ruler of Seville, 131, 150, 151
Al-Mu'tamid, ruler of Seville, 152–3, 161–4, 166–7, 168, 169
Al-Muṭarrif b. 'Abd Allāh al-Amīr, 74
Al-Muṭarrif b. 'Abd al-Rahman II, 55
Al-Muṭarrif b. Ismā'īl b. Dhī'l-Nūn, 103
Al-Mutawwakil, ruler of Badajoz, 131, 153, 162, 164
Mūsā b. Dhī'l-Nūn, 80
Mūsā b. Fortūn b. Qasī, 39
Mūsā b. Muḥammad b. Ḥudayr, 74
Mūsā b. Mūsā b. Fortūn b. Qasī, 47, 48, 53, 58, 65, 72
Mūsā b. Nuṣayr, 5, 6, 10–12, 15, 18, 19
al-Mustanṣir, Umayyad caliph: *see* al-Ḥakam II
al-Mustanṣir, Yusuf II, Almohad caliph, 257–60
muwallads, 39, 50, 56–9, 65, 68–70, 74, 75–6, 77, 143
Muzaynis of Silves, 135

Nabīl, ruler of Tortosa, 145
Nafza, Berber tribe, 31, 34, 73
Najā al-Ṣiqlabī, 86, 94
Nakur, 95–6
Narbonne, 29, 40
Al-Nāṣir: *see* 'Abd al-Rahmān III
Al-Nāṣir, Almohad Caliph, 248, 249–56
Naṣr, eunuch, 45, 47
Naṣr, Nasrid ruler, 286–7
Navarre, 58, 61, 106: *see also* Pamplona
Las Navas de Tolosa, battle, 255–6, 266
Niebla, 26, 51, 134, 137, 144, 191, 203, 209, 248, 271
Niẓām al-Dawla, ruler of Alpuente, 131
Nubdhat al-'Aṣr, 299, 302
Nuño Gonzales de Lara, 299, 302

Ocsonoba, 84, 92: *see also* Faro
Onda, 225, 270
Oppa, 13
Oporto, 61
Ordoño I, 69
Ordoño II, 89
Ordoño III, 100
Oreto, 66
Orihuela, 14
Osma, 93
Otto I, 97

Pamplona, 29, 55, 61, 84, 85
parias, 145–9, 152, 164, 170, 187

Pechina, 76–7, 79, 96
Pedro the Cruel, 282, 298–92
Pedro II of Aragon, 247, 254, 256–7
Padro Fernandez de Castro, 246
Pedro Manrique, 293
Pedroche, 66
Pelayo, 21, 60
Pepin, 29
Picos de Europa, 21, 28
Plasencia, 246
Poitiers, battle of, 22
poll-tax: see *jizya*
Priego, 66, 264, 278, 289
Puerta Macarena, Seville, 260
Porcuna, 300
Puig, 270

Al-Qādir, ruler of Toledo and Valencia, 152–3, 163, 165, 167, 170
Qā'it Bey, Mamluke Sultan, 302
Qand al-Ṣiqlabī, 94
qāḍīs, xiii, 40, 41, 48, 76, 109, 127, 135, 139, 142, 167–8, 178–9, 187, 192–3, 203, 225, 226
Qaṣr Abī Dānis: *see* Alcacer do Sal
Qayrawān, 5, 6, 10, 11, 16, 17, 19, 35, 44, 80, 156, 242
Qays, Arab tribe, 4, 23–4, 27–8, 31
Quesada, 285
Quraysh, 4, 27, 30, 32, 124, 129, 130
Qasī, Banū, 15, 56, 61, 66, 69–70, 72, 80–1, 84, 92
Al-Qāsim b. Ḥammūd, 128–9, 135, 150

Rabat, 198, 204, 215, 218, 244, 246, 251
Rabī 'b. Theodolfo, 42, 44
Rabī 'b. Zayd, 97
Al-Rāḍī b. al-Mu'tamid of Seville, 166
Raḥḥū, Banū, 283
Ramiro I of Aragon
Ramiro II of Leon, 93, 106
Ramon Berengar III, 174
Ramon Berengar IV, 190
Rayyu, 26, 32, 53, 66
Rāzī family, 7, 8, 9
Razīn, Banū, 94, 103, 116, 139
Recemundo: *see* Rabi'b. Zayd
Reina, 66, 252
Riḍwān, *ḥājib*, 289–90
Riḍwān Bannigash, 295–6, 297
Rio Salado, battle of, 281, 288–9
Riyāḥ, Arab tribe, 205, 219, 223
Roderick, king, 8, 10–11, 13, 14, 17
Roncesvalles, 37
Ronda, 66, 72, 73, 143, 144, 166, 197, 204, 220, 278, 282, 298, 301
Rueda de Jalon, castle
Ruṣāfa, palace, 38

Sa'āda al-Fatā, 103
Sābūr al-Ṣiqlabī, 138
Sagrajas, battle: *see* Zallāqa
sāḥib al-madīna, xiii, 65, 74, 76, 101, 113
Sa'd, Nasrid ruler, 298–9
Sa'd b. Mardanīsh, 186
Sa'īd b. al-Ḥakam I, 55
Sa'īd b. al-Ḥusayn al-Anṣārī, 39
Sa'īd b. 'Īsā, *ṣāḥib al-thaghr*, 224–5
Sa'īd b. Khayra, 139
Sa'īd al-Maṭarī, 35–6
Sa'īd b. al-Mundhir, 87, 92
ṣā'ifa, 55, 65–6, 76, 101, 106, 150
Salé, 160, 176, 202, 204, 205
Al-Ṣāliḥa, Marrakesh, 238, 248
Sālim, Banū, 53, 69, 72
Salobreña, 293, 294, 295, 299
Saltes, 137, 144, 234
Salvatierra, castle, 254, 264
Al-Samḥ b. Mālik al-Khawlānī, 13, 19, 20, 21, 22
Sancho I of Castile, 147, 151–2
Sancho IV, 284, 285
Sancho, son of Alfonso VI
Sancho I of Portugal, 241
Sancho Abarca of Navarre, 120
Sancho the Great of Navarre, 136, 149–50
Sancho IV of Navarre, 190, 246
Sancho Garcia, Count of Castile, 120, 123, 126, 128
Ṣanhāja Berbers, 103–5, 142, 144, 155, 177, 182, 183, 207, 239
Santarem, 174, 190, 217, 234–6
Santaver, 36, 69, 92, 103, 147
Santiago de Compostella, 61, 119
ṣaqāliba, 85–6, 98, 100, 103, 105, 107, 112–13, 117, 122, 125, 126, 127, 129, 131, 143, 151

Sanādīd, Banū, 274
Sarrāj, Banū (Abencerrajes), 273, 290, 295–6, 298, 299, 301
Savarico, Banu, 75
Sayf al-Dawla, Hudid, 187, 194
Seville, Muslim conquest, 9, 12
  under the Banū'l-Ḥajjāj, 75–6, 83–4
  Taifa kings of, 131, 135–6, 137, 142, 144–5
  Christian conquest of, 271–2
Sara, dau. Roderick, 17
Setefilla, 234
Shabrīṭ, Banū, 92–4
Shāmiyun: *see* Syrians
Shaqyā b. ʿAbd al-Wāḥid al-Miknāsī, 36
Shuhayd, Banū, 65, 113
Sīdray b. Wazīr, 193, 195, 202, 203, 211, 215, 218, 221, 231
Sijilmāssa, 95, 96, 155, 157, 161, 184, 203
Silves, 135, 137, 191, 192, 202, 232, 235, 241–3, 252
Simancas, 93
Sīr b. Abī Bakr, 160, 163, 164, 172, 176, 177
Sisnando Davidiz, 148
Slavs, 86: *see also ṣaqāliba*
Ṣubḥ, mother of Hishām II, 109, 116, 120
Sufyān b. ʿAbd Rabbīhi, 45
Sulaymān b. ʿAbd al-Raḥmān I, 38–9, 41–2
Sulaymān b. Hūd, 136, 142, 146–7
Sulaymān al-Mustaʿīn, Caliph, 126–9, 136, 141, 142
Sulaymān b. Yaqẓān al-Aʿrabī, 37–8
Al-Ṣumayl b. Ḥātim al-Kilābī, 27–8, 31, 33
Sūs, Wādī, 183, 197, 198, 200, 202, 203, 206, 250
Syrians, 5, 24–7, 31, 33, 34, 38, 50, 52, 66, 107, 118

Tadla, 161, 206
Tahert, 45, 73, 76, 95
Ṭāhir, Banū, 140
Tākurannā, 66
Talavera, 12, 29, 173, 234, 246
Tamīm b. Buluggīn, Zirid, 164, 167
Tamīm b. Yūsuf b. Tāshfīn, 161, 172–3, 181, 185
Tammām b. ʿAlqama, 32, 34
Tangier, 5, 6, 10, 96, 128, 160, 184, 206
Ṭarafa al-Ṣiqlabī, 122, 123
Tarifa, 152, 161, 203, 277, 278–80, 284, 285, 298
Ṭāriq b. Ziyād, 5, 6, 10–12, 15
Tāsgīmūt, castle, 183, 184
Tāshfīn b. ʿAlī b. Yūsuf b. Tāshfīn, 184, 186, 202
Tavira, 204
Teba, 284, 301
Tenes, 76
Teresa, dau. Alfonso VI, 180
Thābit b. ʿAbd Allāh, *qāḍī* of Zaragoza, 181
Tlemcen, 160, 176, 202, 206, 223, 239, 250–1, 284
thughūr, 52–3, 80
Theodemir, 12, 13, 14, 26
Tīnmal, 183, 200, 216, 219, 225, 266
ṭirāz, 45, 76, 112
Toledo, Muslim conquest of, 11
  under the Umayyads, 57, 83, 92
  Taifa kings of, 135, 139, 141, 144–6
  Christian conquest, 152–3
  see also Middle March
Tomar, 242
Torre del Oro, Seville, 260
Torres Novas, 242
Tortosa, 53, 54, 55, 57, 59, 102, 131, 140, 145
Touareg, 4, 155
Toulouse, 22, 56
Trujillo, 220, 246
Tudela, 15, 29, 53, 55, 57, 72, 81, 136
Tudmīr, 12, 26, 47, 53, 66, 75, 85
Tujībīs, 72, 80–1, 85, 92–4, 102, 103, 116, 125, 134, 136–7, 140, 142
Tunisia, 3, 90, 96, 100, 121, 210, 223, 250, 251: *see also* Ifriqiya
Turgūt, Banū, 160, 176

ʿUbayd Allāh b. ʿAbd Allāh al-Balansī, 43, 55
ʿUbayd Allāh b. Abīʿ Abda, 64
ʿUbayd Allāh b. Muḥammad al-Māridī, 189
ʿUbayd Allāh b. ʿUthmān, 31
ʿUbayd Allāh b. Yaḥyā, governor of Tortosa, 59

Ubeda, 69, 209, 256, 292
Ucles, 69, 80, 85, 92, 139, 173, 177
Al-ʿUdhrī, 71, 81
ʿUmar Asnāj, Almohad, 212
ʿUmar b. Ayyūb, Abū ʿAlī, 247
ʿUmar b. al-Ḥājj al-Lamtūnī, 178, 186
ʿUmar b. Khālid b. Khaldūn, 135
ʿUmar b. Saḥnūn, 232
ʿUmar b. Sulaymān al-Massūfī, 161
ʿUmar b. Tīmṣalīt al-Tīnmalī, 232–3
ʿUmar b. Yaḥyā al-Hintātī, Abū Ḥafṣ, 199, 201, 203, 205–6, 212, 216, 221, 222, 223, 227, 233
ʿUmar b. Zarqāj, *qāḍī* Beja
Umayya b. ʿAbd al-Ghāfir, 76
Umayya b. al-Ḥakam I, 55
Umayya b. ʿĪsā b. Shuhayd, 64, 65
ʿUmra, battle of, 240
ʿUqba b. al-Ḥajjāj al-Salūlī, 24
ʿUqba b. Nāfiʿ al-Fihrī, 4, 5, 6, 27
Upper March, 42, 52, 56, 57–9, 71–2, 80–1, 87, 92–3, 100, 102, 116, 125
Urracca, queen of castile, 179–80
ʿushr, ʿushūr, xiii, 20, 50, 59, 68, 79, 158, 161, 169
Utrera, 279
ʿUthmān b. Abīʾl-ʿUlā, *ṣāḥib al-ghuzāt*, 283, 285, 286, 287–8, 290
ʿUthmān b. Jāmiʿ, *wazīr*, 255, 256, 257, 260–1

Valencia, Taifa kings of, 131, 133, 140, 142
  El Cid in, 165–6
  Christian conquest of, 269–71
Vega of Granada, 213, 264, 278, 283, 284, 287
Velez Malaga, 303
Velez Rubio, 79
Vera, 290, 293
Vermudo II, 120
Vermudo III, 150
Vikings, 45, 47–8, 75
Vilches, 226
Viseu, 150
Visigoths, 1–3, 10–15, 17, 19, 21, 39, 60, 61

Wāḍiḥ al-Ṣiqlabī, 117, 121, 122, 126–7
Wajjāj b. Zalwī al-Lamṭī, 151
Al-Wansharīsī, 175
Witiza, king, 1, 10–11, 13, 15, 17

Yaḥṣubis, rulers of Niebla, 137
Yaḥyā b. Abī Bakr, Almoravid, 176
Yaḥyā b. ʿAlī b. Ghānīya, 186, 187, 189, 190, 191, 192, 203, 204
Yaḥyā b. ʿAlī al-Ḥammūdi, 129
Yaḥyā b. Ibrāhīm, chief of Guddāla, 155–6
Yaḥyā b. Isḥāq b. Ghānīya, 244, 250, 251–2
Yaḥyā al-Maʾmūn, ruler of Toledo, 152
Yaḥyā b. Mazdalī, 176
Yaḥyā b. Muḥammad al-Tujībī, 94, 102
Yaḥyā b. al-Mundhir al-Tujībī, 136
Yaḥyā al-Najjār, 303
Yaḥyā b. Rawād, *qāḍī* Cordoba, 182
Yaḥyā b. Sīr b. Abī Bakr, 176
Yaḥyā b. ʿUmar b. Raḥḥū, 288, 289
Yaḥyā b. ʿUmar b. Turgūt, 156–8
Yaḥyā b. Wasinū, 160
Yaḥyā b. Yaḥyā al-Laythī, 41, 43–4
Yaḥyā b. Yūmūr, 204, 209
Yaʿīsh b. Muḥammad al-Asadī, 139
Yalūl b. Jaldās, 215
Yaṭī b. Ismāʿīl, 160
Yemen, Arab tribal group, 4, 23–4, 27–8, 31, 47, 50, 135
Yūsuf I, Abū Yaʿqūb b. ʿAbd al-Muʾmin, Almohad Caliph, 200–36, 237
Yūsuf II: *see* al-Mustanṣir
Yūsuf I, Nasrid ruler, 288–9, 291
Yūsuf II, Nasrid ruler, 292
Yūsuf III, Nasrid ruler, 294–5
Yūsuf IV, Nasrid ruler, 296–7, 298
Yūsuf V, Nasrid ruler, 297
Yūsuf b. Aḥmad al-Biṭrūjī, 191, 203, 204
Yūsuf b. ʿAbd al-Raḥmān al-Fihrī, 27–8, 31–2, 33, 34
Yūsuf b. Bukht, 31
Yūsuf b. al-Fakhkhār, 244
Yūsuf b. Mardanīsh, Abūʾl-Ḥajjāj, 222, 224, 225, 227, 230
Yūsuf b. ʿUmar, Abūʾl-Ḥajjāj, historian, 236, 238, 245, 248
Yūsuf b. Sulaymān, 204, 212, 213
Yūsuf b. Tāshfīn, 159–64, 171–2, 175, 181, 289
Yūsuf b. Wānnūdīn, 234, 235, 236

Zahara, castle, 284, 293, 300
Zallāqa, battle of, 162–3, 164, 167, 175, 176, 221
Zamora, 61, 71, 89, 120, 152
Zanāta Berbers, 96, 103, 121, 142, 144, 155, 160, 161, 167, 228, 245, 275, 282, 283
Zaragoza, under the Umayyads, 57–9: *see also* Upper March, Tujībīs
  Taifa kings of 131, 133, 134, 136–7, 140, 145–7, 162, 166, 170, 173–4
Zāwī b. Zīrī al-Ṣanhājī, 112, 121, 126, 141, 142
Zaynab, wife of ʿAbd al-Muʾmin, 216
Zayyān b. Mardanīsh, 267–71
Zenete, 282
Zīrī b. ʿAṭiya al-Maghrāwī, 104, 120–1
Zīrī b. Manād al-Ṣanhājī, 103, 105, 121
Zirids, 103–4, 105, 121, 133, 141–5, 155
Ziryāb, 46
Zīz, Wādī, 156
Zorita, 69, 153
Zuʿāl b. Yaʿīsh al-Nafzawī, 71
Zuhayr al-Ṣiqlabī, 129, 142